FROM SUBMISSION TO REBELLION

FROM SUBMISSION
TO REBELLION

*The Provinces Versus
the Center in Russia*

**Vladimir Shlapentokh
Roman Levita
Mikhail Loiberg**

WestviewPress

A Division of HarperCollinsPublishers

In memory of our parents:
Vera (Ita) Iakovlevna Gurevich-Shlapentokh,
Anna Zinovievna Donde-Levita, Iakov Froimovich Levita,
Olga Abramovna Loiberg, and Iakov Mikhailovich Loiberg

Published in 1997 in the United States of America by Westview Press, 5500 Central Avenue, Boulder, Colorado 80301-2877, and in the United Kingdom by Westview Press, 12 Hid's Copse Road, Cumnor Hill, Oxford OX2 9JJ

Library of Congress Cataloging-in-Publication Data
Shlapentokh, Vladmir.
  From submission to rebellion : the provinces versus the center in
Russia / Valdimir [i.e., Vladimir] Shlapentokh, Roman Levita, Mikhail
Loiberg.
    p. cm.
  Includes bibliographical references and index.
  ISBN 0-8133-2156-5 (hc.). — ISBN 0-8133-2157-3 (pbk.)
    1. Federal government—Russia (Federation)   2. Regionalism—Russia
(Federation)   3. Russia (Federation)—Politics and government.
I. Levita, R. (Roman)   II. Loiberg, M. IA. (Mikhail IAkovlevich)
III. Title.
JN6693.5.S8S55   1997
320.8'0947—dc21   96-53283
                                                                          CIP

The paper used in this publication meets the requirements of the American National Standard for Permanence of Paper for Printed Library Materials Z39.48-1984.

10   9   8   7   6   5   4   3   2   1

CONTENTS

TABLES

ACKNOWLEDGMENTS

Our greatest gratitude goes to Joseph Kupsky for his meticulous and ingenious editing of this manuscript and to Tatiana Chowdhury for her immense help in checking and rechecking numerous references. A special thanks to Michele Wynn, Joshua M. Woods, Professor Vladimir Zolotykh (from Izhevsk University, Russia), and also a special thanks to Varlen Soskin, whose paper on Siberia has been used. If this text still contains errors, it is the authors' fault.

We also extend our heartfelt thanks to several Russian sociologists who shared their data with us—Yurii Levada, Vladimir Shubkin, and Elena Avraamova, among others.

Vladimir Shlapentokh
Roman Levita
Mikhail Loiberg

1

INTRODUCTION

In 1991, as a result of complicated processes, Russia lost its empire and had to acquiesce in the transformation of its "national republics" into independent states. Millions of Russians bemoaned the end of their empire, but other concerns emerged almost immediately: Would Russia follow the fate of the Soviet Union and be transformed into either a loose confederation of several dozen regions or a much smaller entity? Was it possible that the current Russian Federation could return to the former size of Moskovia, the predecessor of the current Russian state that existed four to five centuries ago?

In order to make predictions about Russia's future, we have investigated the relationship between the center and provinces throughout Russian history, from the emergence of the Russian state to modern times. In this book, we approach this extremely difficult issue from a very broad perspective, looking at developments in Russia as a case study of the relations between the center and the periphery in general.

Indeed, the study of the relations between the center and periphery (referred to here as CP relations) is one of the most important characteristics of any complex system, whether it be social, biological, or mechanical in nature. In the social sciences, these relations are of crucial significance for social entities at the micro- as well as the macrolevel.

In speaking of the *center*, we mean, according to the traditional approach in modern social science, the central administration, including the office of the president and subordinated structures, the government, and Parliament. The term *provinces* embraces all those territories outside the capital of the country, and they have traditionally played a special role in the life of the country. In many countries, the provinces differ from each other in that their residents sometimes have a different ethnic identity than the majority of the people in the country.

There are three types of states that have different forms of CP relations: the unitarian state, the federation, and the confederation. In the first case, the center has a monopoly on all strategic decisions, including the appointment of the heads of local administrations. In the second case, the provinces have a significant level of autonomy, and the selection of the local elite is essentially managed independently of the center. At the same time, however, the decisions made at the center are binding on the provinces. In the third case, the provinces are the major loci of power, and the central administration is shaped by and represents the interests of the provinces.

As noted, the main objective of this book is to study the CP relationship, using Russia as a case study. Each of the three types of states just mentioned is relevant to Russia. In 1985, only one decade ago, Russia was a strong unitarian state, whereas in the post-Communist period that has followed, it tends to act as a federation. At the time this book was in the last stages of preparation in late 1996, there was also a serious internal movement to transform Russia into a confederation in the near future.

We investigate here the relationship between the center and provinces during different stages of Russian history, with special focus on post-Communist Russia. As we progress through the book, we study how historical traditions, on the one hand, and the new market economy and democratization, on the other hand, will shape the major trends in these relations for the coming decades.

Regionalism, however, is not only a dependent variable. It is also a powerful independent variable that exerts tremendous influence on all aspects of social, economic, and political life. In this book, we devote a great deal of attention to regionalism in both of its roles.

In our analysis of CP relations, we also make the distinction between "objective" and "subjective" factors. The globalization of the economy and world communications are "objective" factors immensely affecting these relations. However, such "subjective" factors as ideology and public opinion also have a tremendous impact on CP relations and deserve the same amount of attention.

We discuss herein all eighty-nine administrative units of contemporary Russia, often called the "subjects" of the Russian Federation. However, the main objective of this book is not so much to discuss the non-Russian regions—the so-called ethnic republics—as it is to investigate the "pure" Russian regions, for it is in these regions that 80 percent of the population of the Russian Federation lives.

CP relations can be approached from several perspectives. Among these, the most generally elaborated are the political, economic, and literary viewpoints. Each of these approaches, even though they are interlinked, has its own specific focus. Whereas social scientists, primarily political scientists, concentrate on the distribution of power between the center and regions, economists, who have even created "regional science," are mostly interested in the economic differences among regions.[1] Similarly, literary critics are interested in the role of regional subjects in literary works. We deal here primarily with the political dimension of regionalism. However, we do not ignore economic issues and superficially touch upon literary questions.

Methodology and Sources

We use the comparative approach to the study of regionalization in Russia as our major framework. We assume that without comparing the course of regionalization in various countries of the world it is almost impossible to identify the essence of this process, to separate out the universal and specific factors, and to discover the trends that will influence the shape of Russia in the foreseeable future.

Of equal importance is the use of the historical approach. This allows us to assess whether the powerful trends that determined the character of the CP relationship in the past are affecting the development of current conflicts between the center and periphery. For this reason, an excursion into the prerevolutionary, Stalinist, and post-Stalinist epochs of Russian history is extremely important for this study. Of course, the closer the past is to the present, the more impact it will have on current developments. For this reason, we use the "funnel" principle. As the narrative moves from the remote past to the present, the discussion of regional issues increases in detail. In other words, there is very little detail given about Kiev Rus' and a great deal more detail offered about the developments that have taken place since 1991.

Because we are strong believers in the multisource approach[2] and assume the necessity of bolstering any conclusion by citing several sources, we have done this throughout as much as possible. A number of the surveys conducted by the All-Russian Center of Public Opinion Studies (VTSIOM) in 1994, as well as the unpublished data produced by a number of Russian sociologists, serve as the book's statistical foundation. Our thanks go to those sociologists who kindly permitted their unpublished data to be used in this work: to Vladimir Shubkin for his survey of the Siberian elite in 1995, to Elena Avraamova for her national survey of the elite, and to Fred Borodkin for his surveys of Siberian respondents.

Much important information covering the entire political spectrum was taken from the Russian press. We closely monitored these sources while making our study of Russian regionalization in 1990–1996.

Among those Moscow periodicals used were *Izvestia, Moskovskie Novosti, Segodnia, Komsomol'skaia Pravda, Moskovskii Komsomol'ets, Argumenty i Fakty, Literaturnaia Gazeta, Pravda, Sovietskaia Rossia, Literaturnaia Rossia, Nezavisimaia Gazeta, Megalopolis Express, Kommersant, Ogoniok, Novoe Vremia, and Svobodnaia Mysl'*. Articles and feature stories in the Moscow press were used for content analysis, providing important results for this study. We also regularly studied the local press in various cities, including Ekaterinburg, Saratov, Volgograd, Novosibirsk, and several others.

Another important source of information was Russian television, along with the daily bulletin of Radio Free Europe and daily publications of the Open

Media Research Institute (OMRI), both of which were available over electronic mail systems. Information was also "fished out" from the Internet.

We also collected a significant amount of information in 1991–1995 during our visits to various regions of the country. During these visits, we made contact with different segments of the population, ranging from the head of the administration and regional parliament to workers and peasants. The regions visited included Novosibirsk, Saratov, Cheliabinsk, Murmansk, Tver, Ekaterinburg, Vladivostok, Khabarovsk, and Cheboksary, among others.

In addition to these sources, we have included information from fiction and have tried to capitalize on our casual contacts with knowledgeable people, both those living in the Russian provinces and those in America and other foreign countries.

An Overview of the Text

Chapter 2 serves as an introductory chapter, outlining the major concepts and theories necessary in the analysis of CP relations. This is followed by Part One, which includes Chapters 3–6, in which CP relations throughout Russian history are discussed, covering the period from the center's total domination of the provinces until the years of reform beginning in 1985. Part Two, composed of Chapters 7–9, examines the period when relations between the center and provinces became unstable and turbulent—the years since 1985. In Part Three, the focus shifts from the historical perspective and moves into sociological analysis. Here, in Chapters 10–17, we analyze the conflict between the center and regions in post-Communist Russia in the separate areas of politics, ideology, and the economy. At the same time, we investigate the differences among Russian regions and the varying influence the regions have on the relationship between the center and the provinces in Russia. Part Four, consisting of Chapter 18 and the conclusion, is devoted to the controversial consequences of regionalization on different aspects of Russian society at the end of the twentieth century.

2

THE MAJOR THEORETICAL PERSPECTIVE: REGIONALISM AS PAST AND CONTEMPORARY WORLD DEVELOPMENT

We approach CP relations from a dynamic perspective, supposing that these relationships tend to be conflicting, even in certain historical periods when many societies may indeed be relatively stable. Both participants in the CP relationship—the center and the provinces—can be seen as instigators of the destabilization of this relationship. In this book, the main focus is on the activities of the provinces, and for this reason the main concepts here are regionalism and regionalization.

Chief Concepts

By *regionalism* we are referring to an ideology as well as to a political and economic activity that is geared toward achieving greater regional autonomy, or greater particularization of substate entities.[1] *Separatism* refers to the highest degree of regionalism, in which a province tries to gain complete political independence by leaving the greater nation-state. *Regionalization* stimulated by regionalism as an ideology is a process leading to the growing role of regions, as the country's administrative units, in the life of the given country.

Local, or mini-, nationalism exacerbates regionalism and separatism by providing them with the elements of nationalistic ideology. These beliefs emphasize not only the specific cultural and economic interests of a region but also the radical importance of the region's specific language and long-term cultural traditions.[2]

At the same time, we consider regionalism to be a special case of *particularism*. Particularism is the tendency to oppose the specific features of a social entity that favors universalism, which is the dominance of various patterns of material and nonmaterial behavior. Particularism manifests itself in numerous forms—from the willingness of a minority to preserve its native language and its cultural traditions in clothing or eating habits to a social group's desire to maintain its own rituals. It may even manifest itself in the local jargon. These traits differentiate the minority from other people.

In a broader sense, the regionalism issue involves the relationship between two major principles of organization, universalism and particularism, as elaborated by Talcott Parsons. In Parsons's books, published in the 1950s and 1960s, the axis of universalism versus particularism was used as one of the most important dimensions, or "pattern variables," of any society.[3] Parsons was confident that progress would unswervingly diminish the role of particularism in the modern world. "Value generalization" would be the dominant trend in modern society, a trend he did not consider contradictory to the increasing differentiation of society, with its growing numbers of institutions, associations, and functions of different sorts.[4]

For instance, Parsons argued that the monetary system as a universal means of mobilizing resources is a much more efficient way to appeal to the interests of single groups than appeals to their particularism or ascriptive roots.[5] He was sure that the movement toward the dominance of a single language, mostly through education, in a multiethnic community is a necessary condition for progress, otherwise society would face "disruptive internal tensions."[6]

Parsons's assumption about the progressive curtailment of particularism in the modern world turned out to be wrong. In fact, with the growing complexity and diversity of the world, it has proven to be particularism that has increased its realm at the expense of universalism.

Universal and Specific Characteristics of Regionalization

In a study of any kind of social process, in any society and at any time, we can discern universalist and particularist elements. This holds true for regionalization in Russia. Indeed, each "universal law" manifests itself in an observable context, in the specific interaction with other variables that have their own magnitude. The variables, such as the size of a given country, affect CP relations everywhere, but the size of the Russian Federation makes this factor much more important in this relationship than it is, for example, in Italy or Spain. The degree of influence of all other variables on regionalization in Russia is also different than it is in China, America, or France.

Of course, some "universal factors" are stronger than others, and for this reason they manifest themselves more or less uniformly, whereas others, which are weaker, vary greatly in their strength. The end of the Cold War is an example of a very powerful universal factor. It encouraged regionalization, particularly in those countries that were greatly involved in the confrontation between the two camps. This is as true for Russia as it is for Italy. At the same time, the impact of such a universal factor as the impact of foreign countries on regionalization is significant even now for such big countries as Russia and China but not of great importance for France or Italy.

Dormant and Active Regionalism

Regionalism is always present in any society, even in a totalitarian one that suppresses any of its manifestations. If it does not manifest itself in "real terms," it is nevertheless on the back burner of the political actors.

As will be shown later, Soviet politicians, since the end of the Russian Civil War, have paid very little attention to the conflict between the center and regions, with the exception of occasional vituperations against "localism" (*mestnichestvo*), commentaries that were of ritual character rather than being reflections of real concerns. The same can be said about researchers, Soviet or foreign, who have almost totally ignored the issue.[7]

However, as soon as opportunities emerged, regionalism began to pop up as if it had been waiting for just the right moment. Therefore, in our analysis of regionalism in post-Communist Russia, we shall isolate both the specific developments that triggered the resurgence of regionalism and the long-term factors that encourage regionalism in contemporary societies.

New Regionalism at the End of the Twentieth Century

Under the growing influence of certain factors to be discussed later, the movement for regional autonomy from the center has been rekindled at the end of the twentieth century, in varying degrees of intensity, in various countries around the world. Although universal factors make regionalism a global process, in each individual country it has many particular traits. The history of a country, as well as the country's various specific features, strongly imprints the process of regionalization. Some of these specific national factors are spatial (size of a country), political (degree of democratization), economic (degree of marketization of the economy), and cultural (intensity of national patriotism).

Regionalization has spread throughout the contemporary world. It is quite strong in Europe, particularly in such countries as Spain and Italy,[8] and to some degree in France and England.[9] Whether actual or dormant, it presents a powerful force in India and Pakistan.[10] It is also of special significance in China[11] and is even quite strong in North America, if one keeps in mind the political situation in Canada involving the Quebecois.

The United States faces regionalism in its milder and rather hidden forms, as exhibited in the movement for the expansion of the states' role at the expense of federal authority. However, even here, it is occurring to such a degree that in the opinion of some politicians in the mid-1990s, America is moving "back toward the Articles of Confederation."[12] Various other forms of particularism are of no less significance in the United States, such as the growing cultural and ethnic autonomy (not to be confused with cultural diversity) of various groups in the country.[13]

Regionalization in Russia

Regionalism in the form of ideology, as well as its appearance in political and cultural movements, existed in prerevolutionary Russia. It also existed in milder and veiled forms in the Soviet Union. The collapse of the Soviet empire and the emergence of the Commonwealth of Independent States (CIS) from its ashes exerted tremendous influence on Russian regionalism, making it one of the strongest political processes in the country. Various circumstances, universal as well as specific, have influenced this process.

Since 1991, with the end of communism and the collapse of the Soviet Union, CP relations have become a crucial problem for Russia and for its survival as a cohesive state. These relations are debated in the program of every political party in the country. Several political organizations have emerged for the sole purpose of offering their solution to the regional issues of the country. Almost every edition of any Russian newspaper treats the subject in some way. It will be many years before this process ends with the development of a solid equilibrium in the relations between the center and provinces. This will occur only when all of the CP conflicts are solved through constitutional means.

Regionalism in the Post-Soviet Republics

The collapse of the Communist regime in August 1991 and the subsequent dissolution of the Soviet Union the following December had a tremendous effect on center-periphery relations, not only in the Russian Federation but in most of the other former Soviet republics as well. This was especially true for Ukraine and for Kazakhstan, Georgia, Tadzhikistan, and Moldova. The ethnic factor accounts mostly, but not solely, for regionalization in the other former Soviet republics.

By 1993 in Ukraine, for example, the differences and even the confrontation between the western, eastern, and southern regions (the Donbass, Odessa, Crimea, and Karpat Regions) had already presented a kind of danger to the new state's unity. These differences were determined by the predominance of Ukrainians in the western part of the country and by the great number of Russians in the east and south. The debates on the possible regionalization of Ukraine and its disintegration were popular topics in the Ukrainian and Russian media in 1993–1995.

Regionalization, coupled with the revival of tribalism, became a leading issue in Central Asia in the wake of the Soviet Union's collapse. The most dramatic developments occurred in Tadzhikistan, where an armed struggle broke out between regions. In this civil war, those who supported the Communist authorities (Leninabad and Kuliab were their centers) were labeled the "Rouge Khmers" by the liberal Moscow press in 1992–1993, and their opponents were found in the southern regions (Kurgan-Tiube Region was their center) and were mostly Sunnites, though they also included the Pamir believers in Islam. This struggle put Tadzhikistan's existence as a state in "clear and present danger." Only the intervention of the Russian army on the side of the north seemingly saved the country.

The situation in neighboring Kirghizstan is not far from spilling over into Tadzhikistan. The antagonism between the north and the south in Kirghizstan is deeply rooted. In 1992, the conflict between Bekmamat Osmonov, the leader of the south in Djalal-Abad, and President Askar Akaiev, who represented the northern regions in the opinion of his southern opponents, was quite significant. This political struggle soon erupted into a bloody confrontation.

Along with Kirghizstan, Turkmenistan is also vulnerable to regional conflicts, which for the most part reflect the differences between various tribes. It is probable that the authoritative regime of Saparmurad Niazov was the factor accounting for the dominance of relative calm in the state. In another region of Central Asia, in Kazakhstan, the division between the north and the south can also be ascribed to different proportions of Russians in the population. In the north, there is a majority of ethnic Russians, whereas in the south, they are the minority. Regional antagonisms have become a significant part of politics in the Caucasian republics as well, particularly in Azerbaijan and Georgia.

Regional conflicts in the other former Soviet republics are also quite important. In Moldova, the coexistence of three contrasting populations—the central part populated by Moldavians, the Dniestr Region with its predominant Slav population, and the southern part, where the Gagauzs live—accounts for much of the tension evident in the new state. Such regional tensions have been unavoidable even in the Baltic republics. In northeastern Estonia, the Narva Region has a Russian majority, leading to obvious political clashes. In Lithuania, there is a region in which Poles compose a majority of the population, and this has led to confrontations with the republican government.[14]

The Theoretical Framework

Let us now discuss the theoretical framework of this book. It is greatly different from the theoretical premises on which the analysis of regionalism and regionalization in the last few decades has been based.

Regionalism as a Conservative Movement:
The Modernization Theory Approach

Until the 1980s and, particularly, the 1990s, regionalism and particularism were in general strongly associated with the fading past, which tried to entrench itself in the present, for good or bad. For Parsons, for example, "the resistance to values generalization" was labeled "fundamentalism" and "social conservatism." He insisted that "if a single keynote of a main trend of the development of modern civilization could be selected, I think it would be the trend toward cultural universalism."[15] This viewpoint was particularly evident in literature and the arts, where the virtuous and enchanting past, on the verge of disappearance, was seen as directly opposed to the present.[16]

One of these views can be labeled "historical," since the conflict is perceived as being between both actors, the capital and provinces, and as a continuation of the old struggle for the nation's integration. This struggle started in many countries several centuries ago. It occurred in France in the sixteenth century, in England in the fifteenth and sixteenth centuries, and in Russia in the fourteenth and fifteenth centuries. The transformation of western and central Europe, which had five hundred independent political units in 1500, into an area composed of only twenty-five such units by 1900 was evidently considered to be a strong progressive process.[17]

The conceptual basis of such an approach is the traditionalist theory, which supposes that nation-states emerged around a center, which, over many centuries, has been the main agent of modernization in its fight against backward and parochial territories. Such territories, represented by local elites and other groups, tried to defend their old privileges, customs, values, cultural traditions, and archaic economic and political structures against universal values, the integrative policy of a nation-state, rational organization, and social and technological progress.[18] Traditionalist theory also assumes that regionalist movements are usually supported by people in the periphery, who perceive of themselves as deprived economically or culturally, as opposed to those in the metropolis. Those who live in the periphery also have their old identity, which distinguishes them from the people in the metropolis.

Such an approach, strongly inspired by various modernization theories, has mostly condemned regionalism as a reactionary development. This disapproval of regionalization was in agreement with liberal ideas of the mid-twentieth century, such as the belief in progress and universalism, and, of course, with the ideologies of past nation-states. It was also supported by Marxists, with their focus on the universal model of social development.[19]

An Alternative Approach:
The Focus on Contemporary Trends

In this book, we propose another approach to regionalization in the contemporary world. This approach, without disregarding historical and cultural traditions, assigns more weight to current developments and the most recent past. We assume that at this given juncture of history, regionalization cannot be treated simply as a process harking back to the past, or as a "hangover from the past," to use Michael Keating's locution.[20] Along with several other social scientists, we further suppose that in many cases this process is addressed to the future rather than the past.[21] Even in the late 1970s, some authors spoke about "the challenge to centrality" as one of the most important developments of the times.[22] This shift has been stimulated by the most powerful contemporary trends and the most recent global events, such as democratization, the globalization of the economy, the radical decline in the fear of global war, and the onset of nefarious ecological developments.

It is most often the case that the advanced and not the backward regions are the champions of regionalization.[23] This circumstance holds true for Italy, with Lombardia as the leading force in this process; in Spain, with the same role played by Catalonia; and in Russia, with the key role played by Ekaterinburg. At the same time, the backward regions in some countries, as, for example, in southern Italy, are politically very passive. The animosity of regions toward the center is determined by the willingness of the regions, which are often in no way ranked behind the center in any respect, including statistical measurements of the standard of living, to get their fair part of the economic pie, as well as more freedom to act on their own.[24] For these reasons, attempts to consider the provinces of France, Spain, or Russia as the center's colonies, as do regionalists and a few scholars in these regions, now have no scientific justification, although the term "colonialism" is actively used by leaders of regional movements everywhere.[25]

It is remarkable that in some cases backward regions have demanded the interference of the center in the redistribution of resources in their favor. This places these regions in the role of being advocates of centralization rather than being champions of autonomy.[26] For this reason, we believe that in many, if not most, cases the relations between the center and periphery in the contemporary world are far from fitting the traditionalist model with its focus on the past. The historical factor continues, of course, to exert significant impact on the relationship between the center and periphery, especially in those regions with significant ethnic specificity. It is still an important component of the ideology of regionalization, as it exists in Corsica, in France, or in the Basque country in Spain.

The Enduring Strength of Minor Nationalism

As we focus on the new trends stimulating regionalization in the world, we should recognize that the traditional approach to this issue does not lose all its value. Several developments that abet regionalism are still germane.[27]

There are still developments in a few corners of the world that seem to follow the traditionalist model, most of which retain the ethnic factor as the major bulwark of regionalism. "Minor" nationalism continues to be a powerful force and is the essence of the separatist movements in several locations, for example, in the Basque country in Spain, Quebec in Canada, Corsica in France, Sardinia in Italy, and the Chechen Republic in Russia.[28] Moreover, local elites, including those in regions completely immersed in the contemporary world, such as northern Italy or Scotland, use history to enhance their position vis-à-vis the center.[29]

In order to understand regionalization in almost any country, one should have a great knowledge of the past. It is also necessary to decode the function of historical memory in our times. Local elites, the main driving force in regionalization, try to inspire regional movements by resurrecting old particularities. They "invent traditions" and create "illusory" beliefs and "imagined communities" in their efforts to unite their countrymen.[30]

However, it is not the past but the present political, social, and economic factors that determine the character of these relations. This is particularly true for former Communist countries, where regionalization is not determined by the resurgence of grievances against the capital that have lingered for centuries but by the developments directly related to the recently extinct totalitarian regimes.

Let us move on to the analysis of contemporary worldwide tendencies encouraging regionalization. Some of them are of a spontaneous character. Others are elements of the central elite's policies, which are also affected by various processes, particularly economic ones. Such tendencies push the provinces farther toward autonomy and responsibility for the satisfaction of their population's basic needs.

Democratization of Society and Regionalization

One of the most powerful stimulants for regionalization is the progress of democracy throughout the world. In the last one-third of the twentieth century, this progress has taken two forms. The first form has been the extension of democratic institutions throughout the world, primarily due to the collapse of totalitarian states after World War II and in the period 1989–1992. The second form is the improvement of democracy in Western countries, with their growing focus on minority rights.

The Incompatibility of Regionalism and Totalitarian Regimes

Indeed, the character of the political system and its place on the totalitarian-democracy scale is of crucial importance to CP relations. History provides us with many facts supporting this thesis. At its most extreme, the totalitarian regime destroys the seeds of any regional opposition to the regime, eliminating any politician who challenges the supremacy of the center.

The centralization of the Russian state in the fifteenth and sixteenth centuries was deeply connected with the terror against the local elite, as well as with the opposition in the center. The regional movement did not emerge in Russia until the second half of the nineteenth century. After 1917, it was completely eliminated by the Bolsheviks. Regionalism was almost absent in Nazi Germany and Fascist Italy, despite the fact that the unification of both countries occurred very late and the regional traditions were quite strong.

The Soviet, Nazi, and Fascist regimes eliminated regionalism in their respective countries with the iron hand of mass repression. In the past, the instruments of mass repression controlled the country with the help of the major networks of three chief institutions: the party, the secret police (the KGB, Gestapo, etc.) and the army. The most powerful elements of the center's control over the regions were its cadre policy and terror.

In the Soviet past, the *nomenklatura*, or appointment, system determined the composition of administrative personnel, and it was not only the highest regional officials, such as the first party secretary, the chairman of the local soviet, the heads of the KGB office, and the highest military commanders, who were appointed from Moscow. Even the candidates for slots in the second, third, and fourth levels of the bureaucracy had to be formally endorsed by the Central Committee.

After 1991, this system was discarded. Some high officials, such as governors, were still appointed in 1992–1994 by the president; however, most of them were either elected by popular vote or appointed by local leaders. The weakening of the center was primarily manifested in this revolutionary change of cadre appointments.

The control of Moscow, Berlin, and Rome over the provinces was primarily based on the state security apparatus and the party committees that watched over the behavior of each adult individual in the region, particularly the behavior of apparatchiks and intellectuals.

As soon as the totalitarian regime collapsed, as in Nazi Germany and Fascist Italy, or began to flounder, as in Spain, the Soviet Union, and Communist China, regionalism almost immediately began to flourish and expand. Without the Communist, Nazi, and Fascist Parties' monopoly on power, along with the reduced clout of the political police, the regional elite and ordinary citizens alike lost their fear of being demoted or even arrested. They began to regard the capital without their previous awe and horror.

Democratization Encourages Regionalism

By definition, the democratization of society opens the way for autonomy in all spheres of social life, including that in the provinces. In turn, the existence of a high degree of autonomy in the provinces acts as a significant antidote against antidemocratic tendencies. It is not surprising that in postwar Germany and Italy, the victors enforced provisions in the constitutions of these countries that introduced greater autonomy of the provinces.

However, the correlation between democracy and regionalism is all but simple and linear. The initial foundation of democracy in some nation-states, built as it was on the views of the majority of the population, was often accompanied by an apparent curtailment of regionalism. Regionalism indeed, as was often contended, represented rather archaic and nondemocratic tendencies in society.[31] The American Civil War was the most eloquent example of the willingness of a democratic state to halt regionalism on the road toward separatism.

However, when the rights of minorities moved to the forefront of political life in democratic societies, all forms of particularism, including regionalism, flowered. Particularist phenomena and their tendencies to expand have always been present in modern society, even if appearing mostly in disguised and suppressed forms. However, since the 1960s and especially since the mid-1980s, particularism in its numerous forms has taken the offensive in various parts of the world.

Democratization Undermines
the Unity of the Central Elite

The emergence of democracy in former totalitarian and authoritarian societies, in addition to deepening democratic processes in the old democracies, tends to undermine the unity of the central elite. The number of factions in the central elite under these circumstances tends to increase, as does their tendency to disagree. The same developments also occur in nondemocratic societies, though mostly during transition periods from one form of regime to another.

At the same time, in any political system, totalitarian or democratic, the strength and unity of the center is a primary factor determining the CP relationship. The center's strength is manifested in its ability to enforce its laws and directives using its state machinery. This ability, in turn, is determined by its unity and its legitimacy in the eyes of the population. It can be stated that the stronger the center, the greater its unity will be and the less autonomy the provinces will have. The inverse also holds true: The weaker the center, the more it needs the support of the provinces, which exploit these developments to enhance their autonomy.

World history, including that of Russia, abounds with examples showing to what degree the situation in the capital governs the level of autonomy in the regions. The Russian period of "feudal divisiveness" from the twelfth through the fifteenth centuries was the direct result of Kiev's decline in power as the center of Russia, and the growing power of the Moscow principality ultimately led to the centralization of the country and the loss of autonomy by all previously independent territories.

Even during the Soviet period, there were times when the center became temporarily weakened. This was usually due to unsettled factional disputes. Under such conditions, the role of regional leaders grew almost immediately. This occurred in 1964 when Nikita Khrushchev was removed from power. The same thing happened in 1989–1991. When the power of the general secretary declined, the role of regional leaders again ballooned almost automatically.

However, the decisive increase in regional power took place with the emergence of democracy in the post-totalitarian period, in particular with the establishment of private ownership of the means of production. A number of powerful cliques in the center using various sources of power began to compete with one another for the control of society. This kind of activity weakens the center and increases the strength of the provinces, which try to use the conflict in the capital for the enhancement of their own power. Post-Communist Russia is, of course, a classic example of this sort of development. The same processes are also clearly visible in Hungary and Poland, as well as in such countries as China and Vietnam, which have left the peak of totalitarianism behind.[32] Furthermore, even in democratic countries we can observe periods when conflict among the elite has weakened the center, which immediately increases regional power.

Internationalization of Life, Globalization of the Economy

Another modern trend that provokes particularism and, especially, regionalism is the internationalization of life in the world. The primary factor involved is the globalization of the world economy. This development was predicted by Karl Marx and Friedrich Engels in *The Communist Manifesto* in 1848, an idea that appeared for an entire century afterward to be preposterous.[33] The globalization of the economy and many other aspects of social life have significantly changed traditional territorial identities, even if not radically so. Such identities had previously been based on continuity, homogeneity, and clearly identifiable borders.[34] This process of eroding identity has now reached a level where regions of various states can conduct business among themselves and easily skirt their capitals, ignoring their central governments. Of no less significance has been the rapid growth of multinational companies and the emergence of various multinational organizations.[35]

The case of the European Community is especially significant here. This organization gradually, but inexorably, diminished the role of national states in Europe, enormously stimulating the autonomy of regions in all its member countries. Members of this organization were, for instance, a powerful stimulus for the encouragement of regionalization in each of its member states. As a result of this process, Europe is becoming, as Riccardo Cappellin has formulated, a "Europe of regions." The unification of Europe has led to the emergence, alongside existing administrative and historical regions, of a new territorial conglomerate of "meso-regions," which are based on network relationships among various urban centers. This development is an indicator of many new developments and trends.[36]

The opening of the Russian economy, as well as the immense expansion of economic contacts with foreign economies after the fall of communism, has had a tremendous impact on the relations between Moscow and the provinces. This subject will be discussed later.

It does indeed seem to be a dialectical case that the globalization of social life, a phenomenon that should be considered as spreading "universalism," or the growth of similar patterns of behavior across the world, at the same time promotes "particularism," undermining nation-states and encouraging regions to develop their autonomy from the center.[37]

The World as Interdependent Village

In the 1960s, the theorists of "systems analysis" insisted that the power of the center in big complex organizations lies, to a very great degree, in its monopoly on information.[38] The consequences of the information revolution have confirmed many of their statements. The new electronic means of communication, as well as the rapid intensification of world travel without restraint and often without a visa, has allowed any sort of minority to entertain close contacts with similar groups in other parts of the world.[39] Expatriate communities can also now maintain stronger ties with their countries of origin, which can only enhance their self-identity and separation from their adopted countries.

At the same time, a resident of any region in a large country is no farther from people in other countries than from fellow citizens living one thousand miles away. Today, a resident of the Russian Far East is increasingly more involved with Japan or China than with Moscow or St. Petersburg.

The End of the Cold War

Whatever the limitations of the Emile Durkheim–Talcott Parsons approach to society as regulated by social values, it is true that even a partial consensus on values is extremely important for the functioning of any society. The end of the Cold War significantly changed the value system in the countries that had been active in the confrontation between the two opposing blocks. The fear of a third world war also had a tremendous impact on the minds of politicians and ordinary people. This, in turn, immensely affected life in the Soviet Union, the United States, Western European countries, Japan, and other nations.

When the Cold War ended, there was a significant shift in the value system in many nations. National security and patriotism ceased to play the same role as in the past. This significantly influenced the relations between the center and provinces. The center was deprived of a powerful ideological weapon in favor of centralization. The end of the Cold War clearly accounts, at least partially, for the surge of new regionalist movements in such places as Canada, Italy, France, and Pakistan. Even in the United States, the increased role of the states in various issues, such as welfare and medical expenditures, would have been impossible without the disappearance of the Soviet Union.[40]

The Declining Role of the Center

The trends and events described herein account for much in the declining role of the capitals in many societies. This decline, in turn, enormously accelerates regionalization.

Indeed, most states in the past, particularly those that were nondemocratic, but also those that were once democratic, typically had a cult of "centrality" coupled with negative attitudes, present in official ideology, toward regionalism. Since ancient times, there have been dozens of famous philosophers and social scientists who have praised "centrality" practically as a "sacred phenomenon"[41] and as the necessary condition for the survival of a national state.[42]

There have been many cases in history when centers have declined or even disappeared, some temporarily and some permanently. Such cities as Babylon, Nineveh, and Carthage were once the centers of empires that have since disappeared from the surface of the planet. Cities such as Rome, Athens, Alexandria, Constantinople, Samarkand, and Jerusalem are among those whose role was much greater in the past than in modern history.

The reasons for the decline or disappearance of once-mighty centers are numerous, but the fall of a state, of which each of these cities was the capital, is the most frequently cited cause. However, the decline in the center's role in recent decades is mostly due to regionalization and democratization.[43]

The cult of the center, personified by the capital, was very strong in Russia. This remained true despite the fact that after the building of St. Petersburg in 1703, Russia had two capitals, St. Petersburg and Moscow.[44] However, after 1918, when Vladimir Lenin's government, under the threat of German invasion, moved the capital to Moscow, the cult of one center was fully restored.

Generally, regionalization in the second half of the twentieth century has enhanced the growing contempt for national capitals, seen as places where corrupt bureaucracies ignore the interests of the country and focus almost exclusively on their own perpetuation. Residents in Milan, voting in 1994 against Rome's bureaucracy, were confident that it was necessary to deprive the bureaucracy of the right to interfere in Milanese affairs. The animosity toward central governments by their regions is widespread throughout the world.

Regionalization from Above

Since the 1960s, most of the trends that have forged regionalization into a process very different from any previous trend came "from below." Thus, such

trends appear to be rather spontaneous and not directly aimed at the encouragement of this process. At the same time, there is an important trend coming "from
above," and it is also an important factor accounting for the growing role of
regionalization in the modern world. The modern national democratic state is
itself interested in shifting several of its functions to regional units. It is doing so
for several reasons, such as the effective management of the economy without a
central totalitarian power, a shift that is possible only with the cooperation of
local authorities.

One difficulty in doing this, however, is that national resources, which are at
the disposal of the center, are limited. It is reasonable to ask regions to mobilize
their own efforts to augment their economic and financial potential themselves,
under the condition that additional resources will be put under the region's control. For this reason alone, regional policy has emerged with an important role in
the activities of the central administration in almost all of even the smallest
countries in the world. This trend in the behavior of the central elite has become
visible in many countries around the world during the last two decades of the
twentieth century, including the United States and Russia.[45]

Theoretical Presentation of CP Relations at the End of the Twentieth Century

Our of the CP relationship is based on two theoretical approaches, the theory of
complex organizations and conflict theory. In view of the enormous number of
variables affecting CP relations, it is impossible to build an elegant model with
either theory. However, our approach, unlike the historical approach's focus on
the struggle "between old and new structures," will provide us with the conceptual framework necessary to grasp the essence of CP relations in Russia and
many other countries, not only in recent times, but to some degree in the past.

The Complex Organization Approach

The CP relationship is the crux of any complex organization that supposes the
existence of intermediate bodies between the center and primary units. This
approach to CP relations was initiated by theorists of systems analysis in the
1960s. It was then incorporated into the theory of complex organizations and, to
some degree, into decisionmaking theory.[46]

The paradigm "centrality-periphery" is particularly useful in the analysis of
any "spatial" organization, that is, an organization whose elements are geographically separated from one another. In this case, it is of crucial importance for the
efficiency of an organization with its own goals to determine its best degree of
centralization. This approach can not only be naturally extended to the analysis
of corporations or other individual organizations but also to the large social systems that are controlled by the center.[47]

CP relations in a complex organization are based on two factors, power and cooperation. The center tends to consolidate power, defined as the right to make strategic decisions, as well as to reward or punish subordinates for their success or failure in implementing the center's decisions. At the same time, the center needs peripheral structures for running the entire organization. It is therefore interested in maximal cooperation with the periphery, which in turn is interested in collaboration with the center.

In a totalitarian system, political power, with the omnipresent apparatus of repression, mostly defines the relationship between the center and periphery. The provinces are deprived of any possibility of a direct confrontation with the center. They can only surreptitiously display their displeasure, until discovered, by ineffective fulfillment of directives from above.

Quite often, the secret sabotage of the center's directives by the provinces is treated as proof that the center shares its power with the periphery. American Sovietologists assumed this quite frequently, as will be shown later. In this way, the monopoly of power is confused with the efficacy of power, and these are very different concepts. In fact, the center in a totalitarian organization can adopt various strategies to control the periphery through its agents in the provinces. Never permitting its agents to define the goals of their activity, the center can delegate various degrees of freedom to them in choosing the means to the accomplish their directives.

At one extreme, the center can adopt the policy of total centralization. In this case, the emissaries from the center only have to control the observation of orders, while their opinions are almost completely disregarded by the center. At the other extreme, the center can choose the policy of full decentralization. This is similar to participatory management, to use terminology from the theory of organization.[48] In such an organization, emissaries are summoned to the centers for advice and can do anything they wish in their fiefdoms while trying to achieve the supreme goals set by the center.

In Iosif Stalin's time, regional party secretaries had very little freedom in the selection of methods to accomplish Stalin's orders. In Leonid Brezhnev's society, the situation was radically different. Although Moscow, as in the past, set the political and economic goals for party bosses in the provinces, party secretaries enjoyed much autonomy and could make specific decisions for the implementation of the Kremlin's policy.

For the reasons outlined here, the organizational approach is especially fruitful in the analysis of rigidly controlled societies, in which the leaders have a monopoly on power and can therefore choose one or another form of coordination of the center and provinces. Such was the case with Russian leaders prior to 1989–1991.

To some degree, this approach can help elucidate the relationship between the center and periphery in a stable democratic society with a strong, popularly elected central power, such as that in France. In such a society, CP relations are also somewhat similar to those described by the model of big organizations. Indeed, in these societies, the national institutions have priority over regional and central ones. This is similar to a totalitarian society, in which national institutions have the upper hand in the initiation of significant changes in the distribution of power between the federal and provincial authorities. Of course, the center in a democratic society has to take into account the position of the nation's population as a whole, in single regions, as well as the interests of the national and local elite.

Unstable Societies and the Conflict Approach

CP relations change radically in an unstable society, in which all actors are able to change their status vis-à-vis each other on their own initiative. The actors are relatively free not only to choose the means of their activities but also to choose their goals. This was the case in early feudal societies, such as the Holy Roman Empire, and in medieval England. This also held true in the United States during both its periods of turmoil, the American Revolution and the Civil War.[49]

However, even during more peaceful periods, when the United States undertook significant changes in its life, the two-hundred-year-old debates between Federalists and their opponents flare up again and again. This is evident, for instance, in the aftermath of the Great Depression and more recently in 1994–1995, when the Republican Party began its crusade for radical reforms. During such periods, the relationship between Washington, D.C., and the states could perfectly well be seen from the perspective of conflict theory.

Conflict theory, as it was shaped in the 1960–1970s in the West, borrowed its main concepts from Marxism. Marxism was in turn strongly influenced by the Hegelian dialectic, through which the world was seen as being fraught with various conflicts. There were a number of other authors in the past who viewed the world through the prism of conflict, including Ludwig Gumplowicz, Vilfredo Pareto, and, to some degree, Max Weber. In American postwar sociology, conflict theory emerged as a challenge to functionalism, with its focus on equilibrium in social life.

The sociologists who advanced the conflict approach, such as Raymond Aron, Lewis Coser, Ralf Dahrendorf, and Randall Collins, among others, widened the repertoire of conflicts under study as compared to approaches in traditional Marxist publications. In this way, they elevated the role of the conflict approach in sociological analysis.[50] Furthermore, the search for conflicts in social life was incorporated into modern analysis as its organic ingredient, without special reference to a "theory of conflict." In the same way, no one cites Marx on the analysis of the impact of economic developments on politics. Having lost its status as a special theory, the "conflict approach"—it is better to use this term instead of "conflict theory"—is now a part of the methodology of most social scientists.

The conflict approach found its strongest support in game theory, which also suggested the utility of seeing the world in terms of conflict between participants in a game, regardless of the character of the conflict—whether economic, political, social, or of another type. Game theory provided sociologists inclined to see the world in terms of conflict with several ideas quite useful for conflict analysis, such as zero-sum and non-zero-sum games, coalitions, payoff matrices, and so forth.

The advocates of the conflict approach believe in the ubiquitousness of conflicts in the world at all levels of society, whether they occur between different groups and institutions or inside them. Conflicts can range in size from the family unit to any social institution or corporation and to society on the whole, since the social actors with conflicting interests confront each other in the struggle for resources, power, and influence. It is also assumed that conflicts in society are engendered by all sorts of factors influencing social behavior, including economic, ethnic, political, and cultural factors, as well as all other factors that distinguish people from each other, such as sex, age, language, education (including level and type of education), state of health, and many other characteristics, all of which can produce conflicts of various sorts, both open and hidden. Conflicts generated by differences in place of residence, such as the capital, provinces, cities (large and small), and countryside, are quite significant in our world and are of special importance for this book. The conflict approach also presumes that in each conflict, the participants create their own more or less developed ideology (or at least a simple rationalization) to explain their behavior.

In addition, the conflict approach supposes that most social changes have occurred as a result of conflict. Competition as a major feature of the market economy is one of the outstanding examples of place in the importance of conflict as a source of change and innovation. The conflict approach also assumes that people, in order to pursue their interests and fight their rivals, create various groups, coalitions, and institutions. Mass movements, such as various insurrections, disturbances, and revolutions, are natural outcomes of conflicts of various sorts. Of course, the conflict approach has its limitations, and in some cases the focus on conflict can only mar the analysis, as was, for instance, the case with those Sovietologists who looked for conflicts in Soviet society where there were none. However, it can hardly be doubted that the conflict approach is extremely useful in the analysis of societies in a state of turmoil and transition from one stage to another.

The "ideal" society for the proper application of conflict theory in describing the relationship between the center and periphery is post-Communist Russia. Here, the major political actors were struggling for the distribution of power between the center and regions, as well as for control of natural and human resources.

For an analysis of CP relations, the heuristics of conflict theory, along with some concepts of game theory, is the best theoretical framework, even if no formal models and payoff matrices are to be used in our analysis.[51] Indeed, both entities, the center and provinces, try to maximize their own power, although the struggle is often against the long-term and global interests of each entity. The center tries to maximize its control over all elements of organization, including the individual units that make up the peripheral structures. Peripheral structures, personified by their leaders, try to minimize the intervention of the center, monopolize control over their own elements, and even exert influence on the decisions of the center.[52]

In such cases, the relationship between the center and the periphery, as well as that between individual peripheral units, is by definition only competitive and is based on both the zero- and non-zero-sum game principles. If regional leaders have consistent separatist intentions, as is the case with Quebec or Chechnia, to use only contemporary examples, the zero-sum approach is the most reasonable framework for an analysis.

However, there is often the situation when the non-zero-sum game approach has greater heuristic value than the zero-sum game. This occurs if both parties assume the necessity to divide power between themselves or when the regional elite are not poised toward full separation and do not want the demolition of the existing nation-state or even of the empire. This was the position of a few members of the national elite during the collapse of communism. At the same time, the central elite, aware of its limitations, also wants to delegate some power to local authorities as a condition for the efficient administration of society. In some cases, it may even be a condition necessary for its survival.

But even in the case of the non-zero-sum game, often not until the "saddle point" (a decision about how the power in a country will be divided) is achieved, regions and centers try to maximize their power at the expense of their opponents. Where the leaders of the center and regions find the saddle point is of crucial importance for the fate of a given state. In 1996, it was impossible to predict, for instance, where the saddle point would be for Russia, as well as for several other countries where internal stability had not yet been achieved. Such countries include India, Pakistan, and Canada, among others.[53]

Theoretically, it is possible to suppose that in the period of the formation of CP relations, both actors strive toward a sort of Pareto equilibrium, where each actor is in a better position as compared to the positions they would hold if they were to deviate from it. However, the struggle for power and the actors' concern only with self-interest always tends to cause a departure from the best overall solution.

The struggle for power between the center and periphery, combined with the willingness to set up cooperative relations under conditions favorable to each actor, is the main, but not the sole, conflict developing within an unstable organization. Also quite important are the conflicts that take place within the center. Such conflicts arise when each warring faction attempts to use the periphery, in its entirety or in isolated units, as its ally for gaining supremacy.

The various pressure groups and coalitions formed between actors, such as the coalition of regions against the center, the coalition of the center with some regions against other rivals, and so on, are very important phenomena in the internal struggle of an organization. The heuristics of coalition game concepts as a part of the conflict approach to social relations are quite useful for the description of alliances, both temporary and stable, that systematically emerge in CP relations. Among other things, two concepts—the famous prisoner's dilemma and the free rider concept[54]—suggest how difficult the creation of coalitions is when the eventual participants are trying to outsmart one another or put the burden of acting first on "others." When either of the actors fail to cooperate, both incur losses. The inability of Russian regions to form such a coalition against the center in 1993 resulted in the curtailment of their autonomy, at least in the short run.[55]

The role of external organizations in various internal conflicts can be important, since each actor has the option of looking for allies outside of its organization. In the case of any given society, it is foreign countries, both neighbors and remote but powerful countries, that very much influence that society's CP relations. These external forces either try to aid regions against the center or withdraw their aid in order to help the center maintain the country's unity. The impact of foreign countries on the fate of Austria-Hungary or the Ottoman Empire was enormous. As will be illustrated later, the neighbors' position on the developments in the Russian Federation after 1991 was quite significant and should be fully taken into account in the analysis of the nation's CP relations.

The conflict theory approach is also a reasonable tool for analyzing another phenomenon typical of unstable societies, the interregional conflict. Indeed, regionalism in the present world is often the ideology adopted by movements that advocate the redistribution of resources and power, not only between the provinces and the center, but also between various regions. We can observe this in Italy, where the hostility of the Lombardian League to the Italian south is quite evident, as is Catalonia's hostility to the rest of Spain and Quebec's to the rest of Canada. It is the movement for new forms of a nation-state.[56]

Major Actors in the Game

Numerous actors participate in the struggle for establishing CP relations. Various factions of the central and local elite, the current central and local administrations, intellectuals (or the church, as in the past), and the masses are all participants. In each historical epoch, all parties try to find a saddle point, a state of relative equilibrium, that permits them to maximize their goal or their utility function as much as possible.

All the actors determine their policy toward each other on the basis of what they "want" and what they "can get." Of course, "want" and "can get" closely interact with one another, functioning as both an independent and dependent variable in relation to each other. Seen individually, they often "want" what they "can get," but they also quite frequently "can get" what they "want."

Two actors, the regional elite and the masses, appear first. They are often the initiators and the warriors of regionalization, as well as the adversaries of regionalization.

In most cases, the local elites are the major engines of regionalization, whether we have backward or advanced territories in mind. Only rarely have ordinary people become pioneers of regionalization. This happens most often when the masses fight for democratic transformation, often under existing conditions that are favorable for regionalization. For example, this is what occurred in Russia in 1987–1995. Quite often the masses are either neutral or even inimical toward attempts to sever the ties between the provinces and capital. Even the intellectuals stand out relatively rarely as fervent supporters of political regionalization.[57] This runs contrary to nationalist movements for the reunification of a country, which intellectuals have usually supported. Let us recall from modern history those movements in Italy in the nineteenth century or in Ireland in the twentieth century.[58]

Of course, the local and ethnic elites alike need the support of the masses in their confrontation with the central elite or the elite of other regions. Thus, it is not surprising to see that elites resort to various means in an effort to draw the masses to their side.

In several cases, the interests of the masses and local elite converge. To some extent, the elite could claim to be acting on behalf of the population of its regions. However, even in this case, the angle of separation between the interests of the masses and of the elite is often quite significant. Many of the actions of the elite are dictated by its willingness to enhance and preserve its own power, even if that damages the interests of the entire population. In many cases, regionalism is almost purely the "elite's business" and arouses no support from the population. Certainly, in these cases regionalism cannot develop into a mass movement and seriously challenge the center.

Transition from a Totalitarian Society

The transition from a totalitarian to a democratic society presents us with a transition from one theoretical framework, the complex organization approach, to another, that of conflict theory. This in itself presents a special issue. Indeed, this transition introduces two elements unknown in a totalitarian society, the clash between various ideologies, as opposed to the monopoly of one ideology, and the cost of the maintenance of the state at the given level of unity.

The inclusion of ideology in the relationship between the center and the periphery compounds problems a great deal. It adds emotional and often irrational factors to the process of decisionmaking for any actor. Such factors appear irrational when judged by the interests of the country or the region. However, they often seem quite rational when one takes into account the goals of the actors who pursue these goals.[59] In contemporary Russia, for instance, the unifying patriotic ideology is confronted by various sorts of ideologies. There is the nationalist ideology, encompassing regions with specific ethnic compositions. There are also the antibureaucratic-democratic and pure "regionalist" ideologies.

Another element, which is almost irrelevant in a totalitarian society, is the cost of the center's communications with the provinces and costs of communications between various regions. With the decline in centralized control and the weakening of the "patriotic ideology," each region becomes able to compare the cost of its transactions with its compatriots and foreigners. The cost of communications also becomes a powerful factor entering the decisionmaking process and the choice of strategy for all actors in the country.

Value Judgments of Regionalization

As previously discussed, prior to the 1980s, it was permissible to unequivocally condemn regionalism as a conservative movement. Later, the attitudes toward regionalization became somewhat more flexible, although the spirit of disapproval was still dominant in most publications on this subject.

We are more sensitive to this issue in this book, insisting that modern regionalism is predominately stimulated by the most current trends. But we in no way approve of this movement. The fact that behind this movement there are powerful contemporary trends does not mean that mankind must praise it by definition. The crux of the debates about the consequences of regionalism lies in the appraisal of the role of the nation-state in the contemporary world.[60]

Of course, now there are people in almost all the larger countries who do not consider the traditional unit of the nation-state to be an important prerequisite for the well-being of their population. They contemplate the possible splitting of these states into smaller partitions as a rather positive process that must be encouraged. In this way, as the ideologists of the transformation of the nation-state argue, this process will spread the protection of human rights and increase the efficiency of the economy. They also argue that this would finally eliminate national borders, since people would no longer tend to live in the large, old nation-states but in specific cities and regions that would perpetuate mutually beneficial relations among themselves. This would be the world that Marx and Engels predicted, even though in another context; in *The Communist Manifesto* one and one-half centuries ago, they promised a world without national borders.

However, some people have taken a different stand on the same issue. They have suggested that regionalism, along with other forms of particularism, undermines the fundamentals of a society's unity. Separate people, who live in the same territory and have the same cultural heritage and language, present a danger to the existence of the nation-state, especially if the local elite is able to play its ethnic or cultural cards.[61] The foes of regionalization also point to the geopolitical dangers of the weakening of modern nation-states, since it portends the remapping of the entire world, promising new, horrendous conflicts.[62]

In this book, we will exercise restraint in the direct assessment of the consequences of regionalization in Russia, as well as in other countries. We will take great pains to keep our objectivity, although we are inclined to see democratization and the expansion of human rights as the major criteria in the evaluation of this complex and contradictory process of regionalization. At the same time, we remain aware of the consequences of this process on civil order in Russian society as a value vitally important for the well-being of the people, in some cases even more important than political freedoms and democracy.

PART ONE

The Era of the Center's Dominance Before 1985

History plays an active role in current developments in Russia in several ways. The first manifestation of history's part in current trends is in cultural and ideological traditions. There are also various institutions that stem from the past, and some go as far back as the roots of Russian history. History also plays a role in recent developments through actors, whether political parties or individuals, who were active in previous periods.

The past is of special importance to the life of Russians. There are not many people on earth who are as absorbed with their national history as the Russians. History also plays a far more significant role in the decisions of everyday life for Russians than for others. Russian history, as it has unfolded in the last thousand years, has been quite influential in the struggle between centralists and decentralists in post-Communist Russia. The Russian mentality abounds with the images and ideas of the remote past, which are directly relevant to regionalization as it develops in contemporary Russia. This is why it is necessary to take a brief look at Russian history since the Kievan period prior to examining the most recent epoch, 1991–1995.

The Soviet period itself absorbed many Russian traditions, particularly the traditional relationship between the center and periphery. This is of great significance because the Soviet ideology incorporated in this relationship directly affects developments in Russia after 1991.

Moreover, the political and cultural figures of post-Communist Russia were educated and socialized under the Soviet regime and cannot completely escape its influence, even though they proclaim themselves to be fiery anti-Communists. The Communist Party, one of the most powerful organizations in post-Communist Russia, is the direct heir of the Communist Party of the Soviet Union. Therefore, it would be difficult to understand the complicated processes that have taken place since 1991 without first delving into Russian national history.

3

PREREVOLUTIONARY RUSSIA: THE CENTER UNCHALLENGED SINCE THE SIXTEENTH CENTURY

In order to understand the importance of CP relations in the Middle Ages to contemporary Russia, one must first glance at the administrative map of the Russian Federation.

The Regional Structure of Kiev Rus'

On this map, for instance, there are the neighboring regions of Novgorod and Tver. Novgorod has its roots in the pre-Rurik period of Russian history. Tver has its foundations in the Mongolian period. Furthermore, consider the two neighboring regions of the Black-Soil Center, Kursk and Voronezh. The first dates back to the principality of Kiev Rus', whereas the second is the result of the feudal colonization epoch of the Muscovite state.

The northern part of western Siberia was developed by two waves of immigrants, separated in time by several centuries. The first wave originated in the Yermak period in the sixteenth century. The second wave, which dates back to the 1960s and 1970s, resulted from the development of the Khanty-Mansiy oil lands, after which that area became the main oil-producing region of Russia.

Other regions, such as the Republic of Tatarstan and the Astrakhan Region, were foreign states conquered by Moscow tsars in the mid-sixteenth century and became part of the Russian empire. These were in fact the first conquered territories of the fledgling empire. It should be pointed out that Tatarstan alone has preserved its native ethos, whereas Astrakhan has been turned into a common Russian province. Numerous similar examples can be given.

Before the end of the tenth century, the Kiev state consisted of a number of tribal unions, which preserved their autonomy. Historians name eight of them as the main ones. There was the Polyane tribal union living around Kiev, which also incorporated the tribes of Ulichi, Tivertsy, Volynyane, Duleby and Duzhane. These tribes lived in the territory that is today the western Ukraine. There also were the Drevlyane, who lived in the woods along the Teterev River; the Krivichi, who lived in what are today the Smolensk and Pskov Regions; the Dregovichi, living in Polesye and present-day Byelorussia; the Slovene of the Novgorod Land; and the Rodimichi and Vyatichi, residents of the present-day non-black-soil regions of Russia.

Because none of these settled peoples left their areas over the centuries, it is therefore clear that Polyane, Drevlyane, Severyane, Volynyane, and so on were the ancestors of the Ukrainian people; the Krivichi and Dregovichi of the Byelorussian people; and the Slovene, Radimichi and Vyatichi of the Russian people. This means that there could not have been any disintegration of the allegedly single ancient Russian nation into three separate nations.

According to both domestic and foreign sources, the most numerically strong were the Slavic tribes of Vyatichi, the ancestors of the Russian nation. The land of Vyatichi was mostly inhabited by people "with rather modest means," who jointly built towns with fortifications, lived in log houses resembling Christian basilicas in form, rooted out trees, ploughed the land, organized joint festivities with other villages, burnt their dead together, and if necessary fought with lances, arrows and javelins. Their everyday life was full of primeval prejudices, such as the remnants of matrilocal marriages, widows' suicides, and pagan beliefs.[1]

Kiev Rus' was the first state entity that emerged to control the territories of people in several tribes, which had kept their identity for a long time. The prince's power was a necessary component in the social and political structure of Kiev Rus'.[2] In the eleventh and twelfth centuries, the social functions of the princes were as versatile as were the functions of any socially useful institution serving the interests of society as a whole, including the masses of people.

At the same time, the prince in Kiev Rus' did not become an authoritarian ruler. This is clear from the ample evidence of the activity of people's local communities.[3] It is hardly possible to call such a prince a sovereign, when, upon arriving in a certain *volost'* (principality), he had to seek the support of the *vetche* (people's assembly) community and accept *vetche* decisions, which imposed certain limitations upon him. In this way, the prince concluded an agreement (*ryad*) with the people's assembly. In a sense, the prince became a power of the community, and his function was to protect the interests of the local community. The head of Kiev Rus', although regarded as the ruler of these territories, could not ignore the sort of autonomy that the tribes and some cities possessed.

The conflict between the quest for autonomy, which was often linked to democratic independence, as embodied by the famous *vetche*, and the country's unity, often associated with the prince, led to power struggles, which raged throughout the history of Kiev Rus' and during the ninth through fifteenth centuries following its demise. These power struggles were eventually suppressed with the installation of autocratic rule in Moscow in the fifteenth century. However, they were once again revived in full scale much later, in 1917 after the fall of tsarism and again in 1991 after the collapse of communism.

The Period of "Feudal Splitting"

Even more important for the future development of regionalism in Russia were the events that took place after the decline of Kiev as the leading Slav state. The decline of Kiev was due in part to a loss of trade following the sack of Constantinople by the Crusaders in 1204 and the consequent migration of the people of Kiev to the north. Novgorod replaced Kiev as a flourishing commercial state, rising to a dominant position. In the thirteenth century, Novgorod was chosen as the site for a major factory of the Hanseatic League. Kiev also lost its importance as the great national and cultural center, to be replaced by the cities of Suzdal, Vladimir, and, ultimately, Moscow (founded in 1147), all of which were future rivals for the leading role in the formation of the Russian state.

At the same time, in the period from the twelfth to fourteenth centuries, the number of princes in Rus' grew noticeably. For example, under Vladimir Svyatoslavich there were eight principalities, or *volosti*. Their number grew to fifteen in the mid-twelfth century. Russia became a loose federation of city-states, held together by a common language, religion, set of traditions, and customs, ruled by members of the multitudinous house of Rurik. Members of the royal house were usually at war with one another, and thus they were unable to protect their subjects against nomadic peoples such as the Polovetz and Mongols or against the Teutonic knights and other foreign invaders. After 1991, this period was cited regularly by those who opposed separatist tendencies in the Russian Federation.

One of the Polovetz raids was the subject of the Russian epic *The Lay of Igor's Host*, which bemoaned the inabilities of Russian princes, absorbed with protecting their own independence rather than uniting against foreign enemies. This epic became an important element of the Russian mentality and served as a warning against separatism and the neglect of the national interest. The image of princes fighting with each other and being oblivious to the fate of the people was deeply engraved in the Russian mentality. This image has been evoked countless times in the debates on regionalization in post-Communist Russia.[4]

The regional structure of Rus' in the twelfth century can be described as an aggregate of basic semistates. According to Arsenii N. Nasonov and Lev N. Gumilev, Rus' consisted of (1) the Novgorod Republic with suburbs; (2) Polotsk Principality; (3) Smolensk Principality; (4) Rostov-Suzdal Land; (5) Ryazan Principality; (6) Turovo-Pinsk Land; (7) Russian Land proper, including the three principalities of Kiev, Chernigov, and Pereyaslavl; and (8) Volyn and Chervonnaya Rus', which in the early thirteenth century united to form the Galitsk Principality.[5]

The successful Mongol invasion in the first half of the thirteenth century and the installment of the so-called Tatar yoke over the next several centuries should be considered another terrible price paid for the inability of the Russian princes to put national interests above their own. These events are also embedded in the Russian national memory, despite the fact that Russian politicians and intellectuals in the 1990s derived different conclusions from them. Most of them use the "Tatar yoke" as a warning against the egotistical interests of various elites, both national and regional, referring to these elites as a danger to the survival of Russia. Others, deep pessimists, have suggested that Russia is now doomed to disintegrate as it did in the thirteenth century.

The Regional Structure of Moskovia

Under the rule of the Golden Horde in the thirteenth and fourteenth centuries, Great Rus' remained a country divided into numerous regions independent from each other but not from the Mongol's lands. Great Rus' was a very loose confederation of eleven large Russian principalities, divided into twenty smaller *udelnyi* principalities. The Tatar Mongols governed Great Rus' through the Great Vladimir Principality, which was nominally preserved. The position of the grand prince was used to stir up strife among the other princes. The unique feature of this regional structure was the fact that all the principalities were ruled over by the descendants of a single ancient princely dynasty, the Rurikoviches. The main members of the confederation, the Moscow, Tver, Ryazan, and Novgorod princes, constituted a kind of collective suzerainty of a single dynasty over a nominal center.[6]

It would not be an exaggeration to state that the character of Russian statehood and Russian regionalism was finally determined in the fifteenth century. This occurred when one of the Russian principalities subordinated to the Golden Horde was chosen to play the leading part in the unification of the country. The khans of the Golden Horde considered themselves the supreme rulers of Rus', and therefore they promoted the unification of the Russian princes in order to facilitate the management of their Russian *ulusy,* or districts. This was especially beneficial in the collection of tribute, for it was much easier to entrust this task to a single grand prince and to make him responsible for it. The same was true of judicial functions. Thus, by stirring up competition for the position of grand prince, the Tatar Mongols objectively promoted the unification of the principalities.[7]

By the year 1300, the Tver Principality was considered the strongest, the Ryazan Principality the most militant, and the Novgorod Republic the richest among the principalities of Great Rus'.[8] The existence of powerful independent Russian principalities with their centers in ancient Russian cities, sometimes even stronger than Moscow, was an important fact for those who were involved in the regional movements, fighting for autonomy from Moscow at the end of the nineteenth century, in 1917 and after 1991.

However, by 1400, Moscow Principality had become the strongest, and it managed to capture the capital city of Vladimir in 1364 and, leading the people's volunteer corps, to rout the armed forces of the Golden Horde at the Battle of Kulikovo in 1380. Despite the military victory by Moscow, another century would pass before the Tatar Mongols' rule was completely shaken off, a delay that was mostly due to internal struggle. Once again, this is a fact that Russian historians cite as another argument for maintaining national unity.[9] Eventually, Moscow, under Ivan III, annexed Novgorod in 1478 and the Tver Principality in 1485, and then, under Vasilii III, annexed Pskov in 1510, the Smolensk Principality in 1514, and the Novgorod-Seversky Principality and the Ryazan Principality in 1521.

Of no less importance in the view of later Russian generations was the struggle between the Kremlin and the boyars. The boyars, Russian minor noblemen, were effectively the absolute rulers on their estates. They were inclined to treat the Moscow prince as an equal and, in fact, did not recognize his sovereignty. Local princes and boyars did not want to yield their power so easily to Moscow and used what few opportunities existed to regain their power. This was unsuccessfully attempted by several princes during the reign of Vasilii III in 1521.

All these developments have been engraved in the Russian mentality over the centuries as the most important events leading to the creation of the Great Russian State and, later, the Russian empire. The names of the independent principalities that opposed "Moscow's historical mission," such as Tver or Ryazan, came to epitomize the lowering of national interest in favor of narrower, local self-interest.

The apologists for the Romanov and the later Stalinist empire used to substantiate the rise of Moscow and its establishment of monarchical centralism throughout Rus' by citing the following important objective factors: (1) Moscow's geographical position at the center of the Russian lands and at the crossroads of important trade routes, (2) the absence of intra-Moscow military-feudal strife, and (3) the high political skill of the princes (Stalin's predecessors).[10] The modern supporters of the Eurasian concept of Russia, who praise the alliance between the Russians and Asian peoples, explained Moscow's dominance by pointing to the matrimonial union between Moscow and Tatar Mongol rulers—"Tatar wives in the Moscow palaces of the princes." For instance, the sister of Khan Uzbek was married to Prince Yurii Danilovich.[11]

It seemed that there was no alternative for Russia: Moscow, and Moscow alone! However, this is not the sole possible historical perspective. According to the research of Alexander Zimin, an outstanding Soviet historian, there was an alternative.[12] An analysis of available sources prompted Zimin to conclude that in the early fifteenth century, as far as the formation of a single Russian state was concerned, there were at least three groups, which represented three territorial formations, laying claim to the heritage of the victor of the Battle of Kulikovo, the great Russian unifier Dmitrii Donskoi. The Moscow-centered territorial formation was one of three territorial formations. The second was represented by the trade and handicraft settlements of the Russian north and partially by the Volga Region (Galich, Vyatka, and Ustyug, areas where the salt-extraction industry was developed and which were inhabited by free peasants). The third group was represented by Novgorod and Tver, which became rich thanks to the transit trade between the West and the East.

What was the reason for the rise of Moscow? Zimin refuted the traditional arguments in favor of the rise of Moscow that had been supported by the tsarist autocracy and Stalinism.[13] He managed to prove that there were no easy trade routes in the Moscow region and that the cities on the Volga (Galich, Iaroslavl, Kostroma, Nizhniy Novgorod, and others) were in a much more favorable position geographically for the development of trade.

Additional arguments against these traditional explanations about the rise of Moscow include the observation that the Moscow region was very poor in natural resources and did not have a single well-developed industry. There was also much to be desired as far as suitable farmland was concerned. Moreover, strange as it may seem, Moscow failed to become the center of resistance to the Golden Horde after Dmitrii Donskoi, evident in the fact that a few of his descendants begged the Tatars to be made grand prince.[14] This means that the accepted economic, geographical, social, and political version of the unavoidable rise of Moscow over the rest of the principalities is quite questionable.

Still, Moscow did have a decisive advantage over other principalities. It possessed a cadre of gentry troops, or knights. Since the fourteenth century, the prince's government had settled landowner-soldiers, the Russian version of landed knights, in the center of the Moscow state, which experienced poor trade and was almost completely devoid of natural resources. These landowner-soldiers were the force in this wooded and swampy region that not only subordinated peasant colonists, who later had to render material support to them to be allowed to perform their chief functions, but also promoted the victory of the Moscow unifying group. In this period, we find the first appearance on the historical arena of Russian beneficiaries, whom some historians stubbornly find in Kiev Rus', basing their reasoning on the proposition that there should have been beneficiaries there, although nothing of the sort can be substantiated in historical sources.

Zimin's main conclusion is as follows, though some historians consider it to be too categorical. The victory of the Moscow unification movement greatly predetermined the further development of Russia's centralization as serfdom, whereas a victory of the unification of the north might have brought about the rather rapid development of commodity-money relations. Had the north won, Russia might have developed further along the route typical for western European countries (the victory of the third, Novgorod-Tver movement, was out of the question).[15]

At the same time that the tsar's power was strengthening, an institution called the *Boyarskaia Duma* underwent a very remarkable evolution. This council of boyars, who represented their patrimonial estates and had the ability to challenge the tsar, was gradually transformed into a body of advisers and, eventually, supreme leaders apparently concerned only about national, and not local, interests. Four and one-half centuries later, Russians still watch the supreme leaders and regional bosses struggle over an institution—but this time, the institution is the Federal Council, a body that in 1994–1995 was composed of regional bosses and was referred to by some journalists as the *Boyarskaia Duma*.

Ivan the Terrible

Ivan IV, also known as Ivan the Terrible, delivered the fatal blow, mortally wounding the boyars. His aim was to consolidate his autocratic position by weakening the power of the boyars and the church. Under Ivan the Terrible, the struggle of the boyars against the nobility, considered to be an attack on the remaining "semistates" in favor of a completely united state, reached its peak, although the final blow did not fall until the late seventeenth century.

In his struggle, Ivan IV seized half of Moskovia as his personal property. This territory, called the *oprichnina*, was a separate administrative unit ruled directly by the tsar. This development would later be recalled in post-Communist Russia when President Boris Yeltsin created his own administration, which competed with the government in ruling the country.[16] Ivan distributed this territory among his supporters as rewards for military and personal service, thereby establishing a new service corps called the *oprichniki*. In return for land, the *oprichniki* acted as Ivan's personal police force.

As has happened many times previously in Russian history, battle for the centralization of the Russian state against the regional elite was accompanied by a wave of mass terror. Ivan the Terrible initially directed this wave against the boyars and then extended it to all other classes of the population. The cruel massacre of Novgorod in 1570, prompted by an apparent "boyars' conspiracy," was one of the bloodiest illustrations of the price of centralization under specific conditions. The massacre at Grozny in 1995, another act initiated by the masters of the Kremlin in Moscow for the preservation of the center's control over the territories that it considered to be its own, can be cited as another example of the bloody destruction of a city regarded by Moscow itself as "Russian."

When the boyars, resentful about their diminishing power, plotted against him, Ivan IV resorted to torture, exile, and execution to repress them. These actions were praised by Stalin as a way to create a powerful, centralized state. The elimination of regionalism was a primary condition for the creation of the powerful Russian empire that Ivan IV began to build with the conquering of Kazan in 1552 and Astrakhan in 1556.

After the death of Tsar Ivan the Terrible in 1584, followed by the death of Tsar Boris Godunov in 1605, the Time of Troubles, lasting from the late sixteenth until the early seventeenth centuries, settled harshly on Russia. During this time, the boyars tried to restore their power. They almost reached their goal by first murdering Tsar Godunov's successor, known as the False Dmitrii, and then by ousting Tsar Vasilii Shuiskii in 1610. They installed a government of seven boyars, known as the *semiboyarshchina*, in 1610 and colluded with the Polish army, to which they rendered Moscow.

With a Polish army occupying the capital and a powerful peasant rebellion quickly evolving, the country lapsed into chaos. The situation was at last resolved by the initiative of Kuzma Minin, a Nizhniy Novgorod butcher, who succeeded in raising a national army in northeast Russia. Under Prince Dmitrii Mikhailovich Pozharskii, who gained the help of a few cossacks, this army marched on Moscow and in 1612 expelled the Poles. In 1613, a *Zemskii Sobor* (irregular national assembly) was called, representing the principal chief and the Orthodox Church, elected Mikhail Romanov, the great-nephew of Tsar Ivan IV's wife, Anastasia Romanovna, as tsar. Mikhail thus founded the ruling house of Romanov.

The Time of Troubles and particularly the period of the "seven-boyar government" were often invoked by Russians in the debates surrounding regionalism in post-Communist Russia. Many cited this turbulent time as an example of what was to come if the regions would not recognize the supreme value of national unity.[17]

In 1549, Ivan IV had called the first *Zemskii Sobor*. This precursor of the Russian Duma of 1993 consisted of two houses. The upper house composed the *Boyarskaia Duma*, the council of bishops and the highest officials. The lower house represented all classes of Russian society, except the peasants. The *Zemskii Sobor*, reflecting the mood of the country, was evidently more supportive of state centralization than the upper house. It therefore furthered the diminishment of the role of the *Boyarskaia Duma*.

Military Reforms

The creation of a centralized Russian state in the fifteenth to sixteenth centuries was based on radical changes in military organization, a circumstance that significantly influenced Russian history. The newly centralized Russian state was based entirely on the huge military machine directed against its neighbors, for the state's defense as well as for territorial expansion. For this reason alone, as will be shown in detail later, the end of the Cold War in the late 1980s and the movement toward sincere attempts at coexistence with the West were a revolutionary turn in Russian history—a change that deprived the central elite of the major justification for its power and significantly encouraged regionalism.

The gist of the military reforms of the fifteenth and sixteenth centuries was the creation of a corps of knights, whose members, in return for their service, were given land, creating a local landed gentry. The reform caused a revolution in agrarian relations similar to the one that took place in the eighth to tenth centuries in the West. Valid comparisons include the military-agrarian reforms of Charles Martel, Alfred the Great, and Heinrich the Fowler in the state of the Franks. As in Great Russia, England and Germany, respectively, also carried out such reforms, under conditions of tense struggle against external enemies, such as the Arabs, Normans, and Hungarians.

The establishment of a military system of this type had a tremendous impact in the sphere of politics and state structure, to say nothing of the socioeconomic consequences, such as serfdom and extensive growth of the *corvée* system, which especially flourished following the military victories of Peter I and the emergence of opportunities to export grain to the West.[18] First of all, the absence of the right of primogeniture resulted in a situation in which even the owners of patrimonial estates became quite dependent on the state. They became a kind of nursery, training soldiers who did military service for a landed estate.

As a result of the division of patrimonial estates between heirs, old-time boyars, like children of the princes, lost the basis of their social and political influence and began to rely only on the favors of the grand prince. This explains why the boyars and the nobility failed to bring forth an aristocracy capable of limiting the power of the monarch. Not only landowners but also minor princes and boyars in their petitions called themselves serfs, or slaves, of the grand prince. Observant foreigners, such as Ambassador Herberstein of Germany, used to write that the Moscow princes Ivan III and his son Vasilii III had far greater power over the lives and property of their subjects than any monarch in western Europe (this was written before the time of Ivan IV).[19] Thus, the military-agrarian reforms of Ivan III laid the foundation for the Russian autocracy.

The organization of troops and the search for the means to maintain them were the central problems of the Moscow state government. The entire population was divided into two groups: those who supplied the military men and those who kept the army. Due to the lack of sufficiently developed financial resources, the great estate of the grand prince (later the tsar) supplied the state cavalry, the main troops of Russia in that period. The maintenance of the cavalry at the expense of local landed estates meant the permanent attachment to the soil of the peasants in those villages that had to support cavalrymen. Since the late fifteenth century, the migration of peasants had gradually become limited. By the early seventeenth century, under the Decree of 1607, peasant migration was already considered a state offense. The peasants were attached to their owners in accordance with entries in special books (*pistsovaya*) of 1592–1593.[20] This meant that the peasants in Russia became serfs at the time when their counterparts in western Europe had already been set free.

For the upkeep of an infantry armed with firearms, the need for which became clear in the course of military clashes with the West, a tax system that levied direct and indirect taxes was introduced. Direct taxes consisted of *pishchalnye* taxes for the upkeep of the *streltsy* (military guards who served the tsars from the sixteenth to the beginning of the eighteenth century), *emchuzhnye* taxes for the production of gunpowder, *gorodovye* (town) and *zasechnye* taxes for the building of fortifications, and *popolyanichnye* taxes for ransom.

Indirect taxes consisted of internal customs duties, which constituted a rather complex system of payments and were levied at every stage of the movement of goods from the producer to the customer. In the course of the sixteenth and seventeenth centuries, this system was aggregated but not reduced. According to T. N. Milyukov, the military expenditures of the Moscow government grew in the course of the seventeenth century by at least 200 percent.[21]

The above-mentioned reforms turned the recently unified northeastern Rus' into a military monarchy with an omnipotent center and a population forced into tax-paying corporations tied by mutual guarantees. There were very weak manifestations of public initiative, and the economy was completely subordinated to military purposes. The consequences of these military-agrarian reforms of the fifteenth to sixteenth centuries to a great extent determined the character of Russian centralism and particularism and reached as far as the February Revolution of 1917. Furthermore, the drive for the creation of the best military machine under existing conditions continued to influence Russian domestic life until the collapse of communism.

Regional Structures

The regional structure of the state as it was created in the sixteenth century (Ivan IV's reform of local administration took place in 1555) also fully corresponded to the aims of a newly centralized state and its military organization. The local landowning system replaced the system of "feeding" as a means of maintaining the army. So as not to distract the military men from performing their military duties, a new form of elected local government was introduced in the localities. However, this was a special type of elected government, far different from what is usually implied by the term. The population elected its representatives not actually for the purpose of defending the public interest but rather to fulfill the assignments of the center, that is, the state, on behalf of the voters. In fact, this was a way in which the autocratic government could use its subjects as a sort of cheap surrogate for bureaucrats who were now responsible for the fulfillment of the center's directives, a practice that the later Soviet system exploited to a great extent.

The system was vastly extended during Soviet times, when the political elite recruited millions of Russians into the role of "little bosses," as members of numberless committees, as agitators, and as members of various official organizations. These Russians, who were granted almost no special benefits other than the feeling of belonging to "power," helped local authorities to control the population, reporting on each other and forcing each other to observe official directives.[22]

With the collapse of the Soviet state, this centuries-old system disappeared, leaving behind a power vacuum. It was not filled by the new order based on the new Russian democratic institutions since these institutions did not contain elements of effective self-government, without which it is impossible, as the experience of Western countries shows, to maintain order in the provinces.

In the sixteenth century, local authorities elected by the people not only did not defend the interests of the population but lived directly at their expense. Twice a year, on Easter and St. Peter's Day, the population had to bring them foodstuffs and fodder. Furthermore, local governors received a portion of all duties, trade taxes, and court fines collected.

The administrative staff of the vice-regent consisted of a manager (*tiun*), a judge, a bailiff, and other officials. As there were no established norms as far as the amount of "feeding" was concerned, government by vice-regents and village rulers turned into an actual tragedy for the population.[23]

In the mid-sixteenth century, all of the power in the cities and *uezdy* (districts) was concentrated in the hands of city *voevody* (governors), who replaced the vice-regents and officials of urban departments. They governed completely in the localities and controlled the bodies of local self-government (the zemstvos).

The duties of a *voevoda* were as follows:

To establish the size of a given year's tribute to be paid by the population that was bound to keep the army

To exercise control over the payment of tribute (to detect shirkers)

To perform police functions (both the zemstvo and the *gubnaya izba* [a type of criminal investigation office] were subordinate to him), which consisted of looking for runaway peasants and criminals

To supervise the work done by the customs office, the work of the pubs, petty trade, and the operation of mills through his subordinate officers in these areas and through other *tselovalniki* (officers)

To recruit gentry and boyar children for military service and to compile respective lists, including data on the size and quality of an estate and the way in which service was performed, as well as to organize regular reviews and send recruits to the army upon the first demand of the *Razryadnyi Prikaz* (a central department dealing with military matters)

To organize local hired corps, consisting of *streltsy* and *pushkari* (gunners)

To bear responsibility for all city fortifications, and in border areas, for the organization of border guard services (mounted patrols)

To perform judicial functions, including imposing fines (it should be mentioned that the concentration of power in the hands of *voevody* was accompanied by a serious aggravation of penalties meted out by local Russian courts)[24]

Subordinated to *voevody* were the city commandant, as well as the heads of the *streltsy*, the city prison, the gunners, and so forth. In large cities, *voevody* usually had one or two assistants, called second and third *voevody*, who were also future vice-governors.[25]

It is only natural that the militarized Moscow state, based on the system of landed estates, became overcentralized, and the regions there were deprived of their rights more than in any other monarchy in Europe. Such was the price of state unity, Moscow style. The creation of the Russian empire and the administrative innovations introduced by Peter I failed essentially to change this regional structure.

Peter I's Reforms of Local Government

The reforms of Peter the Great were necessitated not so much by the state's new tasks as by a search for new means to solve a centuries-old task: the extraction of the maximum amount of manpower and monetary resources from the people in order to sharply raise the country's war potential. In this sense, nothing changed significantly. The only changes were the skyrocketing military expenditures connected with the formation of a regular Russian army in order to replace the genteel cavalry and *strelets* infantry and the navy, built not on the system of hiring, as in the West, but on a recruiting system. Greater military expenditures were urged in light of the twenty-year-old war with Sweden, which culminated in the conquest of the Baltic regions and gaining an outlet on the Baltic Sea ("a window to Europe"). Within the period from 1700 to 1710, the size of the Russian army increased by 150 percent (from forty thousand to one hundred thousand), while military expenditures grew in 1710 by 40 million rubles, in sharp contrast with 1680.[26]

The creation of regular armed forces and war industry, as well as huge conquests (during the reign of Peter the Great, the territory of Russia increased by almost 10,500 square miles), required a significant growth in profits in the budget (65 percent of all budget expenditures were delegated to military purposes).[27]

All this entailed the need for a radical restructuring of the state management mechanism. The reform of the state mechanism (as with the reform of the armed forces), carried out in the first twenty-five years of the seventeenth century, established a system of bureaucratic government. This new system was organized on a uniform basis throughout the country with the gentry at the head, as members of the gentry had served earlier on their own estates, though this time they served not as knights of the gentry corps but as officers and officials.

The *Boyarskaia Duma* was replaced by the governing Senate, which ruled over the country in the absence of the tsar. The system of centralized branch management in Russia, in the form of either colleges, branch ministries, committees, departments, or people's commissariats under the Bolsheviks, was destined to outlive the many centuries of the gentry's rule and, almost without a break, the Bolsheviks' rule.

The system of local management, which consisted of *voevody* and *gubnaya* elders, was also unsuitable for the tasks put forward by Peter I. The main reform of local government took place in 1708. Russia was divided into eight *gubernii* (administrative divisions): *Ingermanlandskaya* (located since 1710 in St. Petersburg), Moscow, Arkhangelsk, Smolensk, Kiev, Azov, Kazan, and Siberia (To-bolsk). Five years later, these administrative divisions were further divided to form the Nizhniy Novgorod, Astrakhan, and Riga *gubernii*. In 1725, there were fourteen *gubernii*.[28] Two centuries later, the *gubernia* divisions emerged once again, seen as the ideal administrative structure for Russia.

The introduction of the poll tax required the close proximity of the government to the tax payers. In response, in 1719, forty-five provinces, later to include five more, were formed within the *gubernii*, which were further divided into districts. Governor-generals were placed at the head of the *gubernii* in the capital and on the border, controlling simple governors and vice-governors. Provinces were headed by *voevody* and districts by zemstvo officials, who were elected by the local gentry.[29]

The *gubernia* reform united the central and local government into a single system. Each province now had a branch of the respective central body, typically departments dealing with recruits, forestry, foodstuffs, investigation, and so on, which were the official representatives of the St. Petersburg colleges.[30]

In 1720, an attempt was made to separate the judicial branch from the administrative branch. The provincial court, consisting of *ober-landrichter* (senior judge) and several assessors, was responsible for the rural population, whereas the city court looked after the urban population. The court of second instance was declared to be the *nadvorny* (governor-appointed) court in Moscow and St. Petersburg, and the third instance was the Justice College. The functions of the Supreme Court of the Russian Empire, up to its very end, were performed by the Senate.[31] However, this attempt to separate the judicial and administrative powers, the first such attempt in the history of the country, could not but fail under the conditions of a centralized government. There was no force that could prevent the governors and *voevody*, who ruled over the *gubernii* and provinces single-handedly, from interfering with the work of judicial bodies, which were a significant source of power over the population and a source of personal enrichment.

In the period from 1723 to 1724, a magisterial structure of city government was established, which replaced the burgomaster *izba* system of the beginning of the century. The magistrate was a collective office consisting of a president, from two to four burgomasters, and from two to eight *ratmann* who managed the entire life of the cities, including the activities of the corporations and guilds, which embraced all the craftsmen and merchants.[32]

The local administrative reform did not achieve its goal of creating a system that allowed the capital to effectively control the periphery. The strong power of the governors and *voevody* appeared in practice to be stronger than the central government, which was unable to properly control the localities, with the probable exception of military affairs. This was borne out by a fantastic sum of arrears, which by the end of the 1720s reached 35 percent of the profit in the state budget (consisting of approximately 7 million out of the 20 million rubles of the state budget's profit).[33]

In addition to overt control over the activity of the state apparatus, there was also covert control that was practiced by sneaks whose task was "secretly to watch over all affairs and learn about thieves and power abusers."[34] On numerous occasions, the Senate was forced to send officers vested with special powers and sometimes accompanied by soldiers to *gubernii* to collect arrears, to punish *gubernia* officials and even to arrest governors.[35] Just imagine a soldier arresting the governor! As we will demonstrate later on, the management of centralized government is unthinkable without maintaining both secret and overt control. In any case, there was no stopping the representatives of local governments from stealing and accepting bribes.

As was shown to be true throughout the whole of Russian history until the end of the Soviet system, a monopoly on political power never meant that this power would be effective. In addition, it was not necessarily the case that such a monopoly could enforce the central regime's orders through its agents in the provinces, who, by the logic of the system, enjoyed a significant degree of unofficial autonomy and could indulge in arbitrariness in running their domains.

Later in the first half of the nineteenth century, the powerful and despotic Tsar Nikolai I complained about his inability to curb his governors. Nikolai Gogol's famous novel, *The Inspector-General* (1836), eloquently describes the objective autonomy of the emissaries of the Russian capital.

Decentralization of Local Government, 1775–1800

Under Catherine the Great and the strong influence of the Pugachev riot (1773–1775), which threatened the existence of the empire and its dominant noble class, the tsarist government decided to strengthen the gentry's role in the management of the localities. This could be achieved only through decentralizing local government and placing local gentlefolk in the most crucial positions there. This reform was somewhat similar to those of Brezhnev that supported party cadres and expanded the power of party regional secretaries, mostly as a means to ensure order in the country.

The Resolution on *Gubernii* was issued in 1775. This resolution radically changed the local administration and transformed it into a system that lasted up to the reforms of the 1860s.[36] The basic targets of these administrative reforms were threefold. First, the administrative bodies were broken down into smaller units. At the time of Peter's reforms, Russia was divided into twenty-three *gubernii*, sixty-six provinces, and 130 independent *uezdy*. According to the resolution, all the provinces were abolished. The country was to be divided into fifty *gubernii*, which in turn were to be further divided into *uezdy*. This territorial-administrative division was based on tax and military considerations. As a rule, a *gubernia* embraced 300,000–400,000 "revision souls," whereas an *uezd* contained about 20,000–30,000 people. The specific national and economic features of the territory were completely ignored.[37]

Second, a certain decentralization of the branch system introduced by Peter the Great was needed. Offices were opened in *gubernii* that were to be departments of the colleges.[38]

Third, a certain degree of separation of powers in the executive-administrative, judicial, and financial-tax functions of local government developed. This was done according to the principles of Montesquieu, which Catherine II shared. In particular, a system of local courts, independent from the administration, was introduced. *Gubernia* chambers of criminal and civil law, their members to be appointed by the Senate, served as appeals courts for the lower courts. Courts acquired a purely class character. In the *uezdi*, there were courts for the gentry, the city magistrate for urban dwellers, and lower courts for the peasants. The administrative-police functions in the *uezd* were performed by an elected captain-police officer. There was also a *gubernia* board, which served under the governor, responsible for the management of the territory's social life, including education, health services, and charity. Moreover, the establishments responsible for these spheres could act as banks granting loans on the land securities.

The state chamber in the *gubernia*, headed by the vice-governor, was responsible for the regions finances. These responsibilities consisted of tax collection, financial control, issuing licenses for trade in wines, state monopoly on the sale of salt, auditing, and control over district treasuries, which collected, stored, and distributed money upon the chamber's orders.[39]

City life was also managed on the principles of class self-government. All city dwellers who had reached the age of twenty-five and had an annual income of at least fifty rubles were elected to the City Assembly, from which in turn were elected representatives, with a term of three years, to the City Duma. The City Duma consisted of the city head and six town councillors from each of six estates. Estates were defined as real estate owners located within the city borders, merchants, handicraftsmen united in corporations, visitors from other cities, people of intellectual professions, and the petty bourgeoisie.[40]

The executive bodies were headed by vice-regents, who, as a rule, had two *gubernii* under their supervision and acted as commanders-in-chief of all troops in their territory. This institution, which was probably introduced under the influence of the Pugachev uprising, was the weakest point in the entire local system of government under Catherine II. The vice-regent's office, which in fact was vested with unlimited powers, could not actually be subjected to punishment. It was outside the reach of petitioners and thus almost exclusively consisted of grafters. In actual practice, the absolute power of the vice-regents reduced the elements of self-government and the division of functions—the very foundations of Catherine's reform of local administration—to nothing.

Of the seventy-five people on staff in the *gubernia* administration, the gentlefolk elected one-third, whereas in the *uezd* they chose one-half. It is sufficient to mention that only gentlefolk had the right to elect the chief of the *uezd* police (the captain-police officer), *uezd* judge, and so on. Moreover, candidates for the remaining jobs in the administration were also appointed by the *gubernia* chamber from among the local gentry.[41]

This system was crowned by the institution of the marshals of the nobility, who were approved by the vice-regent (governor) and chosen from among two candidates nominated by the *gubernia* assembly of the nobility.[42] Until February 1917, the marshal of the nobility was second in importance only to the governor.

The ruling position of the gentry as an estate was augmented by the Charter of Rights, Freedoms, and Advantages of the Nobility issued in 1785. Thirty-five articles in this document referred to their rights, whereas only one referred to their duties: "On the first call from the tsarist government not to spare either efforts or life itself in the service for the state."[43]

Thus, in the course of the fifteenth to eighteenth centuries, an important change took place. The order was transformed from a system of obligatory military service in which gentry managed their landed estates at their own expense to a system of privileged estates, with owners free from any military service, with the sole duty of supporting the autocracy. However, things needed to change; the nobility possessed too many privileges, and the tsar, who relied on the spoiled noble class, possessed too much power. The stubborn refusal to change this order led the country to the substitution of the Communists for the privileged social groups of the nobility.

Regional Life in the Prereform Russian Empire

The first half of the nineteenth century was characterized by great innovations in foreign policy and very insignificant developments in domestic policy. In the period between the death of Peter I and the enthronement of Paul I, the territory of the empire grew by thirty thousand square miles. It further increased by almost seventy thousand square miles during the reign of Paul's sons, thanks to the conquest of Finland, Bessarabia, North Caucasus, and Transcaucasia.[44] Inside the country, however, things remained as they were under Catherine II, with the state structure based on serfdom and the decisive privileges of the nobility.

Attempts to change the empire's structure somewhat were made both from the top, as with the long-range schemes of Alexander I and the reformist plans of Mikhail Speransky, and from the bottom, such as the Decembrist uprising, but they were not, in fact, carried to fruition. Thus, the promise given by Alexander I when he ascended to the throne that under his rule everything would be as it had been under his grandmother was actually fulfilled. The changes in the central management system, for instance, the replacement of the colleges with ministries, failed to have any serious impact on the life of the Russian provinces, which continued to be governed in the way they had been at the end of the eighteenth century.

The main reason for this failure to change lay primarily in the sphere of Russian geopolitical policy. After the Patriotic War of 1812 and the liberation of Europe from the Napoleonic yoke, Russia became a true continental superpower. In order to preserve this new Russian status, the tsarist government hampered any democratic reforms in the country. Thus, the revolutionary explosions in Europe in 1830, especially the uprising in Poland, caused St. Petersburg to halt even cosmetic reforms of serfdom and local government in 1848. Revolutionary activities outside Russia were conducive to the strengthening of police supervision over the entire social and political life of the country.[45]

In such conditions, any substantial reforms of a bureaucratic-serf empire were possible only in the case of its military defeat, which would strip the country of its superpower status. This happened as a result of the Crimean War of 1853–1856, after which serfdom was abolished and a series of socioeconomic and political reforms were carried out.

As for the regional life in the country before the period of reforms, it is best described in the works of Russian classical literature, which experienced an unheard-of upsurge in the nineteenth century. *Eugene Onegin* (1831) by Alexander Pushkin, *Dead Souls* (1842) and *The Inspector-General* (1836) by Gogol, and *Poshekhonye Olden Days* (1887–1889) and *The Golovlev Family* (1876) by Mikhail Saltykov-Shchedrin are, without exaggeration, an encyclopedia of Russian life, serving as the most reliable historical sources.

These authors' descriptions of the life of society in provincial towns revealed not only the complete dominance of the state bureaucratic machine but also a certain self-sufficiency of life in the provinces. To lead such a life, as the main characters of *Dead Souls* or *Poshekhonye Olden Days* show us, there was no need for the interference of the central government; they had everything they needed at home. But for those who wanted to make something of their life, to build a career or simply to serve their motherland, as, for instance, young Tentetnikov from the second volume of *Dead Souls* attempted, there was no place for them in the provinces.[46] St. Petersburg was mentioned in *Dead Souls* as a kind of pump sucking all the young people of the nobility out of the provinces. And it was not the very best people who returned home after working in the capital, one example being Iudushka Golovlev, who spent his earlier years in various departments of the capital. Thus, according to Gogol and Saltykov-Shchedrin, the gentlefolk in the provinces lived on their own and in their own interests.

St. Petersburg, home of the central government, was a sort of promised land for the nobility who served as government officials. The second capital, Moscow, was a center that attracted all the provincial gentlefolk not holding jobs. Gamblers were attracted by Moscow clubs, hard drinkers were drawn by pubs, and the pious by an abundance of churches. Moreover, Moscow played a special part in the life of daughters of the nobility, for it was an all-Russia fair of potential brides from the gentry families.

The Moscow winter balls were the meeting grounds for young gentlemen and young gentlewomen.[47] Personal encounters at the balls, although not accidental, were naturally far more effective matchmaking methods than other means, such as meeting through newspapers and so on. In fact, such vulgar methods were not used in Russia in the period preceding the reforms. It was at the ball that Pushkin's famous heroine, Tatiana Larina, met her future husband.[48] It was at the balls that many girls from the provinces found their husbands. Young men in Moscow were in a somewhat better position to begin a family than young men elsewhere, for they usually held government jobs in the capital or had come there to study. In this light, the social life of the ruling estate in the Russian provinces prior to reforms was obviously second-rate.

As for the second most important social sector of that period, merchants, tax farmers, and contractors had already begun to play a special role in that sphere. This also found a vivid expression in literature. The richest and most powerful man in the *gubernia* where Chichikov, the main character of Gogol's *Dead Souls,* tried to engage in a swindle, was the tax farmer Murazov. In the events described by Alexander Ostrovsky, a famous nineteenth-century Russian author, the richest and most powerful man in the *gubernia* was the contractor Khlynov.

The clout of merchants in the *gubernia* was much greater than that of the majority of the local gentlefolk.[49] However, the structure of the local management system, based exclusively on the privileged right of the local gentry to express its will, hampered the development of regional bourgeoisie. Russian writers were very sensitive to the situation in the country and understood that the country was on the eve of great change, thus it was not by chance that Ivan Turgenev named his well-known novel *On the Eve* (1860).

Regionalism in the Reform-Era Russian Empire: The Zemstvo

Russia's defeat in the Crimean War did away with the superpower status of the Russian empire. During the reign of Alexander II (1855–1881), Russia's territory grew by almost seven thousand square miles due to colonial acquisitions in Central Asia and along the Amur River.[50] This military defeat was followed by certain changes, such as the elimination of serfdom (1861), the extension of the powers of locally elected administration (1864), the establishment of a civilized system of courts (1864), a certain alleviation of censorship (1865), the introduction of universal military service (1874), and the introduction of the universities' independence.[51]

The Creation of the Zemstvo

The reforms of local administrations are of special importance for this book. After the abolition of serfdom, the most important elements of local government were the newly introduced zemstvos, which came into existence on 1 January 1864 and were abolished by the Bolsheviks in 1918. Of almost equal importance were the city's self-governing corporations, to which were passed certain administrative functions that had earlier been performed by state bodies.[52]

The abolishment of serfdom made it necessary to create a local administration capable of replacing the leading role of the landlord in the management of the province.[53] It is characteristic that St. Petersburg introduced the zemstvo only in those areas where there were landlords and where Russians made up the majority of the population. For these reasons, zemstvos were absent in Poland, the Baltic territory, Siberia, and Central Asia, as well as in the Arkhangelsk, Astrakhan, and Orenburg *gubernii*.

The Center's Rationale for Zemstvos

St. Petersburg evidently supported the idea of self-government, as seen in the introduction of the zemstvo, a form that resulted mostly from the influence of the British but also incorporated some traditions found in Russian history.[54] Alexander II tried to improve local life, using the energy of members of the wealthy class, though he also wanted to separate local self-government as much as possible from politics. This policy rejected local independence from the center even in provincial dealings on purely local issues, keeping ultimate control in the hands of the tsarist bureaucracy.[55] The zemstvo was therefore only responsible for the local construction business, hospitals, schools, charity institutions, agronomist and veterinarian services, land credit, and zemstvo statistics.

Prior to the institution of zemstvos, there had been neither medical services for the peasants nor a system of primary schools.[56] To a considerable degree, the autocracy accepted the idea of limited self-government because it wanted to shift some of its responsibilities to local governments.[57] More than a century later, Mikhail Gorbachev and, particularly, Boris Yeltsin did likewise, when they realized that the central administration could not satisfy the basic needs of the population.

Procedures Used in Forming the Zemstvos

Zemstvo administrative bodies, the *gubernia* and zemstvo assemblies, were elected for a term of three years and in turn formed executive bodies called zemstvo boards, which maintained permanent offices. The election of deputies (town councillors) took place at congresses of the estates.

The right to vote was strictly limited by certain qualifications. Landowners, depending on the *gubernia*, had to have at least two to eight hundred *desyatiny* (2.7 acres) of land, and town and city dwellers had to possess working capital of at least 6,000 rubles or some real estate, the cost of which should not be less than 500 rubles (in the *uezdy*). Peasants faced a multistage voting screening system beginning with a village meeting, followed by a *volost'* (a small rural district) meeting and a district meeting, a selection process that could be passed only by the most reliable nominees.

As would be expected, the nobility was the dominant group in zemstvo congresses, which made up, along with clerical deputies, more than 50 percent of the population, whereas merchants constituted 10 to 15 percent of the seats, and the peasants 35 to 40 percent. After the murder of Alexander II in 1881, the upper classes became even more preponderant.[58]

Zemstvo district congresses were held once a year, but the current work was done by zemstvo administrative bodies. District congresses sent several delegates to *gubernia* congresses. Although zemstvos were allegedly the first all-estate administrative corporations, the zemstvo assembly was always headed by the local marshal of nobility.

The main burden of special zemstvo duties was shouldered by the peasants. For instance, in 1868 in the Tver *gubernia*, peasants had to pay 9.6 kopecks per one *desyatina* of their land per year, whereas the gentry paid 8.3 kopecks per *desyatina*. In 1882, the figures were 16.5 and 13.4 kopecks, respectively. At the same time, the zemstvo was financially self-sufficient and did not receive subsidies from the government. This aroused the criticism of Soviet and post-Soviet historians, who could not understand the importance of the effect of this on the autonomy of local government, an issue that was very differently debated in post-Communist Russia.[59] Zemstvos had no law-enforcement bodies of their own and thus could not exist without local executive organs, specifically, the officials and police.

The system of city self-government was mostly engaged in town planning. The City Duma was elected by tax payers for a term of four years. The executive body was the city administration, headed, like the Duma, by the city head, or *golova*.

Conflict with the Center

Although weak and far from ideal, contrary to Alexander Solzhenitsyn's opinion more than a century later, the system of self-government in the Russian provinces, as seen in the zemstvos, could not but come into conflict with the autocratic state. Officials in St. Petersburg saw the zemstvo, and with full reason, as a step on the route toward the creation of a constitutional monarchy and the restriction of the center's absolutism. Indeed, from the very beginning the zemstvo was regarded in Russia as a single liberal bulwark against the central government. This was particularly true of Free Economic Society, the main mouthpiece of the zemstvo.[60]

Being determined to halt the evolution toward liberalism, officials in St. Petersburg tried to put zemstvos (formally all-estate institutions) under the control of the apparatus of the gentry and bureaucrats, headed by the government, which remained the sole master in the *gubernia*. At the very least, they tried to eliminate the entire institution of the zemstvo, as Sergei Witte, minister of finance suggested be done in a memo to the tsar in 1899.[61] The governor headed numerous offices: offices of the military (conscription), excise (tax on the sale of alcoholic beverages), and industrial and forest protection, which controlled life in the provinces. Each district had respective offices headed by the *uezd* marshal of nobility.

The district police officer (*ispravnik*) was also appointed from among the local gentry, as well as two assessors for each district police department, the majority of justices of the peace and *stanovoi* police officers (the *stan* was a division of the *uezd*). The system of zemstvo elections ensured that 40 to 50 percent of town councillors were elected from the local gentry.[62]

Simultaneously, the centralization of the system of maintenance of law and order took place. The year 1862 witnessed the merging of the institutions of town and village policemen to form a *uezd* police department.[63] The system of political investigation, as embodied in the secret political police departments of 1903, was rather well organized. The prison system was equally well organized, with each *gubernia* having is own prison inspector. At the same time, large prisons, or centrals, were built, subordinated directly to the capital, of which the Alexander Central near Irkutsk was especially well known. Prisoners who were condemned to penal servitude were sent to these extended prisons (the old Nerchinsk was supplemented by Sakhalin and Iakutsk).[64]

The regional structure of the Russian empire after the period of reform, which combined the elements of civilized self-government and bureaucratic centralism, all-estate citizenship and a privileged group's control, principally the nobility, could not function over a long historical period. A deviation from this path was unavoidable, either toward complete self-government or toward total bureaucratic centralism. Russia was unfortunate enough to have floundered into the latter.

Counterreforms

The reforms of the 1860s did not satisfy some elements of Russian society, and the revolutionary movement, resorting mostly to terror, began to influence the country's political life. After the murder of Alexander II by terrorists in 1881, his successors, his son Alexander III (1881–1894) and grandson Nikolai II (1894–1917), tried to avert the collapse of the state controlled by the nobility.

Alexander III tried to achieve this through counterreforms, which, among other things, greatly reduced local self-government, even though the offensive against the zemstvo had already started in 1866, two years after its introduction.[65] A strong ideological campaign against self-government, which had started shortly after the tsar's death in 1881, was carried out by several publicists, whose spokesperson was Mikhail Katkov of St. Petersburg. Over a decade, many of the institutions that had been created in 1864 were eliminated, and the role of landowners, who were mostly foes of the zemstvo, as the major social basis of the monarchy was significantly enhanced at the expense of all other classes.

Despite these counterreforms and their many limitations even at their peak, the zemstvo was probably the only institution in prerevolutionary Russia that could claim relative success. It left an indelible imprint on Russian history, and even in post-Communist Russia, it was regarded by politicians of all colors as a model of Russian self-government. The zemstvo improved significantly the state of affairs in Russia in the spheres of agriculture, health care, and education.[66] The zemstvo managed to create a group of people—doctors, teachers, and lawyers—who were devoted to the public cause and came to be immortalized in Anton Chekhov's novels and plays.

Russia on the Eve of Monarchy Collapse: The *Oblastnichestvo*

Nikolai II, in his turn, tried to avert the fall of the Russian empire through involvement in external military conflicts. In 1904, Russia was embroiled in a vicious war with Japan and ten years later found itself entangled with Germany. Naturally enough, Russia's defeat in its war with Japan was followed by a second period of restructuring in the wake of the revolution of 1905.

Like the restructuring of the 1860s and 1870s, reform efforts only went halfway. The autocracy was preserved, although some semblance of a parliamentary structure was introduced. The tsar conceded to establishing an elected lower chamber (the State Duma); an appointed upper chamber (the State Council), which basically remained an assembly of the nobility, into which in 1906 one elected representative from each of the *gubernia*'s local administration was admitted; and an executive body (the Council of Ministers), which was subordinate not to the Duma but to the tsar. It goes without saying that such an abnormal combination of parliamentary government and autocracy could not function normally for an extended period of time.

By the beginning of the twentieth century, Russia, for the most part, still retained most of the same administrative-territorial divisions that were in existence under Catherine II. In the early 1900s, there were seventy-eight *gubernii*, eighteen regions, four boroughs, and ten governor-general territories, which were headed by the commanders of military districts, in the capital and outlying *gubernii*.[67]

The entrenchment of the zemstvo in Russian life allowed the emergence of a regionalist ideology and a regionalist movement, a new phenomenon in Russia—the *oblastnichestvo*. This was a social and cultural movement focused on the specific character of individual Russian regions, promoting local customs and culture.

The movement emerged under the direct influence of the abolition of serfdom in Russia in 1861, even if in the past a number of Russian authors had pointed the way, such as the Decembrists Nikolai Bestuzhev (1791–1855) and Gavril Batenkov (1793–1863), as well as Afanasii Shchapov, a prominent historian of Siberia, who asserted that Siberia was a colony and needed autonomy for progress. The mightiest stronghold of regionalism was in Siberia. For the leaders of *oblastnichestvo*, Siberia was a sort of serf for the Russian empire. Consequently, they blamed St. Petersburg for making Siberia a place of exile and accused officials who came from "Russia," that is, from St. Petersburg or Moscow, of arbitrariness and indifference to the fate of the region. The leaders of *oblastnichestvo* were fervent advocates of the creation of a Siberian university and local periodicals. It was only natural that the major figures in this movement were scholars, writers, and literary critics and that their main periodicals were literary magazines.[68] Tomsk and Irkutsk were the major centers of *oblastnichestvo* in Siberia. St. Petersburg was also a site for the movement's activities.

The history of the Siberian *oblastnichestvo* can be divided into two phases, an early period, beginning at the end of the nineteenth century, and a later period. The main figures of the first stage were Grigorii Potanin (1835–1920) and Nikolai Iadrintsev (1842–1894).[69] They created an ideology that suggested that their geography and climate made Siberians a special people. They called for Siberian residents to look at their "small motherland" almost as a colony, though without direct political invectives against St. Petersburg, a viewpoint that their descendants would repeat almost one hundred years later.[70] In the beginning, they dreamed of Siberia's autonomy from St. Petersburg. Later, their dreams changed to include their region's equality with other metropolises. Their main periodical was the *Tomskie Gubernskie Vedomosti.*

The patriarchs of *oblastnichestvo* were under the evident influence of socialist ideas propagated by Russian populists, who believed in the special quality of Russian communities. However, they recognized, unlike the populists, the role of the development of capitalism in Russia, which led some historians to treat them rather as leftist liberals. At the same time, the leaders of the movement were evidently also influenced by democratic ideas. They dreamed of a Siberian regional duma that would control finances, a key factor for Siberian autonomy. The leaders of *oblastnichestvo* advocated that the Siberian "indigenous" people should be proud of their land and try to create their own "Siberian literature" and criticized those writers who were not permanent Siberian residents for their focus only on the dark side of Siberian life.[71]

Both of the leaders of *oblastnichestvo*, Potanin and Iadrintsev, along with other members of their circle, were arrested in 1865 as separatists who nurtured the idea of creating a state like the United States of America. All of those involved were severely punished and sent into exile in Arkhangelsk, although they were carefully kept outside of Siberia. They were eventually pardoned in 1874 and continued their activity until their death.

The second stage of the *oblastnichestvo* movement started with the revolution of 1905. Most members of the movement joined the Liberal Party, led by the constitutional democratic cadets, a group that included such visible figures as the industrialist Sergei Vostrotin, the lawyer Pavel Vologodskii, and the president of Tomsk University, Vasilii Sapozhnikov. A major event of the movement was the convening of the congress of the Siberian Regional Union, which discussed the creation of a regional duma. However, this idea did not reach the level of implementation.

At the same time, Siberian deputies of the Russian Duma after 1905 managed to create their own faction in the parliament where they tried, again without success, to pass laws favorable to their region. It is remarkable that during the free election of the Constitutional Assembly, *oblastnichestvo* gained less than 1 percent approval, since its leaders could not have offered any serious social program that was more important for the population than the idea of autonomy.[72]

The core of the new *oblastnichestvo* movement was confronted with several revolutionary parties whose members were in Siberian exile. These groups accused the movement of being an impediment to the unification of the opposition against the government.[73] However, the movement held out against its critics and continued to insist in its periodicals, the most important of which was *Sibirskie Zapiski*, on the radical differences between Siberia and the rest of Russia, as well as on the special destiny of Siberia.

During the Russian Civil War, many members of the movement supported the struggle against the Bolsheviks, whom they recognized as the enemies of Siberia's autonomy. However, the consequent attempt by the movement's older leaders to create an independent republic later failed.[74]

After the Bolshevik victory, *oblastnichestvo* as a political and social movement came to an end. But as a cultural movement, it remained alive. In fact, in the 1920s and early 1930s, it was still possible to discuss regionalism in literature and even to defend it as a positive development, as did Vivian Itin at the Congress of Russian Writers in 1934.[75] Literary regionalism was most visible in Siberia, where a number of the authors remained.[76]

The growth of mass terror in the mid–1930s completely removed *oblastnichestvo* in any of its forms from public life. "Localism," or *mestnichestvo,* became one of the most serious of political vices. It meant that those who were focused on local issues in this way demonstrated their disregard of national interests, an accusation that could easily land the culprit in the Gulag.

After Stalin's death, *oblastnichestvo* began very gingerly to revive, mostly in the realm of culture and literature, as well as in the so-called *kraievedenie*, the study of local lore, and then in the creation of publications on the history of regions as well.

Developments in literature at the time followed a particularly typical pattern. Several authors began to publish articles, and even books, that claimed the existence of a specific species of Siberian or Volga literature. However, ideologists were often quite hostile toward these publications, requiring their authors to write, for instance, not about a separate "Siberian literature" but "on the place of Siberia in Soviet Russian literature."[77]

4

THE CENTER AND REGIONS IN
THE SOVIET PERIOD: THE PROVINCES
WITHOUT A VOICE

The Soviet system, born between 1917 and 1922, had less toleration for regionalism and regionalization than the previous Russian empire. As before, changes in the CP relationship in Soviet society depended only on the amount of power the political elite regarded as expedient to delegate to its local agents.

The Center and Regions' New Relations
After the October Revolution

The new Russian government that was created in the aftermath of the February Revolution of 1917, which took place in the wake of two and one-half years of fighting during World War I, tried to restructure the old autocratic state. However, this reform failed to result in the creation of democracy in the country. The provisional government, which was at the helm for only eight months, failed to substitute a bourgeois-democratic state for the state of the nobility. All of the bureaucratic apparatuses, in the center as well as in the provinces, remained intact. Only regional governors were replaced with commissars of the provisional government. All tsarist laws were preserved; procurators, judges, and investigators kept their jobs in the capitals as well as in the periphery. The nobility, clergy, and merchants retained their privileges. Even the titles of the nobility were not abolished.[1]

The majority of Russia's population "permitted" the Bolsheviks to successfully carry out a coup. The people did not actively support them, as Soviet historians claimed, nor did they thoughtlessly obey a small group of conspirators, as some people today insist in an effort to explain the easy victory of the October uprising.[2] The Bolsheviks came to power as a political force, promising not only to implement socialist ideals attractive to a significant part of the population, but also to reestablish order in a country seized by anarchy after the February Revolution.

The Role of the Soviets

In the beginning, the Bolsheviks tried to build a new society according to socialist ideas, hoping to see Russia become a society that could be run as a commune. Indeed, at first it seemed that this was actually taking place: Factory and plant committees established self-management in production, the professional army was disbanded and replaced by a voluntary army, an elective principle was introduced, and "Soviets of workers and peasants" were elected everywhere. In fact, power was transferred to the soviets in the capitals and sixty other major cities by the military revolutionary committee (VRK), mostly without violence.[3]

The Bolsheviks considered the soviets to be the highest achievement in democracy since they combined legislative, executive, and judicial powers in the same body elected by co-workers. It was assumed that the soviets would be composed of ordinary workers and peasants, as opposed to professional politicians and bureaucrats. They would run society by means of direct contact with the masses at all levels of the country, from small villages to society as a whole. Thus, the soviets, which spontaneously emerged during the revolution of 1905 in Alpatyevsk, Nadezhdinsk, Ivanovo-Voznesensk, and Kostroma to head the workers' strikes, became the form of a new state structure.

But soon it was discovered that this idealistic system of government, described so vehemently by Lenin in *State and Revolution* (1917) on the eve of the October revolution, did not work. This showed that the state-commune was nothing but a myth, that it was impossible to manage the country without professional bureaucrats. Subsequently, the central government and local soviets began to hire people who were educated enough to perform managerial functions. In a country that was almost illiterate, it was quite difficult to find such people. The victory of Soviet power made this all the more difficult. The local bureaucratic apparatus very soon surpassed the size of the previous tsarist one.[4] It was not surprising that the Bolsheviks began to invite old tsarist officials to work for them.[5]

Toward Centralization

Almost immediately after their seizure of power, the Bolsheviks in Moscow began to try to maximize the centralization of power in the country. It soon became evident that they did not want to share real control of Russia with anybody, and they started to turn local soviets into instruments of the central administration.

During the civil war, at the suggestion of the central government, many soviets created their own military-revolutionary committees. This was done to fulfill the center's directives concerning the mobilization of people and resources for war. These committees ignored the rituals of Soviet democracy, using dictatorial and even terrorist methods to achieve the goals set by the Kremlin.[6]

The Resistance of Local Authorities

The Kremlin could not yet impose its will easily across the entire country as the Soviet leadership wished. Autonomy was therefore somewhat tolerated in 1918–1920 in several regions, even though local Communists did their best to prevent this. A few regions proclaimed themselves independent "republics," for instance, Siberia[7] and Kaluga.[8] In some cases, Moscow itself initiated the creation of "independent republics," if the central leadership could not take full control of the whole territory. This was the case with the Far East Republic.

With all its intentions to control the provinces, the Kremlin had to tolerate many cases of "arbitrariness" from the local authorities, which, in their turn, were irritated by the direct intervention of the center in the region's everyday life.[9] The center intervened mostly through local departments such as the military or economic branches, which, as will be discussed later in greater detail, were subordinated to the Executive Committee of the local soviet and the respected People's Commissariat in Moscow.[10]

It is remarkable that the executive bodies of these regions followed the example of the central government and began to call themselves "Soviets of People's Commissars."[11] They tried to imitate the central government in everything. For this reason, after the Soviet government moved to Moscow in March 1918, local Soviets of People's Commissars were abolished.[12] However strong the local forces were, by the end of the civil war, the Kremlin had established its complete control over all territories that were not occupied by its opponents.

By the end of the civil war, not only local soviets but also local party organizations had very little autonomy in running their own regions. All were obliged to follow the directives from Moscow, even in the regulation of the details of local life.[13] Local party units, including each individual party member, were fully transformed into agents of centralization.

Conflict Between Centralists and Decentralists

As previously mentioned, being consistent centralists, the Bolsheviks searched for the most effective way to control the regional economies. They oscillated between prescribing everything to their agents in the provinces or endowing them with limited liberty to determine the appropriate means to achieve national economic goals, up to the outer limit of relatively free election of local soviets. However, most Bolshevik leaders were against any deviation from centralization, especially in politics.[14] This position was justified in the eyes of many leading politicians by, among other things, the low educational and professional level of local cadres, their parochialism, and their inability to understand the national goals of society, as well as their inclination toward extremism and their barbaric, erratic, and capricious actions.[15] In the post-Stalin era, as will be shown later, there were many among intellectuals who defended centralism and considered the center to be much more enlightened and progressive than local bosses.

In the first decades after the revolution, debates on the best coordination of the center and regions, primarily in the economic sphere, were still possible. In fact, various ideas on this subject were advanced and implemented within the Bolshevik Party.

During the first few years following the revolution, most of the Bolshevik leaders were inclined to give regional leaders significant economic autonomy. Thus, they made the decision in December 1917 to create "regional economic councils," also known as *sovnarkhozy*, which even appeared to have some democratic overtones.[16] Some of these bodies were headed by prominent Bolsheviks, such as Mikhail Frunze of Ivanovo-Voznesensk, Valerian Kuibyshev of Samara, and Inessa Armand of Moscow. Soon, however, the *sovnarkhozy* lost their initial autonomy and were transformed into the instruments of the Moscow Supreme Economic Council, but then after a short revival during the New Economic Plan (NEP), they yielded their power to branch directorates (*glavki*). In 1932, the *sovnarkhozy* were simply eliminated as an obstacle to the branch regulation of the Russian economy, and with the exception of Nikita Khrushchev's attempt to restore them in 1957, they never reappeared during the Soviet system.

The advocates of economic and, to some degree, even administrative autonomy of regional authorities defended their views with some success until the early 1920s.[17] These defenders of regional autonomy were members of a movement called "democratic centralism," headed by Timofei Sapronov, chairman of the Moscow Soviet,[18] and Nikolai Osinskii, chairman of the Supreme Economic Council and chairman of Kharkov's *sovnarkhoz*.

The Subordination of
Local Government Departments

By the beginning of the 1920s, the Bolsheviks, in eliminating "decentralists," had established a rather refined order coordinating the activity of central and local authorities. A special rule was set during the first years of the Soviet order, which allowed for any department of the Soviet executive committees or party committees to be subordinated both horizontally to the local party or soviet boss and vertically to the respective departments of higher bodies.[19] For instance, the district financial department was subordinated to both its own executive committee and to the regional financial department. The regional financial department was subordinated to its respective executive committee and to the Ministry of Finance. The district social security department was subordinated to the district executive committee and regional social security department, with the latter subordinated to the regional executive committee and the Ministry of Social Security, and so on and so forth.

The Structure of the Soviets and Elections

The main bodies of the Soviet government, prior to the adoption of the Constitution of 1936, were congresses of the soviets of a given territory. Delegates to these congresses, from the All-Union Congress to the Congress of Village Soviets, were elected according to a hierarchical principle, where the Congress of Village Soviets elected delegates to the regional congress, the regional congress selected delegates to the territorial congress, and so on. Between these congresses, all power was vested in the executive committees, from the Central Executive Committee of the USSR on down to the village executive committee, whose members were elected by their respective congresses. According to the constitutions of 1918 and 1924, only workers, peasants, and working intellectuals had the right to vote. Former noblemen, merchants, and clergy were deprived of their rights to vote and to be elected to positions on the soviets.

In the mid-1930s, Stalin decided to present the Soviet Union as a "normal" and democratic society that did not need the political institutions of the revolutionary period now that socialism was built. The new "Stalin Constitution" of 1936 replaced the Soviets of Workers' and Peasants' Deputies with the new Soviets of Working People's Deputies, which have been known since 1977 as just the "People's Deputies," and he introduced universal suffrage based on the formal idea of the victory of socialism in the Soviet Union.[20] The multistep system of elections was also replaced by direct elections.

The changes in the administrative-territorial and governing structures of Soviet power did not affect the essence of social and economic life in the regions, for local bodies continued to be completely subordinated to local party committees and the center. The elections of local authorities and national bodies were completely bogus, as they had been since the early 1920s. Even though these elections were carried out regularly, nobody thought they had any significance other than that those who were elected, for instance, to the office of deputy even in a local soviet, gained a status symbol. At the same time, the regime obtained between two and two and one-half million deputies of local soviets (1980) and 30 million people who were considered volunteers of the regime.[21] This powerful network of political activists composed of deputies and, to a lesser degree, their assistants energetically supported party policies in their milieu in order to repay the party for their new privileges although those were small.

The Party and the Soviets

Local governments were subordinated to the center not only directly or through intermediate soviets at higher levels but also through local party committees. Vladimir Lenin was the author of a well-known comparison, further developed by Iosif Stalin, that likened the local and central soviets, trade unions, youth unions, cooperatives, and other structures to the "belts" that connected the Communist Party with the working class and the rest of the country's population. Therefore, there was the inevitable presence in the center and localities of two power structures, one of which, the party, instructs, while the other, the Soviet state proper, obeys.

It was in 1919–1920 that a type of political structure called the "dictatorship of the party," a term first used at the Twelfth Party Congress in 1923, took root. Later, at each party forum during "splits," the opposition mentioned the substitution of party bodies for the bodies of central and local soviet governments. Nevertheless, this principle remained intact during the entire life of the Soviet state. In Stalin's period, it was a moot question, whereas under Brezhnev's rule, it was even included in the 1977 Constitution under the famous Article 6, which was abolished only in 1990, just before the collapse of the Soviet Union.

The separation of soviets at all levels from party control was a leading political issue in the last two years of the Soviet system. Andrei Sakharov, the champion of modern Russian democracy, chose the slogan "all power to the soviets," used by the Bolsheviks in 1917, as the most important political demand of the Russian democrats in 1989. This followed the example of the Kronstadt rebels in 1921, who demanded "soviets without Communists."[22]

Before 1989, any attempts to even weaken the control of the party over local governments could only fail while the party remained the "leading and guiding" force in society. However, in everyday life the majority of the population had to deal officially with local soviets, which possessed power in name alone.

Meanwhile, the local party apparatus was conspicuously the instrument of the central political elite. As Merle Fainsod correctly said, local party leaders were "little lords" who had "to cringe before the great lords in Moscow."[23] Local party committees became "defenders" of local interests only when the poor supply of food could generate, in their perception, public disturbances that could bring with them personal catastrophes, such as being fired or, even worse, being fired by the Kremlin. Only in such cases did they dare to beg their Moscow bosses to help them in either cutting regional quotas for the procurement of food by the state or to send them some staple foods from the central stores. The soviets, being under the full control of the local parties, played practically the same role as the agents of the center.

In the story *Happiness* by Petr Pavlenko (1947), one of the "masters" of Stalinist literature, the chairman of the regional executive committee called the first secretary of the regional party committee, saying, "Give your blessing, Your Holiness, for the start of the day."[24] The reader should not be confused by the tone of these words and assume that they indicate particularly friendly relations between the two regional leaders. That was exactly how the working day of the majority of Soviet leaders began: A minister rang up the chief of the respective department of the CPSU (Communist Party of the Soviet Union) Central Committee, a chief of a department of the regional executive committee called the chief of the respective department of the regional executive party committee, and so on and so forth. The complete control of local party bodies coupled with dual subordination almost completely stripped Soviet government bodies of any semblance of initiative.[25]

Since local governments had to follow instructions from various sources of power, in cases of conflict between directives, they almost always tended to give priority to the commands from the local party committee. In doing this, they also shifted to the local party committees the responsibility for the local government's decision to disobey soviets at a higher level, such as the controlling ministry. The predominance of the party in running local authorities was practically unquestioned until 1989.[26]

The Population and Local Soviets

Russians accepted the inferior role of the soviets as a "normal" phenomenon. However, on some issues the people expected the soviets to perform a variety of functions delegated to them by the party. For example, in the event of an emergency, the people looked to party committees, either local or central, for support.

The analysis of the Smolensk archives, which covers the activity of the regional authorities since before World War II, shows that First Party Secretary Riumiantsev, along with his deputy, "functioned," in the words of Fainsod, "as the ultimate dispenser of mercy and patronage after all other alternatives were exhausted."[27]

However, even more significant is that Soviet citizens did not look for the assistance of local party committees; rather, they looked to the center. The analysis of the complaints sent by the city of Taganrog to the authorities shows that 45 percent of all citizens who sent letters of complaint addressed them only to central authorities. Only 11 percent were sent to city and district bodies, and 22 percent went to bodies at all levels.[28]

The Party Secretary as Stalin's Governor

During the first few years after the revolution, local leaders appointed by Moscow became the chairmen of the executive committee of the local soviet.

The Tver Region, for example, was ruled by Andrei Zhdanov, chairman of *"gubispolkoma,"* the executive committee of the *gubernia* soviet.[29] However, a few years later, all power in every region was concentrated in the hands of the first party secretary. When Zhdanov was transferred to Nizhniy Novgorod in 1924, he was given this position. This arrangement was to last until 1989.

As compared to the tsarist governor, the first secretary of the regional party committee from the early 1920s until 1991 did not head open committees and offices of different types but rather the bureau of the regional party committee, a completely closed body. This body was simultaneously the government and the supreme court of the region, approving all appointments within its jurisdiction and making decisions on all matters.

Despite his powerful image before his subordinates and the population of the region, the party secretary did not have the freedom to act on any domestic or foreign policy issue of the country. He even lacked leeway in the interpretation of political directives. In case of any doubt, he had to consult the Central Committee. During the major political campaigns in Stalin's time and after, all party secretaries strictly followed Moscow's orders regarding the number of peasants who had to be enrolled in collective farms during collectivization, as well as the approximate number of "enemies of the people" who had to be arrested in their regions. Of course, the overfulfillment of these political targets was usually, but not always, greeted positively in the Kremlin.[30]

The powers of the party secretary were also greatly limited in the selection of cadres. The second secretary, the chairman of the Executive Party Committee, the chief of the People's Commissariat of Internal Affairs (later called the Ministry of Internal Affairs and then renamed the Ministry of State Security), the procurator, the representative of the Commissariat of Procurement (later the Ministry of the Commissariat of Procurement), as well as the directors of large industrial enterprises of union importance were appointed by Moscow as the *nomenklatura* of the Central Committee, whereas the regional party committee performed only consulting functions. But with the rest of the huge army of officials, the first secretary of the regional party committee did whatever he wanted; he appointed them, dismissed them, and transferred them to other jobs. It was not infrequent that the service list of one person in a district (regional) *nomenklatura* included the posts of the head of industrial, cultural, and trade organizations. The everyday life of top regional leaders was organized along the same lines as in the capital.[31]

In addition to this ramified system of subordination and coordination, there were also commissions of soviet and party control, at that time called the Ministry and Committee of State Control, subordinate only to Moscow. The task of these bodies was to monitor the fulfillment of the center's decisions.[32]

None of the regional secretaries considered themselves to be representatives of the region where they ruled. Moreover, many regional party secretaries worked in the Central Committee and learned what Moscow expected from its provincial cadres before actually working in the province.[33] All of them regarded themselves as Moscow's envoys and dreamed of a transfer to the capital to a high position on the Central Committee or in the government. Indeed, two-thirds of all members of the Politburo in the 1970s had served in the past as regional secretaries.[34] At the same time, the status of the regional party secretary was very high in Soviet society. In the social hierarchy, he was equal to an all-union minister. Party secretaries of the leading regions were members of the Central Committee, while others were members of the Control Commission of the party.[35] As a rule, party secretaries were at least members of the Supreme Soviet of the Russian Federation, if not deputies of the Supreme Soviet of the USSR itself.

At the same time, first party secretaries were regularly used, with the Brezhnev period being an exception, as whipping boys for the Kremlin. Iosif Stalin, Nikita Khrushchev, and, to a certain extent, Mikhail Gorbachev shifted the responsibility for various problems, from time to time, to the first persons in regions, making them out to be either wreckers or, as in the later, milder times, laughingstocks, firing them mercilessly. Sometimes they were even sent, as in Stalin's period, to the Gulag. For example, regional party secretaries and other local party apparatchiks were used as scapegoats for the mass terror when Stalin decided to somewhat slacken the pace of repression in early 1938.[36]

The Administrative Division of a New State

The administrative-territorial division of the new state was also subordinated to the aims of the most effective party leadership of Soviet government. The Bolsheviks failed by force of arms to preserve a number of colonies, such as Poland, the Baltic states, Finland, and Bessarabia. The rest of the colonies, together with the genuinely Russian regions and colonies of settlers that also became ethnically Russian, that is, Siberia and the Far East, became parts of the new state. The resultant Union of Soviet Socialist Republics, the successor of the Russian empire, was federal in form and unitary in content.

At first, the Soviet government could not manage without a certain enlargement of the regions. Despite a veritable army of officials, there was a shortage of skilled party leaders to manage a large number of regions. In addition, the Soviet government also wanted to manage the life of the outlying provinces of several proletarian centers with strong party organizations, such as Moscow, Petrograd, and Ekaterinburg. This consideration lay behind the decision to designate regions headed by Moscow (seventeen *gubernii*), Ural (five *gubernii* with the center in Ekaterinburg), Northwest Siberia (six *gubernii* with the center in Petrograd), and Central Siberia (five Siberian *gubernii* with the center in Omsk). Among other territorial giants were the Middle Volga, Lower Volga, North Caucasian, Azov-Black Sea, West Siberian, East Siberian and Central Black-Soil Regions (which are now the Kursk, Orel, Voronezh, Tambov, Lipetsk, and Belgorod Regions).

These regions were headed by prominent professional revolutionaries, who combined their Bolshevik mercilessness and fanaticism with heavy political experience, a broad world outlook, and a knowledge of people and their work capacity. Included among these people were Sergei Kirov, Anastas Mikoian, Pavel Postyshev, Iosif Vareikis, Boris Sheboldaev, Robert Eikhe, and Mendel Khatayevich. However, Stalin considered these qualities personally threatening, so after the men had fulfilled their tasks in Stalin's reconstruction of the country, most of them fell victim to his purges and mass terror. The decomposition of giant regions into smaller divisions during the period of mass terror, such as occurred with Iaroslavl, Tula, Kursk, Voronezh, Cheliabinsk, Arkhangelsk, Gorky, and many others, was also a result of Stalin's completely unfounded fears.[37]

By the beginning of the 1920s, CP relations in the Soviet system had been transformed into their final permutation, which was to last until the end of the Soviet era. This form secured Moscow's full control over the periphery, which changed rather insubstantially during the next six decades. The major principle was clear: Each body in the province had to obey the directives from Moscow. The hierarchy of power was clear: The center ruled supreme, then the union republic, territory (region), region (city), and finally, the village.[38]

Lenin's principle of any organization, that of so-called democratic centralism, presupposed the phony opportunity of election from bottom to top and subordination from top to bottom of the minority to the majority. This seemed to supply Moscow with reliable guarantees against local separatism, for it signified the complete dependence of the lower bodies on higher bodies. Thus, from the very first days following the revolution, Moscow received the right to annul the decisions of all lower bodies. Moscow's control was all the more absolute now that all local leaders were in fact appointed by the Kremlin, and any election, inside the party as well outside of it, was prearranged.

Spurious Separatism

However strong centralism was in his time, Stalin claimed that local separatism was among the many threats to the Soviet system. Systematically, various provocative measures were taken that usually ended in violent reprisals against local officials allegedly guilty of attempts to separate a certain local organization from the center.

Among the Russian cities that were the most maligned for sporadic separatism was Leningrad. This city aroused special hatred in the Father of All Peoples, as Stalin used to be called, for in the period of party debate after Lenin's death, its local party organization refused to obey him. The city, headed by Grigorii Zinoviev, joined the opposition against Stalin in 1925. Breaking the dissent in Leningrad demanded much effort by the Kremlin. Stalin preserved his special grudge against Leningrad when Zinoviev was later replaced by Sergei Kirov,

Stalin's close friend, who, however, became so popular among Leningrad party members, and even in the country, that Stalin came to consider him as his rival. All of Stalin's frustrations surrounding Leningrad were vented in the late 1940s. The leadership of Leningrad fell victim to a provocation concocted in the Kremlin. Using the all-Russia wholesale fair organized in Leningrad, allegedly without the permission of the union government, as a pretext, Stalin accused the party leadership of the city and district, as well as some of the Leningrad leaders at the all-union level, of separatist activity. It was stated in the Politburo's decision that Leningrad was guilty of "attempts to build a partition between the Central Committee and the Leningrad organization and in this way to separate the organization from the rest of the party." All of the major Leningrad local leaders, Aleksei Kuznetsov, Petr Popkov, Mikhail Rodionov, Nikolai Voznesenskii, a brother of a Politburo member, and two hundred others were fired and excluded from the party. They were finally executed by a firing squad, and hundreds of others were imprisoned. The city party organization was subjected to a purge, in the course of which thousands of Communists suffered.[39]

A similar provocation was organized almost simultaneously in the Ulianovsk Region. Practically no information was leaked to the press, but one thing was certain—the investigation also ended at the Lubyanka prison.

The Regional Selection of Cadres for Moscow

The only area where the "regional factor" influenced Soviet politics was in the selection of cadres. Even in Stalin's time, high officials who were transferred from the provinces to Moscow tried to recruit their deputies and staff from among their countrymen. Zhdanov, for instance, installed several people from Leningrad in the party and state apparatus, and Lavrentii Beria brought in many of his former subordinates from Georgia.[40]

However, after Stalin, the formation of Moscow cadres on a regional basis increased enormously. Khrushchev invited many of his fellow countrymen from Ukraine: Fedor Kirichenko was installed as a secretary of the Central Committee, Andrei Grechko became minister of defense, Brezhnev was made a secretary of the Central Committee, and several others were brought in. Brezhnev, in his turn, was considered to be the founder of the Dnepropetrovskaia-Moldavian "Mafia," since he had worked in both places. Examples of Brezhnev's cadres include Nikolai Tikhonov as prime minister, Konstantin Chernenko as a secretary of the Central Committee, and many others. Boris Yeltsin, in post-Communist Russia, continued this practice and brought several dozen of his former subordinates to Moscow from Sverdlovsk, such as Gennadii Burbulis as state secretary, and Yurii Petrov as head of his administration, along with many others.

However, there is no evidence that the people who had worked in the provinces used their new job in the capital to protect the interests of their former countrymen. They all considered themselves representatives of the country as a whole, as if putting aside their personal egotistical ambitions.

By the time of Stalin's death, Soviet society had reached the peak of centralism. The periphery and its leaders had no autonomy whatsoever, and regionalism and regionalization were phenomena simply absent in the country.

5

THE KHRUSHCHEV ERA:
THE FIRST MOVE TOWARD
DECENTRALIZATION

With Iosif Stalin's death, various dormant tendencies once again began to rise to the surface. To some degree, this trend also held true for regionalism and regionalization. However, it was the Kremlin that initiated revisions in CP relations in the country.

Khrushchev's Attempts at Decentralization

Stalin's death in 1953 saved Soviet society from serious problems and delayed the threat of a new war. At the same time, conditions were not yet ripe for the restructuring of Stalin's empire, in contrast to the period of reforms attempted in 1861–1905 and in the period of the Romanov empire's collapse in February 1917. But Stalin, in contrast to the tsars, had not lost a single war, either against foreign invaders or against his own people, although his effort had engendered a very great cost.

The change of leadership in the Kremlin during the 1950s took place against a background of the Soviet Union's terrific successes in the arms race, especially in the realm of nuclear weapons production. Stalin's successors at first limited their actions to softening the terrible Stalinist methods of rule in the country. More or less serious reforms started only after the Twentieth CPSU Congress in 1956, which denounced the cult of personality surrounding Stalin for the whole world to see and, for the first time politically and morally, condemned his activities as being criminal.

The Twentieth CPSU Congress gave birth to a rather broad movement among Soviet intellectuals for deep renovation of all aspects of life in Soviet society. However, this makeover was to remain within the framework of socialism, which later became known as liberal socialism, or "socialism with a human face," a famous slogan that became popular in the time of the "Prague Spring" (1968). This movement was especially active in the 1960s and thus was generally referred to as the "movement of the sixties."

Regional Reforms:
Interregional Economic Councils (sovnarkhozy)

Nikita Khrushchev's attempts at reform, from a regional point of view, were also prompted by a desire to raise the efficiency of socialism.[1] He desired greater efficiency in industry and sought to attain it by decentralizing the management structure and bringing it closer to the actual site of production. It was true that the overcentralized Stalinist management system in industry was characterized by outrageous absurdities. The operation of two hundred thousand enterprises and over one hundred thousand construction sites was managed from a single center, the State Planning Committee.

Directing the entire behemoth was practically impossible. Branch ministries and departments were engaged in similar construction projects in the same regions. They also had similar supply and sales operations and brought goods and materials back and forth to different regions of the country. The regions' economies were made up of different departmental patches that did not function as a unitary complex. At the same time, Khrushchev saw in the creation of new regional bodies a means to weaken Stalinists in the central bureaucracy, since hundreds of them were sent to the provinces as heads of *sovnarkhozy* and their departments.[2]

Khrushchev's idea to shift the center of gravity to the localities resulted in the abolition of branch ministries and the restoration of the economic zones, each one of which was headed by an institution called the Council of the National Economy. One hundred and four territorial management bodies of economic regions were created. As a rule, they included several small or one large industrially developed region or territory.[3] Altogether, sixty-eight Councils of the National Economy were formed in the Russian Federation.[4]

The restoration of the *sovnarkhozy* was a great novelty in Soviet society because this was the first deviation since the early 1930s from the hypercentralization of the Soviet system, and it expanded the local emissaries' power, even if they still could only follow commands sent from Moscow. As is recorded in party documents, the same innovation was underwritten with the idea that regional economic administration was better able to cater to the needs of the population, an idea that cast doubt on the center's wisdom.[5] For the first time in the Soviet era, local interests emerged as a significant factor in the country's economic life.[6]

The creation of *sovnarkhozy* met with the disapproval of many party apparatchiks who saw in them a threat to the central planning system and the impetus for "local patriotism." Quite soon, the reality of the situation began to provide them with the necessary arguments against the decentralization of economic management.

Indeed, the transformation of management in accordance with the territorial principle could not but bring forth autonomistic tendencies in the economic regions. For instance, to build one's own plant for the production of certain types of spare parts for machines and mechanisms was much easier than to wait for the delivery of these parts from another economic region that already had a similar plant. It was argued, and not without reason, that the reform inhibited techno-logical progress since most research institutes were located in Moscow and the local authorities had to pursue their own parochial technological policy.

The Division of Local Party Committees

Khrushchev did not stop with the *sovnarkhozy* in his restructuring of the coun-try's provincial life. In 1962, he enlarged the economic regions and initiated one of his most complicated experiments, the division of the ruling party and the state government bodies in accordance with the production principle. The idea was based on the assumption that with modern economic conditions, the territo-rial principle of party organization did not satisfy the requirements for economic management, since the party bodies were incapable of simultaneously paying equal attention to both industry and farming.

According to the decision made at the November 1962 Plenary Meeting of the CPSU Central Committee, all village party committees were abolished and replaced by the collective farm–state farm territorial departments. At the same time, the party committees and the Soviets of Working People's Deputies of each region or territory were each divided into two equal bodies—industrial and agri-cultural. These two bureaus were created in all regional committees responsible for industry and agriculture.

For instance, the Gorky Region (now called Nizhniy Novgorod) had a popula-tion of 3,671,000, of which 170,000 were members in the party organization, which was divided into forty-six village party committees and twelve city party committees, including six city district party committees. This structure was replaced by two independent regional party committees, one of which was responsible for industry and included eighteen city party committees, six city district party committees, and 2,416 primary party organizations, making a total of 126,000 Communist Party members. The second bureau was responsible for agriculture and incorporated eighteen party committees of production collective farm–state farm departments, instead of the former district party committees, including 1,614 primary organizations, coming to a total of 44,000 Communists. In addition, two independent regional soviets (councils) and eighteen soviets of production departments were established.[7]

When asked in the 1990s about the party reorganization, Alexei Adzhubei, Khrushchev's son-in-law, who played an important role in the leadership of that period, described the two equal regional party committees in each region as an embryo of the two-party system, which, presumably, was a feature consciously introduced by Khrushchev himself.[8] Regardless of Khrushchev's genuine intentions, it is obvious that this innovation significantly undercut the power of party bosses in a given region since there were now two, rather than one, regional party secretaries, which meant one of them could somewhat neutralize the other's arbitrariness. In any case, for the first time in Soviet history, with Khrushchev's step, it became evident how effectively changes in regional politics could promote movement away from a totalitarian regime.

However, the step toward the division of party and state leadership failed to push society to some sort of liberalization. On the contrary, it tended to create mostly disarray in the provinces. The apocryphal history of that period (intellectual eyewitnesses remember it very well) is full of stories about the clashes between the regional, or territorial, agricultural and industrial party committees in the same region or territory, and they became quite common. Despite these struggles, no mention of such clashes appeared in the mass media of the USSR, as a scan of the 1960s press illustrates.

The aggravation of the economic situation, especially in the agricultural sector, forced the government to raise prices on meat and dairy products in 1962. In addition, poor harvests and the resultant grain purchases, in exchange for Soviet gold, from Canada in 1963 (the first transaction in a series of such purchases that stretched over almost thirty years) forced the leader of the Soviet empire to search for new stimuli to bring greater efficiency to socialism.

However, at the October 1964 Plenary Meeting of the CPSU Central Committee, Khrushchev was relieved of his post. His accusers did not directly discuss the problems of the regional policy in relation to Khrushchev's own regional policy.[9] All the same, it was evident that Khrushchev's critics saw in his regional policy, as in many of his other actions, a serious threat to the centralized character of Soviet society. To them, this policy, and later developments would prove them right, was a vital condition for the central elite's preservation of their monopoly on political power.[10]

In any case, the new leadership annulled all of Khrushchev's major innovations in regional policy. The October Plenary Meeting made a special decision to eliminate Khrushchev's directive to split the regional party committees.[11] Almost one year later, upon the decision of the September 1965 Plenary Meeting of the Central Committee, the regional economic councils were also abolished and the branch system of management restored.

Regional Planning and Studies

Regardless of the final results of Khrushchev's regional politics, it opened the way for a renewal of regional studies in Russia. This is quite significant in light of the fact that they had practically been stopped in the 1930s, along with other empirical social research.

As a matter of fact, the "spatial factor" was never ignored in the Soviet planning system. Since the 1920s, each Soviet textbook on planning, as well those on "political economics," always contained a few chapters about "territorial planning," including discussion on the allocation of "productive forces" and on the necessity for planners to take into account the specific character of each region in the country. Planning committees at all levels had special units to deal with the allocation of resources and local issues.[12]

However, with the exception of a short period of time in the late 1950s, branch-ministerial planning always dominated territorial planning. Since *mestnichestvo*—the preference of local interests over national ones—was at the very top of the Soviet Union's roster of major vices (not to mention separatism), regional studies in the 1930s practically disappeared from Russian academia.

The party leadership, which took the path of modest modernization of Soviet life after Stalin's death, was not seriously afraid that permitting the resumption of regional studies, even if only of an economic character, could foster *mestnichestvo*, as Stalin would have, with his paranoid fears of everything. The Kremlin was still so strong that it could snip even its slightest traces in the bud.

At the same time, the leadership assumed that regional studies would be able, without undermining the centralization of the system, to raise the economy's efficiency. This feat would be accomplished primarily as a result of the better distribution of production forces among regions, as the studies would take into full account the specific character of each region and its natural resources, geographical location, climate, and the population's composition.

This willingness to include the "regional factor" in economic policy was an action similar to several other government initiatives after 1953. This willingness manifested itself in the restoration of sociology, in the repeal of the ban on cybernetics, and in some extensions of freedom of actions for managers and others.[13]

The obscure Council of the Allocation of Productive Forces, which had been a part of the Academy of Science since 1930, became a part of the State Planning Committee in 1960 and gained high recognition in the country under the guidance of Vasilii Nemchinov, a well-known statistician. Resuscitating the council was one of the first events signaling the emergence of regional economic studies. After that, those in the field were permitted to translate Western theoretical books on regional economics into Russian, despite the fact that Soviet scholars continued to speak of "regional science" in quotes, accusing the discipline of various vices, including "geographical determinism."[14] Soviet scholars were also allowed by the government to participate in various international conferences on regional issues. Even more important was the emergence of departments of regional studies in various economic institutions, particularly in the Institute of Economics in Novosibirsk, and the publication of the first Soviet books and articles on regional issues.[15]

Regional studies from the 1960s until the 1980s were still far removed from discussions on the political relations between the center and regions and were evidently concerned with the improvement of the central planning system. Most regional studies scholars concentrated on the coordination of the so-called branch principle of Soviet planning with territorial planning in the interaction of enterprises belonging to different ministries within the same region. The numerous facts on the ineffective transportation of goods from one region to another, which resulted mostly because enterprises could not requisition parts or raw materials from neighboring firms since they belonged to "another" ministry, were a major inspirational force for regional studies and for the debates over the role of regions as "subjects of the economic management."[16]

Regional studies in the 1960s and 1970s were also encouraged by mathematical economics, which emerged in the Soviet Union in the late 1950s. The most popular direction in mathematical economics was optimal programming in general and linear programming specifically, both of which were aimed, among other things, at reducing costs while determining the best distribution of resources in a given territory. The first publications in optimal programming were devoted to the "transportation problem," and they offered algorithms for finding the best future allocation of producers and consumers or the best transportation connections for existing economic units with given production and transportation costs.[17]

Mathematical economics also initiated the elaboration of each region's economic balance and the computation of each region's contribution to the gross national product (GNP).[18] It was also permitted to speak about the "criterion of efficiency of the regional economy" in the economic literature under the influence of mathematical economists.[19] All these developments heightened interest in regional economic issues.

However, most of the economic publications on this issue were quite scholastic and irrelevant to common practice, instead serving propagandistic goals. These works usually underlined the region's submission to the country's interests and substantiated the necessity of using the region's specific character, such as its natural resources and geographical location, as well as the necessity of smoothing out the economic differences between regions.[20] If economists touched on the issue of economic decentralization in the country, they, as a rule, referred to managers of individual enterprises. This was particularly true after the dismantling of Khrushchev's regional policy.

All in all, however, the practical contribution of regional studies to Soviet economic policy was minimal. Decisions concerning the building of new enterprises did not involve the recommendations of experts if they did not quickly adjust to the intentions of the Soviet rulers. These leaders, with their political goals, wanted first of all to increase production by all means possible and refused to accept the various regional factors as constraints on their will.[21]

6

THE BREZHNEV ERA:
STABILITY OF REGIONAL CADRES

As has previously been pointed out, the October 1964 Plenary Meeting of the CPSU Central Committee, at which Nikita Khrushchev was forced to retire, restored the centralized management of the economy through branch ministries and departments, as well as through single party bodies in localities. From this moment on, Soviet society lived under the leadership of Leonid Brezhnev. In 1966, he left his position as first secretary to assume his new post as general secretary of the CPSU Central Committee. In 1978, Brezhnev added the post of chairman of the Presidium of the Supreme Soviet of the USSR to his list of accomplishments.

The second half of the 1960s was spent on the restoration of the pre-Khrushchev order and the installation of a new kind of relationship between the Moscow seigneur and his regional vassals. The Kremlin decided, in contrast to Khrushchev's era, to guarantee regional secretaries a sort of stability while it maintained full central control over all strategic decisions. Indeed, even if the stability of the upper leadership happened to be illusory,[1] the regime's promise to guarantee the regional secretary full tenure was on the whole brought about. Never in Soviet history, either before or after Brezhnev, did regional secretaries hold onto their positions for so long.[2]

Of the first secretaries of the regional (territorial) party committees of Russia present at the Twenty-Third CPSU Congress in 1966, the first congress held under Brezhnev, 32 percent remained at their posts for ten years and were present at the Twenty-Fifth CPSU Congress, and another 30 percent moved on to higher posts in the capital. Five years later, at the time of the Twenty-Sixth CPSU Congress, the last one under Brezhnev, 22 percent of the former first secretaries who had taken part in the first Brezhnev congress still held their jobs.[3] This means that almost every third regional head held his job for at least ten years and, again, every third secretary was promoted to a higher post in Moscow.

At the same time, 20 percent worked in their regions for the entire period of Brezhnev's rule, which was practically impossible for party leaders of the pre-Brezhnev period.

Among the most "stable" secretaries of regional party committees were the first secretaries of the Vladimir, Kaluga, Novosibirsk, Vologda, Tula, and Tomsk Regions—the first secretary of Tomsk, Egor Ligachev, was later the second secretary of the CPSU Central Committee.[4] It is possible, of course, that sometimes these people were not promoted to higher posts because of their personal qualities. However, this was not always the main reason, for as the Russian proverb goes, it is better to be the first guy in a village rather than the second one in a town.

The Tenure of Regional Leaders in the Brezhnev Era

The stability of regional cadres, along with, of course, the supposedly active participation of the regional secretaries in Khrushchev's ousting, was interpreted by several American Sovietologists as evidence that regional leaders were autonomous actors and were able to influence, and even exert pressure on, the Kremlin. Furthermore, many scholars even contended that the October 1964 coup particularly meant the victory of bureaucracy and regional bosses, who were able to put their representative on the throne and who, after that time, were controlled by them.[5] However, there is a mountain of evidence showing that in the conspiracy against Khrushchev, those party secretaries who had been informed mostly indirectly about the plot played more than a secondary role. At the meeting of the Central Committee, which rubber stamped the decision of the Politburo, party secretaries, as they had in 1957, simply joined those leaders of the party who were tasting victory.[6]

Referring to the presumably active political role of regional leaders, certain Sovietologists argued that this showed evidence of political pluralism emerging in Soviet society; others saw signs of a "bureaucratic society." These interpretations of events suggest that the central and regional political and economic elite—not just the general secretary and few other members of the Politburo—made the strategic decisions. Some authors suggested that regional leaders even formed a "pressure bloc" and were thereby able to extricate some concessions from the Kremlin, which, by the way, did indeed happen, though only in post-Communist Russia.[7] In fact, nothing like this occurred in the 1970s.[8]

Many Western Sovietologists did not understand that the power monopoly was not declining when power holders actively backed their subordinates (not only as personalities but also as implementers of their policies), whose support could be particularly important in cases of state emergency, when the position, and even the life, of the leader could be in jeopardy. Of course, subordinates, including secretaries, bodyguards, and mistresses, can also heavily influence their superior, though this does not change the fundamental fact—the superior has the real monopoly on power.[9]

Reliance on Local Party Bosses
for Fear of the Masses

There were two main reasons that Brezhnev "stabilized" the regional cadres, as well as the other echelons of bureaucracy in the country. The first explanation was indeed connected with the circumstances surrounding Khrushchev's political demise. Brezhnev, as Gorbachev did later on, evidently drew a valuable lesson from this spectacular and unprecedented event in Soviet history. He apparently decided not to treat the regional cadres in such an unceremonious way as his predecessor had and thereby diminished the likelihood of their participation in an eventual plot. He was also able to justify his new cadre policy by stressing the need for conservative stability in society.

The second reason for Brezhnev's cadre policy was of more importance. In the opinion of the conspirators, Khrushchev, with his reforms and particularly with his denunciation of Stalin, had perched society on the edge of anarchy. Most members of the Politburo and those around them did indeed believe this.[10] Developments two decades later somewhat confirmed that their fears were well founded—the Soviet system turned out to be very fragile when its leader embarked on the road of reform.

The new team in the Kremlin decided to do everything necessary to stop the process eroding party power in Soviet society. It should be noted that Soviet leaders since the civil war have maintained a permanent fear of mass riots. This was particularly true after the Stalin era. As subsequent events showed, including developments in post-Communist Russia in 1992–1994 with the drastic deterioration of life in the country, the misgivings of Soviet leaders were strongly exaggerated. However, Soviet leaders did not know the magnitude of their people's patience and were in a state of incessant apprehension about public disturbances.[11] The Kremlin immediately received information about the most trivial strikes in remote cities. And, in 1962, a few extraordinary riots, even if modest in scope, did indeed occur—one in Novocherkask and another in Karaganda. The first disorder greatly impressed the Kremlin.[12] This event was declared a classified state secret and, until glasnost, was unknown to the Russian people. There is little doubt that Novocherkask contributed to Khrushchev's "resignation."[13]

Among other measures taken to prevent the collapse of the system, of which the significant rise in the standard of living was one such, Brezhnev and his comrades chose to strengthen the power of local party governors, who were thereafter delegated immense power from above and became directly responsible for maintaining order in the country.

This was an alternative to Khrushchev's, and later to Gorbachev's, policy to garner support for the regime by siding somewhat with the masses against local authorities, whom the masses so hated. It was a fixture of the Khrushchev regime, as it also was to some degree of Stalin's, to publicly pummel regional party secretaries and make fools of them at conferences and meetings, even in the presence of foreign dignitaries—actions that aroused the ridicule and gloating of ordinary people.

The Brezhnev Kremlin calculated that promising party bosses a lifelong position in the *nomenklatura* and total support in the implementation of discipline on their territory would restore order in the country. Regional leaders therefore had free rein in the selection of local cadres, even if Moscow formally had to endorse people chosen for the second and third levels of the local hierarchy.[14]

Regional emissaries were essentially free to dispose of the region's wealth, to promote favorites, and to create a kind of regional Mafia. It can be stated outright that during the period of Brezhnev's stabilization, Mafia-type structures appeared in almost all the localities.[15] However, no matter what crimes occurred in the regions and what measures were taken by Moscow in this respect, nothing appeared in the press.[16]

Tenure Without Political Independence for Regional Leaders

Although Brezhnev endowed the regional *nomenklatura* with lifelong tenure and the freedom to act on behalf of Moscow, it was deprived of any opportunity to make even remotely political decisions that could endanger Moscow-based centralism.[17] As had been the case in the past, the vigilant surveillance on the part of the Central Committee immediately put an end to any attempts at regional independence and initiative, even if these attempts involved such an innocent sphere of management as the formation of approved public organizations, such as the councils of "elders," pensioners, and nurses in any particular region. Such occurrences immediately became the topic of discussion in the party press, whereas the more serious initiatives evoked more serious reactions, although they were not mentioned in the press.

None of the regional party secretaries or leaders of national republics, displayed any political initiative in the Brezhnev era. They never even tried to create any sort of informal organization or pressure the general secretary in any way, even though they formed the largest (making up more than one-third of the Central Committee's membership in 1976), most professional group in the Central Committee.[18] With their apparently more stable positions, regional party secretaries did not play any documented role on the three occasions when the

Central Committee formally endorsed a new leader of the country—Yurii Andropov (1982), Konstantin Chernenko (1984), and Mikhail Gorbachev (1985)—even if those members of the Politburo who supported a particular candidate referred to the support of this decision by "the mood of the many first regional party secretaries, members of the Central Committee."[19]

This did not happen even during perestroika after 1987, by which time the Kremlin had lost much of its power and prestige. Even then, regional secretaries who hated Gorbachev, although not hiding their hatred as had been necessary in the past, did not dare to plot against him hoping to evict him from the Kremlin. They invariably followed the lead of the general secretary in all public actions.[20] It was only at the last CPSU congress in July 1990 that unsuccessful attempts to unseat Gorbachev were made.

The efforts of some Sovietologists to confirm the devolution of "political and economic decision making authority to local elites" are ill founded.[21] Indeed, they have misconstrued some extension of the power of local elites to choose the means of accomplishing Moscow's directives as their full exercise of freedom in political matters. Even the leaders of big republics like Ukraine, not to mention the regional secretary of a Russian region, were deprived of any right to participate in the political decisionmaking process. In fact, when Piotr Shelest, the Ukrainian first secretary and a member of the Politburo, showed his discontent with Brezhnev's foreign policy, he was fired on short notice on the eve of President Richard Nixon's visit to Kiev in 1973.

Another theory suggests that regional party secretaries, along with the rest of the *nomenklatura* as agents of the "bureaucratic market," had exercised much autonomy and had evolved inside the Soviet system into private owners, but this view, again, is nothing less than modernizing the past. In fact, there is no evidence of the accumulation of wealth by the regional party elite, nor were there signs that they were "alienated from its order," as Egor Gaidar suggested in his book *The State and Evolution* (1995), or that they greeted capitalist "thermidors" with perestroika and subsequent developments.[22]

Everything that Western experts attributed to regional leaders in the 1970–1980s indeed happened—but these things did not happen until the time of post-Communist Russia, when the regional political elite entered into an all-out confrontation with the Kremlin, a fundamental development we will turn to later on. Furthermore, even the slogan of "stability of cadres" was ultimately relative. When it was necessary, Brezhnev fired regional secretaries on short notice, albeit much less frequently than Khrushchev and, of course, without publicizing the reasons for their removal. For instance, between 1966 and 1971, he replaced thirty-one regional secretaries. Only one year before his death, he ousted almost 10 percent of all regional secretaries. His successors were no more afraid of the regional bosses. Andropov managed, during one year of his rule, to expel one-fourth of all regional secretaries. Gorbachev, in his first year, replaced one-third of them, and, even more interesting, he found 78 percent of their successors not among regional cadres but inside of the Central Committee.[23]

Another issue is the attempts of various groups and institutions in Soviet society, which have existed all throughout Soviet history, to influence the Kremlin, the monopolist on power, in order to get benefits for themselves. There is no doubt that regional leaders, for instance, tried to persuade, but would not dare press, the Kremlin to build a projected big automobile plant in their own region.[24] In trying to extricate a necessary decision, regional leaders, as well as the heads of various institutions such as the KGB or the army, used various arguments, mostly related to the defense of the country and the strengthening of the Soviet state and the party. However, whatever they requested and suggested, they behaved as humble subordinates and not at all as "pressure blocs." It is ludicrous, for instance, to speak about the "conflict between the central government and local governments . . . as endemic" to the Soviet Union as well as "to all modern political systems."[25] The pressure groups, including regional leaders, were to emerge partially after 1989 and in full scale after 1991.[26]

A Brief Portrait of
the Regional Party Secretary, 1960 to 1989

Despite all the corruption in the Russian provinces, it would be wrong to ignore the fact that most regional party secretaries were quite competent and hardworking politicians, usually with good organizational skills.[27] Many of them in the late 1970s and early 1980s still wanted to build their careers or to preserve their positions with deeds that were useful, in their opinion, to the might of the state. Most of them were indeed concerned with their region's economic success and expended much effort, using their power and connections in Moscow, trying to overcome various obstacles for the fulfillment of state plans, particularly in the arena of the military-industrial complex. It is enough to mention Gorbachev and Yeltsin, who, as regional party secretaries, tried to improve the economy, within the framework of the Soviet system, in their respective Stavropol and Sverdlovsk Regions.

Of course, the average regional boss was far different than those idealized party men that hack writers described in their novels.[28] Many of them were deeply conservative and were admirers of Stalin. They almost unanimously hated Khrushchev and heartily helped the Politburo conspirators toss him out of the halls of power. They also enthusiastically greeted a sort of restoration of Stalinism, a movement that started in the late 1960s, and were frustrated when the Kremlin halted this process in 1973.

Moreover, being in general much more conservative than their leaders in Moscow, regional party secretaries carried out much more antidemocratic policies than the center. Leningrad, for instance, with Grigorii Romanov, was much more reactionary than Moscow. Later, during perestroika, the regional secretaries resisted reforms as much as possible and enthusiastically supported the August 19, 1991, coup.

Many regional secretaries felt themselves, of course, to be almost unrestrained rulers over their subjects in the region, encouraging a modest cult of personality, much milder in form than the cults of regional leaders before the mid-1930s. In addition, they enjoyed various legal privileges, though these were much less luxurious than the perks of those who replaced them as governors in post-Communist Russia.

A Regional View of Economic and Social Processes Under Brezhnev

In the first few years of his regime, Brezhnev apparently wanted to introduce some economic reforms that would improve the efficiency of the Soviet economy. To this end, the so-called Kosygin reform was endorsed in September 1964 in a Plenary Meeting of the CPSU Central Committee. The main thrust of the reform was to transfer the national economy from an extensive to an intensive form of development through the decentralization of economic management and the expansion of enterprise powers.

Kosygin's reforms were very soon stifled by the party apparatus at the central and regional levels, because the party feared even the relative independence of enterprises. However, the downpour of "petrodollars" made it possible to improve the standard of living in the country, due to some progress in agriculture, housing construction, the services sphere, and the import of consumer goods.

After a period of some progress, however, by the mid-1970s the Russian economy had entered a period later dubbed the "period of stagnation." The growing inefficiency of the Soviet economy and its inability to cope with technological progress, along with growing military expenditures and the Kremlin's willingness to continue the arms race, caused deterioration in many areas of social life. Progress halted, and sometimes even regressed, in most sectors of the economy, including agriculture and the leading branch industries. The stagnation of the civilian economy was, naturally, accompanied by other phenomena that became especially pronounced in the 1970s: fluctuation of manpower, contempt for labor and labor morality, alcoholism, and the corruption of the party and state apparatus, which began to merge with bands of thieves of state property.[29]

Reviving Interest in Regional Issues in the Late 1970s

In the late 1970s, with the growing stagnation, the Kremlin started to flirt again with the idea of expansion, in the wake of Khrushchev's initial attempt to create greater regional economic autonomy. This time, however, it was to be strictly under the control of party secretaries, not under the aegis of the *sovnarkhozy*, whose head under Khrushchev had been able to challenge the highest party official in the region. By the end of Brezhnev's regime, the Kremlin had started to discuss multibranch regional industrial and agro-industrial complexes, which were combined with local enterprises and were able to cooperate with each other whatever their subordination; under discussion as well was the necessity to increase the role of local authorities in managing the economy.[30]

These initiatives, however, were typical "spurious innovations," appearing along with others, such as the implementation of the "automatic system of management" (ASU), which served mostly ideological purposes and described the aged leadership in Moscow as "dynamic" and "progressive," while affecting very little in real practice.[31] Soviet economists, as a rule, praised each new official initiative, despite the evident fact that this "innovation" had brought no real progress to the Soviet economy.[32]

Regional Life in the Period of Stagnation

Meanwhile, regional life in Russia during the period of stagnation was determined mostly by two main factors: (1) the poor supply of foodstuffs and consumer goods in general, and (2) stable local leadership. The growing shortage in supply, stemming from specific features of the totalitarian economy, led to the establishment of peculiar relations between the capital and the rest of Russia, including even Leningrad.

Moscow groceries became stable sources of meat, meat products, and various delicacies for nearby regions, such as Kalinin, Iaroslavl, and Kostroma. A journey to the capital for foodstuffs became a common phenomenon, like a trip to a distant store in one's own town. Relatives and neighbors would often gather for regular weekend jaunts to Moscow. In fact, enterprises and offices rented tourist buses for such purposes, and one could often see several such buses parked near Moscow shops—no other Moscow city sights interested these "tourists." A business trip to Moscow was considered a bonus, for by spending a day in a queue to get into *GUM* (a major department store) or other supermarket one could buy two pairs of imported boots (the second pair to sell at home for a higher price) and thus compensate for the traveling expenses. Later, after the institution of market reforms and free prices in 1991, the Yeltsin regime regularly reminded provincial Russians of how they had had to travel to Moscow in order to buy a sausage.

The Brezhnev era was the best of times in Soviet history for the regional elite, a time when they enjoyed relatively high status. All the same, during this era they were not afraid now of each call from Moscow, wondering if it could mean a demand for their resignation, if not something worse. For this period of about twenty years, the Kremlin was able to combine full political and economic control over the provinces with the active support of its policy by its appointed regional elite.

PART TWO

The Center and Regions in Conflict Since 1985

In the previous chapters, we discussed regionalization and regionalism in Russia mostly from a historical perspective. Now we will discuss these phenomena in rather theoretical terms to see how worldwide trends and, more specifically, Russian national trends stimulated regionalism and shaped its specific forms in 1991–1995. In addition, we will also consider the consequences of regionalism for Russian society in this period.

As before, the most appropriate heuristic framework for the analysis of the relationship between the center and regions in post-Communist society, and to some degree in any nontotalitarian society, is conflict theory. We will also discuss the struggle between the center and regions along ideological, political, and economic planes.

7

THE GORBACHEV ERA: DESTABILIZATION OF CENTER-PERIPHERY RELATIONS

Regionalism as a political phenomenon was in no way on the agenda of perestroika during its first years of operation. In 1985–1989, this issue was simply ignored in the media and not present in any political actions. Moreover, beginning with Mikhail Gorbachev's first year in office, he often spoke of the "plan's" importance and even the advantages of centralization, leaving no room for regional issues.[1]

The "territorial issue" evolved out of the relations between the center and Soviet national republics in late 1986. The relationship decidedly turned sour as Alma-Ata students rioted against the appointment of Gennadii Kolbin, a Russian emissary, as first secretary of the Kazakh Communist Party. The ethnic issue was gradually advancing to the forefront of Soviet politics with the outbreak of the Nagorno-Karabakh conflict and the initiation of the national movement in the Baltic republics in 1988–1989. However, in 1987–1988, regionalism continued to remain dormant. Only after 1989 did regionalism begin to intrude upon the Soviet political scene, becoming a vital issue to the future of Russia after 1991.

It is reasonable to make a distinction between the "subjective" and "objective" aspects of regionalization. Indeed, the Gorbachev regime's attitudes, as well as those of liberal intellectuals and the troubadours of perestroika and other major actors—the local party elite and the masses—toward decentralization were very ambivalent and succumbed to various, seemingly contradictory acts. Whatever their subjective views on the democratization of political life in the country were, the objective processes in the country had moved since the very beginning of perestroika toward decentralization and weakening the Kremlin, opening the way for regional party leaders to expand their autonomy.

Gorbachev's Contradictory Position

Until 1989, the extension of regional autonomy was almost never mentioned in the documents of the highest bodies of the CPSU. In the chapter on the improvement of the management of the national economy in the Resolution of the Twenty-Seventh Party Congress' "Guidelines of the Economic and Social Development of the USSR for 1986–1990 and for the Period Ending in 2000," there are only conventional stock phrases typical of the entire post-Stalinist period.[2]

There is not a single word referring to regionalism in Mikhail Gorbachev's famous book, *Perestroika and New Thinking for Our Country and the Whole World* (1988), although a section of the second chapter is titled "New Understanding of Centralism." This section deals with the democratization of planning, the reduction of the number of indicators to be used to judge the performance of enterprises, the extension of their rights, in other words, the relationships between the central departments and economic units. The only exceptions are three phrases on the necessity of having a firm, centralized principle as the basis of a planned economy's advantage, but these comments, too, are addressed not to the regions, but to national republics.[3]

This slack reaction is perhaps due to two interwoven causes. As soon as Gorbachev charted a course toward glasnost and democratization, the power of regional party secretaries immediately began to rise. The new, open spirit throughout the country lessened popular fear of the Kremlin. This was also true concerning the Kremlin's emissaries in the regions.

At the same time, the Kremlin, in the person of Gorbachev, was quite aware that regional secretaries posed potential dangers to the existing regime and to the reforms that it initiated. This danger was rooted in the selection system of the party leadership, which was inherited from past regimes and once seemed to be purely a formality, but now with democratization of political life in the country, it had to be taken seriously—another ironic development of perestroika.

Distinctly separated from the system of soviets, the party election system was multistage. City or district party conferences sent their deputies to regional (territorial) party conferences, whereas the latter sent representatives to the party congress. Regional (territorial) conferences elected the Central Committee, which in turn elected the Politburo and the general secretary. All the first secretaries of the regional party committees were represented on the Central Committee. In Stalin's lifetime, especially after 1934, this did not mean a thing. The decision about who was appointed general secretary was not the responsibility of the secretaries of regional party committees, but it was the general secretary himself who appointed first secretaries of the regional party committees.

As soon as totalitarian power had weakened somewhat, as became evident in 1985–1989, the threat of such an electoral system became quite real to party leaders. The real election of party officials almost immediately became quite an important factor in the political process. Most party activists—the electors of first party secretaries and even of major city party secretaries—were conservatives and open enemies of reform. Under the existing circumstances, they preferred to support first secretaries who shared their negative attitude toward reforms. The growing political power of local party organizations was clearly revealed during the election of delegates to the Nineteenth Party Conference in 1988. The so-called election was reduced to the appointment of delegates by the regional party committees, which ostensibly ignored the candidates chosen by the various groups of people in factories, research institutes, universities, and offices. In many cases at these meetings, party officials openly tried to yank people by the hand in order to "pull" their own people to their way of thinking. Only in a few regions, such as in Sakhalin, Astrakhan, and Iaroslavl, did people manage to influence the election of candidates, mostly "killing" the candidacies of the incumbent or former first party secretary.

The major tribunes of perestroika, such as *Moskovskie Novosti, Sovietskaia Kul'tura, Ogoniok* and *Literaturnaia Gazeta*, seemingly egged on by Gorbachev, lambasted party committees for violating democratic rules. However, in general these efforts were to no avail. Only in a few cases, in regions such as Iaroslavl, Kamchatka, and Omsk, did the forces of perestroika manage to affect conservatives, insisting on their candidates and foiling their political opponents.[4]

Indeed, in 1987–1989, the relationship between Gorbachev and regional party leaders was very complicated. The general secretary could still dissipate some of the emerging freedoms of the party apparatus to elect regional officials and remove any one of them, which he did quite frequently. For this reason, among others, regional secretaries did not dare to challenge Gorbachev at the meeting of the Central Committee until summer 1990. Therefore, Gorbachev continued to ignore their views on essential issues of domestic and foreign policy. However, he was quite aware that as had happened after Nikita Khrushchev's dismissal, in the ensuing state of emergency, the political role of party secretaries could rise enormously, when they had a crucial impact on the course of events that led to his political demise. As matter of fact, Gorbachev, along with a host of Moscow politicians and Sovietologists, turned out to be wrong. Even during the August 1991 coup, regional leaders remained mostly passive, and not one of them directly defended the junta, even though they almost unanimously approved of its program.

However, in 1987–1989, Gorbachev was still unwilling to tolerate any increase in the power of regional leaders, who were still mostly conservatives and openly harassed the advocates of reforms in their regions.[5] Gorbachev could not significantly change the situation by replacing the first secretary, since the second secretaries and chairmen of regional soviets, who were the natural candidates for succeeding the first secretary in the Soviet system, favored the same views as their predecessors. In this way, the great party reformer failed to create a new cohort of local leaders devoted to continuing reforms.

Of no less importance was another factor, one that explains the Kremlin's refusal to include regional autonomy in the program of reforms. It was also clear to Gorbachev that the rise of regional autonomy, leading to the weakening of the center's might and its inability to easily resort to repression as in the past, could also contribute to the dissemination of anarchy throughout the country. This became particularly evident when nationalist movements began to develop in most of the Soviet republics.

The Inevitability of Decentralization

Although he was trying to slacken the move of regional leaders toward autonomy, Gorbachev himself was encountering increasing difficulty in running the country and was thus forced to give them more leeway in ruling their regions, thinking that in this way he could enhance the economic performance of the country. There was a growing consensus in society that it was impossible to run an economy from the center and that it was important to involve people in both the management and government at the local level. All ideas of the automation of management (the so-called ASU) and the use of mathematical methods for the drastic improvement of central planning, which had been important ingredients of all party documents on economics in the 1970s, totally disappeared from Soviet life in the mid-1980s. In its place, the concepts of the early 1960s on the importance of decentralization in economic management reemerged.

Besides reluctantly accepting the growing autonomy of the local *nomenklatura*, Gorbachev was also buying their support against the central bureaucracy, which was in many cases even more hostile than local leaders to his reforms. Several times, Gorbachev played regional cards against his enemies in Moscow. Such was the case at the Nineteenth Party Conference in 1988, when Gorbachev exploited this regional card and used it against his enemies in the Politburo and the Central Committee. Pretending that this measure was a condition for democratization, Gorbachev proposed that the positions of regional party secretary and chairman of the local government be held by the same person, and certainly, by a party secretary. This idea aroused the democrats' anger, but was heartily accepted by members of the local *nomenklatura*, who were a majority of the delegates, since it evidently increased the power and autonomy of the party secretary. However, with the congress's support, Gorbachev was able to initiate free elections for Parliament in 1989, radically changing the political situation in the country.

Amid the growing disorganization of economic life, in the words of Russian authors, "local authorities began to face 'alone,' without the support of Moscow, their population," and this was because Gorbachev's regime started to shift economic responsibility for provincial development onto the regional bosses.[6] He advanced, in 1988–1989, the almost absurd economic idea that each region had to satisfy all the needs of its population with the products of its own agriculture and industry. The so-called regional *khozrashchet* idea, also known as "self-suffi-ciency" or "regional cost accounting," was forgotten very soon, since most regional enterprises were under the direction of Moscow ministries.

There was yet another factor that made the new Kremlin regime a hostage to regionalization. It was the process of democratization that Gorbachev initiated in 1987. With the purpose of supporting not only glasnost but also the wider participation of the public in the nation's government, Gorbachev backed the increasing role of people in running their own districts, cities, and regions. Indeed, in the process of expanding democratization, Gorbachev began to call for the expansion of the soviets' power, an evident challenge to the political monopoly of party apparatchiks. This call could only enhance the autonomy of the regions, even if it involved the same apparatchiks who at this stage could exploit this process in their own interests.[7] Because of all these contradictory developments, it was not until 1991 that the regionalization and decentralization of Russian regions came to the forefront of official policy.

The View of Democratic Intellectuals Before 1991

Democratic leaders and publicists differed very little from party leaders and ide-ologists in their attitudes toward regionalization during perestroika. As a matter of fact, before 1989 most Russian liberal intellectuals ignored not only regional-ization but even ethnic problems, despite their growing significance since late 1986. Moreover, even in 1989–1991, when it had become impossible to ignore the conflicts between Moscow and the Soviet national republics, as well as the conflicts between various non-Russian ethnic groups, Russian liberals continued to disregard the CP relationship.

Strange as it may seem today, up until the disintegration of the Soviet Union there was not a single word referring to regionalism in the writings of the most popular warriors opposing the totalitarian power. Speakers at meetings of demo-cratic-minded intellectuals also kept silent about regionalism, as did the radio and television services, which were becoming increasingly more daring. The rea-son for this state of affairs lies not in censorship or in Communist Party pressure on the authors, publishers, and editors, for by that time the ideological power of the CPSU had already been undermined and censorship was not yet abolished but had been seriously weakened.

A typical example is a series of serious collective works called "*Perestroika: Glasnost'*, Democracy, Socialism," the first volume of which is *There Is No Other Way*, published in 1988 under the editorship of the popular democrat and doctor of history, Yurii Afanasyev.[8] This is, in fact, an anthology of the progressive (for that period) social thought of Russia, although the presentations are not uniform and are sometimes contradictory.[9] In this encyclopedic edition of over five hun-dred pages, there is not a single paragraph, to say nothing of an article, on the

problems of regionalism, excluding several generally known references and citations from the works of the Marxist-Leninist classics concerning the benefits of
local self-government or the combination of centralism and democracy.[10]

What is the reason for this silence, this striking absence of such topics as "the
center and the regions" and "the centripetal and centrifugal forces in Russia" in
the democratic press during this time period? First, as previously mentioned, the
advancement to the fore of problems concerning the fate of national republics in
the Soviet Union was never really addressed. The problem of "the center and the
regions" was perceived instead as the problem of "Russia, its satellites, and its
younger brothers—the union republics." The relationship between Russia and
other union republics was only later moved to the forefront by history itself.

A second possible explanation is, in fact, a continuation of the first—the main
emphasis remained on national relations, but this time within Russia. However,
the nationalism of the non-Russian regions in the Russian Federation, even if it
did begin in 1990 to draw the public's attention, was interpreted then as a benign
kind of nationalism, weaker in comparison to the virus of national separatism
that infected Lithuania, Estonia, Georgia, and even the fraternal Slavic Ukraine.

Only a person with a very vivid imagination, prone to apocalyptic revelations,
could have conceived in 1989–1991 that Chechnia and Tatarstan would seriously
demand separation from Russia in order to form their own states. Certainly, there
were such prophets, but they had little say in democratic circles about the euphoric
grip of the forthcoming liberation that took hold of all the peoples from the Communist regime, a regime that had brought about not only stagnation, national strife,
and the center's imperial ambitions but also a striving for freedom in the localities.

The third reason was rooted in the widespread, simplistic notion that the
rejection of the existing system of management, aptly called "administrative
command" by Gavriil Popov, and the establishment of a self-regulating market
economy would automatically lead to the optimization of CP relations. Political
scientists, sociologists, workers in the legal profession, and Soviet intellectuals in
general, even those who were hostile to the official Communist ideology, were
basically trained in an atmosphere of orthodox Marxism. Voluntarily or not, they
were all under the influence of primitivized Marxist teachings on the basis and
superstructure of society and on the decisive role of the economic relations of
production, which supposedly determined all life in society. From this belief
came their confidence that many important social problems were by nature secondary and derivative, which resulted in their underestimating these problems
and even in their complete ignorance of the process of analyzing the real world
and working out program requirements for its transformation. From this Marxist
perspective, it was thought that not only regional but national problems as well
would disappear after the economic problems were solved.[11]

Experience has shown that this was far from the truth. Both national and
regional problems were rooted in more than just economic inequality, although
such inequality does play a very significant part in creating these problems, not
only under totalitarianism.

Managers and Regionalization

The position of managers—the directors of big enterprises—was also full of con-tradiction. On the one hand, they, more than anybody else, were interested in independence from the center or at least in weakening their current dependence. They viewed the tough guidance of the State Planning Committee and the dic-tates of the ministries as too dear a price to pay for the guaranteed sale of their produce, whether or not the consumers needed this produce. On the other hand, Soviet directors during the Gorbachev period generally wanted freedom from Moscow, but a peculiar freedom with guaranteed orders, supply of materials, subsidies to cover their losses, and extended production.[12]

But this is not the main point. The directors striving for freedom from the center had no intention of substituting their subordination to Moscow with sub-ordination to local authorities. They liked the heavy hand of the regional party committee no more than the ministerial fist. The corps of directors was clearly aware that the strengthening of local authorities at the expense of the center would not bring them any relief.

Naturally, managers differed from one another. The directors of the largest industrial plants, even under the Communist regime, were "industrial barons," who mostly ignored local authorities and sometimes even ruled over them. It was precisely this group that held the potential of becoming a silent, if not active, supporter of regionalism.

"Agrarian barons," directors of state and collective farms and those dependent on them, were among those who benefited from the greater rights of regions. They wanted the right to dispose of their production and to sell it at free market prices. During Gorbachev's era, agrarian barons were extremely successful in using the expansion of regional autonomy to widen their own power. It is remarkable that in 1985, state purchases accounted for 40 percent of the gross yield of grain in the Russian Federation. It is symptomatic that during Gor-bachev's perestroika, despite significant differences in the yield of grain,[13] the share of state purchases as part of the gross national yield was steadily declining. Thus, in 1986, the state share was 39.2 percent; in 1987, 35.6 percent; in 1988, 31.2 percent; in 1989, 29.8 percent; in 1990, 29.1 percent; and in 1991, it had sunk to 25.5 percent. This is clear testimony to the strengthened position of the regions and the weakening of the center's possible options.

Local Party Leaders and Regionalization

The position of the local party apparatchiks was as contradictory as that of the other actors. Local party bosses educated in the cult of centralism and obedience to Moscow thought that they could both pay the high price of undermining the fundamentals of the Soviet system and gain greater personal power. But most of them understood that augmentation of their power could only be temporary because the required reforms would ultimately destroy the party and perhaps even the Soviet Union.

However, the short-term benefit—more power today—outweighed apprehensions about a dangerous future, which looked quite distant. As a result, as stated above, the local party apparatus, which had resisted most elements of Gorbachev's political and economic program, enthusiastically embraced almost everything that could lead toward decentralization, hoping that with their new power they would be able to stifle reforms at home and in Moscow.

As previously mentioned, the Nineteenth Party Conference provided a perfect example. While arguing against many of Gorbachev's innovations, particularly glasnost,[14] the delegates, mostly provincial apparatchiks, unanimously supported the idea of decentralization. Their critiques of the central authorities were as acerbic and rabid as their attacks on the mass media. Local party officials clearly regarded the ministries and the Moscow press as enemies who could potentially reduce their power and limit their ability to make arbitrary decisions.[15] Thus, Gorbachev, as stated earlier, knew that he could somewhat rely on local bureaucrats to support him in his fight against the Moscow Stalinists, who saw decentralization as the road toward anarchy and the disintegration of the empire.

The ambivalence of regional party apparatchiks toward Gorbachev continued until the spring of 1989. Then, during the first relatively free elections for the Soviet Parliament, first party secretaries were not elected as deputies in forty cities, even in those cities where they were the only candidate on the ballot. A procedure that had long been regarded as simply ritual turned into a devastating debacle for the local party apparatus. Party secretaries who clearly did not anticipate the possibility of such event moved radically and almost unanimously against Gorbachev and took the side of the centralists in Moscow, preferring their previous status as Moscow emissaries in the provinces to the demise of the whole system.[16]

During the last party congress in July 1990, regional apparatchiks were the most hostile group among the delegates. At this point, the conflict between them and the general secretary had reached a level of unbelievable intensity.[17]

It is only natural that during the August 1991 putsch against Gorbachev and reform, local party apparatchiks almost unanimously supported the conservatives. However, only a few regional party secretaries, without any tradition of independent political activities, were bold enough to support the putsch openly. Almost all of them waited to see who would come out on top.

The Masses

In Soviet times, local Communist authorities, local Soviet bodies, and local KGB authorities aroused no less public criticism than was given to the CPSU Political

Bureau, the Supreme Soviet, or the central KGB in the dreaded Lubyanka. Every person living at that time in Russia would probably testify that reactionary tendencies, stupidity, and the desire to block all progress were greatest in the lowest power structures. The slightest manifestations of free thinking, which were routinely ignored in Moscow, were still punishable in the regions.

During perestroika, the local party committees and their leaders were, as a rule, much more conservative than the Moscow party apparatus. Never in the history of the Soviet Union did local apparatchiks look so reactionary in the eyes of the population as during perestroika.[18] For this reason, it is clear that while in 1987–1991, when there were mass demonstrations in the streets and squares of many cities throughout Russia, the slogans read "Down with the CPSU!" and not "Down with the CPSU Central Committee!" Nowhere did the people demand "All power to the local authorities!"

For this reason, the masses were, in 1986–1991, in general indifferent or even hostile toward the autonomy of regions. However, some categories of the population had specific attitudes on this issue. The majority of the workers in the industries, unlike a certain part of the directorate, failed to see any advantage for themselves in a weaker center. Such advantages, however, were apparent to state farm workers, and especially collective farmers. The weaker the center, the fewer the resources it would be able to pump out of the countryside and, conversely, the greater the materials that would remain available to the rural population. Whether these expectations were likely to be realized was quite a different matter. Nevertheless, they formed the breeding ground for regionalistic tendencies.

The part played by the countryside should not be exaggerated. The countryside had greatly fallen apart after collectivization not only materially but also spiritually, as it had lost its most active, independent, and clever people and had become older in terms of its population's age composition, many of whom were hopeless drunks. It was therefore not an active political force and was capable of only silently agreeing with the decisions of the "Soviet feudal lords."

The Struggle Between Gorbachev and Yeltsin

In 1990, a new factor began to exert a growing impact on the relationship between the center and regions in the Russian Federation. This factor was no less than the struggle for power between Gorbachev and Yeltsin, who in the beginning was the head of the democratic opposition to the Soviet president, then became the chairman of the Russian Parliament, and finally became the Russian president.

Gorbachev was on the defensive after 1989, thus it was Boris Yeltsin who took the initiative. As one of his major trump cards in this political card game, Yeltsin used various nationalist and regional forces, along with democratic ideology. The mechanism used to disband the Soviet Union, which was initiated by the logic of the struggle between Gorbachev and Yeltsin a few years later, was considered by many people as a blueprint for the disintegration of the Russian Federation and as the stimulus for separatists of all sorts, for whom the collapse of the USSR showed that the Russian Federation could follow the same fate.[19] Indeed, Yeltsin combined his democratic program with the element of sovereignty for the national republics, including Russia, the non-Russian regions, and Russian regions in the Russian Federation, and he declared that all these separatist moves were directed at the destruction of the Soviet system.[20]

By announcing the crusade for Russian sovereignty, Yeltsin exploited Russian nationalism in an unexpected way. He used Russian nationalists' complaints about the exploitation of the Russian people by the non-Russian republics for his own political purposes. Yeltsin's slogan, "sovereign Russia," also attracted democrats, who saw the Kremlin as a major obstacle to reforms and were ready to use any means available to crush Gorbachev.[21]

In any case, Yeltsin's call to achieve the "independence of the Russian Federation" was the core of his political activity in 1990–1991. He encouraged various industries to emancipate themselves from the center's yoke and "go under the jurisdiction of Russia." He declared that Russian laws were superior to all-union laws, sealing the Russian empire's fate in a political move that caught even the liberals by surprise.[22]

Yeltsin's "Russia card" was extremely successful, since the belief that Russia was exploited by the non-Russian republics was accepted almost unanimously by the Russian people. Later, a similar idea about the exploitation of Russian regions by the non-Russian ethnic regions inside the Russian Federation also played also an important role in the evolution of the relationship between the center and provinces in Russia after 1991.

Another parallel between the developments in 1990–1991 surrounding the fate of the USSR and the events in 1992–1994 concerning the fate of the Russian Federation was also striking, even if the similarity between the two processes was not perfect. Yeltsin was able to use anti-Russian sentiments, which were growing stronger in the former Soviet republics, in his struggle for the "emancipation" of Russia from the Soviet Union. Russians, who had been persuaded by Soviet propaganda of the strength of the "friendship of the people" and the deep love and gratitude of all non-Russians for Russians, met the harsh evidence of ethnic hatred directed toward them in the national republics with amazement and anger, as they also did later when they encountered strong nationalism in Chechnia and Tatarstan.

A nationwide poll, conducted in early 1990 by VTSIOM, the All-Russian Center of Public Opinion, revealed not only that nearly three-fourths of all ethnic Russians denied in one way or another that they had a right to interfere in the business of other peoples but that nearly the same proportion regarded the secession of the national republics as inevitable, in the same way that they later supported the secession of Chechnia from the Russian Federation.[23]

Looking for allies in his struggle for "Russian sovereignty" with the central authorities, Yeltsin lent his support to the nationalist movements in all of the Soviet republics. Because of this, he was met in Vilnius, Kiev, and Alma-Ata as a hero and friend of local nationalists.

In his fight against the central administration, Yeltsin then made another fundamental step that would have enormous impact on future developments in the Russian Federation. This time, looking for additional allies in his fight against the Kremlin, Yeltsin started to encourage each ethnic region, particularly Tatarstan and Bashkortostan, within the Russian republic "to take as much sovereignty as possible," an offer he came to regret one year later.[24]

The Debates on the Sovereignty of Autonomous Republics, Summer 1991

In competing with Yeltsin, Gorbachev also contributed to the regionalization of the Russian Federation. He did not object to the decisions of a number of autonomous republics in the Russian Federation, such as Tataria, Bashkiria, Kalmykia, Mari, and Chuvashia, and even small national districts to proclaim their "state sovereignty" inside the Russian Federation in October 1990.

Moreover, viewing the release of the autonomous republics as a sort of antidote to trouble in the "big republics" of which they were a part, Gorbachev decided to invite Tatarstan, Tuva, and a few other autonomous republics in the Russian Federation to become "full-fledged members." They joined the national republics in summer 1991 in debating the All-Union Treaty (the so-called *Novo ogarevo protsess*), which was envisioned as the means of transforming the USSR into a true federation. Furthermore, during the *Novo ogarevo protsess*, Gorbachev introduced as his own the idea of "sovereignization of the autonomous republics." This referred to the notion that the relationship between the autonomous republics and the "big republics" had to be of the same character as the relationship between the USSR and the national republics, that is, with a contractual basis as laid out in the Constitution of the Soviet Union and in the constitutions of the "big republics." In fact, this idea was supported by Yeltsin, then already president of the Russian Federation. He was evidently no less interested than Gorbachev in supporting the sovereignty of autonomous republics, with the backing of Parliament, which was also involved in the fight with the Kremlin. In addition, Yeltsin even wanted to eliminate both constitutions, viewing them as constraints on the regulation of the relationship between small and big republics.[25]

It is evident that by involving autonomous republics in the negotiations, Gorbachev and Yeltsin both greatly contributed to the animus toward regionalization in Russia, as well as in the other Soviet republics, particularly Georgia.[26]

8

Developments in
Post-Communist Russia:
First Moves Toward
Autonomy, 1991–1992

Soon after the abortive coup in August 1991, regionalization swept across the country. Two early occurrences account for the increased regionalistic fervor. First, the weak center's inability to solve the various social and economic problems in the provinces further aggravated an impatient populace. Second, the ethnic regions' desire to immediately exploit the existing situation, in order to enhance their own status and gain full sovereignty, further exacerbated these regionalistic feelings.

An Initiative from Above

Yeltsin's new regime was quite weak upon entering the new era in Russian history, and Gorbachev's policy of shifting responsibilities to the regions was continued. The dominant democratic ideology also fostered this process.

Indeed, the expansion of regional rights fitted very well with the democratic ideology that dominated the Kremlin in 1992. During this year, with Egor Gaidar as the democrats' leader and virtual prime minister, various groups highlighted the negative role of the centralized state and even the state in general. Therefore, the democrats increasingly saw the regions' large and growing role as a necessary condition for the reformation of Russian society.

Probably even more important was the further weakening of the center's power. After the August revolution of 1991, it was evident that Moscow would never again have the same magnitude of power over the provinces. Certainly, the relations between the center and provinces would ebb and swell, but they would never be as they were in the socialist or even tsarist eras.

To a greater or lesser degree, the Kremlin had already recognized this historic shift in the center-periphery relationship before 1991, probably shortly after 1989. This fundamental change was an important motive, though of course, it was far from being the sole one, for the decisions of the ruling Russian politicians. The majority of them realized that a confrontation with the regions, even if successful, was of no advantage in post-Communist Russia, and this led them to the conclusion that the best policy had to be cooperation with local elites. Otherwise, the chances for generally chaotic conditions or the temporary victory of the extremists would be quite high.[1]

To this end, both Mikhail Gorbachev and Boris Yeltsin tried to co-opt the movement toward Russian autonomy. Gorbachev wanted to use the autonomy of the other Soviet republics in his fight against their rising separatism,[2] whereas Yeltsin wanted to use the Russian Federation's ethnic units, as well as those of the other Soviet republics, in order to oust the first, and last, Soviet president from the Kremlin.[3]

It is not surprising that under these circumstances the center chose to follow Gorbachev's policy and shift a portion of its economic responsibility to the regions.[4] Of course, regional leaders systematically used these circumstances to further expand their own rights.[5]

The Initiatives of Ethnic Republics

In 1991–1992, even if regionalization embraced, to one degree or another, all areas of the Russian Federation, it was the non-Russian ethnic republics that played the leading role in this process. They entered the political struggle in 1990 at the height of the conflict.

The collapse of the Soviet empire and the transformation of the former Soviet republics into sovereign states immensely impressed the non-Russian regions in the Russian Federation. After August 1991, these regions almost immediately redoubled their efforts to win greater autonomy from Moscow. Soon, they even tried to gain true state sovereignty. Almost all of them, with the exception of the Jewish Autonomous Region, proclaimed themselves republics, requiring others to take into account their specificity and special relations with Moscow.[6]

The new Russian administration in Moscow in 1992–1993 was very weak and had no clear plan for reorganizing a new Russian state, and this disarray accounts for the radical changes in the relationship between the republics and Moscow. A sort of legal confusion emerged between Moscow and the national republics. Along with the Soviet Constitution of 1977, each republic claimed to have its own constitution, and these constitutions did not coordinate with the federal Constitution. Republics were free to introduce any law, even if they were contrary to the Russian Federal Constitution. Several republics even proclaimed that a few federal laws did not apply to them. For example, North Osetia and

Ingushetia ignored the law endorsed by the Russian Parliament concerning the elimination of illegally armed units in 1992. In these cases, there was no legal mechanism that allowed, for instance, the removal of republican presidents who even demonstrably violated federal laws.

Zones of Ethnic Separatism, 1992–1995

By the beginning of 1992, it was clear that there were four zones of ethnic separatism, consisting of twenty-one ethnic enclaves, that threatened Russia to different degrees: the North Caucasian, Volga-Ural, and Siberian-Baikal zones; the champion of separatism of the zones, and even of all Russia, was Chechnia.

The North Caucasian Zone: Chechnia

Inspired by its leader Dzhokhar Dudaiev, a former Soviet air force general, Chechnia declared its complete independence from Moscow and even initiated a rebellion against the capital and the central government. At the end of 1991, as the Russian leadership contemplated military solutions for squashing Dudaiev's uprising, the Chechen president promised to declare *Gazavat* (a sacred Muslim war) against Russia and even to launch terrorist attacks against nuclear installations close to Moscow.[7] The relationship between Moscow and Chechnia soon became one of the most critical political issues of the next several years, endangering from time to time the mere existence of the country's ruling regime.

Among the other significant actors in the North Caucasus at that time were the Adygei block, the Karachaiev block, and North Osetia. The Adygei Region, which also proclaimed its sovereignty in 1992, stands out as one of the smallest administrative units in the country, populated by approximately five hundred thousand people, among whom the titular group, the Adygeis (also known as the Shapsugs), make up only a small minority of the population. The Confederation of the Caucasian People was also an important participant in the separatist movement. On several occasions, the leaders of the confederation made inflammatory anti-Moscow speeches. These actions contributed to the fomenting of separatist tendencies in this region.[8]

The Volga-Ural Zone: Tatarstan and Bashkortostan

Tatarstan in the Volga zone was another principal model, along with Chechnia, for the Russian Federation's "small republics" to follow. In August 1990 in Tatarstan, the Tatars, the titular group that composed up to about one-half of the entire population, issued their Declaration of State Sovereignty. This act signaled a renewal of their struggle for the elevation of their region's status to that of a Soviet republic. They also demanded to be allowed to participate as a full member in the negotiations on a new all-union treaty.

In March 1992 the republic carried out a referendum on state sovereignty, which was approved by 62 percent of the voters. Later, Tatarstan elected its president, Mintimer Shaimiev, and the Tatarstan republic's supreme Soviet endorsed its own constitution in November 1992.

The constitution declared Tatarstan to be a "sovereign state and a subject of international law associated with the Russian Federation on the basis of the agreement on their mutual division of power." The constitution also introduced dual citizenship for both Tatars and Russians in a move unprecedented in Russia's history since the conquest of Kazan by Ivan the Terrible in 1550. It is not surprising that in 1992–1993 some journalists called Tatarstan the "center of Russia's disintegration."[9]

In 1991–1992, the Tatar nationalists, headed by Marat Muluikov and Fazia Bairamova, went so far as to demand the right to create their own currency and the withdrawal of Russian troops from the republic's territory to make way for the creation of their own armed forces. They strongly criticized the official republican leadership for cooperating with "imperial Russia" and even "sentenced" Shaimiev to death for his cooperation with Moscow.[10]

The Volga zone's second most significant region was Bashkortostan, which modeled its actions on Tatarstan in conducting its relations with Moscow. It proclaimed its sovereignty in the referendum held on April 25, 1993.

Other republics of this region, such as Mordovia, Udmurtia, Mari-El, and Chuvashia, did not become quite as active, although their elites still never miss an opportunity to gain more autonomy.[11] There were also movements advocating the creation of a Federation of Muslim Republics, aimed mostly at coordinating the efforts of Tatarstan and Bashkortostan in this zone.[12]

The Siberian-Baikal Zone: Tuva and Iakutia

The third zone, Tuva, already had a tradition of independence and was thus a leading entity in the fight against Moscow. This small republic, which had been formally considered an independent state until 1944, drew attention to itself by harshly attacking Russians in 1990–1991.

As in the cases of other republics of the Russian Federation, Moscow in 1992 also demonstrated a lack of will in dealing with this republic, which forced thousands of Russians to leave the region. After the exodus, the tension in the country declined. However, Tuva's drive for greater autonomy continued to grow even though its leaders preferred to remain very loyal to Moscow and were concerned, unlike many other republics, about supporting the integrity of the Russian Federation.[13] The other regions in this zone, such as Buriatia and Khakasia, were relatively passive in 1992 and later.

Another leading ethnic republic in the fourth zone was, without a doubt, Iakutia (Sakha). The tactics of the regional elite in this republic was to use its natural resources to grab as much autonomy as possible without proclaiming complete secession from the Russian Federation. However, Iakutia did not take such an aggressive stance (even underscoring its loyalty to Russia)[14] as Chechnia or Tatarstan. Nevertheless, in 1992–1995, Iakutia demanded state sovereignty and participation in international negotiations on various issues, including agreements on environmental protection, thereby achieving relatively high status among other "small republics."[15]

On the whole, the ethnic republics that have played the most significant roles in Russia's political life in 1993–1995 are as follows (listed in order of importance): Chechnia, Tatarstan, Bashkortostan, Iakutia (Sakha), and Kalmykia. A second set of ethnic republics that have been active in Russia includes Mordovia, Tuva, Ingushetia, Dagestan, and Altai.[16]

Kremlin Policy Toward Ethnic Republics: 1992–1994

In 1992, Yeltsin's government, after some wavering, rejected using repressive measures to quiet the seditious republics in favor of negotiations. Moscow also behaved in the same manner toward Chechnia. At a number of meetings, particularly the August 13, 1993, meetings in Petrozavodsk and Cheboksar, Yeltsin vowed to respect the sovereignty of the republics.

The intense political struggle between the president and Parliament in 1992–1993 pushed Yeltsin to make concessions to the ethnic elites in the hope of gaining their support. Yeltsin endorsed the Federal Treaty on March 31, 1993, which legalized the almost complete sovereignty of many ethnic units, evidently hoping to draw them to his side in the confrontation with Parliament.[17] At that time, Moscow even planned to open offices in Kazan in Tatarstan, which would represent various Russian institutions while that republic installed diplomatic missions in other countries, an extraordinary development in Russian history.

In 1992, encouraged by their growing independence from Moscow, ethnic republics began to nurture relations among themselves in a sort of mild alliance against Moscow. In the beginning, they established special relations with each other. For instance, Tatarstan signed agreements for cooperation with Udmurtia, Bashkortostan, and Mari-El.[18]

In 1992–1993, the Kremlin encouraged the rapprochement of national republics. Overall, one of the most significant developments during this period was the acceptance in October 1992 of the idea of creating a new republican institution, the Council of the Heads of the Republics.[19]

Russian Regions Join the Struggle for Autonomy

The former "big" Soviet republics that had achieved independence were models for the non-Russian "small" republics in the Russian Federation. In their turn, these larger administrative units served as models for other Russian regions in their fight for revised relations with the center. The Russian regions, even if they first possessed separatist sentiments in 1991–1993, now dreamed only about a new form of federalism.

In the beginning, the Russian regional elites were furious about the privileges of ethnic republics in comparison to their own, particularly in regard to state tax revenues and subsidies.[20] The ethnic republics' special privileges became the Russian local elite's main argument for justifying the need to elevate their regions' status. This tactic was used to place pressure on the center as well as to persuade their populations to support them in their struggle with Moscow.

In early 1992, as in a chain reaction, one region after another began to demand the radical extension of its right to the level of conditional sovereignty. All of the regional elites supported their regions actions against the center, even if they did not claim to have become the center's "colonies," as the Siberians had done. Quite soon, several Russian observers realized that the Russian regions' efforts to obtain greater autonomy bordered upon separatism, which was considered as the highest threat to Russia's continued unity.[21]

First Steps, 1992

Having taken the initiative, the provinces in 1991–1993 started to encroach with growing impertinence on the political power of the center. Following the example of the non-Russian republics, the ethnic Russian regions began to abolish or ignore the laws adopted by the Russian Parliament, the president's edicts, the constitutional court's decisions, and the government's directives. As the attorney general reported, in 1992 his office found thirteen thousand edicts issued by local governments to be illegal. In addition, he indicated that twenty-three territories had introduced some form of customs duty against other regions of the Russian Federation.

At the same time, the local administrations continued to complain, as in the past, that they were "deprived of real leverage of power," as Ivan Shabunin, head of the Volgograd administration said in 1993.[22] Many regions in this period composed various statutes and constitutions that did not mention anything to do with the Russian Federation, which significantly abridged the center's power.

During this period many regional leaders declared, as did the chairmen of the Altai and Cheliabinsk Soviets in early 1993, that "they have the right to cancel on their territories any edict of the president."[23] Also in early 1993, the political parties of the Kuzbass, for instance, vehemently discussed the draft of the regional statute that, among other things, declared a political strike be a legal action against the Moscow authorities. Further developments prevented many local politicians from realizing their intentions. Nonetheless, these developments were a significant phenomenon in Russia's political landscape during this period.

Regional separatism became an important component of the political and economic processes in the "new Russia" of 1992. It became "normal" to hear and read throughout the year about the regions' appeals for separation from Russia and even for the creation of independent republics. Siberia and the Russian Far East proved to be the leaders of the pack. Conferences that met to discuss regional separatism, directly or indirectly, meshed with the contemporary political landscape of the new Russia. One of them, the Congress of the Deputies of Siberian Regions, convened in Krasnoiarsk in March 1992. The federal institutions seemed to be undisturbed by them.

The dominant feeling in the periphery in 1991–1992 was that Moscow lacked any coherent political power and that the only way to save the regions was for the local elite to take total control. The reflections of Valentin Fedorov, then governor of Sakhalin, were typical: "The state has been destroyed . . . if there is some power it is only in the hands of local administrators. Foreigners have realized it and want to deal not so much with the government but with regional authorities."[24]

The Ethnic Elite Versus the Russian Local Elite

Not surprisingly, the leaders of the non-Russian republics were enraged at their equivalence with the Russian regions, understanding that this would diminish their own influence in Moscow and undermine their drive for independence.

During the constitutional court's meeting in Moscow on June 5, 1993, there was a real battle between the two groups of elites. The local leaders from the Russian regions demanded that the term "sovereignty" should also be applied to their regions, while the leaders of the ethnic republics complained of the hostility of some regions against them. Eduard Kubarev, chairman of the Chuvashia Republic, in complaining about such hostility, said that the ethnic regions wanted to maintain their monopoly on such "sovereignty."

The Center's Ambivalence
Toward Regionalization, 1991–1992

The policy of the central administration toward the regions proved to be quite ambivalent and indecisive. First, the administration continued Gorbachev's policy of shifting the responsibility for the population's standard of living to the regional administrations. Second, the Kremlin tried to recruit the regions' support in its conflict with Parliament and the regime's opposition. Third, the center wanted to simultaneously regain its control over all of the regions.

While watching the centrifugal processes, as well as the local authorities' animosity to Yeltsin during the abortive coup of August 1991, the Kremlin quickly undertook actions to check regionalism in the provinces, hoping to stop its growth. One of the first such actions was a presidential edict, endorsed by the Russian Parliament on November 1, 1991, that gave the Kremlin the right to appoint the heads of administration, a decision that was received with hostility by the local soviets. These groups consisted primarily of members of the ancien régime and used democratic terminology in their critique of the president's decision.

This edict also banned elections for local administrators for one year. However, on December 1, 1992, the ban was extended by parliamentary decision until the election of the new local parliaments, even in the event of a vote of no confidence. During the next few years, Yeltsin tried to preserve his right to appoint the heads of administration and governors for as long as possible, postponing the elections quite a few times. At the same time, however, he did not object to the presidential elections in the non-Russian republics, a fact that again angered the local elite in many Russian regions.[25] Only in summer 1995 did he permit gubernatorial elections, first in the Sverdlovsk Region and then in other regions.

Another measure used to counteract the growing autonomy of the local authorities was introduction of the post of presidential representative in the provinces in 1992. This official's obligation was to ensure proper execution of the laws and commands of Moscow in the regions.[26]

Despite all of these measures, seemingly directed at the restoration of the center's authority, the Kremlin did very little to curb the impertinence of regional leaders, especially the heads of the local councils (soviets), who were popularly elected and thus felt particularly independent from the Kremlin. They challenged, usually successfully, the actions of the governors, the president, and his government. The press was full of articles describing the conflicts between the various branches of government in the regions.

Moreover, during this period of intense struggle against Parliament, the Kremlin did much to ingratiate itself with local leaders and to elevate their status, even against their own desires. The president and other high officials began to convene various meetings of "consultation" with local bosses, who, like Viktor Stepanov, chairman of the Karelian Supreme Soviet, were behaving more and more impertinently towards Moscow.

In trying to demonstrate its respect for the local elite, Yeltsin's leadership encouraged the formation of the Association of Governors. This gave the green light to the further decline of the national state. Thus, by late 1992, Moscow's control over all the regions had weakened drastically. It became evident that regional autonomy would strongly increase as provinces attained the right to elect their own leaders.

The Federal Treaty, March 1992

Yeltsin's regime sought to mitigate the consequences of rising regionalism and to establish some amount of stability in the relations between the center and the periphery through the Federal Treaty, which clearly reflected the ambivalence of the central administration toward regionalization. It offered the "subjects" of the federation a special treaty, to be signed along with the current Constitution. The treaty was supposed to outline the rights of the Russian administrative units and the center, while also serving as a guarantee that Moscow would observe the rules in dealing with the provinces. The economic issues—subsidies and taxes—were central to the treaty.

The treaty's preparation, by itself, was unprecedented in Russian history. For the first time since the creation of the Moskovia state, the regions steadfastly bargained with the center about various privileges and expectations. The non-Russian republics were particularly discontented with the ethnic Russian regions' demands for equality with them.[27] They were quite aggressive in demanding that they retain their special status and even their special contract with the federal authorities, initially rejecting the idea of equality between ethnic Russian and non-Russian units.

The treaty was signed on March 31, 1992, by eighty-seven units (Chechnia and Tatarstan refused to do so). The treaty was then reaffirmed in the Constitution of the Russian Federation, which was approved by the people in a national referendum held on December 12, 1993.

In the past, the Russian Federation, according the January 1918 Constitution, acted as a federal entity in its relations with non-Russian republics, whereas it took on unitarian aspects in its relations with the ethnic Russian provinces. Contrary to this constitution, the Federal Treaty signified that the federal government would now maintain federal relations on an equal footing with all eighty-nine administrative units. This measure failed to reassure anybody.

The Federal Treaty included three agreements on the differentiation of powers and responsibilities among the federal bodies of the Russian Federation and bodies of the (1) sovereign republics within the Russian Federation; (2) territories, districts, and cities of Moscow and St. Petersburg; and (3) autonomous regions and areas.

According to the treaty, the national republics were recognized as state entities, which joined the Russian Federation with all of the ensuing consequences. As the treaty states, the republics would enjoy complete authority, both legislative and executive, over their territories. However, the regions were deprived of such rights. At the same time, not only the republics but also all of the regions, along with Moscow and St. Petersburg, would adopt their own statutes, which would not contradict federal laws but which would demand the conclusion of special treaties between them and the center on an individual basis.

The Federal Treaty was a compromise measure that tried to solve two problems—to satisfy the demands of both the national republics and the Russian regions. It did indeed enhance the status of both of these actors; however, it did not achieve equality between the non-Russian and Russian entities. Nor did the new Constitution of December 1993 eliminate the main sources of the Russian regional elite's dissatisfaction, even though Article 5 of the section on "The Foundations of the Constitutional Structure" states: "5. All the subjects of the Russian Federation enjoy equal rights in relations with federal bodies of state power."[28] At the same time, the new Constitution dropped the term "sovereignty," which was widely used in the Federal Treaty, thus arousing the anger of the nationalists in all of the republics.

The Federal Treaty, as well as the new Constitution, was unable to harmonize the relationship between the center and its administrative units. In 1993–1995, the republics systematically violated both the treaty and the Constitution. In many cases, the republics violated these agreements by writing their own constitutions so that they stated that republican laws took priority over federal laws, even in those spheres of responsibility typically assigned to the central government, such as foreign policy, the judicial system, and maintenance of national borders.

9

THE GROWTH OF REGIONALISM
AND THE CENTER'S
COUNTERATTACK, 1993–1996

The economic reforms started by Boris Yeltsin's administration in January 1992 resulted in soaring inflation, a decline in production, and a steep drop in the standard of living. These reforms encountered strong opposition among the people and in Parliament, which was generally a foe of reform. These antireform leaders in Parliament tried to use the negative public mood to curtail the president's power and even tried to impeach him.

The Campaign for Regional Support
by Liberals and Centrists

The power struggle between the president and Parliament radically influenced the policy of all the major political actors toward the regions, causing the regional leaders to feel for a time that they were the real power brokers in the country.

As previously mentioned, the president courted the regional elite, trying at the same time to maintain his control over the periphery. Liberal politicians outside the government, who opposed the Kremlin in varying degrees, also tried to attract the regions to their side by supporting their demand for greater autonomy.

Grigorii Iavlinskii, a leading politician and economist, contended then that the government's main task was to "shift the essential activity necessary to ensure the satisfaction of the population's basic needs, from the center toward regions." Iavlinskii also argued that regionalization was a worldwide process that was impossible to stop. He later emphatically spoke about regionalization in October 1992.[1]

Iavlinskii was seconded by Alexander Vladislavlev and Sergei Karaganov, two prominent political figures then belonging to the Civic Alliance, a party that, in 1992, had wanted to reinforce its status on the Russian political scene with the support of the local elite. Vladislavlev and Karaganov declared that "the sources of strength for a country are its provinces, not the capital" and referred to the democratic traditions of self-government in the prerevolutionary Russian provinces. Both these authors demanded that the Kremlin "recognize the right of regions to their own political order [local self-government], their own forces for the maintenance of order, and their own foreign economic activity." The centrists Arkadii Volskii, Nikolai Travkin, and Alexander Rutskoi also saw the regional elite as a potential part of their power base and advocated extending that group's power mainly through economic policy changes.

The Opposition's Hesitant Search for Regional Allies

Like their opponents, the "democrats" who were Yeltsin's supporters—the Russian nationalists and Communists—were torn by their mutually exclusive attitudes toward regionalization. For one thing, regionalization further illustrated Russia's deepening crisis. The opposition's deeply rooted belief in authoritative rule as the only solution to Russia's problems made them impassioned foes of this process. The critics of Yeltsin's regime, mostly Communists, were also those who, unlike the vast majority of Russian conservatives, were uncompromising foes of regionalization and denounced it as a subversive strategy of the democrats.

Pravda's editor, Viktor Trushkov, compared the situation in Russia at that time to that of Russia in the twelfth century, when the country was split among feudal princes who disregarded the dangers of regionalism in regard to foreign enemies. Trushkov denounced Yeltsin's regime for "its strategy aimed at the collapse of Russia" and the "foreign instigators." At the same time, these Communists criticized other Communists who, in regions such as Cheliabinsk, for instance, supported separatist tendencies.[2]

Communist authors were sure that Ekaterinburg, President Yeltsin's hometown and his most loyal city, could only have taken its step on July 1, 1993, declaring the Ural Republic's independence, if prompted by the Kremlin. The ultraconservative newspapers, *Sovietskaia Rossia* and *Pravda,* asserted that it was a Kremlin ploy in a complicated constitutional game that counterbalanced the role of the ethnic regions.[3] The almost patent endorsement of the Ural Republic by Sergei Alexeiev, a close aide to the president, only a few days after its emergence could only support this suspicion.[4] These people also saw an American hand in regionalism, insinuating that the United States was gloating over the inevitable disintegration of Russia.

The other side of the coin was that the confrontation between the regions and the existing central authorities they hated drew the conservatives to the regional leaders as comrades-in-arms. Nationalists and, to a lesser extent, Communists supported the regionalism of the new Russia as another argument against the "anti-Russian policy of Yeltsin's regime" (after all, why should the ethnic regions enjoy more autonomy than the Russian regions?) and as a basis for future crusades against Yeltsin.[5]

At the same time, the opposition justified regionalism as a temporary expedient until the "true power in the Kremlin" could be restored. In this period, a devoted enemy of the regime such as Aman Tuleev—one of the candidates in the June 1991 presidential elections—was also a champion of regionalism as a weapon against the hated liberal center. He argued that only complete regional autonomy could help "alleviate the life of citizens while the government is doing nothing for this."[6]

Anatolii Salutskii, a prominent ideologue of conservatism, saw regionalism as the best hope for the renewal of Russia as a great nation, if only because it was a clear rejection of the cosmopolitan group headed by Yeltsin. Pointing to the regions that were strongly influenced by nationalists and Communists, such as Krasnoiarsk and Volgograd, he reminded everyone that Russia was always saved by the provinces in times of turmoil. For example, during the Time of Troubles, Prince Dmitrii Pozharskii and the simple commoner from Nizhniy Novgorod, Kuzma Minin, saved the motherland from a Polish invasion. This view was developed even more forcefully by Alexander Kazintsev, an aggressive leading nationalistic columnist for the Russian newspaper *Den'*, in his article "Minins Are Not Born in the Capital."[7] He asserted that the opposition would gain one regional center after another, ultimately freeing Russia from the democrats' grip.[8]

Parliament's Attempt to Pit the Provinces Against the President

At this time, the confrontation between the executive and legislative branches was steaming ahead at full speed. The ongoing struggle between Parliament and the president became the axis of the country's political life. The Parliament also tried to ingratiate itself to local elites by passing several laws that expanded their powers.

In 1992–1993, Ruslan Khasbulatov, the chairman of Parliament who had headed the opposition against Yeltsin in 1993, and Vice President Rutskoi actively looked for the regions' support in the political struggle in the center. Khasbulatov warned that with the centralization of the state budget the Kremlin would "stifle the republics and regions; pushing them objectively toward flouting the law, separatism and regionalism." At the same time, during his visit to East Siberia in late 1992, Rutskoi demanded that the Russian regions' rights be elevated to those of the ethnic republics.[9]

Like Yeltsin, Khasbulatov traveled across the country, doing his best at various meetings to enroll the support of the local elite. At one such meeting, the Conference of the Deputies of All Levels (from the district soviets to the All-Federation Supreme Soviet) in June 1993, he encouraged the local soviets to resist the executive power and the democrats in their regions as well as in Moscow.[10]

The March 1993 Confrontation
and Regional Power Growth

The regions' crucial role became evident in March 1993, when the confrontation between Yeltsin and Parliament reached its first climax. Both camps did their best to gain the support of the regional elite as well as the masses. Both the president and Parliament attempted to outmaneuver each other, reduce the other's power, and generally present the other as the enemy of the people. In the meantime, the regional leaders felt that their time had come and that they should establish themselves as the real power holders.

By March 1993, it had become evident that the split among regions and inside regions in their attitudes toward the conflict in the center was quite strong. The local councils in many of the regions favored Parliament, whereas the heads of administration demonstrated their loyalty to the president. Interestingly enough, most of these heads of administration were appointed by Yeltsin, including the mayor of St. Petersburg, Anatolii Sobchak, and the governor of Nizhniy Novgorod, Boris Nemtsov. Such a split also occurred in Samara, where the head of the local administration, Konstantin Titov, supported Yeltsin's edict against Parliament while the so-called small council of the local soviet refused to comply. Similar developments occurred in Tomsk, Voronezh, Tula, Krasnoiarsk, Khabarovsk, and other places. These developments also revealed with great clarity how fragile the regional political structures really were. Until the showdown in October 1993, the Parliament certainly enjoyed greater support from the regions.[11]

Even though internal conflicts were raging almost everywhere, it is possible to list the regions and cities where political sympathies focused particularly on one or another rival. For instance, Krasnoiarsk, one of the largest Siberian cities where the Communist and Russian nationalist movements are much stronger than in Moscow, was one such locus of support. Russian nationalists were also active in 1992–1993 in Vologda, Irkutsk, Perm, and a few other cities. Only in a few regions and cities, including Moscow and St. Petersburg, did the president's faction prevail.

The Ethnic Republics' Renewed Attack

The leaders of the non-Russian republics, of course, enjoyed the clashes in Moscow the most. The parliaments in Tatarstan, Bashkortostan, Karelia, Khakasia, and in several other republics were on Khasbulatov's side or at best remained neutral, as in the cases of Buriatia or Kabardino-Balkaria.

In trying to exploit the political conflict gripping the country, the ethnic republics renewed their offensives for extending their autonomy in spring 1993. The many concessions made by Moscow could not slake the appetite of the local ethnic elite for more power. They chose the new federal Constitution, which gave overwhelming power to the president, as their battleground, since the Kremlin wanted to pass it as soon as possible.

Feeling Yeltsin's dependence on their support, the heads of the ethnic republics tried, after May 1993, to force the president to include in his draft of the new Constitution the concept of republican sovereignty. This provision was absent in the first version of the Constitution but was present in the Federal treaty. For this reason they rejected Parliament's draft of the Constitution in December 1992. The regions also demanded the removal of those articles that established the prevalence of federal over republican laws from the draft Constitution.

On May 12, 1993, the heads of eleven ethnic republics, followed by sixteen more on May 27, went so far as to give the president an ultimatum. They demanded that Yeltsin adopt new procedures for the endorsement of a new Constitution within one month.

The heads of the republics behaved very aggressively (Tatarstan even left the meeting) during the constitutional meeting, at which Yeltsin hoped to endorse his new Constitution. These regional leaders demanded the center's confirmation of their "state sovereignty," the recognition that they "voluntarily joined Russia," their "right of self-determination," and their "right to secede the Russian Federation without any constraint." At the Constitutional Assembly, the republican leaders were also able to extricate a promise from the president to regulate the center-periphery relations using bilateral negotiations with the republics on an individual basis. Thus, each republic was to be treated like a foreign state.[12]

The political situation in March was so tense, illustrated by the fact that the Parliament lacked only a few votes needed to impeach the president in March 1993, that many politicians smelled a civil war, particularly because the loyalty of the regions was divided between the president and the Parliament. In fact, it was possible to predict their allegiances in any future civil war from their ideological slogans at that time.

Whither Russia? A Second Collapse or the Provinces as Russia's Savior

The movement toward autonomy and separatism in Russia was so unusual and so alarming that the fear of imminent collapse spread like wildfire throughout the country in 1992–1993. Most politicians and journalists saw the major threat to the Russian Federation not so much in the separatist rhetoric of the ethnic republics as in the aspirations of the Russian regions, whose view was also supported by a few Western observers.[13]

Nikolai Travkin, a prominent politician, said at the end of 1992 that the disintegration of Russia was "an evident fact."[14] A typical article of this period was titled "Will Russia Collapse?"[15] Leonid Shebarshin, former KGB chief and head of the Soviet foreign intelligence services, was also very pessimistic in mid-1993. He wrote, "Unfortunately, the process of the splitting of Russia is continuing and the fears of some sincerely concerned people that Russia will break up into several independent principalities does not seem fantastic to me."[16]

Andrei Migranian, a member of the presidential council and a prominent political scientist in late 1992, also lamented the impending collapse of the country.[17] Protesting against the possible dissolution of the Russian Parliament by the president, Migranian said, "The disintegration is going on its own, but without the body [Parliament] which is the symbol of the unity of the Russian state, it is difficult to imagine how Moscow will be able to keep control over the regions and republics."[18]

Pessimists were especially concerned about the effect of regionalization in regions bordering foreign countries, such as those in the Far East. Pointing to the tremendous economic and social differences between regions, they envisioned interregional conflicts, initially based on economic disagreements, that would escalate into military confrontations as a part of an overall civil war. Russian pessimists also imagined regional alliances directed against Moscow, an idea once found only in the realm of science fiction that had now become a potential reality. In addition, they raised questions about the ability of regional leaders to guarantee the safety of nuclear power stations, chemical plants, and oil pipelines. In the view of these critics, regionalization would hardly serve the population, since its beneficiaries would be the regional elite and the Mafia.

In a survey of two hundred experts conducted by the Moscow Center of Public Opinion Studies in April–May, 1993, 53 percent envisaged "a growing number of regions that would proclaim their sovereignty," and 5 percent even predicted the full disintegration of Russia. Whereas 52 percent predicted that separatism would grow or at least remain at the same level, only 18 percent believed in the integrative process. Another survey of "the leaders of public opinion," conducted by Boris Grushin's polling firm Vox Populi in November 1993, found that 38 percent of those polled who answered the question "What is the probability of the division of Russia into several independent states?" responded with "very high" or "high."[19]

Many ordinary Russians were quite pessimistic about the consequences of regionalization. According to a March 1993 poll by the Institute of Sociology, 34 percent of all Russians saw regionalization as a danger to the integrity of Russia.

Pessimists were confident that Russia would follow the example of the Soviet Union, but a few people were optimistic about the center-periphery relationship, looking at regionalization not as a direct route to national catastrophe but rather as a promising progression. Since the central authorities were unlikely to restore their power and bring order and prosperity back to the country, the single hope, in their opinion, was the provinces. The greater their autonomy from the helpless, conflict-ridden city of Moscow, the better off the country as a whole would be, since only regions were able to restore the country.

The nationalists and Communists, as previously mentioned, supported the regions as a temporary vehicle for the restoration of a strong central power. The optimists, in contrast, saw in the vast autonomy of the provinces a guarantee preventing Moscow from slipping toward totalitarianism. Western observers were also somewhat cynical about developments in Russia and regarded them as being quite dangerous for the future of the country.[20]

The Exacerbation of Regionalism in Early 1993

Without meeting significant resistance from Moscow, the regions continued in 1993, particularly after March 1993, to probe the limits of their autonomy. In summer 1993 in an article titled "The Brown Movement in Russia," one columnist in a Moscow newspaper stated, "In July, Russian regions ultimately abandoned their submission to central bodies."[21]

As key participants of meetings during which the draft of the new Constitution was discussed, regional leaders sent one ultimatum after another to President Yeltsin and threatened to boycott and disrupt the constitutional process if their demands for equal status with the ethnic republics were not included in the Constitution.[22] In addition, in 1989–1992, the emergence of eight interregional alliances, all of which were evidently aggressive toward Moscow, also indicated the growth of regionalization in Russia.

Throughout the winter and spring, several regions probed to test just how far they could go. Siberia, one of the regions where *oblastnichestvo* emerged, was initially a leading force of regionalism. For instance, during this period a few regionalists in Tomsk formulated a draft of the "Constitution of the Tomsk Region," which was inspired by the "advocates of *oblastnichestvo* with its idea of the sovereignty of Siberia."[23] An article, quite typical of this period, in a Siberian periodical denounced "Russian imperialism" and called for the creation of the "Siberian Federative Republic" as "the best flower among the flowers of one hundred independent states" to emerge from the territory of Russia.[24] Even the emergence in Tomsk, regarded as the spiritual capital of Siberian regionalism, of the "Party of Siberian Independence" headed by Boris Perov, which only lasted for a short time, did not arouse popular amazement, in Russia's public opinion.[25]

Several regions, both non-Russian and Russian, declared early in 1993 that they would not participate in the national referendum on the public's confidence in the president and Parliament and in discussion of the ideas that had been hotly debated since the end of 1992. As a result of these and other developments, a few regions did indeed prevent their subjects from taking part in the April 1993 referendum.

An Emerging Phenomenon: New Russian Republics

The idea of creating republics based on the unification of several districts had already emerged in 1992 but did not climax until early 1993. A number of Russian regions, represented by politicians of various ranks, in one way or another declared their intention to elevate their region's status to that of a republic.

A new wave of events was set loose on May 14, when Vologda, an agricultural region close to the White Sea, declared "*urbis* and *orbis*" that it wanted to see itself as a sovereign Russian republic.[26] However, this bold declaration of the Vologda rulers was ignored by Moscow and the "republic" gradually evaporated from the public consciousness. However, further developments will show that this idea did not completely disappear.[27]

Russia then watched as an epidemic of sorts swept across several regions, a regionalist domino effect that seemingly progressed without consultation with the president or other central bodies and without either an announcement by the regions on their new political status or on their intention to make such a proclamation in the near future. The new republics mushroomed everywhere. European Russia saw the formation of the Pomor Republic, centered in Arkhangelsk;[28] the Central Russian Republic, presumably formed of eleven regions, centered in Orel;[29] and the Leningrad Republic, centered in St. Petersburg, as well as the city republic in St. Petersburg known as the Neva Republic.[30] In the Urals, the Ural Republic was formed around Ekaterinburg and the Southern Ural Republic grew up around Cheliabinsk.[31] Within Siberia were formed the Siberian Republic, centered in Novosibirsk, and the East Siberian, or "Enisei," Republic, centered in Irkutsk.[32] In the Far East, the Maritime Republic was formed with its center located in Vladivostok.[33] Of all these republics, only the Ural Republic and, to some degree, the Vologda Republic materialized somewhat politically.

No local leaders or prominent Moscow theorists and law experts, including those who were close to the Kremlin, seriously considered this trend or were even supportive until summer 1993. One of them, Sergei Alexeiev, wrote an article entitled "The Province Wants Freedom: Do Not Dramatize the Creation of Regional Republics," in defense of this more positive view in the aftermath of the announcement of the creation of the Ural Republic. Alexeiev argued that with a growing number of republics, such as "the Middle Russian, Moscow, Ural, Siberian, Maritime Republics, and the 'free' city of St. Petersburg," "the recitation and the blossom of the Russian people" will become possible.[34]

The Case of the Ural Republic

The history of the founding of the Ural Republic deserves some elaboration since it was the most interesting episode during the formation of the new relationship between the center and provinces in 1993. The first such attempt was made in the Sverdlovsk Region, President Yeltsin's home territory.[35]

The leaders of the region had begun to prepare for the proclamation of the republic beforehand. On April 25, 1993, a referendum was held in the region. The region's population was presented with the following question: "Do you agree that the Sverdlovsk Region should have equal rights with the republics making up the Russian Federation?" The overwhelming majority (84 percent) of the people who voted on the referendum answered with a resounding "yes!". Regional authorities then prepared drafts of the presidential decree and the resolution of the Council of Ministers on giving broader rights to the region, thus making it equal to the national republics. These drafts were basically approved by Yeltsin and Viktor Chernomyrdin. However, nothing concrete had yet been done.

On June 26, 1993, the draft Constitution was completed,[36] and on July 1, a session of the District Soviet of People's Deputies was hastily convened, at which it was decided by a majority to proclaim the creation of the Ural Republic within the district's territory. So many people considered this deed to be of such historical importance that *Moskovskie Novosti*, in a remarkable article titled "The Pathfinders from Ural," felt it necessary to report the exact time of the republic's formation—6:10 P.M., July 1, 1993.[37] In general, the Moscow press hailed the event with enthusiasm.[38]

Governor Eduard Rossel and the chairman of the district soviet, Anatolii Grebenkin, the "founding fathers" of the Ural Republic, emphatically stressed that the formation of the republic was prompted by Moscow's encouragement of separatism in the national republics and the general disillusionment in the presidential draft of the Constitution, which preserved the federation's administrative-territorial division into first- and second-rate subjects.[39]

The leaders of Ekaterinburg insisted that the necessity of extending the Ural's autonomy to the level of republic was dictated by the difficulties of cooperating with the central administration. They also pointed out that the new republic could better dispose of local resources than the ministries in Moscow, which usually ignored the territorial dimensions of economic management, and in general could overcome "the alienation of the population from power."[40]

The Kremlin's Position. The other Ural regions did not support Ekaterinburg's bid for greater autonomy.[41] However, much more significant for the future of the Ural Republic was the position of the Kremlin rather than the reaction of neighboring regions.

In the beginning, the Kremlin seemingly prodded Ekaterinburg toward becoming a republic, through an idea that began to develop in 1993—the rejection of all ethnic divisions in favor of pure territorial divisions.[42] The use of the term "republic," as applied not only to ethnic units but also to pure Russian units, could be regarded as the first step in this direction.[43]

In his struggle with the Supreme Soviet, which flirted with the national republics and autonomous regions, the president relied first and foremost on the support of the regional administrations. Hence emerged his promise to support their intentions to achieve equality with the republics. The leaders of the ethnic republics perceived the emergence of the Ural Republic exactly in this way and were confident that it was a move arranged by the Kremlin to curtail their claims.[44]

However, the Kremlin changed—at what seemed like the last moment—its mind and came to the conclusion that official support of the Ural Republic risked spoiling its relations with the republics. This not only put in doubt the fate of the future Constitution and the outcome of the president's struggle with the Parliament, as well as the recently signed Federal Treaty, according to which the republics, in contrast to the regions, had received the rights of sovereigns, but it destabilized the situation in the country even more.[45]

After some hesitation, the Kremlin took a harsh stance toward Ekaterinburg. The procurator of the Sverdlovsk Region declared the proclamation of the Ural Republic to be illegal.[46] This had no effect. The higher authorities then expressed their dissatisfaction with the Ekaterinburg leaders. The president himself called the proclamation of the republic "a hasty step," and the chief of his administration, Sergei Filatov, declared outright that the actions of Rossel and Grebenkin were a serious blow to constitutional reforms.[47] Finally, Rossel was fired from his position as governor.[48]

It is noteworthy that the rejection of the idea of transforming regions into republics found the enthusiastic support of Yeltsin's lifetime opponent, the speaker of Parliament. Khasbulatov declared the Sverdlovsk experiment "a conspiratory form of sovereignization," whereas according to Rutskoi, who hastened to support Khasbulatov, Ekaterinburg was placing Russia on the brink of an abyss.

The Ural Republic After Its Cancellation. The dissolution of the Ural Republic by Moscow was in no way the death of the idea itself. The Sverdlovsk Regional Soviet decided before it was forcibly dissolved in late 1993 to again demonstrate its allegiance to the "Ural Republic," despite the presidential edict. The Soviet endorsed its constitution restoring the Ural Republic, enraging Yeltsin in "an attempt to blackmail the Federal authorities."[49]

The new regional parliament elected in 1993 elaborated in 1994–1995 the "Statute of the Sverdlovsk Region," which, as the local newspaper *Respublika* affirmed, inherited most of the ideas of the Constitution of the Ural Republic and was praised by the official newspaper *Rossiiskaia Gazeta* as the model for other regions.[50] The statute treated the Sverdlovsk Region in some respects as a sovereign state again. For instance, the statute followed the example of the federal Constitution and introduced a bicameral regional parliament and significantly constrained the power of the governor.[51] The first chamber of this new regional parliament was to reflect the interests of a single stratum of the population and territories (much like the Federal Council), and the second chamber was to represent the interests of the entire population (much like the State Duma).

The developments that surrounded Rossel in the aftermath of publishing the statute were remarkable. All of the leaders of the administrative units of the Sverdlovsk Region actively backed him up. Rossel was also supported by the heads of administration of the Ural regions, which elected him president of the Association of Economic Interaction of Ural Regions. After Yeltsin sacked him as governor, Rossel was elected speaker of the regional parliament and, even more significant, as a member of the upper chamber of the Russian Parliament on December 12, 1993.[52]

In late 1993, Rossel created his own alliance, called Transformation of Ural, as his social base of support. This organization united people who supported the idea of large regional autonomy.[53] Furthermore, when Yeltsin permitted gubernatorial elections in Ekaterinburg in summer 1995, Rossel's major campaign plank was greater autonomy for Ural to guard against its exploitation by the center. Using this tactic, Rossel defeated his main rival, Evgenii Strakhov, the head of regional administration, who was strongly backed by the Kremlin.

Undeterred by the negative reaction of the government toward the institution of the Ural Republic, Rossel continued to propagate the idea of a greater Ural republic in various forums. However, he later underscored that the fathers of the republic always considered it a part of Russia and in no way demanded full political independence.[54]

The Cossacks: A Special Case of Particularization

As the Russian regions began to extract concessions from the Kremlin, a specific and somewhat extraterritorial movement for autonomy made significant headway. This movement was driven by the Russian Cossacks.

The movement for the revival of Cossack communities began in the period of Gorbachev's perestroika. In the late 1980s, in those regions that were inhabited by the descendants of an old military legacy—the Cossacks—military-historical and cultural-educational societies began to appear that promoted the revival of the Cossacks. In the early 1990s, prior to the disintegration of the Soviet Union, the movement for the restoration of the Cossacks began to assume institutional forms. The Union of the Cossacks was established, whose charter declared that the group united representatives of Cossacks from all districts, territories, and communities. This was tantamount to laying claim to the Cossack territorial formations within Russia.

A series of various official acts were adopted by Parliament and the president that endowed Cossacks with special rights.[55] It was soon possible to revive the so-called Cossack way of life on specially allocated lands governed by their own administrative bodies.

The Cossacks Before the Revolution. The Cossacks as a class were characterized before the October Revolution of 1917 by the combination of military service and a specific way of farming. Before the Bolshevization of Russia, the territories inhabited by Cossacks formed the respective districts of particular Cossack regiments,[56] which were subordinated to the Chief Department of Cossack Troops. The present-day administrative-territorial division does not coincide with the borders of the former districts inhabited by past Cossack troops. For example, parts of the territory, earlier included in the district of the Don troops, became part of the Rostov, Voronezh, and Volgograd Districts, whereas another part was incorporated in one of the "near abroad" states, Ukraine. In several cases, Cossack lands were included in the autonomous republics.

Cossack Claims in 1992–1993.   Cossack leaders in 1992–1993 came forward to advocate the restoration to them of these traditional Cossack districts as administrative units with the same rights as normal subjects of the federation.

During this period, the Cossacks in different regions set themselves different political goals, reflecting the different ideologies within the Cossack movements.[57] One of these factions claimed to defend the interests of the state as a whole, even stating that Cossacks have a monopoly on being the best Russian patriots. Another group focused on separating the Cossacks from other Russians as a specific cultural, and even ethnic, formation.[58] However, there was not sufficient unity among those Cossacks who wanted to create their own territorial entities.

It was the Don Cossacks who tended to support, even aggressively, the idea of a sovereign Cossack republic within the Russian Federation. They wanted a very high level of autonomy as well as the formation of special Cossack military units as an autonomous part of the Russian army. Kuban Cossacks seemed to be more inclined to see themselves as a part of the Russian Federation and wanted only limited autonomy within the existing administrative structure.[59]

In the other regions, some Cossacks behaved as aggressively as the Don Cossacks, demanding the complete and unquestionable revival of the Cossack districts within the boundaries of 1916.[60] Other Cossacks were closer to the Kuban Cossacks and came forward in favor of the formation of Cossack regions that would not impose on the interests of neighboring nations, thus avoiding armed confrontations.[61]

Still others held an intermediate position, perhaps only for the time being. They put forward the concept of forming a series of small Cossack republics, including separating land from neighboring national republics to be used in forming them. For instance, three Cossack republics were proclaimed in the territory of the former Karachaevo-Cherkesskii Autonomous Region: Batalpashinskaya, Abazinskaya, and Zelenchuksko-Urupskaya.

It is not surprising that in 1992–1993 relations between Cossack bodies and local authorities were quite tense. Issues of particular concern were land distribution and official attitudes toward non-Russians populations, such as Chechens and Armenians, who had come to the regions as migrants.[62]

However, over the next two years, the Cossack movement lost its aggressiveness and began to advocate playing more of a role in "normal" public activity and the creation of a territorial structure under the control of the state, rather than supporting Cossack secession from the rest of the country. Even during the Chechen War, Cossacks in the North Caucasian regions were relatively passive and, despite some threats against Chechens and other non-Russians, were not involved in serious violent actions. The government, in its turn, issued a number of edicts that legalized some Cossack activities, particularly Cossack associations.[63]

Controversy over a Russian Confederation and the New Constitution

In the first half of 1993, as previously mentioned, some experts and politicians were confident that the fate of Russia as a strong state had been sealed, that its disintegration was almost fatal. At best, they said, Russia would survive only as a loose confederation or as a "cooperative Federation."[64]

Without meeting serious resistance from the Kremlin, regional leaders, in spring and summer 1993, began to demand the transformation of the federation into a confederation. This would mean the re-creation of the Russian state "from below," in order to form a central authority that "the subjects of the Federation" endowed with some degree of power with regular revisions in its size. Grigorii Shamin, the chairman of the Tomsk soviet, declared that "federal authorities are not the subject of the Federation," meaning that the power of these authorities was determined only by the will of the regions "that control the territory."[65]

In a display of unprecedented behavior, almost all the regional leaders looked down on Moscow and all of its political institutions and leaders. Many regional leaders, such as Boris Nemtsov of Nizhniy Novgorod and Valentin Fedorov of Sakhalin, were sure that "real life" and "real progress" were possible only in the provinces.[66] This contempt for their Moscow colleagues was an important element in the political process and would affect the foreseeable future of the new Russia. The general feeling in the country at that time was that if the country actually disintegrated, the regional elite would probably take over enough control in their territories to prevent widespread anarchy.

In this context, the political struggle in Moscow throughout summer 1992 centered, to a great degree, around the adoption of the new Constitution. Not being able to pass his draft of the Constitution through the Parliament, Yeltsin looked for the support of regional leaders who, before the events of October, appeared to be the nation's power brokers. The president was considering the creation of the Federation Council, which would be the highest political body in the country, consisting of heads of territorial units, both Russian and non-Russian regions and republics. By downgrading the role of Parliament and its members elected by popular vote, he was ready to concede more power to local leaders.[67]

Yeltsin began to discuss the idea of the Federation Council, as a body consisting purely of regional leaders, at a meeting in August 1993 with the republican heads first in Petrozavodsk and then in Cheboksar. Whereas the regional bosses saw in this body a new institution able to effectively run the country, unlike the Parliament and the government, the president saw in it an antidote against an increasingly rebellious Parliament.[68]

The first meeting of this council, whose existence was not stipulated in the acting Constitution, took place in September, on the eve of the direct confrontation between the president and Parliament. It was evident that Yeltsin wanted to replace Parliament with this body, to which he had personally appointed a significant number of members. It was only natural that Khasbulatov strongly objected to the creation of the Federation Council. In September, many observers felt that the council was poised either to become a rubber-stamp body of the Soviet type or a sort of Politburo, an oligarchic organ that would make all important decisions without consulting anybody else.[69] At the same time, feeling their powers growing, local leaders, Russian and non-Russian alike, went so far that summer as to demand that succeeding Russian presidents be elected from their ranks.[70]

The Political Struggle in Russia Climaxes, September 1993

Yeltsin's Edict No. 1400, issued on September 21, 1993, radically changed the course of events. With this edict, Yeltsin declared war on Parliament by ordering its dissolution. Parliament in turn impeached him as president, making civil war quite likely.

In this showdown in Moscow, most of the governors of the Russian regions appointed by the president gingerly took Yeltsin's side, though with many caveats and demands for the extension of their powers as a reward. Some of them, like Governor Evgenii Nazdratenko of Vladivostok, threatened both the president and the Parliament with his territory's secession if they both did not find a compromise. The governors of Novosibirsk (Vitalii Mukha) and Krasnoiarsk (Valerii Zubov), and a few others were obviously in the Parliament's camp. The heads of local soviets and presidents of national republics were conspicuously on Parliament's side.[71]

Despite the extreme division of the country's politicians into two distinct camps, regional leaders generally wanted to play an independent role in the conflict, a role that both conflicting parties imposed upon them. However, encouraged by their new role, regional leaders were in general rather inclined to support the Parliament in September, with or without reservations. They had decided that their role as power brokers had increased to a crucial level, so their mission was to prevent civil war and restore the authority of the law and the Constitution destroyed by the president.

Evidently, their course of action was contrary to Yeltsin's expectations, as the president hoped that after having been courted by him for so long, they would join him in his war against Parliament. Instead, without Yeltsin's invitation, forty heads of local administrations gathered on September 27 in St. Petersburg, and this gathering was followed by another meeting of the representatives of sixty-three out of eighty-nine administrative regions on September 30 in Moscow. These regional leaders sent ultimatums to Yeltsin and the Parliament, demanding that they adopt the "zero alternative." This act called for the nullification of the decisions made by both antagonists after September 21 and for the simultaneous election of both powers—the executive office of the president and the legislative offices of the Parliament.[72] The president refused their ultimatums as hostile actions, which opened the way for a military confrontation triggered by the opposition, resulting in the seizure of the parliamentary building, also known as the White House, by Yeltsin's people after it had been shelled by troops loyal to the regime.

It is also worth remembering that during the political confrontation between the president and Parliament on September 29, the leaders of fourteen Siberian territories threatened Yeltsin with the blockade of the Trans-Siberian railroad, a vital rail route spanning the country. These leaders demanded the removal of the blockade surrounding the White House.

During the siege of Parliament between September 21 and October 4, the determination of the opposition's leaders to fight Yeltsin was to great degree based on their belief that the "regions would support them." When the confrontation with the Parliament reached its peak and turned into a bloody struggle, once again there were very few regional leaders who considered themselves able to play the role of mediator between both camps; among those who mediated were Kirsan Iliumzhinov, president of Kalmykia; Ruslan Aushev, president of Ingushetia; Leonid Potapov, chairman of the Supreme Soviet of Buriatia; and Vadim Gustov, chairman of the Leningrad Soviet of Leningrad.[73]

The Aftermath of October's Bloody Showdown

Almost the very day after his victory, President Yeltsin radically changed his attitude toward the regional leaders, forgetting his declaration on their special role in the life of Russia, giving up the idea of a federal council as a body of regional lords.[74] Yeltsin also included in the draft of the new Constitution a new version of the federation council, one that would now consist of two popularly elected representatives from each region. He also eliminated the Federal Treaty from the draft of the Constitution, which proclaimed the sovereignty of the non-Russian republics, and he ordered the exclusion of the term "sovereignty" from the Constitution.

Furthermore, a few days later the president declared war on the regional elites and their administrative bodies, most of whom had been terrified watching the shelling of the White House.[75] Yeltsin's administration began to purge many among the regional leaders and regional soviets. Several governors, including Governor Vitalii Mukha of Novosibirsk, and Governor Alexander Surat of the Amur Region, were dismissed. In a televised appeal to the nation on October 6, the president called upon the local soviets posed against him to denounce their previous resolution supporting Parliament and dissolve themselves. Several soviets followed this advice and did indeed dissolve themselves.

On October 9, 1993, the president, again defying the Russian regions' autonomy, issued an edict. This time he was not asking but demanding that all local soviets dissolve themselves, on the basis that they were a vestige of the old Communist system. This edict was proclaimed as putting an end to the old "Soviet system."[76] This decision meant an immense increase in power for the governors. Even the election of new local legislatures to replace the soviets did not significantly diminish the power of governors who enjoyed Moscow's support.[77] The president then declared after this point that all governors would be appointed by the president.

Yeltsin also signed a decree on the use of economic sanctions against those territorial formations within Russia that failed to pay taxes to the state treasury. This decree gave the government the right to stop financing enterprises and offices located in those districts, territories, and national republics that underpaid their taxes to the federal budget. The government was empowered to stop deliveries of state resources to disobedient subjects of the Russian Federation, halt allotting export and import quotas for those wishing to engage in foreign trade, and reduce the amount of allocated centralized credits by the sum of taxes underpaid to the budget. The Central Bank of the Russian Federation also received the president's instructions to deduct from the current accounts of the budgets of these republics, territories, and districts the sums underpaid to the federal budget. The gravity of the proposed measures was justified by the amount of harm inflicted on the state budget by the regions' greed. For example, within nine months in 1993, the federal budget lost eight hundred million rubles in underpaid taxes.

On February 24, 1994, Yeltsin addressed the Federal Assembly with a message titled "On Strengthening the Russian State." The third section of this message was specially devoted to federalism, regional policies, and the dangers of regionalism to the state. In the very first paragraph, the president wrote that he was "worried about the signs of the country's disintegration, about internal tendencies threatening its territorial integrity."[78] Other leading officials also immediately began to deal with regions aggressively and even arrogantly.[79]

Regionalism on the Retreat

The regionalist theme that flourished in the Russian mass media before October 4 soon all but disappeared for some weeks from newspapers and television. Some journalists were even in a hurry to announce that this phenomenon now belonged to the annals of history. But these were only superficial perceptions of the processes going on in Russia. For every soviet that decided to follow the presidential order, several others behaved contrarily.

Many soviets continued to regard the president's edict of September 21 as "unconstitutional." A typical case was that of Briansk, where the local soviet was harshly and unsuccessfully fighting for the Communist Yurii Lodkin, who had been replaced by Yeltsin's appointee, Vladimir Karpov, to become the head of the local administration. Determined resistance to Yeltsin's policies was also found in Novosibirsk and Blagoveshchensk. Soviet resistance took on milder forms in Arkhangelsk, Kursk, Cheliabinsk, Volgograd, Voronezh, Nizhniy Novgorod, Krasnodar, and several other regions.[80] The national republics were even more adamant in preserving their own soviets and preferred their own constitutions. For example, North Osetia and Bashkortostan declared their determination to keep their political structures intact.[81]

Some publicists also continued to praise regionalization, especially those who were among Yeltsin's critics. Alexander Tsipko, a harsh critic of Yeltsin's handling of developments during the political crisis, called for regional forces and regional intelligentsia to help save Russia.[82]

The Emergence of the "Gubernia" Approach

While the political conflicts between the center and regions were becoming more convoluted, the Yeltsin regime tried to outline a new Constitution that would be able to stabilize the nation's political life, including the regional issue. During this debate, the idea reemerged to liquidate the existing administrative divisions in the country, especially the national non-Russian regions, and to transform Russia into a unitarian state.

In the Bolshevik empire, the political division into national and autonomous republics, autonomous regions, and simple regions was no more than a simple formality—embellishments on a prison robe common to all. Only after the collapse of the Communist regime did the judicial status of a certain territory begin to assume real meaning.

It may seem easy to do away with this inequality by using one of two means: either (1) liquidate the republics and introduce a uniform division of Russia's territory into administrative-territorial formations with equal rights, or (2) raise the regions' status to the level of republic. However, since 1992, the debates about the best administrative structure for a new Russia were strongly tied to the economic inequality between the Russian and non-Russian regions. When the question of the equalization of the republics' and regions' positions was put on the agenda, each of these two possible ways to achieve this found its own group of supporters. And the distribution of support was not at all accidental. The politicians in the center preferred the first method, especially those who were not at the helm and could thus voice their proposals without any risk of being entrusted with their implementation—implementation that might result in the escalation of local nationalist aspirations and anti-Russian manifestations in the republics. The regional elite in the Russian regions preferred the second method, for in their opinion it is more realistic and simplistic; moreover, it flatters their vanity to entertain the thought of becoming presidents, ministers, procurator generals, and so on.

By the end of 1992, sensing the threat to the existence of the "small republics," or national republics, President Mikhail Nikolaiev of Sakha-Iakutia began to look for arguments defending the existing status quo. Referring to international law, he said that its principles presumably also protected the sovereignty of the "small" national republics.[83]

During the preparation of the new Constitution, two versions of the plan for administrative divisions circulated throughout Moscow. The first version supported the status quo, with the national republics remaining special units within the nation. The second version rejected the national-territorial principle of administrative division. This version gained the support of ideologists and politicians who adhered to various, and at times completely different, political points of view. Among the supporters of this second version, the *gubernia* (province) approach, were some centrist parties as well, which had rejected federalism even before 1993 and now enhanced their propaganda of unitarism.[84] Included here were the Party of Russian Unity and Concord and the Democratic Party of Russia.[85]

Many supporters of a unitarian Russian state among the democrats and centrists focused on economic efficiency as incompatible with "the national-political principle as the basis for Russian statehood."[86] Gavriil Popov saw, and not without reason, that granting national sovereignization might threaten human rights and freedoms in these regions and might instigate conflicts among the new nations.[87]

Of course, the most fervent fighters for the *gubernia* version were the overt Russian nationalists, the supporters of a "unique and undivided" Russian great power, who appeal to the traditions of the Russian monarchy and are often pro-Fascist Russian chauvinists. Such was the position held by the ultranationalistic National Republican Party of Russia, led by Nikolai N. Lysenko, which supports "the gradual change of the principle of the federation . . . from national-territorial to geographical-zemstvo, provided that there is a constitutional guarantee of the rights and freedoms of the national cultural-economic autonomies." Vladimir Zhirinovsky was also a strong advocate of the "gubernization" of Russia.

In demanding that the national republics be dismantled, many democrats and centrists manifested their respect for the non-Russian peoples and raised an old idea about national-cultural autonomy (as opposed to national-state autonomy), a subject that had been taboo in Soviet politics since 1917.[88] In their opinion, the present-day situation necessitates the transfer of the center of gravity from the national-territorial to the national-cultural principle of organizing national autonomy.

It is remarkable that the advocates of the *gubernia* solution ignored an essential question at the time. What did unitarism mean for the *gubernia?* The participants of these debates in 1993, however, almost totally concentrated on non-Russian entities.

The first solution to the administrative division in 1993–1994 was discussed not so much in the press as in various meetings and conferences held behind closed doors, in view of its sensitivity. The most important of these were the debates held during the drafting of the Constitution, which were conducted by the Constitutional Commission of the Russian Supreme Soviet. However, here the status quo position was evidently dominant, even if many leading people in the Constitutional Commission, including its secretary, Oleg Riumiantsev, as well as representatives of a number of Russian regions, favored the *gubernia* solution. At the same time, it was also evident that the term "sovereignty" would not be used with respect to the non-Russian republics as had been done in the Federal Treaty.

On June 26, 1993, the work on the draft Constitution was considered finished, and it became evident that the status quo would be maintained. Although it became apparent that it was now impossible to eliminate the national republics, a new idea began to emerge—the consolidation of all Russian regions into a powerful "Russian Republic." Several authors pointed to regional insurgencies as attempts by ethnic Russians to find their own identification and to create a genuine Russian state through regional alliances.[89] The Russian Republic would by definition dominate the federation, and the president of the federation would simultaneously sit as president of this republic.[90] However the "Russian" project did not last long, and the advocates of unitarism returned to a relatively "old," albeit more radical, idea—the abolition of the ethnic administrative unit in favor of the *gubernia*. These *gubernii* were to be territories of relatively the same size, just as had been done in France after the revolution of 1789.

The Center and Self-Government

The ambivalence of the Kremlin's policy toward the regions was also manifested in this period clearly in its attitudes toward local self-government in cities and villages, institutions that were separated from the regional government.

After October 1993, it also became evident that the Kremlin's feelings on the creation of true democratic self-government in cities and villages was somewhat lukewarm, much like the tsarist regime's feelings about the zemstvo. In 1995, there was still no legal basis for self-government in the country, although the Kremlin ostensibly displayed an interest in effective self-government. It even convened meetings on this issue and promised to transfer to local city and village authorities some "municipal property."[91]

In various regions, local authorities, mostly the regional dumas, tried to create their own laws on self-government. However, these laws had little chance of being implemented due to Moscow's indifference and even hostility to them.[92]

Meanwhile, a number of Russian intellectuals, in a desperate quest for a magic solution to Russia's problems, pointed to the prerevolutionary style of Russian self-government, the zemstvo, as the key institution for the country. The most passionate advocate of the zemstvo was, upon his return to Russia in 1994, Alexander Solzhenitsyn. In his numerous speeches, one of which was before the

State Duma in October 1994, televised presentations, and articles, the famous writer insisted that "the salvation of Russia is in the zemstvo."[93]

The New Constitution and Non-Russian Republics

The final draft of the new Constitution, which was supposedly approved by the Russian population during the national referendum held on December 12, 1993, can be seen as a sort of compromise between the *gubernia* and the "sovereign national republic" approach. The new Constitution did not abolish the national republics, but at the same time it did not use the term "sovereignty," somewhat equalizing the Russian regions and national republics.

At the same time, the Constitution reflected the changes that had developed over the preceding years in the relationship between the center and provinces. The new Constitution endorsed the Federation Council, which had been so hotly debated in summer and fall 1993, and, as the regional leaders wanted, made it the body of regional barons. The December election showed that these barons could easily secure their own election.

In comparison to the heady prospects of regionalism and divorce from the center that had been envisioned a few months earlier, a new element was that most of these barons—governors of their administrative units, unlike the presidents of national republics—were appointed by the president. Among other things, the Constitution stated that the members of the federation had the right to form organs of legislative and executive power in the regions in accordance with their own choices and traditions. They could even name their official bodies as they wished.

In the aftermath of the 1993 referendum, several ethnic republican leaders denounced the new Constitution as unitarian and as undermining their sovereignty.[94] The population of seven republics, Adygeia, Bashkiria, Dagestan, Karachaevo-Cherkesiia, Mordovia, Tuva, Chuvashia, and ten regions, mostly from the "red belt" in the European parts of Russia, did not endorse the Constitution.[95]

The Ambivalent Results of the December Election

The December elections, in which the nationalists and Communists were victorious, greatly changed the political climate in the country and had a significant contradictory effect on regionalization. During the election campaign, regional bosses had already partially reverted to their previous arrogance once it became evident to them, as well as to Moscow politicians, that the election's outcome depended upon the local elite. Indeed, in the election campaign for the new Parliament, several leading politicians, including those who were already in the government, such as Sergei Shakhrai, the leader of the alliance called the Party of Russian Unity and Concord, used "the regional card." They "let the provinces save Russia from Egor Gaidar's propresidential alliance, Russia's Choice," promising that if they won, they would rely mostly on the regions in their future policies.[96]

The State Duma and local government election results whipped up regionalist fervor throughout the nation. After a short respite, the regions again assumed the offensive, putting forward their claims. As previously mentioned, Governor Rossel was elected as a member of the Federation Council and the chairman of the district duma.

The Second Stage of the Antifederalists' Offensive

At the same time, the election significantly strengthened the position of the antifederalists, particularly scaring the national republics. The December 1993 elections brought Vladimir Zhirinovsky, the leader of the ultranationalistic Liberal Democratic Party of Russia, an unexpected victory, in which he defeated the democrats. His party was able to make up one of the strongest factions in Parliament. In this new political context, the debates on the best political structure for the Russian Federation took a new course. The move toward unitarism, after its retreat only a few months earlier, was again revived. The future of non-Russian entities, rather than the Russian regions, was now on center stage.

After the election, Zhirinovsky became one of the most aggressive foes of federalism.[97] He opted to use the "zero hour" plan to do away with the national republics. If he gained power, he would issue the decree to form the massive *gubernii*, arrest republican presidents, and, if necessary, take hostages. The goal he envisioned was that on the second day of his rule, Russia would awaken quite united, unified, and undivided into smaller administrative units, with the exception of the governors and governor-generals of the *gubernii*.[98] Moreover, even Yeltsin's administration, as well as several of the democrats who had created the new Constitution based on the old administrative divisions, defended the *gubernia* as the single administrative unit most likely to be fruitful.[99]

One can hear in this political chorus the bass of the great exposer of Communist totalitarianism, Alexander Solzhenitsyn. Solzhenitsyn cherishes both civil rights and the principle of a "united and undivided Russia" and has said, "In the past, Russia was firmly divided into *gubernii*. This situation existed for at least two centuries. This mechanism operated smoothly. Instead of these *gubernii*, Lenin divided the country into autonomous republics . . . and after the collapse of the Soviet Union, all these national republics decided, due to very high opinion of themselves, that they were sovereign and free."[100]

Extreme Regionalism, 1994–1995

The Kremlin could afford to persist in its contemptuous attitude toward regional leaders only for a short period after the October 1993 debacle in Parliament. Only a few short months after his October victory, Yeltsin realized that he could in no way assume that the country was now stable and under his control. In fact, the extremely poor economic situation, the key factor in the political processes in Russia, persisted in 1994–1995, and the national situation was far from being "a Russian miracle (*chudo*)."

As it soon turned out, Yeltsin's October victory only temporarily strengthened his regime. Yeltsin's base of support among the Russian population gradually waned in 1994–1995, and his regime therefore gradually weakened. Thus, it did not come as a surprise after the 1993 results that the December 1995 parliamentary elections brought about the opposition's victory. This victory forced the current regime to make a number of concessions to the Communists and nationalists, who, during the election campaign, tried to present themselves as the provinces' defenders against a Westernized and corrupted Moscow.

With the regime's internal weakening in 1994–1995, regionalization entered a new phase. The public was already accustomed to the regions' growing role in the country's political and economic affairs, leading to the media's disinterest in this issue, in comparison to the events of 1992–1993. However, the non-Russian republics continued in 1994–1995 to gradually gain greater autonomy.

Pacts Between Moscow and the Ethnic Republics

One of the most important events in this period was the signing in February 1994 of a treaty stipulating twelve special agreements between Moscow and Kazan. This treaty was purportedly to recognize both the "statehood of Tatarstan" and the republic's subordination to international law. The treaty was also seen as a method of demarcating the powers of federal and local authority.[101]

However, the treaty did not satisfy the extremist groups in Moscow or in Kazan. Russian nationalists denounced the treaty as too large a concession to the Tatar separatists. Tatar nationalists saw the treaty as the Tatar elite's retreat from its previous position, since the term "sovereignty" was not even mentioned. In addition, they considered it a contradiction of the Tatar Constitution, treating Tatarstan as an ordinary subject of the Russian Federation.

Despite this debate, the treaty between Moscow and Kazan became a desirable model for all the other republics. In 1994–1995, Moscow signed similar agreements with Bashkortostan, Buriatia, Kabardino-Balkaria, Sakha-Iakutia, Udmurtia, and North Osetia.[102] As a rule, the separation of power between the republics and Moscow in these treaties was quite ambivalent, leaving both parties the opportunity to interpret the treaties as they wished.[103]

Negotiations with Russian Regions

Many Russian regions also required similar relations with Moscow. Following the events of October 1993, the Kremlin rejected the pressure exerted by most of the larger regions, such as Nizhniy Novgorod and Ekaterinburg, to sign the special pact with them.[104] However, two years later, Moscow retreated from its position and started to make similar agreements with the pure ethnic Russian regions. Remarkably, Sverdlovsk was the first such region. Then, in late 1995 and early 1996, special agreements "on the separation of powers" with the Kremlin were signed by Nizhniy Novgorod, Orenburg, and Kaliningrad.

At the same time, several regions, mostly those with weak economic potential, declared in 1993–1994 that they did not seek special agreements with the center, preferring standard rules in the relations between the center and their provinces, assuming that such a procedure would not put them in a disadvantageous position in comparison with stronger regions.[105] A few regional leaders, like Khabarovsk governor Viktor Ishaiev, even continued to make flamboyant statements on their desire to see their region become a republic, being careful, however, to underline the economic and not the political motivation for the stance.[106]

Gubernatorial Elections
Stimulate Regional Autonomy

Under the pressure of democratic values, Yeltsin reluctantly reconciled himself to the idea that the governors of all the regions had to be popularly elected, like the chairmen of the regional legislatures in all the regions, who had been popularly elected since the very beginning. After the summer 1995 election in Ekaterinburg, a series of gubernatorial elections was held throughout the country, in Nizhniy Novgorod, Vladivostok, Novosibirsk, and several other regions.

Using his remaining clout over those governors whom he had appointed, in February 1996 Yeltsin fired the governors of Saratov (Yurii Belykh) and Vologda (Nikolai Podgornov), accusing them of illegal activities, mostly related to the use of money that they had received from Moscow. This development aroused the Federation Council's anger. Yeltsin could afford to ignore the "senate," since both governors had been personally appointed by him. However, he definitely could not do the same if senators were popularly elected. It became evident that the situation would change significantly when all the members of the Federation Council were popularly elected.

The Chechen War and Regionalization

In November 1994, facing the growing defiance of Dzhokhar Dudaiev, Chechnia's president, the Kremlin hesitantly started to make war against the rebellious republic in order to show its determination to preserve the country's territorial unity. Yeltsin felt that he needed to do this in order to halt the spread of separatist tendencies in the country and to attain greater leverage in the Kremlin's relationship not only with the non-Russian republics but also with the ethnic Russian regions.

The president was sure that an invasion involving a huge army with vast resources would crush the Chechen resistance in just a few days, perhaps even in a few hours. However, the Russian army, demonstrating an unbelievable ineptitude, was unable to achieve its goal. After an entire year of bloody guerrilla fighting, the whole operation was shown to be a complete failure, provoking many hostile reactions against the Kremlin's master.

With its contradictory effects, the Chechen War initiated a new stage in Russian politics and in the relationship between the center and region.[107] Most of the developments related to this ongoing war are chronologically beyond the scope of this book, and we will therefore dwell only on those events that occurred prior to spring 1996.

All the actors in the political drama surrounding the Chechen War observed four essential elements: (1) Moscow's determination to use brute force in Chechnia, without hesitation killing of thousands of people, including civilians, in order to attain its goals; (2) Russian military defeats that severely damaged the nation's respect for the army, previously the epitome of Russian might; (3) the ineptitude of the central administration in coordinating the activities of its various agencies; and (4) the corruption of the Russian bureaucracy, which extended to the soldiers and officers in the conflict.

First, the manner in which the war was conducted aroused the nation's anger, particularly in the non-Russian republics, and evidently increased their suspicion and hostility toward the ethnic Russians. These anti-Russian feelings increased not only among non-Russians in the Caucasian republics, such as Dagestan, Ingushetia, and Kabardino-Balkaria, but also in non-Russian republics in other areas of the country.[108]

Reflecting this mood and trying to use this situation for their own purposes, some regional leaders attempted to defy Moscow in various ways. Nikolai Fedorov, president of Chuvashia, openly challenged Yeltsin's right to start the war in Chechnia and even issued an edict releasing Chuvashian recruits from participating in this war. Moreover, Fedorov convened a meeting of the heads of seven republics in January 1995, in order to elaborate a common policy toward Moscow in connection with the ongoing war. Fedorov's defiance, however, was left unpunished, allowing the Kremlin to continue to invite him to various meetings in Moscow. Fedorov, in the first half of 1995, granted numerous interviews in which he presented strong criticisms of the Russian president.[109]

None of the regional leaders did anything resembling this. However, several actions against the Chechen War were taken by officials and public organizations in other republics, and particularly strong actions were taken by Tatarstan. Boris Nemtsov, governor of Nizhniy Novgorod, who collected one million signatures from his "subjects" who were protesting the war, also exemplified the involvement of a regional leader in "high politics" at the expense of the Kremlin.[110]

At the same time, Moscow's gloomy firmness in the decision to employ destructive weapons on its own territory, its ability to destroy cities and villages, and its flagrant disregard of any human life, including that of ethnic Russians, scared many non-Russian leaders, showing them the limits of Moscow's tolerance of their insolence.[111] Moreover, some non-Russian peoples, despite their anti-Russian mood and their sympathy for the Chechens, also felt the threat to their own existence that would result if Russia left the North Caucasus, which could lead to the disintegration of the Russian Federation. Dagestan was among the republics that began to fear the evacuation of Russia from Chechnia.[112]

The Chechen War also exacerbated the conflicts in the Moscow political establishment over the relationship between the center and periphery, enhancing the position of the nationalists and their demand for the "gubernization" of Russia. At the same time, the war somewhat weakened the federalists, those defenders of greater autonomy for the national republics and Russian regions in Moscow.[113]

By the middle of 1996, the relationship between the center and periphery in Russia was not much more stable than it had been in 1991. Governor Nemtsov correctly summarized the shape of the Russian political situation as this book went to press in late 1996: "The life of the Russian regions, their relations with the center, remain fragile, arguable, and not regulated."[114]

PART THREE

The Center and Regions in Confrontation

In post-Communist Russia, the center and the provinces have been involved in permanent confrontation, the intensity of which has risen and ebbed under the impact of various political, economic, and social factors. Each player has had its own strengths and weaknesses in the struggle for the upper hand in this conflict. On the one hand, the center has its big state machine, even if it is not very effective; it also has control over the national budget, tempered by its inability to satisfy the basic needs of the population. On the other hand, with their high level of autonomy, the provinces can control the election of the president and Parliament and are able to directly influence Moscow policy. However, the relationship between the center and the provinces is far from being uniform, mostly because of the high differentiation among Russian regions in level of economic development.

The major force of regionalization in Russia is the regional elite. It is this elite that shapes the ideology of regionalism and tries to outsmart the central government in the fight for power and money. From time to time, this elite forges various alliances among different regions in order to extract additional concessions from the capital; and it is this elite that benefits most from the privatization of the Russian economy.

10

THE CENTER AND REGIONS
IN POLITICAL STRUGGLE

Two specific developments in the Soviet Union after 1987, and particularly after 1991, enormously stimulated regionalization: (1) the decline of the center's power, and (2) the democratization of society. Both of these political factors made the relationship between the center and regions radically different as compared with both Communist and prerevolutionary Russia. It is impossible to exclude the possibility, at least for the time being, that Russia might revert to an authoritarian or even a totalitarian state; in any case, however, the center will never again be able to control the Russian provinces as it did for five hundred years.

To a greater or lesser degree, all political actors in Russia had realized by the mid-1990s that the confrontation with regions, even if it could be worked out in some cases, would not continue in post-Communist Russia. Thus, the best policy had to be pursuing further cooperation between the central and local elite. Otherwise, the chances for chaos or the temporary victory of Russian extremists would be quite high.[1] At the same time, all of the actors were also aware that this cooperation would be intertwined with temporary conflicts of various degrees of intensity. In addition, they realized that Russia faced various alternatives in forming the relationship between the center and the periphery in the future.

Explaining the Center's Weakness

The chief cause of the growth in regional powers in post-Communist Russia is the center's political weakness.[2] The center is unable to sustain its historical control over the periphery. There are several causes for the center's contemporary weakness in post-Communist Russia.

First, the center no longer controls the most powerful networks of the three major institutions of coercion: (1) the party, (2) the KGB, and (3) the army. These institutions made it possible for the center to impose its will on the provinces in the past. Furthermore, the center cannot protect its citizens from criminal and terrorist acts, and in 1991–1995, it suffered the experience of watching as local authorities took more and more control over security apparatuses in their regions.[3]

Second, the recognition of democratic principles of government makes it necessary for the center to accept the political struggle for power in the capital as a normal phenomenon. This forces the current administration and its opposition to look for the support of the regional elite.

Third, Russia has become an ideologically fragmented society in which three distinct ideologies—democracy, communism, and nationalism—vie for influence. The center, regardless of its official ideology (in 1991–1995 it was the democratic ideology), must share influence over the minds of its citizens.

Fourth, having been deprived of direct control over the economy due to greater privatization, the center has to shift the responsibility for the satisfaction of the population's basic needs to regions and, therefore, delegate a lot of power to them to perform this function.

With the loss of the old ways of controlling the provinces, the center must now recognize the new role of local elites as independent political powers. It must also cooperate with them in order to preserve the country's unity and proper functioning.

The Center's Clout

Although the center has recognized the new reality in its relationship with the periphery, it still has at its disposal many means of confronting regions that want to expand their autonomy and that thereby increase general separatist sentiments.

The center of the Russian Federation is still the seat of all the national institutions: the presidency, the national Parliament, and the government. These institutions issue laws and directives and are able to, at least partially, effect political changes.

The center has at its disposal a large standing army, a police force, troops of the Ministry of Internal Affairs and of the federal security agencies, as well as military personnel of various agencies, including the president's special military units. Of course, the efficiency of the center's military power is limited, as the Chechen War has demonstrated. Nonetheless, this military power in the hands of the Kremlin is quite impressive and will continue to be a major factor in Russian domestic and foreign policy.

Another of the center's most powerful weapons in its game against the provinces is its authority over the Russian economy, especially the financial, tax, and foreign trade levers. Even if the budget, which is controlled by national institutions, became much smaller than in the past, the center would still operate with a significant part of the national income. Official investment and credit policy can favor one region and disfavor another. With control over taxes and foreign trade licenses, the center also possesses powerful economic instruments that affect regions.

After 1991, the center had a limited and steadily declining ability to shape the composition of the regional elite. However, in a political struggle within a particular region, the center may still support one faction while undermining the position of others.

The Decline of Moscow in the Political Arena

The contradictory status of the central administration vis-à-vis the periphery has determined Moscow's place in the post-Communist environment. As in many other countries today, the status of Russia's capital is declining.

Moscow in the Soviet Past

In the Soviet past, Moscow was one of the few leading centers of the world, along with New York, London, and Paris.[4] It was not only the center of the "internal Soviet empire" but also the capital of the "external empire," or the "socialist camp" (also known as the "Second World"), which included Eastern Europe and, to some degree, Vietnam, Cuba, and several Third World countries. It was a city attractive not only to Soviet satellites but also to people who believed in the advantages, if not the superiority, of socialism.[5]

Moscow was the seat of a central political power so strong that any significant decision in any area of life outside of it was impossible. Even Moscow's party secretary, who held a position apparently of "regional" and not "national" character, was one of the most prestigious political officials in the country. He was also usually a member of the Politburo and had the opportunity to rise to the position of general secretary.[6]

The quality of life in Moscow was the highest in the country, and to live in Moscow was the dream of every provincial resident. The supply of consumer goods, the quality of medicine and public transportation, and the intensity of cultural life was much higher than in any other city in the country. Even Leningrad, the former Russian capital, was far behind Moscow in many of these respects. For any ambitious man or woman in the country, to live and work in Moscow was the ultimate goal, and Moscow attracted, and got, the best talents from all corners of the country. Moscow was not only the center of Soviet science and culture, but in it was concentrated more than two-thirds of all scientific institutions, national periodicals, and publishing houses in the country.

The true idolization of Moscow was one of the essential elements of Soviet ideology. As Yurii Poliakov, a prominent historian, noted, "The love of Moscow became a part of the Russian national conscience, since Moscow was an inalienable part of the emergence of Russian statehood."[7] Among the most popular songs in prewar Russia were those that were devoted to Moscow, songs in which the capital was endowed with features of a living being. A major refrain in one such song of praise was "Moscow—you are the most beloved being."[8]

Nonetheless, the feelings of Russians about Moscow cannot be painted in only one color. The veneration of Moscow was combined in the minds of provincial residents with deep envy and even inimical feelings about Moscow as the exploiter of the country. Millions of people flooded into Moscow in order to obtain food and other consumer goods, but at the same time, many Russians loathed their capital, thinking that its residents unfairly enjoyed a much better life than the majority of the population.

Moscow in Post-Communist Russia

After 1991, Moscow's role in the life of the country declined drastically, though the city continued to be the repository of political power able to change the country's fate. However, in the eyes of most Russians, Moscow lost its role as the major agent of political and economic progress in the country, along with its monopoly in culture and science. With the provinces' direct access to Western technology and financing, in combination with the general decline of scientific, educational, and cultural institutions in the capital, Moscow has almost totally lost its authority as the main source of new ideas—much more so than other global capitals. Young provincial people, at least the very talented or rich among them, now have wider access to Western education, thus Moscow universities and colleges have lost their previous allure.

Moscow has also lost its monopoly over international communication. Because of recently introduced means of electronic communication, each Russian region feels closer to many cities around the globe. Gavriil Popov was justified in contending that "the role of the national center and the capital will fall in the new era."[9]

The dismantling of the central planning system immensely reduced the dependence of provincial bureaucrats on their connections with high officials in Moscow's innumerable offices, in which major decisions were made about the plans for individual enterprises and regions.

To be openly hostile toward Moscow used to be one of the most terrible sins in Soviet public life, but in post-Communist Russia, it became possible to sling any sort of criticism at the capital. For example, in a manner typical of the new times, the governor of the Omsk Region delivered a speech in which he referred to Moscow with irony, using such terms as "our dear and beloved." His speech was laced with contempt as he described Moscow as a citadel of "anemic" bureaucrats and politicians unable to understand how one must run such a big country as Russia. In general, Moscow was accused by the provinces as a parasite that lived at their expense.[10]

The regions' resentment of Moscow was so high that one-fifth of the Russian Parliament's deputies voted for a proposal advanced by a well-known politician, Vasilii Lipitskii, in March 1995, which called for the transfer of the capital to Novosibirsk. Ever since 1991, this idea seems to constantly hover over the capital.[11] In addition, further ideas began to circulate in favor of transferring the constitutional court from Moscow to Cheboksar. Many other similar projects, just as unrealistic, reflect popular sentiments in the provinces toward the Russian capital.

It goes without saying that Moscow has also lost its distinction as the primary Russian venue for various dignitaries from East European countries and, of course, from the non-Russian republics—the place in which they received their instructions, which further added to the city's grandeur. Moscow has also lost its claim as the sole haven of "progressive mankind"—a place where intellectuals from many countries in the world, until the beginning of perestroika, sincerely searched for inspiration and moral and material support. Moscow, of course, has also ceased to be the capital of a superpower in which its leaders' whims could have directly influenced the earth's fate. This Moscow is now gone forever, with tremendous implications for the character of Russian statehood and of the world.

The Decline in Appeal of a Post in Moscow

In this context, it is not surprising that Moscow ceased to be the dream for many local officials and politicians. Indeed, for the past several centuries, all ambitious local citizens desired to spend their lives in Moscow or St. Petersburg, occupying a leading role in the government. In Soviet times, these aspirations were encouraged by the Kremlin's cadre policy, which showed a sort of preference for provincial cadres over Moscow residents. This policy was inspired by suspicions of Moscow liberal intellectuals, whose pernicious influence embraced even party apparatchiks born and educated in Moscow.

In any case, none of the general secretaries following Iosif Stalin were Muscovites, and only two of them—Mikhail Gorbachev and Nikita Khrushchev (though only partially)—received a higher education in the capital. Most members of the Politburo were also people who had come to Moscow from the provinces.

With the collapse of the Soviet Union, the process of selection for high offices changed radically. Local politicians and businessmen in the new internationalized world made their plans with places other than Moscow in mind. Several of them, such as Boris Nemtsov and Aman Tuleev, achieved popularity in the country as local politicians. A few of them even rejected, at least for a time, the invitation to assume a position in the central apparatus.

Of course, Moscow still attracts a number of challenging people, especially if they did not succeed in the provinces and did not leave the country. And Moscow is still the biggest and wealthiest city in the country, promising much for career and wealth seekers and even for very ambitious politicians. In the Middle Ages, the imperial court, even during a period of weakness in the empire, lured many who craved a higher status. Indeed, some local officials were ready in 1992–1995 to relocate to Moscow, as Yurii Shafranik did when he left his position as Tiumen's governor to become the minister of energy in the federal government. Similarly, Nikolai Egorov moved in 1995 to Moscow from Krasnodar, where he was the head of the administration, in order to take various positions in the Kremlin. This pattern holds particularly true of those who found themselves in Moscow as former deputies of national parliaments with no serious chances of reelection. With these dim prospects in mind, they relocated in the hope of finding a niche in the capital.

The Weakening of Economic Ties with the Provinces

Moscow not only lost its political and cultural significance for the provinces but its role as an economic partner also diminished notably. As a result of the country's increased openness and the globalization of the Russian economy, the role of the provinces in supplying consumer goods to Moscow declined enormously. Moscow had also imported food from abroad in the past, but evidently never to such a degree as in the post-Communist period. In 1995, the delivery of goods from the Russian regions to the capital was two times less than in 1991. Furthermore, in 1995, the Russian regions were only able to supply significantly less than one-half of all foodstuffs consumed by Muscovites.

In 1994–1995, supplying Moscow with food became one of the hottest conflicts between the capital and the provinces. The local leaders, supported by the Agrarian Party leaders, representing mostly the managers of collective farms, accused the Moscow government of being unpatriotic in its indifference to the fate of Russian agriculture, due to its focus on the import of foreign foodstuffs. It is not surprising that a fierce battle was waged around the levels of customs tariffs, with Moscow demanding their diminution and the agrarians calling for drastic increases. Boris Yeltsin's government oscillated, in 1994–1995, trying to please both parties, resulting in decisions that satisfied neither party.

Moscow's Second Ascension

Whatever the decline of Moscow in comparison to its past status, it is still the center of a large country. As noted, all of the central administrative bodies, as well as the most prestigious scientific and cultural institutions, continue to be concentrated in Moscow. Most political parties are headquartered in Moscow and of one hundred leading politicians, almost 90 percent are Muscovites.[12]

Moscow is still able, albeit to a much lesser degree, to impose on the provinces its own candidates for their parliaments.[13]

However, Moscow's new role in post-Communist Russia exists in the context of a city that managed to become the financial and trade center of the country on a new basis. Some authors have even spoken of the "second ascension of Moscow."[14] About one-half of all financial capital in the country in 1995–1996 was concentrated in Moscow's region, which consequently now possesses about 35 percent of all banks in the country as well as the lion's share of various foreign, private, and joint companies. With many of the leading companies engaged in foreign trade, Moscow controls one-third of all the country's revenues in hard currency. Tiumen, the main producer of oil and gas for export, has only 12.3 percent.[15]

Moscow is also the site of numerous foreign government and public agencies. All of the leading Russian banks are located in Moscow, as are all of the leading holding and insurance companies.[16] Along with the oil and gas industries, Moscow services attract the greater part of foreign investment in Russia.

With the concentration of financial capital and foreign companies in Moscow after the immense degradation of the standard of living in 1992–1993, in 1994 Muscovites started to have a much better life than people in the provinces. Nowhere in the country did so many people have so many opportunities to simultaneously hold several lucrative jobs—mostly in banks, trade firms, and foreign and joint companies, and in the highest echelons of power—and, beyond this, often have the opportunity to travel abroad with the financial support of foreign institutions. All of these circumstances, and a few others besides, explain why the average per capita income in Moscow in 1995 was almost three times higher than the national average.[17] However, the flow of money to Moscow simultaneously caused it to be the most socially polarized city in the country, where the wealthy flouted their wealth while millions of retirees, scholars, students, single mothers, and clerks working in state offices were fighting for their physical survival.[18]

Moscow Versus Russia

Despite its diminished political power, Moscow developed new financial sinews and a population that for the most part supported democratic and Westernized political parties. By 1994–1995, Moscow had become a city in conflict with provincial Russia, a circumstance never before seen in Russian history.

Several factors contributed to the mutual alienation of Moscow and Russia. First, as just noted, in 1993–1995 Moscow's economic life generally outstripped the rest of the country. Moscow again became the object of envy for the provinces; the object of hatred was not so much the bureaucrats as the "New Russians," who tend to be bankers and heads of trade companies and other lucrative businesses, all of whom are considered by most Russians to be swindlers and crooks. And the Moscow New Russians have done their best to foment the provinces' envy, with their innumerable "presentations," their lavish, prodigal receptions and parties with unlimited consumption of champagne and caviar. These displays were often broadcast on TV, and the lifestyle of these fortunates was reported in various periodicals, which described in detail their multiple homes, Mercedes, twenty-thousand-dollar mink coats, vacations in the Bahamas, and other extravagances. This all aroused the ire of millions of poor people in the provinces. Nothing like this occurred in the provinces, since the same New Russians, quite less numerous than in the capital, have been afraid to reveal how rich they are. The new radical difference between the standard of living in Moscow and the provinces, which is not ideologically legitimized as it was in the past and is today glaringly conspicuous as compared to the *nomenklatura's* "hidden consumption," accounts for much of the capital's alienation from the provinces.

Second, Moscow, represented by ambitious leaders like Yurii Luzhkov in 1993–1996, has actively opposed the interests of Russia and considers itself to be a separate administrative unit similar to any other region in the country. In 1993–1995, Moscow's authorities actively demanded various privileges for its city, including exceptions from federal laws, and was often in conflict with the government. For instance, Moscow came into conflict with the government over privatization procedures and refused to follow the rules designed for the entire country, particularly those rules requiring enterprises to sell stocks to their collectives at symbolic prices.[19]

Third, the differences between the political views of Muscovites and views held in the provinces were, in 1993–1996, extreme. Indeed, in the Stalinist era, there were no visible political differences in mood between Muscovites and provincial residents. In the post-Stalinist era, however, the situation has changed significantly. In the 1960s, Moscow, in the country's and world's mind, was not only the capital of the USSR but also a haven for dissidents, the enemies of the Soviet system. In all this, the average Muscovite shared the same views as the rest of the country. But after 1985, particularly after 1991, the political differences between Moscow and the rest of the country increased enormously.

For example, Moscow residents were the most active fighters for perestroika and were avid supporters of Gorbachev. Later, in 1990, Muscovites sided with Yeltsin, who succeeded Gorbachev as the major engine of change in the country. Moscow elected Yeltsin as a deputy in the first relatively free election of the Soviet Parliament in 1989 and then continued to actively support Yeltsin in all of his confrontations with the Kremlin in 1990 and, particularly, in March 1991. It was the Muscovites who stymied the putsch against the democrats in August 1991, while the rest of the country, with the exception of Leningrad, demonstrated its indifference to events in Moscow or even showed sympathy for the leaders of the conservative putsch. Moscow's fervor for reforms was perceived by the country and the world in general as a demonstration of its vanguard role and as new evidence of the capital as the engine of progress. The provinces later came to look upon the role they played during this period with a sort of repentance and regret for their failure to completely follow the example of the brave Muscovites.

The situation changed drastically in 1993 when the provinces and Moscow realized how different their political sympathies were. During the bloody showdown between Yeltsin and Parliament, several thousand Muscovites demonstrated in the streets in support of the democratic regime, whereas the number of Muscovites who actively backed the opposition's leaders was much lower. However, the provinces remained passive and only watched the battle in the capital with a degree of detachment and little compassion for Yeltsin.

In the 1993 parliamentary elections and especially in the 1995 and 1996 presidential elections, Moscow's voting pattern was markedly different than that of the provinces, more so than ever before.[20] Indeed, in the December (1993) elections, the most democratic party, Egor Gaidar's Russia's Choice, got only 15.5 percent of the vote in the country but received 34.7 percent of the vote in Moscow, more than any other party. At the same time, Vladimir Zhirinovsky's aggressive nationalist Liberal Democratic Party was supported by 22.9 percent of all Russians and gained first place, but it received only 12.8 percent of the vote in Moscow.[21] In the next parliamentary election, Moscow and Russia again went in different directions, despite the general trend in favor of the Communists: Although 22.3 percent of all voters supported the Communists, only 14.4 percent backed them in Moscow. At the same time, less than 4 percent of the country voted for Russia's Choice, whereas 11.9 percent of Muscovites voted for this party; and the liberal party *Yabloko* earned 7 percent nationwide and 15.4 percent of the vote in Moscow.[22] During the presidential election, Yeltsin received 35 percent of the national vote in the first round but got 70 percent in Moscow alone.

This process of the capital's growing political alienation from the country as a whole is a development that evidently undermines the cohesiveness of the Russian state, and it will influence many aspects of Russian development over the next few decades.

11

REGIONS ON THE OFFENSIVE

The collapse of the Soviet system almost immediately transformed regions into powerful actors able to confront the center on many issues. In the conflict with the center, regions had numerous cards to play.

Power Sources of the Regional Elite

To begin with, the power of regions is proportional to the center's political stability. The less stable the center, the stronger the regions and their elite. In addition, various characteristics of post-Communist Russia are deeply rooted in political instability, which stems from the lack of consensus in the country on major social and political values and is manifested in the fragmentation of political life.[1] With the almost permanent political instability in the capital, fundamental order cannot be kept without the center's active cooperation with regional bosses. This political instability leads to the regional elite's significant role in sustaining the country's unity and its order.

History shows that the regions' role increases immensely in periods of crisis. This happened in 1917, when the monarchy fell and Petrograd was engulfed in a fierce political struggle. Almost immediately, hundreds of cities and regions proclaimed their autonomy and even formed independent republics. Likewise, post-Communist Russian history provides us with various examples that support this statement. As previously discussed, the might of regional barons reached its peak in 1993, when the confrontation between Boris Yeltsin and Parliament climaxed.

Another source of the regional elite's power in Russia is Moscow's inability to satisfy the population's basic needs or to even regularly pay the salaries of millions of people working in the state sectors (also referred to as being on the "budget"), including teachers, doctors, and the police. The center needs to have the regions be responsible for the sustenance of a more or less normal life in the country.

A third source of power for the regional elite in Russia is the democratic procedure employed in presidential and parliamentary elections. In a country with very weak and fragile democratic traditions, the possibility for the local elite to influence the election results is quite high. An indirect indicator of the local elite's power to influence elections is the prevalence of incumbents in gubernatorial elections. In the December 1995 and February 1996 elections, most governors and mayors, including those appointed by Boris Yeltsin, were elected despite the president's extremely low popularity. In the gubernatorial elections of December 1995, governors for twelve regions were elected and of these, nine were incumbents who were reelected. Five of the six heads of local administrations in Stavropol were reelected, as were the majority of the administrators in Iaroslavl.[2] Therefore, the center very much depends on the regions in pursuing its political goals. In fact, Moscow experts asserted in 1995 that "the leaders of regions can change the results of any election on their territory by up to 15 percent." This seems to indicate that in many cases the governors control the outcomes of the election.[3]

Almost openly, regional leaders negotiated with the Kremlin, offering their support of the central government during the elections in exchange for various concessions that would be made to them.[4] Mintimer Shaimiev, Tatarstan's president, quite seriously mentioned, not without a touch of irony, that after the December 1995 elections, Viktor Chernomyrdin "as a sign of gratitude to the republic for its correct behavior during the election promised to relieve military industrial enterprises here from taxes." "Under such conditions," added Shaimiev, "it is reasonable to have another election."[5]

On the eve of the December 1993 parliamentary elections and, particularly, in December 1995, the Kremlin built up a political strategy based on support from regional officials and the political parties representing the government, which, in 1993, included Egor Gaidar's Russia's Choice, and in 1995, included Chernomyrdin's Our Home Russia. This strategy was only partially successful; however, without it the election results would have been even more disturbing for the regime than they were.

The regions' power in post-Communist Russia is manifested in its role in the Duma, the lower chamber of the Russian Parliament. Several parties that competed in both parliamentary elections in December 1993 and December 1995, staked their political hopes on the regions by promising to defend their interests in Parliament. They even differed significantly among themselves in their attitudes toward federalism, primarily as it concerned the non-Russian republics and the degree of the Russian regions' autonomy. Among these parties in 1993–1995 were Sergei Shakhrai's Party of Russian Unity and Concord; Chernomyrdin's Our Home Russia; the Congress of Russian Communities, headed by Yurii Skokov and Alexander Lebed; and particularly Eduard Rossel's Transformation of Russia. All of these parties, to various extents, played with the idea that the real repository of power should be the province, a point of view rejected by the Communists who opposed the building of statehood "from below."[6]

Moreover, in both the 1993 and 1995 Dumas, there were regional factions that vowed to defend the interests of the provinces. In the 1993 Duma, a faction called the New Regional Policy, headed by Vladimir Medvedev, was quite visible. However, in the 1995 Duma, the faction that replaced it, Regions of Russia, was one of the most powerful factions, with forty-one deputies in January 1996, including prominent politicians such as chairperson Vladimir Medvedev, Sergei Shakhrai, General Boris Gromov, and former vice chairperson of the Federal Council in 1993, Ramazan Abdulatipov.[7] Another important feature is that several regions started, after the elections of 1995, to create their own special lobbies in the Duma, the lower chamber of Parliament.[8]

The Role of the Federation Council

In post-Communist Russia, regional leaders also find a source of power in their active roles as members of the upper chamber of the Russian Parliament. The role of this chamber, the Federation Council, is quite significant. It endorses laws passed by the Duma and approves the appointments of leading officials such as the attorney general and the members of the highest judicial bodies, including candidates submitted by the president for the constitutional courts, the Supreme Court, and the arbitration court. It is the Federation Council that endorses the decisions of the president to declare national states of emergency and to use the armed forces outside the country. This chamber also plays a crucial role in the presidential impeachment process.

However, the real might of the Federation Council lies in the fact that its members are the powerful local bosses who, in post-Communist Russia, indeed control the country. With their popular election to regional positions rather than their merely being appointed by the president, their power and independence, as well as the power of the Federation Council, increased enormously.[9] By the end of 1995, the Federation Council was a center of power in the country somewhat equal to the government or even to the president. It is evident that in the case of a large political crisis, it is this body, not the Duma or any other institution, that would assume full power in the country.[10]

These complex relations between the Russian president and regional leaders remind us of the relations between the German emperor and local feudal fiefdoms in the post-Carolingian empire in the tenth to thirteenth centuries. In that case, the German emperor wanted to simultaneously curb his barons' desire for independence and gain their support, so important for him in his struggles with individual rulers of other European fiefdoms, particularly in his struggle with the Pope.[11]

Regions and International Economic Relations

The globalization of international life, as previously mentioned, was a strong factor accounting for the regions' increasing power vis-à-vis the center. As soon as possible, the regions started to shape their own foreign strategies and dealt with foreign countries on their own terms. Remarkably, Moscow actually encouraged these developments. In 1995, the Ministry of Foreign Affairs even elaborated the statute regulating interactions of the "Federation's subjects" with foreign countries.[12] Russian and foreign scholars began to recall how single Russian regions in the sixteenth and nineteenth centuries, such as the European Russian North, established direct contact with foreign countries and intensively traded with them.[13]

In the beginning of 1991, the idea of "free economic zones" was a sort of obsession in the provinces. More than 150 administrative units, such as regions, districts, and cities, demanded the right to create such zones where producers were free from taxation. However, it soon became evident that only a few territories in Russia would be attractive to foreign investors, and this idea was mostly forgotten. Nevertheless, foreign economic activities became an important part of life in many regions.

Not only regions and cities close to international borders, such as the Russian Far East and St. Petersburg, but also other regions began to initiate foreign trade activity.[14] For instance, the Tiumen Region signed an agreement on September 23, 1993, outlining long-term economic cooperation with the Republic of Tadzhikistan. In particular, this agreement envisages a most-favored-nation system for the transportation of goods through border control points, the free flow of all monetary resources through commercial banks of Tiumen and the Central Bank of Tadzhikistan, and the use by both sides of the necessarily strong means to ensure the agreed-upon supply of products.[15] At about the same time, Cheliabinsk organized a special seminar in Vienna in November 1993 to discuss investment opportunities in this Ural region.[16]

By 1992, Nizhniy Novgorod had already entered into direct economic exchanges with various regions in Kazakhstan, Tiumen, and North Rhine-Westphalia in Germany.[17] Also in 1992, Iaroslavl concluded special agreements with Uzbekistan, which opened a trade consulate in Iaroslavl; and Iaroslavl also opened direct contacts with German firms.[18] By 1994, almost every large Russian city had established direct trade contacts with several dozen foreign corporations, and nobody was surprised, for instance, when Ekaterinburg began buying roses from Israel.[19]

The national republics were, of course, particularly active in establishing their own international connections. Tatarstan's leaders, in 1992–1993, visited officials in various countries and international organizations, including NATO, trying to represent their republic as a sovereign state.[20] The Komi Republic has also established direct relations with German banks. In addition, since 1995, Chuvashia has had direct air connections with Istanbul.[21]

The regions' power is strengthened by their intensive contacts with foreign countries without Moscow's control. The rapid growth of travel without restraint, often without a visa, and new electronic modes of communication have permitted all Russian regions to easily and directly foster contacts with any country in the world. Russian cities, in stark contrast to the past, are now open to the world and in no way see Moscow as a key to their accessing foreign countries.

12

The Regional Elite as Advocate of Regionalization

As an important process in Russian society, regionalization involved almost every political actor in the center and the regions. Among these actors, the regional elite played the most important role in this process. This has also been the case in such diverse countries as Italy and India and has held especially true for post-Communist societies. It is somewhat paradoxical that in Russia, regionalism, which in the second half of the twentieth century has thrived mostly on democratic ideas, chose as its main standard-bearers not liberal intellectuals or workers' organizations but local bureaucrats, who had in the past docilely served the unitarist regime that had fought democratic tendencies and the people and groups that represented those tendencies.

The Local Elite as Champion of Egotistical and Public Interests

The term *elite* in this book, according to traditional views, is understood to represent the more or less stable group of people in a society who make strategic decisions in major areas of social life. We reject the view that the ruling class can be treated as belonging to the elite only if its members are able to transfer their status completely or partially to their descendants. We include in the local elites the high officials in the regional administrations, deputies of regional parliaments, directors of enterprises, and the leaders of local businesses.

As is the case with any elite, the Russian regional elite in 1991–1995 pursued mostly egotistical goals. Members of the local elite dreamed of becoming presidents; they wanted to enjoy international recognition and the highest privileges accorded to heads of state and to play a special role in the governing of the Russian Federation. They also wanted their own piece of the pie in terms of bribes and other semilegal and illegal privileges controlling business, foreign trade, and other forms of economic activity. The period after 1991 was the first time since the physical liquidation of the boyars—the feudal Russian barons—by Ivan the Terrible in the second half of the sixteenth century that the local elite could claim such power.

The first step taken by Russian regional leaders—the heads of the non-Russian republics and large Russian regions—was to increase their status and material well-being to unbelievable levels, compared to the previous excesses of the first party secretaries in the Soviet past. Most of them built themselves luxurious multistory homes, gave themselves enormous incomes, provided their wives, relatives, and friends with lucrative jobs, and made frequent business trips abroad, as well as making routine the numerous gala receptions for foreigners, artists, and dignitaries from Moscow.

The Russian population held the local elite in the same contempt as Moscow politicians, considering its members corrupted and absorbed with their own enrichment. According to VTSIOM's data collected in May 1995, only 9 percent of Russians "fully trusted" regional authorities and 13 percent felt similarly about their city and village authorities. However, they trusted the Russian president even less, with only 6 percent responding that they trusted him and only 4 percent expressing trust in Parliament and the central government.[1] Russian governors, even if they were popularly elected and ranked as most popular with the public, were perceived by the masses as power-hungry money seekers.[2]

In the period 1991–1995, in order to better serve its own egotistical goals, the local elite tried to exploit the mood of the masses, particularly people's discontent with the drastic decline in the standard of living. The local elite chose Moscow as the main culprit, promising the amelioration of people's situation by pursuing greater autonomy or even, as with a few non-Russian republics, separation from Russia.

Since the decentralization of political and economic life in the country was a historical necessity, the regional elite, whatever the personal motivations, played a somewhat "progressive role." However, as will be shown farther on, in many cases the gap between the elite's egotistical interests and the people's interests can widen too much, causing regional leaders to be perceived more as enemies of their territories' population than as benefactors. The situation becomes particularly dramatic when the center acts as the main engine of progressive reforms while the local elite uses regionalization as a weapon against democratic and market transformation. To a very great degree, this is exactly what has happened in post-Communist Russia. With some exceptions such as Nizhniy Novgorod and, to some degree, Ekaterinburg, which were considered in 1992–1995 to be bastions of reform, the Russian provinces were much less enthusiastic toward reforms than Moscow, even being, in many cases, simply hostile to them.[3] The political views of the local elite quite evidently reflected this regional conservatism.

The Local Elite's Political Conservatism

The democrats' victory in August 1991 significantly strengthened democratic ideas in the provinces. On the one hand, "democrats" seized many of the leading positions in quite a few regions. On the other hand, a number of local politicians who were formerly Communists publicly changed their views, some sincerely and others not, and they joined those who praised democratic values and a market economy. At the same time, the majority of regional leaders kept their views to themselves and watched the developments in the country with animosity. The number of the regime's open or hidden enemies was especially higher in the local soviets whose membership had been elected before the events of 1991.[4] The radical deterioration of the economic situation in 1992 and 1993, along with the rise in the crime rate and other negative developments such as the decline of culture, science, health services, and other public sectors of the economy, could only encourage the old enemies of reform to go on the offensive against "democrats."

The new ideology of the still-authoritative Russian society was based on a mixed economy, but it retained the state's active role in all sectors of society. In addition, Russian nationalism was promoted in Moscow by various conservative parties and movements. In its milder form, this ideology of post-Communist Russia was referred to as the "social democratic ideology." In its harsher, modernized Communist form, the ideology was often called the "socialist-patriotic ideology," or, in sociological terms, the "paternalistic ideology."

In all of these forms, the ideology began to spread among local elite as well as among ordinary people in 1993–1995. Some "democrats" in the provinces and the center were also moved to support this ideology. As many polls indicate, the local elites espousing this ideology reflected to a considerable extent their electorates' mood.

The Meaning of *Nomenklatura* Outside the Soviet System

Some authors have attributed the dominance of conservative views among regional leaders in 1991–1995 to the high proportion of old apparatchiks among them.[5] Indeed, many regional leaders in post-Communist Russia had held high positions in the Soviet hierarchy. Some of these dissenters had even been regional first or second party secretaries in the regions and, in the post-Communist era, had become the chairmen of local legislatures or had been elected governors or had even been appointed governor by the president, for example, Egor Stroiev in Orel or Vitalii Mukha in Novosibirsk.[6] Several authors have been inclined to think that their past experience in the Communist Party determined the behavior and mentality of former apparatchiks now among the elite in post-Communist Russia. However, it would be a mistake to overestimate the *"nomenklatura factor,"* even with respect to those regional leaders who indeed served in the party or state apparatus in Soviet times.

Of course, it would be equally erroneous to dismiss the period of socialization of former party secretaries or the influence of the party bosses' experience. Nonetheless, as conspicuous as the return to power of many apparatchiks in 1992–1994 was, they still could not form a majority in any sector of social life. The natural elimination of people who had held high positions in the regions in the past and the mass intrusion of a younger generation turned the apparatchiks into only a large minority. In fact, by using the formal criterion of membership in the regional *nomenklatura* in the Soviet period, we find that nowhere in post-Communist Russia do former apparatchiks make up more than 30 to 40 percent of all new regional rulers.

Indeed, according to Olga Krishtanovskaia's data, among members of the local elite in 1993 in Russia, on the average, only 17 percent were of *nomenklatura* origin, whereas 25 percent of them surrounded the president, 40 percent of them were members of Parliament, 26 percent were in the government, 42 percent were leaders of political parties, and 59 percent were in the business elite. Vladimir Shubkin's data on the Altai elite, collected in mid–1994, show that among twenty of the highest officials of the executive branch, 35 percent had belonged to the *nomenklatura*. Furthermore, from the same data, it was found that of twenty legislators, 26 percent had been in the *nomenklatura*, as had 66 percent of directors, but no members of the business elite had been in the *nomenklatura*.

It is even more important that we consider another set of circumstances. Outside of its system, the *nomenklatura* has little meaning, much as one cannot imagine the landlord's role without an estate, the bankers' role without banks, or the capitalist's without money. The might of the *nomenklatura* membership was bestowed upon them by the totalitarian state, and when it disappeared, the *nomenklatura* faded away.

All of the members of the former *nomenklatura* had to adjust to a new social reality in post-Communist Russia, which could be labeled anything but a Soviet society. Even those former party apparatchiks who declared war on the new regime in order to restore the old one, like Viktor Anpilov, had to accept the new rules of the political game and behave accordingly. But what concerned the majority of apparatchiks who managed to surface—and they are only a minority of those who were in power before 1989–1991—was their desire for personal success under the new circumstances. This need is similar to that of the former nobles who adjusted to the bourgeois reality in France or England or to that of the members of the former "dominant classes" in the socialist order, if they managed to survive the terror.

Of course, in the political and economic struggle in post-Communist Russia, some former apparatchiks preferred to join the conservative or even nationalist ranks because of their past or because of the opportunities to forge more or less cohesive alliances for mutual aid with people whom they knew in the context of the past system. However, even these party apparatchiks did not want the restoration of the old system and supported other projects, whether authoritative or nationalistic in nature. In any case, these people are definitely not of "pure Communist" belief.

Differences Between Local Administrations and Legislatures, 1991–1993

The more conservative character of local politicians in general as compared to that of the ruling elite in Moscow was already evident in the aftermath of August 1991. However, even then there were significant differences between the views of two types of local politicians—members of the administration and the members of the legislature.

This division in viewpoints had no precedent in the Russian provinces. Of course, such distinctions also formally existed in Soviet times, but they had no significant political meaning since each member of the local elite was appointed by party committee and even endorsed, if necessary, by the Central Committee. In 1991–1994, most heads of the administration were appointed by the president, whereas legislators were elected by the local population. The different constituencies significantly predetermined the political and economic views, as well as the behavior, of the two types of local elite.[7] Of course, the distinction between the two types of elite should not be exaggerated, though it is still quite significant.

Many of those who worked in the administration supported the democratic model of society and the marketization and privatization of the economy. Those who were elected as deputies were mostly hostile to the Yeltsin regime. Members of local soviets that had existed prior to October 1993 were openly inimical to Yeltsin's regime. With the exacerbation of the conflict between the president and Parliament, most of the local soviets unswervingly took the legislators' side, whereas the governors appointed by Yeltsin supported him. Yeltsin's victory in the confrontation with Parliament in October 1993 pushed local elites even farther toward supporting authoritative and nationalistic views along with the masses.

After Yeltsin eliminated the local soviets via his decree, new elections were carried out in many regions in 1994–1996. As a result, the conservative opposition increased its representation in the new local assemblies, or "dumas," that replaced the old soviets. Almost all of the opposition's leading figures were reelected.

According to Shubkin's data, during the local election in Altai in March 1994, 63 percent of all the elected legislators were Communists or were aligned with the Communists' ally, the Agrarian Party, a figure that had increased from the 61 percent elected on December 12, 1993. The democrats fared worse, gathering only 10 percent of the vote for Russia's Choice, a pro-Yeltsin party, whereas in

December 1993 they had received 28 percent of the vote. At the same time, of all the officials in the administration, 31 percent voted for Russia's Choice, which had previously garnered 68 percent, and 8 percent voted for the Agrarian Party, whereas 5 percent had voted for them in December. The remaining votes were split among various small parties.[8]

In 1994–1995, the conservative ideology gained additional influence among local elite. Two circumstances accounted for this process: the continuing economic and political turmoil in the country and the gradual replacement of governors appointed by President by people elected by the masses. In most regions, the Communists were victorious in local elections. In Volgograd in 1995, for instance, the Communists received twenty-two seats of the twenty-four seats available in the city government. The Communists' successes in the other regions were also very impressive along with the Communists' and Russian nationalists' victory during the December 1995 parliamentary elections.

Attitudes About the Center and Autonomy

Regardless of the views of local elites on democracy and the market economy, all of them had to determine their attitudes toward another fundamental issue—whether they supported a strongly centralized Russia or a country in which regions would enjoy a great deal of autonomy.

As in any other nontotalitarian society, members of the regional elite in post-Communist Russia had to choose between the following four major orientations:

1. To seek maximum autonomy from the center and be mostly indifferent about their participation in the decisionmaking process in the center; in a word, to be "autonomists."
2. To seek the same degree of autonomy but, at the same time, to claim a crucial role in the ruling of the country; to act as "confederalists."
3. To seek only the right to participate in the decisionmaking process in the capital, supporting the centralist character of the Russian state; to become "patriots."
4. To seek only their survival as regional leaders without engaging with the center on issues such as its autonomy or its participation in ruling the country; to be "survivor-conformists."

The distribution of the regional elite among these four groups in 1991–1995 was changing, depending upon various factors, of which the most important were the political and economic situation in the nation as a whole and in the capital, the economic and political might of a region, the popular mood in the nation and the regions, and the manner in which regional leaders gained their office—by appointment or election.

Whatever the changes in the composition of regional leaders with their vary-ing attitudes toward centralization and decentralization, there were at any given time the "survivor-conformists," those members of the elite who were passive in regional and national affairs, preferring the status quo to any reforms. This group was primarily composed of the leaders of smaller regions that were, as our con-tent analysis of Russian press in 1992–1995 showed, almost never mentioned in the Russian press. For example, regions such as Murmansk, Novgorod, Pskov, Kostroma, Tver, Kirov, and Astrakhan, along with their leaders, were very infre-quently mentioned in the Russian media.

There can be no doubt that from 1991 to mid-1993, the majority of the elite from the non-Russian republics and from almost all of the powerful Russian regions gravitated to the first group, which demanded maximal autonomy and, in the case of some non-Russian republics such as Chechnia, even separation from Russia. At the same time, many of the regions in this category were almost pas-sive about their role in "big policy" in Moscow. Indeed, in 1993–1994 the most active regional leaders, such as Mukha of Novosibirsk or Valentin Fedorov of Sakhalin, called for greater latitude in their regional business but did not make an issue of their role in the decisionmaking process in the country as a whole, though this situation changed somewhat in 1995–1996.

Sociological data support the thesis on the predominance of the first type of regional leader—who were autonomists in the first years after 1991, though again with some differences showing between the two branches of power, the executive and legislative. As Shubkin's surveys found in the first half of 1993, in the Altai Territory, only 5 percent of all legislators supported the previous role of the center and the complete submission of all regions to its will. By contrast, among the members of the executive branch, 37 percent preferred the previous condition of the regions' submission to the center.

When politicians directly face economic issues, their positions on regional autonomy became more specific. Often, the number of people voting for greater independence from the center diminishes, and at the same time, the distinction between different groups of local politicians becomes more pronounced.

In Elena Avraamova's national survey conducted in 1993, in answering a ques-tion on the distribution of the funds from the national budget, 71 percent of local administration heads insisted that "this money had to be distributed according to the needs of individual regions," recognizing in this way the economic depen-dence of their regions on the center. Eleven percent of the survey's respondents supported the comparable view that "the distribution of money should be deter-mined by negotiations between the center and regions," and only 7 percent shared the view that money received by the region should be proportional to its contribu-tion to the national budget (11 percent did not answer this question). Legislators showed more confidence in the economic potential of their regions, with only 36 percent of them supporting the idea that the center should distribute the budget according to the needs of regions and 44 percent claiming that the influx of budget money should be determined by regional contributions to the national income. Another 4 percent of legislators voted for the older, fully centralized style of financial distribution, and the final 5 percent did not answer. Eleven percent abstained from answering the question. However, when asked about the resources for economic development, almost all of the local politicians, legislators, and administrators focused on the internal potential of their regions, and no more than 2 to 4 percent laid their hopes on federal investment.

In October 1993, when the political confusion in the country began to accelerate and the country was on the edge of civil war, many regional leaders began to drift over to the second group, the "confederalists," demanding even more autonomy than in the past. Only a handful of politicians in the Russian regions described themselves, in mid-1993, as true separatists, even if some prominent local leaders, in a moment of anger, said something to the center on this account, which is, of course, remarkable from a Freudian point of view, in that it is a manifestation of suppressed feelings and desires.[9]

Many regional leaders raised their ambitions, claiming to be national leaders, too, and, playing the role of "confederalists," began to interfere in Moscow's politics. In 1992–1994, several of them even tried to install their own ruling bodies, musing about the election of a president from their own ranks, a president who could take control of the country. With the defeat of Parliament, regional leaders went underground for a while, but a few months later they again began to claim the role of national leaders; among these politicians were Eduard Rossel, Boris Nemtsov, and Egor Stroiev.[10]

In 1995, regional leaders took various initiatives with nationwide implications, evidently to demonstrate that the political establishment in Moscow was unable to cope with the urgent problems of the country.[11] The intervention of the Nizhniy Novgorod governor in favor of immediate peace with Chechnia, in February 1996, was a direct reproach to the central administration, showing it to be unable to solve the problem by itself.[12]

It is remarkable how many regional leaders are ranked among the one hundred most influential politicians in Russia, as determined by the experts at Grushin's polling firm Vox Populi. In 1995, they made up 12 percent of all influential politicians, whereas in the Soviet Union it was impossible to name any regional party secretary who could claim such a national role.[13] In another survey done by the Russian Biographical Institute, of nine "people of 1995," four were regional leaders.[14]

In 1994–1995, with the success of the Communists and nationalists in the election, a number of regional leaders began to join the third category of regional leaders—the "patriots"—who preferred centralism as the single basis for the survival of Russia as a great power and were ready to sacrifice the autonomy of their regions somewhat to preserve the nation. These people regarded their work in the provinces only as a step on the path to the highest positions in the capital, a pattern of behavior recognizable as that of past regional leaders in the Soviet

Union. Among such leaders in 1995, were Yurii Luzhkov, mayor of Moscow, Piotr Romanov of Krasnoiarsk, and Aman Tuleev from Kemerovo.

More important, most of the great regional leaders in 1994–1995, with the evident widening of their power (of which the signing of a special agreement with President Yeltsin for the division of power is only one example), continued to belong to the "confederalists" and wanted to be participants in the management of the country. This essential circumstance diminished the threat to the country's unity. But it also sustained the trend toward confederalism because the regions, in the persons of their leaders, were becoming as important an element of the ruling establishment as the central political elite. The further evolution in the composition of regional ideology, or to state it another way, the shifting ratio between regional autonomy and national unity, will have a radical impact on the future of the country.

The Specificity of Ethnic Elites

The ethnic elite differs in various respects from the local Russian elite. The ethnic elite is much more aggressive and self-perpetuating than its colleagues in the Russian regions. The cause lies in the character of the ideology that is used by the ethnic elite to legitimize its status. In this ideology, the nationalist component is much stronger than in the ideology espoused by most members of the Russian local elite, with the exception of those who support Russian extremists. These nationalistic overtones in the ideology maintained by the Tatar, Bashkir, or Adygei elites, with a focus on the importance of their republics' sovereignty, explain why the members of a title nation, or those carrying the non-Russian republic's name, support the elites in their republics, who mostly belong to the same ethnic group and garner more support than Russians or those of other ethnic groups.[15]

There is a representation problem here, however. Whereas members of the Russian local elite are of the same ethnic origin as the majority of their population in Russian regions, in the elite in the non-Russian regions, a disproportionately small percentage of Russians represents, in most cases, the Russian ethnic minority in the population. In Tatarstan, for instance, Tatars make up about 80 percent of the political elite, though Tartars account for only 48 percent of the population.[16]

Much more so than the Russian local elite, the members of the non-Russian elite are former apparatchiks, a direct result of the relatively weak democratic movement in the non-Russian republics. Among the Tatar political elite only 8 percent had not belonged to the *nomenklatura* in the past. The most prominent leaders of the national republics, such as Mintimer Shaimiev of Tatarstan, Mikhail Nikolaiev of Sakha-Iakutia, Viktor Stepanov of Karelia, Nikolai Biriukov of Mordovia, and Murtaza Rakhimov of Bashkortostan, were former party dignitaries, some of whom, for instance, Biriukov in Mordovia,[17] were quite successful in preserving many elements of the former system in their republics.

However, there were quite a few people among the leaders of these republics who were not of this ilk, such as Akhsarbek Galazov of North Osetia, former rector of a local university; Kirsan Iliumzhinov of Kalmykia, who, a few years before his election as president of the republic, had became a millionaire businessman; and Dzhokhar Dudaiev of Chechnia and Ruslan Aushev of Ingushetia, who had both been Soviet generals.

Unlike the Russian local elite, whose members are city dwellers, most members of the national elite, for example, up to 75 percent of those in Tatarstan, are of rural origin. This circumstance, as shown by Midkhat Farukhshin, increases their antidemocratic orientation even if they have had a higher education, as most of them have, usually in agricultural study (44 percent in Tatarstan). Farukhshin's study bears out the nationalist tendencies of this elite, showing that 52 percent of all Tatars in the Tatar Republic in January 1994 "trusted the highest leaders of the republic" but only 32 percent of Russians and 30 percent of people belonging to other ethnic groups did the same.[18]

There are some hints of democracy in these combinations of ideological beliefs, since these elites have been forced to make some concessions due to new trends. In some of the republics, the elite carries out privatization and accepts some democratic initiatives. However, the degree of democratization varies quite a bit, ranging from a quite significant degree, as in Tatarstan, to a minimal degree, as in Mordovia or Buriatia.

The Charisma of Local Leaders

In 1992–1995, the region's status in the game with the center depended quite a bit on the popularity of its leaders. The greater the regional leader's charisma, the greater the chances the Kremlin would look for a compromise. To a great degree, Moscow would compromise because of these leaders' ability to affect elections and recruit the support of other regional leaders. The special status that such regions as Orel, Ekaterinburg, or Nizhniy Novgorod achieved in the political drama in Russia in 1992–1995 must be ascribed, to a significant degree, to the popularity of their leaders, even if the moral reputation of these leaders was far from impeccable, as was the case with Luzhkov, Stroiev, Rossel, and Nemtsov. To some degree, this is also true of the national republics, such as Kalmykia with its flamboyant president, Iliumzhinov; Tatarstan with President Shaimiev; and Iakutia with President Nikolaiev.[19]

The Masses as Actors

The regional elite was the major force behind regionalization. In contrast, the role of many other political actors was much less significant. This can also be said of the masses. The turbulent currents of Russian public opinion on regionalization in 1992–1995 were quite complicated and contradictory.

After 1991, the hostility to the center lingered in people's minds, though the perception was basically subconscious, as it had surfaced a long time before that when the regional movement emerged, headed by officially recognized politicians. The great turmoil throughout the country in 1991–1995 accompanied the drastic decline in the standard of living for a majority of Russians and the growing corruption of the central bureaucracy. These sentiments made Russians even more hostile to the center and more supportive of local leaders, who were exploiting the popular anti-Moscow mood, as previously discussed.

Economic factors significantly helped increase this alienation from Moscow. The quality of daily life began to depend more on decisions made in regional centers than on those made in Moscow, and interest in Moscow political life decreased tremendously. Moscow newspapers almost disappeared as reading fare for people living in the provinces, who now regarded local periodicals as their main source of information. Only national television remained to link the provinces and the capital.

Several surveys and various anecdotal projects have showed that with the alienation from political power, particularly in Moscow, many Russians felt much closer to their local authorities than to central authorities. This fact sharply contrasts with the situation in the Soviet era, when the Kremlin appeared to be more benign to ordinary people than local administrations.

As part of the project of ROMIR, a Russian polling firm, Andrei Melville and Galina Bashkirova conducted a study in which they based their results on two-hour interviews with focus groups of eight to ten participants in eleven regions of the country conducted on 9–10 September 1993. According to their study, "local politicians and local political institutions, in contrast to central ones, are generally perceived as being 'closer' to the people and in a much better way expressing their needs." The authors cite the following as "typical comments": "Local powers can do at least something for the people" (from Dmitrov); "problems are at least partially being solved by regions themselves, though not always successfully" (from Pskov); and "the Moscow bureaucracy crushes down everything, it denies the regions the right to initiate and choose by themselves their own fate" (from Khabarovsk).[20]

Because of the immense rise in transportation fares to Moscow, as well as to other regions, it became a rarity for most Russians to travel to Moscow, a fact that also accounts for the gradual isolation of the regions from Moscow and other provinces in the country. With the new political developments, people increasingly began to identify themselves as residents of their region and less as citizens of Russia.[21]

These developments pushed a certain part of the population of provincial towns to the side of the "champions of regional interests." It is not at all surprising that 84 percent of voters in the referendum in the industrial Sverdlovsk District cast their votes for the formation of a Ural Republic. The nationalistic attitudes of the population played a role as well. People pondered such issues as whether those who lived in the Ural or Novosibirsk Regions were worse off than the Tatars or Iakuts, with their own republics.

Nonetheless, even with their alienation from the center and their absorption with their private and regional interests, most Russians in post-Communist Russia continued to be somewhat concerned about their country's unity and reflected quite positively the patriotic overtones of the major political parties that participated in the parliamentary elections of 1993 and 1995, in which the nationalists and Communists were very successful.

13

THE IDEOLOGICAL STRUGGLE
SURROUNDING REGIONALIZATION

In 1991–1995, the ideological battles being fought between centralizers and decentralizers over regionalism, or over the degree of autonomy for individual Russian territories, were influenced by numerous factors. Among these many factors were the Russian cultural and historical prerevolutionary traditions, the heritage of the Soviet period, the collapse of the Soviet Union, the changes in attitudes toward several dominant values, the debates over which political system would be most appropriate for Russians, and economic efficiency.

In 1991–1993, the Russian advocates of regionalization shaped their own ideology and developed their own arguments for this process. The most authoritative regional ideologist in 1993–1995 was Eduard Rossel, the Ekaterinburg politician whose movement called Transformation of Russia was based on the idea that progress in Russia would be possible only with regions as the leading political force in the country.[1]

Regardless of what the regional ideology is—whether "progressive" or "reactionary"—and regardless of whether it is the regional or central elite or the intellectuals who use this ideology to their own ends, regional ideology plays a very important role in the political and social processes in Russia. It defines and justifies the behavior of various political actors in contemporary Russia, helping them to rally support for their cause, such as for the expansion of regionalism or for the strengthening of a more centralized state.

There are two main supporters of regionalization—the regional elite and most of the Moscow intellectuals with democratic orientations. The ideology of regionalization consists of several elements, some of them rather temporary and others more fundamental and permanent. The ideology of regionalization, as is any other serious ideology, is based both on the specific interpretation of certain objective facts and on some myths. The main supporters of antiregionalist ideology consist, for the most part, of the central government's political elite and Russian intellectuals with Communist and nationalist orientations, who, as previously mentioned, support regionalism as a way of fighting the democratic regime.

The Russian Past

The Russian past immensely influenced the ideological battle surrounding regionalization in 1991–1995. This past exerted a contradictory pressure on the ideological debates about regionalization. All participants in these debates took for granted that from the fifteenth century until the late 1980s, the dominant classes in Russia strongly promoted centralism and were foes of regionalism.

However, this past was used differently by advocates and foes of regionalism. For one thing, Russian regionalists had to break with the traditions of autocratism and confer a certain degree of autonomy on the regions. For them, the creation of the free cities of Novgorod and Pskov represents a glorious page in Russian history, whereas Ivan the Terrible, as well as other centralizers and autocrats, is condemned as a horrible figure of the past. The prerevolutionary precursors of the Russian democrats of 1991–1995, such as the Russian liberals from the Cadets, as well as Western figures like Max Weber, also praised the prerevolutionary zemstvo as a bastion for the defense of human rights.[2] At the opposite end of the spectrum, the foes of regionalism consider the period of "feudal divisiveness" in the Middle Ages to have been the most dismal time in Russian history and think for that reason, it is a crime against the Russian people to encourage autonomism and separatism.

The Democrats' Argument About the Soviet Experience

The ideology of the Soviet period was even more centralist than the official ideology of tsarist Russia. The centrally planned economic system, with its touted advantages over the "chaotic market economy," was an additional powerful argument for Moscow's absolute control of the country. Advocating the so-called *mestnichestvo*—the preference of local interests over national ones—was considered one of the most dangerous political vices. The rigid centralization of society was tightly combined with the totalitarian regime and its political repression of even the weakest resistance to the regime.

For this reason, and only because of the past association of centralism with Soviet totalitarianism, many Russians, particularly democrats, supported regionalization as an antidote to the repressive regime. Of course, the most important fact for them was not the history of autocracy in Russia but the historical experiences of the Soviet period, when the lack of freedom and the absence of local autonomy were coupled together.

The theorists of regionalization insisted that in a democratic society, regions could not be as subservient to the center as in a totalitarian society and that the essence of democracy itself demands the introduction of self-government and the radical extension of the rights of each administrative unit in the country, from the largest regions to the smallest village. The slogan "democratism and centralism are incompatible" was a principal battle cry for many regionalists. Further, references to Western experiences, particularly the autonomy of the American states and the German lands, were a necessary appendage to any ideological justification of regionalization.

The expansion of regional rights fitted very well with the democratic ideology that dominated the Kremlin in 1992–1993. During this time period, with Egor Gaidar as a leader of the democrats and actually a prime minister, the democrats focused especially on the negative role of the centralized state and even on the state in general.[3]

For the democrats' opponents, the Soviet Union was a symbol of a united society in which regional interests were reasonably subjugated to national goals. From their perspective, in Soviet times, each region and each regional official felt a part of a greater country and worked to promote its might. This vision stood in stark contrast to post-Communist Russia, with its prevailing local interests over national ones.

The Collapse of the Soviet Empire

The collapse of the Soviet empire had a tremendous ideological impact on regionalization, not only on the ethnic republics but also on the Russian regions. People, particularly the elite, realized that Moscow's power was limited and that it was possible to wrench away much of the power from the capital. Therefore, the disintegration of the Soviet Union and the emergence of the Commonwealth of Independent States (CIS), with some of the states economically weaker than some of the other Russian regions, became a powerful ideological element, both for regional ideology and antiregional ideology.

A monograph by a group of authors, published in 1993 under the editorship of Eduard A. Bagramov and titled *Will Russia Follow in the Steps of the Soviet Union?* was typical of the time period. The apprehensions expressed by alarmists at that time seem to be justified by Chechnia's proclamation of complete and unquestionable independence and by the almost offensive campaign of separatism used by Tatarstan to divorce itself from the Russian Republic.

The democrats referred to the collapse of the Soviet Union as a justification for the necessity to tolerate regionalism and to even encourage it. They used the example of the separation of Ukraine from the motherland as convincing evidence in favor of autonomy.

Communists and nationalists, who sometimes supported regionalism for their own current political purposes, saw a portentous omen for the Russian Federation in the dissolution of the Soviet Union. These antiregionalists even began to look for the same signs of collapse that they thought caused the Soviet empire's collapse. They spoke about the intentional instigation of regionalism, about the inflation of separatism by democrats, and about Jews and Masons.[4]

The foes of regionalization also pointed out that the situation in Ukraine and Byelorussia constituted an argument against autonomy, underscoring the economic decay in the former Soviet republics and the obliteration of the myth that the provinces "fed" Moscow.[5]

Anticentrist and Antibureaucratic Arguments

One of the most powerful validations of regionalization was the accusation that the center was plagued by bureaucratism, ineptitude, and incompetence, all of which stifled development in the provinces. The decadence and corruption of Moscow politicians and the general moral decay of Muscovites in general was included in almost any major text or speech defending regionalism.[6] The regionalists also saw the inefficiency of the centralized state in managing society as one of the major arguments in favor of decentralization, particularly after the center had lost its willingness to resort to repression against those who did not bend to its will.

Regional ideology further supposes that not only is the center unable to run the country through centralism but only regional leaders with their joint efforts are really able to preserve the unity of the country. In other words, this ideology assumes that the focus of power in general has been shifted away from the center to the province and that, using Igor Kliamkin's words, it is "the claim of the local elite to be the sole defenders of national interests."[7] This signifies the transition from the primacy of the idea of a Russian nation-state to that of a Russian confederation. In 1991–1995, several regional leaders, as mentioned earlier, came to the foreground in their roles as the mouthpiece not so much of their own regions but of the country as a whole. The regional elite were also proclaimed to be the driving force behind privatization as well as a force able to overcome many problems Moscow could not cope with, including corruption.[8]

Developments in 1992–1993, when the country was on the edge of catastrophe as a result of market reforms, added to the regionalists' convictions. The abrupt fall in the standard of living and the evident inability of the central administration to prevent it was the basis for regionalism's popularity among Russians living in the provinces. They, of course, were being used by the local elite.[9] Millions of people in these years stopped receiving their salaries, and their savings were practically decimated due to the astronomical inflation. Under these circumstances, regional leaders claimed to be, along with enterprise directors, the country's saviors. Local leaders resorted to barter exchange and in this way were able to provide food for their people. In some regions, the regional government started to issue its own money and to conclude trade agreements with other regions and even foreign countries.[10]

The foes of regionalization rejected the arguments that the growth of the local bureaucracy was beneficial, pointing out that it was becoming much more arbitrary and greedy than the central government apparatus. For them, regionalization meant the expansion of the bureaucracy and the significant deterioration of the protection of individuals' rights. These critics of regionalization also pointed out that without a powerful central bureaucracy, which has at its disposal an army and law enforcement forces, a nation cannot pursue its national goals, maintain the order and the unity of the country, and protect it against foreign enemies.

Democrats as Centralists

The new democratic and market trends in post-Communist Russia encouraging regionalism also aroused the strong resistance of conservatives in the provinces. These conservatives, especially former apparatchiks, who correctly viewed Moscow as the major instigator of reforms in the country, at least temporarily supported regionalist ideology as the antithesis of Moscow's ideas. This, in turn, caused some democrats to become concerned about the fate of their reforms, as they saw regionalism being used by conservatives as a weapon against the building of a new society in Russia. Vladimir Lukin, a leading democrat, insisted that regionalization and, especially, the trend toward autonomization of non-Russian republics "leads to their progressive backwardness."[11]

It is remarkable that Anatolii Chubais, the main "privatizer" of the Russian economy during his term in the government, was enmeshed in permanent clashes with such regional leaders as Evgenii Nazdratenko in Vladivostok and Yurii Luzhkov in Moscow. The existence of "conservative regionalism" was an important factor in the ideological and political battles in the country in 1991–1995.

The Radical Decline of Patriotic Ideology

Patriotism, an essential part of Soviet ideology, with its emphasis on the might and well-being of the entire country, including its dismissal of local interests, was accepted by most Russians in Soviet times. The people, labeled as pursuing their local, and thus egotistical, interests, were regarded in Soviet society almost as traitors.[12] Therefore, in 1989–1994, patriotism as a part of Soviet ideology was under strong attack by the media and official ideologues of the Yeltsin regime. The drastic amelioration of international relations in Gorbachev's era, the process of disarmament, the intensive international contacts between Russians and foreign countries, the disappearance of fear—all of these factors removed many of patriotism's pillars of support.

However, only the opposition to the regime—the nationalists and Communists—continued to promote the idea of state patriotism. Most Russians in this period shared the regime's hostile attitude to the opposition and virtually excluded patriotism from their set of "positive values." Russian nationalists bemoaned the indifference of Russians to the future of their country, to the "Russian idea"—a euphemism for the special role of Russia in the world.[13]

Patriotism probably reached its nadir in 1994, when Russian nationalism and "statism," meaning "state patriotism" or the ideology of a strong Russian state, began to restore somewhat the importance of patriotic attitudes in the country. However, there was no reason to think that in whatever scenarios were being prepared by fate for Russia, patriotism would ever reach 1985 levels.[14] The decline of patriotism very much encouraged regionalization and its ideology.

The Individualization of Personal Ideology

The decline of patriotism was only part of the more general process of the growing indifference of Russians to public values as a whole and of the privatization of the Russian mind, a mental process that very much strengthened the ideology of regionalization in 1991–1995.

Indeed, privatization not only transferred the bulk of the Russian economy into private hands, but it also privatized the social and political life of the nation in the extreme. Through the centuries, the conviction about the superiority of public interests over private ones reigned supreme in Russia. In the Soviet period, the focus on national interests as being preeminent reached its peak, particularly in the first decades after the revolution when the Bolsheviks sought to eliminate all facets of private life.

The anti-Communist revolution of 1991 led Russia to jump from a society with a powerful collectivist and centralist ideology to a society where public interests were removed from the mind of almost everybody—from ordinary citizens to the highest officials in the country. Of course, private interests were always present in Soviet society, even in Stalin's time.[15] However, even in the last decades of the Soviet Union, when the privatization of social life made significant progress inside Soviet society, the individual's concern about the national welfare of the country was still quite strong. It greatly influenced in various ways the conduct of the Soviet people, particularly the political establishment, the army, and the KGB.

The overarching role of public interest in the mind of Russians was always a necessary condition for the function of the Soviet Union as a highly centralized state. In any case, by 1985 the Russian people could lay claim to being the world's most patriotic people, not only in words but in deeds as well.[16]

History, it seems, likes to move from one extreme to another. In 1989–1995, Russians were transformed into a people almost totally indifferent to any social value or to any public issue and became reluctant to make even the slightest sacrifice for the public good. According to data collected by VTSIOM in 1994, no more than 3 to 7 percent supported any particular "ideological slogan," including "social justice" (no more than 3 percent) or a "strong state" (7 percent). Of a list of twelve values, Russians chose mostly the "conditions of normal civil life," as it was formulated by the authors of this survey; "order" was chosen by 19 percent; 18 percent chose "stability"; and a "decent life" was selected by 10 percent.

In another VTSIOM survey in 1994, it was found that the number of people who said that they "do not bear responsibility for the developments in their country" and that they blatantly support "jungle individualism," almost doubled between 1989 and 1994, moving from 17 to 33 percent. At the same time, no less than two-thirds of Russians in the past looked to the "collective" (people in their firms) or to various party organizations for support in cases of emergency. Today, three-fourths of Russian people who were asked "whose support you would hope to find in difficult circumstances" answered that they would "count only on themselves."[17]

In such a mood of "jungle individualism," with private interests almost completely destroying interest in public affairs, Russians refused to trust any national political institution in the country or any Moscow politician. In the eyes of the Russian people, almost all politicians, especially those in Moscow, were corrupt and concerned only with their own private interests, power, and enrichment. Russians were particularly dissatisfied with law enforcement agencies, which, in their opinion, openly colluded with criminals. Russians infrequently addressed the police when they become victims of crimes, and they have lost all confidence in the judicial system.

Most Russians did not identify with any single national political party in the country, a circumstance that contributed to the alienation from the center and aided the spread of regionalist ideology. According to various surveys, in 1992–1995 no more than 5 to 10 percent of all Russians considered themselves members of any political association or even sympathized with any particular politician, either in the current government or in the opposition.

However, even more significant is the indifference of Russians to the fate of their country. Russians in the provinces are openly hostile to Moscow and refuse to see it as the capital of a united state. The resounding victory of Rossel in August 1995 in the governor's race in Ekaterinburg is quite remarkable, since this politician was the founder of the Ural Republic. The Ural's status as a republic was canceled by the Kremlin because Rossel's supporters argued that the Ural was a colony of Moscow.

Although they have a strong nostalgia for the "old country," meaning the Soviet Union, in 1992–1995 Russians did not want to accept even the slightest sacrifice for the restoration of the old empire. For this reason, ordinary Russians were very lukewarm about the possible reunification with Byelorussia and Ukraine, seeing in both of these Slavic republics poor relatives whose alliance with Russia would only fuel inflation.

Russians were also unconcerned about the fate of their compatriots living abroad in the Commonwealth of Independent States. Only a tiny percent of them expressed any sympathy for their sufferings and discrimination; the majority would not even lend a helping hand to their brethren.

Russians were not only uninterested in the restoration of the Soviet Union, but they were also rather indifferent to the integrity of the Russian Federation. The Chechen War was a revelation on this issue. Most Russians did not support the official justification of the war as an action necessary to save Russia as a nation and refused to sacrifice their sons and money for this purpose. In contrast, they voted for the expulsion of Chechnia from Russia. Only a minority of Russians (no more than 20 to 25 percent) accepted Yeltsin's justification of the war as a necessary condition for the preservation of the territorial integrity of the country.[18] Russians were evidently not scared by the idea of an almost independent Chechnia and did not want to make the sacrifices needed to stop national separatism. The media castigated the Kremlin, denouncing Yeltsin's policy in the North Caucasus not only in the non-Russian republics but also in the pure ethnic Russian regions.[19]

Most amazing were the attitudes of Russians toward the army, a sacred institution for Russians throughout the centuries. However, in 1992–1995 it had become an accepted norm to avoid compulsory military service as well as to defect from military units deployed in Chechnia.

Russian Nationalism and the Russian Versus Non-Russian Standard of Living

The ideology of Russian regionalism was somewhat influenced by Russians' feelings of being discriminated against and by the privileged status of non-Russians in the Soviet Union and in the Russian Federation. This point of view was shared not only by typical Russian nationalists but also by politicians from various camps, including the democratic camp.

The idea that Russians had been treated unfairly in their own country, as an element of regionalist ideology, was formed to a great extent by the conduct of the rulers of the Soviet Union and, more recently, of the Russian Federation, which has followed the pattern of many of the empires in the past. Indeed, the empires, or semiempires such as the Russian Federation, have often tried to ingratiate themselves with the ethnic minorities, particularly when society enters a period of turmoil and the ruling elite must try to save the existing order. For example, the Austrian and then the Austro-Hungarian empire, from 1848 until its end in 1918, tried to accommodate all of its major ethnic minorities, such as the Hungarians, Czechs, Poles, Italians, and others. The central administration's policy of favoring ethnic minorities outraged the dominant ethnic group (Germans in Austro-Hungary fiercely fought the Habsburg's national policy) and the regions with this group's population demanded the same or even more autonomy than the ethnic minorities.

Many Russians, mostly politicians and intellectuals, pointed to two other forms of discrimination: first, the comparison of the political status of non-Russian territorial entities with that of Russian regions; and second, the economic exploitation of Russians by non-Russians.

Both these ideas were actively used by Boris Yeltsin in his struggle with Mikhail Gorbachev in 1990–1991, and their role in the collapse of the Soviet Union was quite significant. The same ideas, a political and economic substantiation of the autonomy of Russian regions, reemerged again in 1992–1993 as a part of the ideology of regionalization. These concepts became, as it has been indicated, the basis for the high autonomy of the Russian regions as discriminated against in comparison to non-Russian "small" republics in the Russian Federation. The unequal status of the Russian regions was one of the important themes in the nationalist ideology of many Moscow politicians like General Alexander Lebed.[20]

Accusing the non-Russian elite of abusing its status as a special ethnic group, Russian nationalists pointed to the fact that in most non-Russian republics, the "title" ethnic groups, which gave their name to the republic, were a minority, whereas Russians were often a majority in the republic.

Russian nationalists also rejected the identification of non-Russian republics in the Russian Federation with the former Soviet republics. Indeed, with the exception of Kazakhstan, the title nations constituted the majority of the population. According to a 1989 population census, the total population native to the region exceeded 70 percent in Ukraine, Byelorussia, Georgia, Azerbaijan, Armenia, Uzbekistan, Turkmenia, and Lithuania. It is somewhere between 60 and 70 percent in Moldova, Tadzhikistan and Estonia, and 52 percent in Latvia and Kirghizia. In Kazakhstan alone, the native population constituted only 40 percent of the total population.

The picture is completely different in the national republics, which are political divisions in the Russian Federation. Here, with the exception of several republics in the North Caucasus and Chuvashia, the title ethnic groups do not constitute a majority of the population. In 1989, the Bashkirs made up only 23 percent of the republic's total population; the Mari made up only 43 percent; the Udmurty only 33 percent; and the Tatars only 48 percent.

The rage of the Russian nationalists was particularly directed against those small units that became "republics" after 1991. All of the new republics and, of course, district units have populations of much less than one-half million people, and the "title" ethnic groups make up only a small fraction of the whole population. In Khanty-Mansiy, they make up only 0.4 percent, and just 4.2 percent in the Iamalo-Nenetsky District.[21]

The economic argument was probably an even more important part of the discrimination-based Russian regionalist argument. Nikolai Shmelev, a well-known economist, ascribed the rebellion of the Russian regions to their desire to get their "fair share" of the products made in their territories.[22]

The thesis about the economic exploitation of Russians by non-Russians and about the inferior status of Russians in the Soviet Union (Russians did not have their own republic inside the USSR as fourteen other nations did) was one of the most important elements in the Russian nationalists' platform both before and after 1991. After the collapse of the Soviet Union, this thesis was appropriated by the regionalists.

In more specific analysis of the differences between Russian and non-Russian regions, many advocates of Russian regionalism examined the flow of money from the center to the regions and vice versa. This investigation seemed to suggest that the differences in the direction of the money flow of the federal budget predetermined the differences in the quality of life—Russians seemed to be worse off than non-Russians.

In fact, the real situation is much more complex. Indeed, the budget's money flow to the non-Russian republics was much higher than to the Russian regions. Regionalists who used this argument to accuse the center of the unfair treatment of the Russian regions usually ignored the direct data on the standard of living, which did not support their thesis about the plight of the Russian regions.

The available data show that, on the whole, the standard of living in most of the Russian regions was higher than in most of the national republics. This is because several other factors besides financial relations with the center determine the quality of life in the country. Of course, there are some exceptions for this rule.

Let us first compare the data on the average monthly wages of workers and office employees, even though these data, like many other indicators, have significant limitations as a characteristic of the quality of life.[23] In 1993, of nineteen republics, only five—Karelia, Komi, Buriatia, Khakasia, and Sakha-Iakutia—showed an average monthly salary higher than the average in the Russian Federation. Let us dwell a little on those republics that stand out by having a higher average salary.

In 1970–1993, the average wage in the Komi Republic was much higher than in the Arkhangelsk and Vologda Districts. In 1992, Komi outstripped the Murmansk District, which lies mostly beyond the Arctic Circle, in terms of this indicator. But the reason for such success lies not in the sovereign status of the Komi Republic but in the specific features of its economic development. The Komi Republic is a land of miners and oilmen, whose wages cannot be compared with the wages of workers in other industries.

The case of Sakha-Iakutia in the Far East, which does not correspond to the typical scheme, is explained by its diamond industry factor. Although the wage level there is much higher than in all of the other regions except one, it still lags behind the Magadan Region, which has a similar production structure.

The wage level in the Russian regions, during the period of 1985–1992, was much higher than in other areas, such as the Volga-Vyatka, North Caucasus, Ural, Western Siberian, and Eastern Siberian Regions.[24] Statistical data also disprove the allegation that rural populations in the national republics received better wages than in the Russian districts.[25]

Other indicators support the same conclusion. If we take as an indicator of the standard of living "the proportion of the value of a minimal basket of nineteen foods in the individual money income" in 1993, we find that in eighteen of nineteen non-Russian republics, this proportion was higher than the national average. This means that the population in these republics had to spend a much higher proportion of their income on food than the average Russian citizen. Only in Sakha-Iakutia was income proportion at the average level.[26]

Most of the other indicators also indicate the lower quality of life in non-Russian republics as compared to the national average. The number of cars per one thousand people was, in 1993, less than the country's average in twelve republics. The number of telephones per one hundred city families was lower than the average in fourteen other republics.[27] Even more important is the fact that housing conditions in non-Russian republics were much worse than in Russian regions. Of all the republics, only four—Karelia, Kalmykia, Mari-El, and Adygeia—had better housing conditions in 1993 than the average in the Russian Federation.[28]

Russian Versus Non-Russian Budget Benefits

The non-Russian regions would have lived much worse if they had received from the center proportionally the same amount of financial support as the Russian regions. In fact, and here Russian nationalists have a point, non-Russian regions enjoy a much more beneficial status with respect to budget and taxes than Russian regions.

In 1992, the subsidies from federal funds to national republics exceeded the receipts from these republics by 170 billion rubles, which means that the federation paid two and one-half rubles for every ruble received from the republics! Indeed, the relationship between the center and the Russian regions is completely different. Here, the positive balance for the federal center's budget amounted to 1.607 billion rubles, which meant that for each ruble contributed to the national budget, the regions received only 31 kopeks in return. Among the regions, only the Kamchatka and Chita Regions got more from the center than they gave back.

The picture was much different as far as the republics were concerned. Only the Mordovia, Udmurtia, and Chuvashia Republics had a negative balance in their relations with the center. The rest of the republics got from the latter much more than they gave to it. The national republics accounted for approximately 15 percent of the population of the Russian Federation, whereas their share of the total taxes paid by the regions to the federal budget was less than 5 percent. By contrast, their share of the subsidies from the budget was 9,670 rubles per person. Two different indicators were hidden in this figure: a negative figure of −12,680

TABLE 13.1   Financial Relations Between the Center and Regions for 1992

	Percent of RF Population	*Taxes Paid to the Federal Budget*		*Subsidies Received from the Federal Budget*		*Balance*	
		Millions of Rubles	*Percent of Total*	*Millions of Rubles*	*Percent of Total*	*Millions of Rubles*	*1,000 Rubles per Person*
National republics	14.75	118,265	4.85	288,035	28.72	−169,770	−7.74
Regions and territories	85.25	2,321,679	95.15	714,579	71.28	1,607,100	12.68
Total in RF	100.00	2,439,944	100.00	1,002,614	100.00	1,437,300	9.67

SOURCE: Data published in *Segodnia*, 25 June 1993. The mistakes in the publication have been corrected by the authors.

rubles per person in the Russian regions and another negative figure of −7,740 rubles per person in the national republics (see Table 13.1).[29]

For example, the Sverdlovsk District, whose population is four times the population of the Komi Republic, got from the federal budget four times less in subsidies than the Komi Republic. The per capita balance in relation to the budget was positive in the Komi Republic and amounted to 59,000 rubles, while in the Sverdlovsk District it was negative, at −14,000 rubles, which means that the difference reached 73,000 rubles.

We should also take climatic and natural conditions into consideration, which ultimately affect the living conditions in the Komi Republic and the Sverdlovsk District and also obviously affect the size of federal subsidies and other privileges. Let us therefore compare Komi this time with the Arkhangelsk and Murmansk Districts, where climatic conditions are the same if not worse than in the Komi Republic. In these regions, with a considerable portion of their territory within the Arctic Circle, the per capita balance in financial relations with the federal authorities is also negative and differs only slightly from the indicator for the Sverdlovsk District: In the Arkhangelsk Region it almost reaches a negative of −10,000, and in the Murmansk District it is also negative, at about −13,000 rubles.

On the whole, the ethnic republics paid two times less in taxes than the Russian regions. Karelia received the president's permission to keep 90 percent of all collected taxes. Komi and Iakutia enjoyed almost the same privileges, which prompted Russian authors to write about their "financial separatism." At the same time, one-half of the expenditures of the republics of the North Caucasus, Southern Siberia, and the Northeast were covered by federal allotments.[30]

These data prove without a doubt that the republics do have favorable financial relationships with the center. It is not the Russian regions that are milking the national republics. On the contrary, they serve as a milking cow for the national republics.[31] In addition, it is also clear that these financial relationships with the center greatly promote the ideology of privatization advanced by the Russian regions.

Ecology and the Conservation of the Old Culture

As the heirs to the old *oblastnichestvo*, regionalists have expressed their deep interest in the conservation of nature in their territories and are strongly convinced that the center is completely unconcerned about the dramatic and even catastrophic ecological developments in the provinces. Furthermore, in many cities the first political activities in 1988–1990 that can be viewed as having regional overtones involved the issue of the conservation of their provinces. Again, as the resuscitators of the *oblastnichestvo*, the regionalists included various actions in their programs aimed at the preservation of the old culture, including the protection of buildings and artifacts.[32]

14

THE CENTER AND REGIONS
IN THE PERIOD OF MARKETIZATION
OF THE ECONOMY

One of the most important areas in the struggle between the center and the regions was economics. For the most part, this struggle concentrated on the disposal of the taxes collected in the regions and on the property issue—that is, what property should be considered federal or local.

Taxes and the Budget

For moderate regionalists, a main point in their program was economics, with the focus on taxes. In 1993, the Russian regional budget made up about 15 percent of the GNP (gross national product). Most regional leaders found this to be too low. As in any other society, the regions, even in Soviet times, tried to eliminate the amount paid in federal taxes and to increase subsidies from the center.[1]

After 1991, regional demands for the redistribution of tax incomes became one of the most important elements in the regionalists' programs. The regions, especially the so-called donor regions, or economically powerful regions, demanded the radical diminution of the amount of money transferred to the center. These powerful regions were prepared to reject the center's subsidies, which usually made up a smaller portion of the money transferred to the donor regions from the federal budget. In 1992, for instance, transfers to the Russian regions totaled 3,518 billion rubles (budget transfers: 274 billion rubles, budget investments: 443 billion rubles, budget subsidies to agriculture: 358 billion rubles; direct credits: 1,980 billion rubles), whereas the transfers from these regions to Moscow amounted to 4,018 billion rubles.[2]

The donor regions regarded subsidies as a powerful form of leverage wielded by Moscow over local government and preferred to have independent financial resources. In 1993, they received only about one-half of all revenues given to the state treasury that had come from their regions.[3] Many regions, especially the more well-to-do ones, considered this unacceptable.

In the struggle for financial independence, a few regions achieved some significant successes in 1993–1995. Ultimately, they made some legal progress, increasing the portion they received of taxes even before the 1990s. In the late 1980s, for instance, they earned the right to retain the previous fiscal year's surplus and to introduce some additional local taxes.[4]

The next step in the legal extension of the regions' rights came on December 22, 1993, when the president issued the decree "On Certain Changes in the Taxation System and Relationships Between Budgets of Different Levels." This edict reduced the capabilities of the federal treasury, giving more opportunities to the regions.

In accordance with this decree, the part of the tax on profits to be channeled to the federal budget was rigidly fixed at 13 percent of all profits. As for the part to be channeled to the local budget, the regions got the right to vary it from 0 to 12 percent of the profits to be paid as tax. It was expected that in 1994 the implementation of this decree would result in the redistribution of resources between the federal and local budgets in the amount of 4 trillion rubles (in 1993 prices).

This presidential decree, while formally extending the rights of the regions, in fact made poorer regions even more dependent on the center than before. Since 30 percent of their enterprises did not make a profit, they consequently could not collect enough in taxes on profits to pay the budget, no matter what the tax rate was. Their only hope was to rely on subsidies from Moscow.

But as the capabilities of the federal budget, in this respect, were now reduced (in favor of those regions where there were less profit-losing enterprises), the chances of receiving a subsidy fully depended on a region's "exemplary" behavior. It can therefore be said that the greater the number of unprofitable enterprises in a region or territory, the lower the probability of regional separatism taking root there. The regions gained the right to seriously increase their revenues through fifteen federal taxes (on profit, a value-added tax, an excise tax, and other taxes). They were also allowed to set up an additional twenty-seven regional and local taxes that were at the total disposal of local authorities. At this point, in contrast to past practices, the regions gained full control of their budgets. Regional authorities continued in 1993–1995 to "bargain" with Moscow about their budget, but such bargaining only took place because these authorities tried to get additional subsidies and exemptions from the capital to balance their own budgets.[5] In general, the total portion of the consolidated federal budget allotted to the regional budgets changed from 28 percent in 1992 to 40 percent in 1993.[6]

However, most regional leaders—of course, mostly those from the "rich" regions—were dissatisfied with the existing situation. Thus, the year 1993 witnessed the regions' so-called tax coup. A number of regions (Volgograd, Iaroslavl, Samara, Krasnoiarsk, Altai, and several others) either stopped paying all taxes to the federal treasury or sharply reduced the amount contributed.[7] By the middle of 1993, thirty regions had not remitted their taxes to the Federal treasury on time.[8]

Regions tried to introduce a de facto system, legally called the "one-channel system." In this system, a region or, especially, the national republics would collect all taxes in its territory, sending a portion of them to the center. According to many Russian politicians, this was an idea that could undermine the unity of the country.[9] Indeed, such a practice would have caused the center to lose the ability, as in the past, to obtain money directly from its producers and citizens.

The impertinence of the regions was seemingly without limits. In 1993, Krasnoiarsk authorities decided to sue Moscow over various laws that had been passed encumbering the region's budget with additional expenditures that the regional authorities considered the center's responsibility to pay.[10]

It is remarkable that a few relatively rich regions since 1991 have revealed a tendency—a rather weak, though clearly pronounced tendency—to try to develop some level of independence from the official currency. In 1992, Boris Nemtsov, in order to cope with the lack of rubles for salaries in Nizhniy Novgorod, tried to replace them with regional obligations (they were named "Nemtsovki" by the populace), and in 1995 he also nurtured the idea of creating the region's own gold reserves in order to guarantee foreign investment.[11]

The non-Russian republics were the most aggressive in the tax war. Chechnia, Tatarstan, and Tuva virtually ceased paying their taxes in 1993.[12] Sakha-Iakutia and Bashkortostan regularly postponed the payment of their taxes, whereas Ingushetia and North Osetia declared themselves bankrupt and practically stopped transferring money to Moscow.[13]

In 1992–1993, the center began to negotiate with individual regions about their debts to the federal budget and yielded to many of the regions' demands. The outcome of these negotiations between the center and regions on taxes in 1992–1993 depended on various factors, including the personal relations between the regional and Moscow leaders and each region's political weight.

Of course, only relatively economically powerful regions could afford the tax war. Many Russian regions were so poor that they were totally dependent on Moscow and could not make ends meet without subsidies and credits on favorable terms from the center. Budget expenditures exceeded revenues by over 30 percent in the Amur, Chita, Kamchatka, Sakhalin, and Altai Regions, along with a few other regions.

By the end of 1995, both the center and the regions were discontent with each other. The regions continued to insist that the center was still trying to grab as much as possible for the federal budget and was still postponing the fulfillment of many of its obligations to the regions.[14]

The Struggle for Property

Property was a very formal issue in Soviet society. In the public mind, the single owner of all the means of production was the state—or the "society," according to official propaganda. In fact, the only serious distinction was between "socialist" and "personal" property. Although the individual could possess "objects of personal consumption, house, garden [or small plot] and labor savings," the rest of the country's wealth was declared to be "socialist."[15] "State" and "cooperative" properties were declared to be important but foreordained to disappear in the not-so-remote future. The distinction between the two (state property as "owned by the whole Soviet people" was "superior" to property owned by an individual "collective"), however, did not have implications for everyday life since the state controlled everything anyway.

The territorial dimension of property relations was also not of serious significance. Indeed, state enterprises were divided into three categories depending on who controlled them: "all-union" enterprises, which were under control of the all-union ministries; "republican" enterprises, controlled by the republican ministries; and "local" enterprises, controlled by the local authorities.

All-union enterprises made up two-thirds of industrial production and the others made up the remaining one-third.[16] From this one-third, no more than 7 to 10 percent was controlled by republican and local bodies, whereas the rest was controlled by the enterprises of the all-union republic. This meant the predominance of Moscow in running these types of enterprises.[17] At the same time, the concepts of federal, republican, or municipal property did not exist.

In post-Communist Russia, property relationships changed radically and, as in many other countries, several types of property emerged: public property in four forms—federal, republican, regional, and municipal—as well as private property of the Western type. Each type of property has its personal correlation—owners and managers. Public property is run by the bureaucracy, which controls property under its jurisdiction, and private property is owned by individuals or a collective of individuals.

The bureaucracy's struggle for the expansion of property under its command is one of the most important dimensions of regionalization. As one Moscow author contended, the whole issue on "sovereignty" is nothing more than "an episode in the fierce struggle for property that has embraced the entire former Soviet society."[18]

If, in the West, the division of resources between federal and local authorities is of secondary importance (the lion's share of resources belongs to private owners, although this division has little significance for tax policy), in Russia, the volume of public property is much higher and the types of administrative control over the means of production and natural resources—central or regional (especially in the first stage of privatization)—was of vital significance in Russia in 1992–1995, for the central as well as the local elite. For this reason, the program of serious regionalists included the establishment of maximum control over public assets in the region's territory.

As soon as regionalization took its first steps, the local elite immediately put the question of regional property rights before Moscow. Facing the necessity of having to revise property relations between the center and the periphery, Moscow was under pressure from the regionalist movement to become more willing to shift responsibilities for economic development to the provincial authorities. Ultimately, the Kremlin accepted many of the republics' and, to some degree, the regions' requirements on property issues.

At the same time, however, the central administration tried not to lose control over the country's major natural resources. In any case, the Russian Constitution of 1993 (Article 72.1) acknowledges that "the possession, usage and disposal of land, minerals, water and other natural resources are in common control of the Russian Federation and the subjects of the Federation."[19] The vagueness of this article, exemplified by the term "common control," reflected the fact that property relations between various levels of the administrative hierarchy, in the first years of the post-Communist era, were yet to be resolved and remained deeply complex in character and a continual source of permanent tension and conflict.

The National Republics

It was the non-Russian republican elites that particularly demanded the extension of their control over the means of production in their units.[20] Several times, the leaders of these republics openly declared that for them the distribution of property rights between the republics and the Russian Federation was the most important issue.[21]

In 1991–1992, the national republics tremendously increased the amount of production facilities and utilities under their jurisdiction. Whereas up to 80 to 90 percent of all enterprises in the republics were run by the ministries in Soviet times, in 1993–1995, 60 to 70 percent were directly controlled by local, republican authorities. In the Russian Federation in 1993, "the subjects of the federation" possessed, on average, 22 percent of all "privatized property," but some localities had a much greater percentage under their control: Kalmykia had 96 percent of all assets under its control; North Osetia possessed 83 percent; Iakutia and Altai had 81 percent; Dagestan controlled 65 percent; Tuva gained 52 percent; Mordovia commanded 41 percent; and Komi had 38 percent.[22]

Of special importance was control over natural resources. Iakutia, for instance, demanded and actually received partial control over its diamonds and gold, with only one-third of these resource rights going to Moscow. Moreover, Iakutia obtained the right to have access to the international diamond market. Bashkiria gained control over all its natural resources, such as its oil and a considerable part of its industry, including oil-processing and chemical industries.[23]

On the one hand, Moscow formally accepted the republics' claims for almost full control over their natural resources. Thus, the respective treaties signed in early 1995 between the Russian Federation and Tatarstan, Bashkortostan, and three other republics acknowledged that the land and its resources were the wealth of the republic. On the other hand, these treaties, stating that federal authorities had common control over at least some portions of the republics' natural resources, left Moscow with the legal opportunity to preserve or even increase its command over the resources of these administrative units.

The Russian Regions

Russian regions followed the patterns of the republics and also declared their need to have their regional resources under their jurisdiction. However, in this case Moscow was much more adamant in protecting its monopoly on natural resources than in its confrontation with the republics.

The case with the Orenburg Region is typical in this respect. In October 1994, the legislators of this region included in a statute an article concerning the rights to natural resources similar to the article in the national republics' constitutions. However, the Russian Ministry of Justice refused to accept this article, and Orenburg was forced to limit its control over these resources.[24]

Relations between Moscow and the Sverdlovsk Region were of the same character. In the aftermath of the parliamentary defeat in 1993, legislators simply repeated in the region's statute an article similar to that in the new Constitution, which spoke in a vague and murky way of "the Federation's and region's common control over natural resources." However, later in 1995, particularly after Eduard Rossel's victory in the gubernatorial election, legislators went on the offensive and began to fight Moscow, demanding its permission to include in the statue an article similar to the article in the republican constitutions underscoring the monopoly of the territory over its own resources.[25]

In addition to the larger regions claiming a monopoly over the resources located within their territory, the smaller ethnic districts began to claim sole ownership over their territories' resources. In 1994–1995, the Khanty-Mansi District fought for these rights with its superior regional authority, the Tiumen Region, which was itself "a subject of the Russian Federation." Via Sergei Sobianin, the chairman of the local parliament, the Khanty-Mansi District demanded full control over its natural resources, mostly oil (it supplies Russia with 30 percent of its hard currency), and direct contact with Moscow on the distribution of revenue.[26]

The center's and the provinces' antagonistic interests over property were wholly revealed during the process of privatization of state property in 1992–1995. Each side fought for control of this process. Since the composition of the Russian Parliament, in many cases, more accurately represented the interests of the provinces and not those of the center, several of the laws adopted by it rather helped the regions to gain control over this process. One such law was the "Law on the Privatization of State Enterprises and the General Principles of the Privatization of Municipal Enterprises of the Russian Federation," adopted by the Duma in October 1995. An expert on this subject qualified this law as one that permits "regions to fully regulate privatization."[27]

Local Administrative Control over Producers

In post-Communist Russia, the local political elite significantly increased its power not only over natural resources but also over private companies. This was accomplished in the main by using financial levers and local law enforcement forces now under complete control of the elite. Operating with a grip on taxes, energy prices, water, and other services, along with the power to grant or deny licenses and other "authorizations" and with the option to threaten to cut off energy and water supplies, local authorities possessed tremendous leverage over the local economy, power far more extensive than that of any first party secretary of the past.[28] The local authorities, using legal or illegal means, were able to extort from local businesses money for public projects as well as for personal gain.[29] In Toliati, for example, local authorities used their new power on a grand scale to pressure the local car industry in order to obtain additional money for the local budget.[30]

Regions Struggling for Economic Particularism

As they fought for autonomy in 1992–1995, the Russian regions came to be ardent agents of economic particularism. Indeed, the Russian provinces confronted Moscow as a united entity, as in summer 1993, when the Russian regions demanded that they be granted equal status with the non-Russian republics, and to some degree, also during the debates on the new Russian Constitution. However, in several cases, many individual Russian regions conducted their game with Moscow separately from the others, often demanding that they alone be granted special status and special privileges and completely ignoring the rest of the provinces.[31]

The "small republics" were, of course, the initiators of this economic particularism. Kalmykia demanded and received the right to keep for its own needs one-half the oil, gas, wool, and raw leather produced within the republic, whereas the export licenses became the prerogative of the republic. North Osetia was completely released from export duties on goods to be exported according to additional quotas; Bashkortostan won the right to keep 75 percent of its currency revenues for the republic; and Iakutia asked for special privileges in exporting diamonds.[32]

The Russian regions again followed the example of the non-Russian entities and, from 1989 on and particularly after 1991, have crusaded for "special treatment" on an individual basis. The Russian regions, most of them wealthy, fought with the center for various individual "exemptions."[33] For example, they demanded (and in many cases got) export privileges, whose profits would go to the regional, and not the state's, purse. Following suit, Irkutsk demanded special quotas for the export of timber; and Tiumen received oil and gas concessions. Many other regions, such as Kaliningrad, Arkhangelsk, Kemerovo, Ekaterinburg, Murmansk,[34] Cheliabinsk, Chita, and a few others, also demanded quotas for the export of their products.[35]

An important development in 1992–1993 was the participation of interregional associations, such as the Siberian Agreement, in pressuring Moscow to obtain the right to export raw materials abroad without the center's permission and to gain other privileges, as well.[36] The privileges obtained by certain regions only served to increase the general chaos and the widening gap between regions.

Remarkably, Moscow, which was supposed to be the champion of universalism, began to support particularism in its relationship with regions, with the probable rationale that the benefits of breaking the regions' unity were greater than the costs of promoting legal chaos in the country. Apparently moved by the above consideration, Moscow signed special agreements in 1994–1996 with individual republics and regions, arousing protest from those who saw these actions as a serious danger to the country's cohesion.

15

DIFFERENTIATION BETWEEN REGIONS IN THE STRUGGLE FOR AUTONOMY

As previously mentioned, on numerous occasions the Russian regions differed from each other in their relations with the center. The scale of these differences, which illustrates the degree of a region's "visibility" (by which we mean the amount of discussion that region received in the media) on the Russian scene, is quite lengthy. This statement is confirmed by our analysis of the visibility of individual Russian regions in the Russian media in 1992–1995, an indicator that indirectly reflects the regions' political activity. Seven hundred and sixty-six articles in thirteen leading Russian newspapers were included in the analysis.[1] The results are illustrated in Table 15.1.

To a very great degree, the visibility of the regions is connected with their activism in the regional movement. Indeed, all four of the most visible regions are champions of the struggle for autonomy. All three regions that rank second in degree of visibility are also renowned for their political activities, places such as Kemerovo, Vologda, and Novosibirsk, all known for their confrontations with Moscow on regional rights. Let us now study the factors that determine the intensity of the regions' claims for autonomy.

Population Size and Economic Might

The most powerful variable that determines the political activity of a region is the size of its population and its economic power. The variation in the size of the Russian regions is enormous (see Table 15.2).[2] Of the most visible regions in the country (see Table 15.1 for those regions that were discussed in ten or more articles), almost all, with the exception of Vologda, have populations of more than 2 million. In comparison, many of the least visible regions have populations of less than 2 million, and a few have populations of less than 1 million residents. Only

TABLE 15.1   Visibility of Russian Regions in the Media

Number of Articles Written	Name of Region
20 or more	Sverdlovsk, Nizhniy Novgorod, Maritime Territory, Moscow
10–19	Vologda, Kemerovo, Novosibirsk
5–9	Tambov, Samara, Arkhangelsk, Stavropol, Rostov, Perm, Krasnoiarsk, Khabarovsk, Kaliningrad
2–4	Tomsk, Tiumen, Cheliabinsk, Irkutsk, Novosibirsk, Orel, Tula, Iaroslavl, Voronezh, Lipetsk, Penza, Leningrad, Briansk, Saratov, Uilianovsk, Krasnodar
0–1	all others

Kaliningrad, of the eight regions with populations of less than 1 million, was quite visible in 1993–1995, in the Russian media.

The population size is correlated with the volume of economic activity in a region. The economic differences between regions were high even in the Soviet Union. We used data collected in the first half of 1995 to determine the relative economic might of the Russian regions (see Table 15.3).[3] Of the five regions with a maximal volume of industrial production, two were shown to be the most visible in the Russian media: Moscow and the Sverdlovsk Region. Among the six regions of the next group, two were also of primary visibility: Nizhniy Novgorod and the Moscow region. Three regions of the third group, Krasnoiarsk, Irkutsk, and Perm, ranked at third order of visibility, whereas Cheliabinsk was of the fourth order of visibility.

Differences in economic success had widened significantly, compared to the Soviet era. Using per capita incomes in 1990 as a comparison, we found that the most economically efficient region, Samara, surpassed the least economically efficient region, Kalmykia, by 6.5 times. With 1992 figures, we discovered that Tiumen, with the highest per capita national income level in the Russian Feder-

TABLE 15.2   Population Ranges of Russian Regions

Number of Regions	Population Range (in millions)
2	less than 0.5
6	0.5–1.0
25	1.0–2.0
9	2.0–3.0
11	3.0–5.0
2	more than 5.0

SOURCE: *Rossiiskii Statisticheskii Ezhegodnik* (Moskva: Goskomstat Rossii, 1994), pp. 441–443.

TABLE 15.3   Volume of Industrial Production in Russian Regions

Number of Regions	Volume of Industrial Production (Billions of Rubles)
5	more than 15,000
6	10,000–15,000
9	5,000–10,000
19	2,500–5,000
18	less than 2,500

SOURCE: *Gosstatkom Sotsialno-Ekonomicheskoie Polozhenie Rossii, January–June 1995* (Moskva: Goskomstat, 1995), pp. 158–160.

ation, outdid Dagestan by twenty-seven times. This per capita income gap was mostly a result of the changing structure of the Russian economy in 1992–1995.

The Higher Status of Larger, Wealthier Regions

The size of a region had some political importance even in the strongly central-ized USSR. For example, the Sverdlovsk Region was regarded as much more important than the Kursk or Kurgan Regions. The status of the regional party secretary in the country was also strongly proportional to the economic weight of the secretary's region.[4]

In post-Communist Russia, the larger a region's population and GNP, the greater the degree of the regional elite's political activity. The economically stronger regions become donors to the federal budget, whereas weaker regions need subsidies for their continued survival. Therefore, the higher a region's inde-pendence from the center's subsidies is, the greater that region's quest for auton-omy will be.

Since the economic factor is not the only one that influences the degree of regionalism in a region, there were cases when economically weaker regions could be highly visible for a short period of time as active participants in the regionalization effort, whereas economically powerful regions, such as Tiumen, could be almost totally passive.[5]

In general, the large, wealthy regions are not only more politically active than the small, poor regions, but they also act as the economic pioneers and models for the next tier of regions. From time to time, even a few of the relatively weaker regions joined their "big brothers" in the crusade for autonomy. However, these regions were quick to quit the struggle with the center as soon as they received its censure.

The cases of Vologda and Voronezh are characteristic of this trend. In mid-1993, Vologda tried to join the vanguard in the struggle for full regional auton-omy. Voronezh also joined the regionalization movement at the same time. Both regions, however, lacked promise from the "republicanization" point of view. These are small regions, the largest being the Voronezh District, which is only one-half the size of Kentucky or Tennessee. They also lag far behind the majority of the Ural and Siberian districts in population size. They have no natural resources to speak of, except for Voronezh's iron ore deposit in the area of the Kursk magnetic anomaly, which is mined in insignificant quantities in the Kursk and Belgorod Regions.

Both regions have nothing to boast of concerning their manufacturing industries. This is true not only for Vologda, which is mostly an agricultural region traditionally famous for its butter, but also for Voronezh, which has the reputation of an industrial city. After 1991, Voronezh's manufactured products, such as metal cutting lathes and even its famous aircraft, as well as forge-and-press equipment, excavators, agricultural machines, TVs, and radio sets, all of which fail to comply with world market requirements and are sold even within the country with great difficulty, were not in great demand. Despite these economic straits, the Voronezh District Soviet of People's Deputies adopted a declaration on September 3, 1993, to raise the district's status to the level of republic.[6]

However, the rebellions in Vologda and Voronezh, which had some political significance in 1993, gradually tapered off in October of that year. This was not the case for larger regions, such as Sverdlovsk or the Maritime Territory, which continued to play a significant political role after Yeltsin's victory over Parliament in 1993.

The Role of Economic Potential in Non-Russian Republics

Economic might, along with population size, is one of the factors that explains the great diversity of the political activities of the non-Russian republics. As the scores for the indicator of visibility of non-Russian regions (see Table 15.1) illustrate, the most prominent regions in the media were Chechnia (139), Tatarstan (57), Bashkortostan (33), Sakha-Iakutia (29), Kalmykia (26), and Chuvashia (23). Among the first four republics, two (Tatarstan and Sakha-Iakutia) owe their visibility mostly to their important economic power.

The economic potential of these republics helped them in their relationship with the center. The other republics' prominence was due to other circumstances, such as separatist movements (Chechnia) or unorthodox leadership (Kalmykia).

Moreover, analysis based on a region's visibility shows that most of the advocates of centralism in Russia were in relatively small or economically weak regions. Orenburg, Perm, Orel, Smolensk, and Volgograd were among the regions whose leadership supported the maintenance of a strong central government in 1993–1995. However, this list does not include the "strong" regions such as the Maritime Territory, Nizhniy Novgorod, Kaliningrad, and Sverdlovsk.

The economic regional differentiation in post-Communist Russia also brought new elements, such as the conflict between Moscow and provincial private businesses, to the forefront. Having lost much of its power as the administrative center of the country, Moscow was able to rally its economic power, particularly through financial institutions. The expansion of these institutions in the provinces met with the resistance of a significant number of the local businesses in the economically rich provinces. Local businesses that did not resist the center were ready to serve Moscow as its representative in the provinces. In other words, the higher the level of investment is in a region, the more willing the region is to protect itself against the capital.

The experience of the Ural Region best illustrates this statement. Local authorities and businessmen, besides those who represent Moscow money, were continually confronting Moscow companies that tried to seize control of Uralmash, a leading factory in the region. The Ural financial corporation InVur was supported by local forces as the main defense against Moscow expansion.[7]

Natural Resources as
a Factor of Regional Power

The economic gap between the strong and weak regions widened during the transition from a centrally planned economy to a market economy. Although some regions weathered the bad times quite well, others were not able to survive 1993–1994 without constant help from the all-Russian center. The variance in the number of insolvent enterprises across the country illustrates how much the regions differed from each other during the process of adjustment.[8]

The climate of the transition process to a market economy was most favorable for regions that produced raw materials and much less favorable for those that had a highly developed manufacturing industry, particularly those that produced weapons or machinery, especially agricultural machinery. Among the consequences of this process, the "weight" of the Russian economy shifted to the east, to regions rich with natural resources, and away from the west, from regions dependent upon manufacturing industry.[9]

Official unemployment data from the end of 1993, even if it underestimates by at least two to three times the real unemployment rate, is also a good indicator of the adaptation of the Russian regions to the new economic order. Indeed, in twenty-eight Russian regions the official unemployment rate was less than 1 percent of the labor force, whereas this number was two to four times higher in nine of the other regions. In Ivanovo and Iaroslavl, it had almost reached 5 percent.[10]

Not only the general size of the region's economic potential but also its structure is of the greatest importance in determining the region's role in Russian politics, in regionalization, and in its relations with the center. The most important role to a region is foreign trade.

After the Soviet Union's collapse and the demilitarization of society, the Russian economy entered the entire world market. Very soon, it became evident that Russian survival depended upon the export of raw materials, such as gas, oil, and semiprocessed products like iron and nonferrous metals. At the same time, with the Russian economy's inability to compete with foreign producers of consumer goods, Russia became dependent on mass imports of these products. This orientation of the Russian economy, toward exporting raw materials and importing consumer goods, determined, to a great degree, both the economic status of the regions and the elite's policy.

The key role of exports in the Russian economy benefits only regions rich in natural resources, which therefore have the opportunity to export. In post-Communist Russia, export potential thus became the leading indicator of a region's prosperity and standard of living.[11]

A number of regions in Russia radically distinguish themselves from the rest of the country with their special export possibilities: Of total Russian exports, the Volga Region had 17.8 percent (including Samara, with 12.4 percent); Western Siberia had 22.4 percent (including Tiumen, with 17.2 percent); Ural had 14.6 percent; the Central Region had 7.7 percent (including Moscow's 2 percent); the Far East had 6.3 percent; and the Northwest Region had 2.4 percent.[12]

The export potential significantly increases the local elite's leverage in its relations with the center. But at the same time, it also increases the willingness of the center to maintain control over regions rich in natural resources. It is the regions with high export potential (these regions are extroverts, using the terminology of a Russian geographer) that fight for maximum autonomy, whereas regions with weak export potential (these regions are described as introverts) are more likely to be on the centralists' side. These weaker regions also advocate a state-regulated economy and, of course, high state subsidies from the center to aid the regions.[13]

In general, all other things considered, the greater a region's export possibilities, the greater its desire for autonomy. The case of Sakha-Iakutia serves as an excellent example. Due to the territory's prosperous diamond industry, this republic's leadership, despite its small population, was as politically active in 1991–1995 as the leadership of several other large republics and regions.[14]

Distance from Moscow as a Determinant of Regionalism

One of the most powerful factors influencing the intensity of regionalization is the country's size and the region's location if the country is relatively large. The Soviet Union, building on the foundations of the Russian empire, emerged as the largest country in the world. With its totalitarian society, the unity of the country was secured by a gigantic, coercive apparatus and a strong patriotic ideology. After 1991, Russia entered a new stage in its history, and its size began to conflict with the new political and economic order.[15] Post-Communist developments jeopardized many areas of the actively demanding sections of the budget, and the regional focus, using Vladimir Kontorovich's phrase, shifted "from the Russian ballet, the best in the world, and Russian science to the various remote territories."[16]

Two intertwining circumstances are also extremely important in this respect: distance from the capital and proximity to foreign borders.

The size of the country has always been a powerful factor in determining the nature of relations between the center and the provinces. Regions located far from the capital, such as the Russian Far East, Kaliningrad, and the Northern Territories, tended to be alienated from the mother country merely for geographical reasons, even if their leaders did not harbor separatist feelings or the desire to join another country, although, of course, nobody could have predicted the future circumstances that would cause these feelings suddenly to emerge.

Distance began to play a special role when the country started to move from a totalitarian state with a centrally planned economy to a liberal society with a market economy. Transportation costs were also quite important for the Soviet and the pre-1917 Russian economy. As previously mentioned, Soviet economists tried, particularly in the post-Stalin era, to discover how to minimize transportation costs, mostly by trying to allocating production better. The Kremlin was always aware of the strategic importance of cheap, quick transportation, particularly via railroad, to the strength and unity of the country. Ignoring real transportation costs by granting gigantic subsidies, the Soviet system made transportation services affordable for producers as well as for ordinary Russians.[17]

With the transition to a market economy and the inability of the state to subsidize transportation costs as in the past, the Russian transportation system proved to be unable to adequately perform its previous functions. The volume of transportation declined immensely. As a result, the transportation of commodities decreased in 1990–1993, by 40 to 50 percent (the railways by 37 percent). The transportation of passengers by rail has decreased 26 percent, and air passenger transportation has fallen 54 percent.[18]

More important for the country was the excessive cost of transportation between the European and Asian parts of the country. These costs account for the reason the remoter regions of the country have significantly changed their economic structures and their trading partners, whom they now search out primarily among foreign countries.

High transport costs, along with several other factors, including the lack of information and the obstacles created by local administrations against the free flow of commodities, explain why Russian "economic common space" was significantly curtailed in 1992–1994. Evidence of these developments lies in the increased disparity in prices of almost all goods and in the emergence of "the fragmentation market for these same goods," using the expression of many Russian authors.[19] The same goods of the same quality were sold in different regions at very different prices. The disparity in prices of some goods, for example, coal and electricity, reached a 1:6 ratio. Let us now speak specifically of these three remote territories: the Northern Territories, Kaliningrad, and the Russian Far East.

The Question of the Northern Territories

Russia's Northern Territories envelopes a huge portion of northern European Russia and Asia, from the Kolski Peninsula to the Chukotka Peninsula as well as to the eastern reaches of the Far East, which makes up one-third of the Russian Federation's territory. There are thirty-five relatively large cities in this region, including Murmansk, Norilsk, Vorkuta, and Magadan. In the Soviet Union, this territory was considered to be both strategically important and a source of extremely valuable raw materials, such as oil, gas, coal, gold, diamonds, and furs, among others. No less than 50 percent of the total national income was generated from this region. The Soviet state generously subsidized this region, which attracted millions of Russians, since incomes were high.

With the collapse of the Soviet Union, the well-lubricated mechanism sustaining these territories almost immediately corroded. Left to its own care, the northern region began to quickly fall apart. Personal incomes dropped tremendously. New housing construction declined significantly.[20] The high price of energy paralyzed the network of many social institutions, such as kindergartens, hospitals, and various other services. The delivery of consumer goods during the short period in the summer when the Arctic Ocean is navigable, a very important campaign in the Soviet times, was not carried out on time, creating incredible problems in satisfying the basic needs of the local population.

From time to time in 1993–1995, the local authorities in various northern cities—Arkhangelsk in 1994 was one of them—declared the situation to be critical and predicted severe catastrophes, mostly because of the lack of oil or coal for power stations. Fortunately, these catastrophes did not materialize.

The steady decline in the number of residents had already begun in 1993. This toll would have been even higher if the economic situation in many of the regions to which residents wanted to return, such as Ukraine or other areas in Russia, had not also been in bad shape. The increasing numbers of desperate people from Ukraine who moved north looking for seasonal work also somewhat diminished the decline in the number of people living in the north.

In the highest echelons of power in 1993–1995, there were discussions about the future of the Northern Territories, which could not sustain itself without gigantic subsidies. It appears that some factions were able to convince many of the others that it was in the highest interest of the country to support the region by all means possible.[21]

The Fate of Kaliningrad

The Kaliningrad Region, dating from the time of East Prussia, was seized by the Soviet Union as one of its prizes in its victory over Germany in 1945. As long as the Soviet political and economic machine was strong and Lithuania remained a part of the Soviet Union, the region did not differ from the other remote territories of the Soviet Union. However, when these conditions disappeared, the fate of Kaliningrad immediately became problematic. At the same time, the importance of this region as the sole Russian port on the Baltic Sea only increased with the collapse of the Soviet Union.

In 1992–1993, the region stood out in the country in several key aspects. Almost immediately after 1991, communication difficulties between the Kaliningrad enclave and Russia emerged. Since Russian trains must cross the sovereign states of Lithuania and Byelorussia, a number of problems were created for passengers and commodities. This was particularly important in that it led to increases in the prices of goods from Russia to such an extent that in 1994–1995 Kaliningrad was one of the most expensive cities in the country.

Foreign firms became particularly active in this area, probably more so than any other region in the country, including the Far East, with which Kaliningrad has been always compared. In the beginning it was particularly German businessmen who were active in entering the economy of the region. This huge influx of foreign business interests caused many Russian politicians to speak out about the "Germanization" of Kaliningrad. However, the period of prevailing German activity diminished, though it did not cease to play an important role. This role inspired an article published in *Pravda* that prophesied that Kaliningrad would suffer the same fate as Alaska—to be sold at a ridiculous price to foreigners.[22]

The Kaliningrad Region was then turned into a dumping ground for illegal transfers of Russian raw materials at artificially low prices designed to undercut all other prices. At the same time, in 1994, the number of drug-related crimes there was six times higher than in Russia on the whole. The number of smuggling-related crimes increased to twenty times higher than previous levels.

The Separation of the Far East Region

The transition from a command economy to a market economy almost immediately raises the question of how Russia, as a country stretching from the Baltic Sea to the Sea of Japan, can maintain its cohesiveness at the end of the twentieth century. Transportation and communication costs, by themselves, make the economic interaction between the Far East and the European portions of Russia, in many cases, inefficient.

Trade between the Far East and its neighboring countries, such as China, Japan, and South Korea, surpasses economic connections with western Russia more and more. As Viktor Ishaiev, governor of the Khabarovsk territory, declared, "Here is horror: It is not profitable for us to trade with Russia and gradually we turn our back to it." Furthermore, as the governor added, "the separation of the Far East is already a fact."[23] At the same time, the reduced resources at the disposal of the central administration do not allow Moscow to subsidize its remote territories as much as in the past.

The gradual alienation of the Far Eastern Russian population from the European parts of Russia is also a serious factor. Residents of the Far East and even Siberia are gradually receding psychologically from Moscow and travel to the European parts of Russia and even speak on the phone with their compatriots less and less often. Airline tickets from the Far East to Moscow are several times higher than the average monthly salaries of Russians in the East. Most residents of this area do not read Moscow newspapers and journals and have become almost completely apathetic about Moscow political life.

The Importance of Close Proximity to Foreign Countries

The distance from foreign countries also significantly influences regional life and a region's relations with the center. Certainly, in combination with a region's remoteness from the capital, this factor can very much affect feelings of regionalization and even separatism.

After the collapse of the Soviet Union, the number of Russian administrative units that share a border with a foreign country increased from twenty-nine to forty-six. This circumstance, in the opinion of a Russian expert on regionalization, portended significant developments for the future, unless some preventive measures were taken.[24]

The character and degree of the foreign influence depends very much on the sort of country the Russian region shares a border with—that is, whether it is an "old" country (one of the "remote abroad" nations) or a "new" country (the "near abroad").

The propensity of an "old" foreign country to interact significantly affects the life of a border region and its relationship with the center. These Russian border regions can promote foreign trade and get hard currency much more easily than the Russian inner regions. These circumstances make a region less economically dependent on the rest of the country, and because of this, its desire for self-government increases.

The "Old" Foreign Countries

St. Petersburg's proximity to Finland and the other Scandinavian countries has strengthened its position in post-Communist Russia in its quest for more autonomy from Moscow. It also explains, at least partially, why the idea of separation from Russia could emerge, even if only half seriously, in the minds of St. Petersburg politicians in summer 1993, when Russian regionalism reached its peak.

The closeness of Vladivostok and Khabarovsk to foreign countries, especially China, Japan, and South Korea, and the extreme distance from Moscow became an extremely important factor in the economic and political processes in both the Maritime Territory and the Khabarovsk Territory.[25]

Of course, the closeness to the "old" foreign countries is not enough to explain the variance of regionalism across the country, since several dozen variables shape the intensity of regionalization.[26]

The "New" Foreign Countries

As previously mentioned, after 1991 several Russian regions became the immediate neighbors of the Commonwealth of Independent States. Although the proximity of the "old" foreign countries became a factor in stimulating foreign trade and, ultimately, autonomist tendencies, the emergence of the CIS had a rather adverse effect on the economic situation and tended to support anticentrifugal tendencies. Indeed, almost all of the regions neighboring Ukraine or Kazakhstan saw their economic transactions with these republics curtailed.[27]

However, even more important is the fact that in all of the CIS, with the exception of the Baltic republics, the economic recession since 1991 has been much higher than in Russia. The influx of seasonal workers and emigrants into these regions from former Soviet republics, particularly from the Russian regions in the North Caucasus, has created a lot of problems in increasing the tensions and conflicts in their territories.[28]

As a result, the closeness to former Soviet republics, especially those with Muslim populations, is in no way a factor encouraging the Russian regions to challenge the center. Rather, this proximity affects these regions in the opposite way and causes them to support a powerful, centralized state.

The Russian Regions in the North Caucasus

The Russian regions in the North Caucasus, including Stavropol and Krasnodar, have to be included in this category of Russian regions, even if their greatest preoccupation is not only their proximity to Georgia, Azerbaijan, and Armenia but also their closeness to "Russian" republics, such as Chechnia, Dagestan, and several others. For this reason, the political mood in 1992–1995 in Stavropol and Krasnodar was significantly different from the rest of the country. The populations here voted for Communists and nationalists more actively than in many of the other regions, and the antagonistic attitude toward non-Russians was much stronger than elsewhere. The presence of Cossacks in these areas also significantly contributed to the transformation of these regions in 1992–1995 into a stronghold for those promoting a "great and indivisible" Russia.

The proximity of these foreign countries and particular non-Russian republics had a contradictory influence on Stavropol and Krasnodar, both enhancing autonomist and even separatist tendencies and cultivating procenter feelings. In general, this effect is particularly true for those regions whose neighboring countries have deeply alien cultures, such as those in the Russian Far East.

The Role of Cultural Homogeneity in Regionalization

It is almost certain that the greater the cultural heterogeneity of a country is, the greater the potential for regionalization and even separatism becomes. However, cultural specificity is not the same as ethnic specificity. Ultimately, we identify Samuel Huntington's differences between civilizations.[29]

Ethnic minorities living in the Russian Federation differ from each other only in the degree to which they have been assimilated into the Russian culture or in their degree of active alienation from it. They also differ in the degree to which they accept the civilization to which the Russians belong, which can be described as a subclass of the Western civilization.[30] There are big differences between people such as Chechens (along with several other Caucasian people) and Tatars, along with several other peoples in the Volga area. For example, the Tatars are much more integrated into Russian culture than the Chechens, even if they now live outside their republics.

Seemingly, the history of every empire, almost without exception, including multinational states, supports the thesis that heterogeneity leads to regionalization. Of course, the quest for autonomy is always present even in relatively homogeneous countries such as Germany or Japan. However, regionalism increases with the growth of ethnic and cultural diversity.

Modern regionalization is provoked not so much by ethnic and cultural specificity as it is by new global trends. However, ethnic and cultural factors, vigorously used by regional elites to strengthen their cause, foment feelings of hostility to the center and the dominant ethnic group.

Of course, the greater the ethnic and cultural specificity of a region or a group, the greater the quest for more autonomy. The case of Chechnia, where the Caucasian ethnicity and Muslim culture is quite alien to Russia, is a prime example. The most consistent fighters for greater autonomy and even full independence are the regions with non-Russians as either the majority, as in Chechnia, or at least as the largest ethnic group, as in Tatarstan or Bashkiria. Greater variation from the Russian culture accounts for many of the differences in the role of local nationalists in Chechnia and Tatarstan.

The cultural factor also plays a significant role as an accelerator of regional tendencies in pure Russian regions. The Cossacks' case demonstrates this correlation well. Another good example is the case involving the Pomors. The Pomors are much less demanding than the Cossacks. They have neither the traditional Cossack militancy nor ancient claims to neighboring national republics. However, the movement called Pomor Renaissance still bears a cultural character. As

Alexei Bednov, one of the leaders of this movement, said in spring 1994, the Pomors do not lay claim to territorial redivision. In their opinion, the Arkhangelsk Region should be given the Pomor Republic's status. The Pomor leaders never insisted on a differentiation of rights between the native inhabitants and the rest of the population.

Furthermore, regionalism caused the emergence, and in some cases a renewal, as in Siberia, of interests in the region's cultural traditions. In this way, it contributed to the spiritual retreat from Moscow and the national culture. The process is particularly prominent in Siberia and in several Russian cities in European Russia, including Tver and Iaroslavl, among others.

16

THE REGIONALIZATION AND POLITICAL FRAGMENTATION OF RUSSIA

Significant differences among the Russian regions in size, economic power, and location, along with the declining role of Moscow as an uniting force, led to a strong differentiation among regions in the quality of life and, particularly, in politics. This, in turn, brought about the significant political fragmentation of the country.

Regional Differences in the Quality of Life

In a totalitarian state, regional differences in the quality of life have minimal influence on the country's political processes. However, in a semidemocratic or fully democratic society, their significance is high and very much affects the ability of regions to cooperate with each other in political actions. Indeed, in the Soviet Union, as in any other country, regional differences in the standard of living were quite high.

Differences During the Soviet Period

The main cause of these differences was not variations in prices and wages. The Soviet central planning apparatus set almost the same rigid prices and wages for all regions in the country, although they were somewhat higher for the more remote regions. The main reason for the different quality of life was the variable attitude of the center toward a region, that is, the determinant was whether the center considered a region, or a given city, to be important to it. The center's attitude determined the supply of goods sent to the region and the amount of investment for the construction of houses and various residential facilities, such as schools, hospitals, and cultural institutions.[1]

In the post-Stalin period, the country was divided into a number of zones, which were further stratified into an hierarchy of the quality of life. Moscow was the most privileged city, followed by Leningrad and several other industrial centers such as Sverdlovsk, Volgograd, Novosibirsk, and a few others.[2] Many large cities, such as Saratov and Voronezh, were included in the next supply zone. The medium-sized and small cities were on the lowest rung in the center's hierarchy of attention to human needs and were only a little better off than villages.

There were also a few other factors, such as climate, ecological conditions, and free markets for food, that accounted for regional differences in the quality of life.[3] Some of these factors—such as the ecological conditions of life and climate—could only exacerbate the differences, despite the state's attempts to compensate for the hardships of life in such regions. Some factors, such as less expensive food in the countryside than in large industrial cities, which enjoyed a better supply of goods, could, to some degree, mitigate the "unfairness" of the state's policy toward the regions.

In any case, differences in the quality of life in Communist Russia were enormous.[4] According to some calculations, these variations in standards of living, on average, had a ratio of 1:3.[5] Additional data show that a Moscow resident's standard of living was three to four times higher than his counterpart living in a village or in a small city, with the same salary.[6]

Regional differences in housing conditions,[7] as well as differences in climate and ecological conditions, were enormous in Soviet times,[8] and these differences were "transferred" to post-Communist Russia.[9] Although the differences between the country's cities and regions were extreme in the Soviet era, they had no political significance, since any grumbling about the quality of life was a state crime.

Income Differences as the New Determinant

Differences between the center and regions changed radically in post-Communist Russia. Certainly, the supply of consumer goods regulated by the state ceased to be a factor in determining the quality of life. In post-Communist Russia, residents of the most remote regions can buy goods that were previously only available to members of the Politburo.

In addition, income became a major factor in explaining the regional differentiation in standards of living in post-Communist Russia. The variation of prices, a factor of insignificant importance for a developed market economy, also became a considerable factor affecting the country's standard of living.[10]

The Growth of Interregional Differentiation

By all accounts, interregional differentiation increased significantly in 1992–1995 in post-Communist Russia. The ratio of regions with the highest to lowest levels of consumption was 1:3 in the Soviet Union, but it increased in post-Communist Russia to 1:7. In 1993, the ratio of "expensive" to "cheap" regions was 1:5, whereas in the past it was 1:3.[11]

Europe and Asia

In general, life in Russia's Asian possessions is significantly worse than in European Russia. According to a VTSIOM survey conducted in 1993, people's satisfaction with different elements of their life gradually declined as one moved eastward in the country. The survey found that ecological conditions were considered to be "very bad" by 25 percent of the residents of Central European Russia, by 29.4 percent of residents in the Ural Region, by 32.9 percent of those in Siberia, and by 34.8 percent by residents of the Russian Far East. In addition, 23 percent of the residents of Central European Russia expressed their "complete dissatisfaction with their life," as opposed to 27 percent in Siberia and the Russian Far East.

Some Consequences

The ever-increasing differences in the population's standard of living have contradictory effects on the integrity of Russia. These differences are now a factor that threatens the national unity and at the same time makes difficult the broad alliance of regions' solidarity in pursuing political or economic goals against the center.

These regional differences in the quality of life increase the mutual animosity between people living in poor and rich regions. People in poor regions blame the rest of the country for their "exploitation" or, at best, "neglect." People in rich regions accuse others of possessing a "welfare mentality" and of unwillingness to work as hard as they do.

These same debates also took place during the last years of the former Soviet Union, when all of the republics blamed each other for their own problems. They evidently contributed to the growing interregional animosity and final collapse of the USSR.[12]

The Territorial and Political Fragmentation of Russia

The large differences in the standard of living among regions is not the sole factor accounting for the high political fragmentation in Russia. Other factors include the population's social stratification, the region's political traditions, and the charisma of political leaders with different political orientations. All these factors explain why the political climate in the Russian regions varies so much. In 1991–1996, the differences between regions in their popular attitudes toward various political parties and leaders were quite high.

There have been three politically very different zones in the country. The first zone, consisting of Moscow and St. Petersburg, were the democrats' strongholds in 1992–1996. During the parliamentary elections of 1993 and, particularly, 1995, as well as during the 1996 presidential elections, both Russian capitals voted radically differently from the rest of the country. Moscow, the symbol of Russian power over the centuries, appeared to be "against Russia," during the 1995 elections.[13] It is interesting to note that some of the larger Russian cities, like Ekaterinburg and Nizhniy Novgorod, are very close in political behavior to the capital.

The second political zone is the "red belt," including Belgorod, Briansk, Voronezh, Kaluga, Kursk, Lipetsk, Orel, Smolensk, Tambov, and Volgograd—all European regions located in the black-soil and non-black-soil regions, where Communists and nationalists won in local elections in 1994–1995. The populations of these regions were more negative toward Yeltsin's reforms and more critical of the president himself during the referendum in April 1993 than the rest of the country.[14] In twelve regions, mostly in black-soil and non-black-soil areas, significant numbers of people voted against the Yeltsin Constitution on December 12, 1993.[15]

The third political zone was located in Siberia and the Russian Far East, where nationalists were particularly successful and the people's opposition to Yeltsin's regime was much more active than in European Russia.[16] For example, the variance in the results of the December 1993 election was quite high. The percentage of people who voted for Egor Gaidar's Russia's Choice varied from 4.7 percent in the northwest area to 16.1 percent in Moscow, whereas the same indicator for Vladimir Zhirinovsky's party oscillated between 4.2 percent in the central area to 27.2 percent in the Far East.[17] The results of the December 1995 parliamentary election and the 1996 presidential election were the same: The variance in voting behavior was immense.

The 1994–1995 local election could only confirm this regularity, which revealed even more conspicuously than the parliamentary or presidential elections the existence of various zones with different political orientations. The victory of the Communists and local bureaucrats was overwhelming in Krasnodar, Ivanovo, Chuvashia, and, of course, the regions of the black-soil zone. The "red belt," in 1993–1995, contained the most ardent and consistent foes of Yeltsin's region and reforms.[18]

In 1991–1995, the non-Russian republics had occupied special positions on the Russian political map. Most of them were conservative. In March 1995, Communists and old local bureaucrats in virtually all ethnic republics, such as Tatarstan, Udmurtia, North Osetia, and Bashkortostan, gained a majority in the election of local legislatures.[19]

There are also some differences by locality in people's readiness to take part in mass demonstrations. According to VTSIOM's survey, in answer to the question "Will you take part in protests against the rising prices and the falling standards of living," the average percentage of people who answered "quite likely" was significantly higher in Siberia and the Far East than it was in European Russia.

Indeed, in 1994, belief in imminent spontaneous popular demonstrations against the authorities was growing, according to VTSIOM polls, its frequency moving eastward, from 44.1 percent in European portions of Russia to 45.4 percent in Ural, 49.8 percent in Siberia, and 50.4 percent in the Far East. When respondents were asked whether they would take part, the answer "yes" was given by 21.3 percent of the European Russian residents, 25.3 percent of Ural residents, 29.6 percent of Siberian residents, and 27.6 percent of Russians in the Far East.

Regional Differences in Post-Communist Politics

Regional autonomy opened the way to stronger policy differentiation in a period when Russia was changing its economic structure. In some regions, members of the local elite staked their political careers on accelerating privatization and marketization of the local economy. Simultaneously, in other regions, the same elite chose a policy of diminishing the rate of economic transformation as much as possible, waiting for the moment when Moscow's ruling regime would change. The high autonomy of the local elite permitted such differentiation in policy, in the economic and other spheres. To some degree, the differences in the regional elite's stance toward the metamorphosis of Russian society reflected the differences in the population's attitudes toward reform.

The degree of privatization of apartments is a good indicator of the differentiation among regions in economic policy. It oscillated between 9 percent (Ulianovsk) and 43 percent in Altai.[20] The privatization of small businesses also varied significantly in the country. In Krasnoiarsk, 57 percent of all small business workers were employed in private enterprises in 1993, yet in Moscow, this figure was 95 percent.[21] According to available information for mid–1993, in thirty Russian regions, prices were essentially free market; in ten other Russian regions, prices were strongly regulated; and in the rest of the Russian regions, the authorities used a mixed policy.

A Comparison of Two Radically Different Regions

The Nizhniy Novgorod and Ulianovsk Districts are classical examples of the two different approaches—of the regional elite's two forms of behavior in the stormy sea of economic shock. The Ulianovsk District is mostly an agrarian economy, whereas Nizhniy Novgorod has an industrial emphasis. The former is, to a certain extent, self-sufficient in foodstuffs. For the latter, a policy of agrarian autarchy was ruled out. In 1992, the Ulianovsk District produced 70.6 kilograms of meat per capita, compared to the Nizhniy Novgorod District's production of

46.7 kilograms of meat per capita. Their respective production of milk was 439.6 kilograms and 330.7 kilograms; of eggs, 406 kilograms and 345 kilograms, respectively.

Nizhniy Novgorod was headed by the young intellectual, Boris Nemtsov, an active democrat who chose to follow a liberal economic model in 1991.[22] The regional authorities declared their full orientation toward the Western model of economic development.[23] They actively promoted entrepreneurship and persistently carried out small-scale privatization. In 1993, they invited Grigorii Iavlinskii, a famous advocate of reforms, to visit and even claimed to be ahead of Moscow in establishing radical reforms.[24]

The local administration was initially very proud of its privatization of trucks and then of its elaboration of the special privatization program for collective farms. Prices were freed, and subsidies were used not to keep prices at low levels but to either raise the income level of people who were in the low-income brackets or to provide subsidies to those whose incomes fell below the subsistence level to bring their incomes up to this minimal level. In the same manner, subsidies were given not to the housing economy but to tenants for their rent payment. The creation of mixed private-municipal enterprises was encouraged in the priority branches of agriculture, such as in the production of combined fodder.

The style of political and economic life instituted in Ulianovsk was radically different from the Nizhniy Novgorod experiment. Within a very short period of time, Ulianovsk leaders first followed the same Western rituals as Nizhniy Novgorod, then returned Ulianovsk to the rules of Soviet life. Yurii Goriachev, former first regional party secretary, rather than playing the role of reformer, chose to function instead as the population's paternalistic leader, or father. In this capacity, without rejecting moderate egalitarianism, he became absorbed with the desire to make his people's lives at least tolerable, and he was not ashamed to resort to the old Soviet instruments, such as regulating prices and rationing food.

Economic policies in Ulianovsk were based on entirely different principles than in Nizhniy Novgorod—and these principles were also those supported by the Kremlin. Goriachev sought his base of popular support from among the masses, taking on the role of "leader of the masses," even though he had tried to ingratiate himself with the democrats at the beginning of his career as governor in post-Communist Russia, a strategy he abandoned in 1993.

In 1991–1995, the Ulianovsk leaders managed to keep the old network of party apparatchiks and managers in the countryside almost intact. The regional leaders also decided to retain the collective farm system as long as possible. Ulianovsk's leaders actively blocked privatization, and as previously mentioned, the regional rate of privatization of apartments was the lowest in the country.

In order to earn the population's support, the Ulianovsk leaders generously subsidized food in their region, making prices of basic goods in the region the lowest in the country. In 1992–1995, they widely used rationing with a coupon system, where people were entitled to buy food at a lower price than in free markets.

Obviously, it is possible to have permanently low prices on foodstuffs only if two conditions are observed: Distribution must be rationed, and exports to other regions must be prohibited.[25] Prices in the Ulianovsk District were much lower than in Nizhniy Novgorod, whereas per capita monetary incomes were practically equal, which made it possible to maintain the standard of living and social peace.[26] For these reasons, the attitude toward privatization in Ulianovsk is much more reserved.

The Ulianovsk authorities found money for their subsidies in a new local tax on each type of industrial good exported to other regions, primarily cars and aircraft, which amounted to 10 percent of the cost and was intended "to stabilize the social and economic situation." They also introduced a number of other taxes on banks, on vendors, and on market and other economic institutions.[27]

Ultimately, in 1993–1994, the competition between the two regions over raising the standard of living was watched by the whole country. Ulianovsk, with much lower levels of privatization, provided a better life for its citizens.[28] Ulianovsk and Nizhniy Novgorod, which both became myths in the Russian political struggle, were the object of harsh attacks from the democrats and Communists in 1994–1995 and have followers among regional leaders.[29] Of course, the democrats condemned the leadership of Ulianovsk, whereas it was primarily the Communists, although there were others as well, who encouraged that district's policies.

Democrats praised the "Nizhniy Novgorod experience," presenting it as the "capital of Russian reforms," while asserting that Ulianovsk was a "Communist preserve" and that its prevalence was only temporary.[30] Likewise, the Communists spoke of the "degradation" of Nizhniy Novgorod and accused Nemtsov of political exhibitionism and personal favoritism toward the businessmen who had generously financed the 1993 election campaign that brought him to the Russian senate.[31] At the same time, Communists described Ulianovsk's success as further evidence of the Yeltsin regime's failure. In 1994–1996, Russian newspapers systematically published articles predicting economic collapse in both regions, though, of course, for different reasons.[32]

The greatest challengers to Moscow's economic policy were the non-Russian republics. Among them, of course, was Tatarstan, whose leadership stubbornly rejected ideas of "shock therapy," and, until 1995, the region was supported by large collective farm subsidies.[33] Strong resistance to economic reforms, particularly in regard to the privatization of land, was quite prevalent in Bashkortostan.[34] In any case, the differences in economic policy of the various regions contributed to an increase of heterogeneity throughout the Russian Federation.[35]

17

REGIONS IN COALITION AGAINST THE CENTER

In their permanent confrontation with the center, open or hidden, regions resort, as in any game with a number of participants, to forming coalitions among themselves.

National Bodies Representing the Provinces

Russian regions created a number of organizations that strengthened their power in the struggle for dominance with the center. Many of these organizations, as a result of the convoluted character of the Russian political processes, even emerged at the initiative of the Kremlin, which always tried to use any political organization as its own instrument of power.

In 1992, at the very beginning of the center-periphery confrontation, there emerged, as previously mentioned, an organization of Russian regional leaders called the Association of Governors, which began to play a visible political role in the country.[1] In their turn, many presidents of non-Russian republics actively supported the Council of Republican Leaders.[2] Irregular meetings of the heads of the national republics were also held, creating another in which they could communicate and cooperate in the elaboration of a common policy toward Moscow.[3]

More important, there were similar bodies that emerged in the Russian Parliament. Various factions in the Duma thought it important to defend regional interests and joined the emerging movement Russian Regions in 1995.[4]

However, the most important body representing the regions came to be the Federal Council, which consists of two representatives from each region in the Russian Federation, as discussed earlier.

Regional Consolidation: An Idea from Above

Along with organizations that represented all the regions, there emerged several associations that united regions in the same geographical areas.

As previously mentioned, when Nikita Khrushchev wanted to increase the regions' role in economic planning and management, he ordered the establishment of large economic zones with the *sovnarkhoz*, the Council of the National Economy, as the controlling economic body in all administrative regions included in a given zone. After Khrushchev's dismissal from his post, the *sovnarkhozy* and the economic zones were liquidated.

In 1992, the same idea reemerged, but in a new historical context. In the beginning, the idea was primarily supported by a few Moscow politicians. Even before the adoption of the Constitution of the Russian Federation, the notion appeared in a few parties' program documents of "lands," which were rather vaguely determined but obviously intended as a replacement for districts and territories.[5] However, the position of the regime toward the consolidation of the regions was of much more importance.

In the light of growing regionalization, the Kremlin hardly wanted to strengthen the provinces, since large territorial blocks could then make claims for their autonomy much more effectively than the smaller regions. In such a confrontational situation, it was preferable to have many subjects who could be played off against each other, who could be dealt with one by one, by using a carrot today and a stick tomorrow. In a word, the smaller and weaker the regions were, the stronger the position of the center would be, and therefore the easier it would be to divide and conquer.

Even the idea of economic integration looked dangerous to the Kremlin. Indeed, it feared not integration itself but the fact that the initiative originated in the lower echelons and that this integration was to be implemented not from the top, that is, from the center, but from below. Moscow had reason enough to view the emergence of several large superregions—strong units both economically and politically—as threatening to Russia's territorial integrity.[6]

However, the Kremlin also saw some positive elements in the consolidation of regions. First, aggregating the regions could serve as a centralization and economic integration factor, suppressing regional separatism and the willfulness of small "independent principalities." In some cases, it would be easier for the center to deal with a limited number of administrative-territorial subjects instead of eighty-nine smaller units.

It is not by chance that the Constitution of the Russian Federation contains Article 78, which reads that "the federal organs of state power shall have the right, in order to perform their responsibilities, to form their own territorial bodies and to appoint respective officials."[7] Despite financial difficulties, Moscow was ready to take on the maintenance of these associations and the centralized financing of their undertakings. In addition, however, the Kremlin wanted to use these large territorial units as its own instruments, in order to preclude the appearance of a kind of Siberian parliament or Ural duma assembly.

Second, after this point in time, Moscow took seriously the separatist movements of the national republics, seeing in the large Russian territories a good antidote against separatism. As we mentioned earlier, this was exactly the motivation of the central authorities when they pushed Ekaterinburg to proclaim itself a republic, a dangerous signal to the national republics.

The Initiative from Below

The major stimulus for developing large administrative entities, however, was found below. In consolidating regions, the regional elite saw a major antidote to control by the central bureaucracy, a way to create semistate entities able to challenge Moscow almost as equals. The initiators of new regional conglomerates were the larger regions such as Ekaterinburg and Novosibirsk, which, by definition, had to play the leading role. The leaders of smaller regions supported either the status quo or the creation of relatively loose associations able to challenge the center in defending their interests as well as to coordinate the economic efforts of individual districts.[8] The process of forming big territories "from below" was manifested in 1992–1994, in the creation of interregional associations.

Interregional Associations

Regional consolidation started with the emergence of various associations. Despite the disagreements between local leaders of neighboring regions, the tendency toward consolidation gained momentum in 1992–1994. Many alliances of regional politicians emerged in different corners of Russia and ranged from relatively solid to very loosely formed bodies. Among them were the following: Alliance of Russian Cities; Alliance of Northern Cities; Association of Regions and Republics of Ural; Far East Regional Association, centered in Moscow; Northwest, in St. Petersburg; Central Russia; Association of the Regions of Central Russia, centered in Belgorod; Siberian Agreement, located in Novosibirsk; Association of Territories and Districts of the North Caucasus, concentrated in Rostov on Don; Great Volga, active in Samara; Ural Regional Association, with its center in Ekaterinburg; and Association of Eastern Territories, located in Khabarovsk.[9] By the end of 1995, eight interregional associations appeared to be quite active.[10] Along with these associations, from time to time there also emerged other bodies that claimed to coordinate the activities of different regions, though not necessarily contiguous regions.[11]

All the associations that emerged in 1992–1994 claimed to pursue only economic goals. However, in 1993–1994, they tried to play a significant role in the political relationships between the regions and the center.[12] The Achilles' heel of the interregional associations was the contradicting interests of the various regions. The membership of practically all of these associations included both strong and weak regions, as well as both rich and poor.

With the restoration of presidential power in the aftermath of the election of December 12, 1993, interregional associations' activities declined almost immediately. They forgot about their ultimatum to Moscow, which they had been bold enough to send only few months previously.[13] However, in a few months' time, the interregional associations resumed their activities.

It is significant that the leaders of non-Russian republics followed the example of the Russian regions and began to form their own associations. Negotiations were conducted between Tatarstan, Bashkortostan, and Udmurtia in summer 1993 to coordinate their economic activities. The leaders of these republics directly connected their initiative with the emergence of regional Russian republics.[14] However, an alliance between these three republics never materialized.

The Siberian Agreement

Of all the numerous interregional associations, only a few were able to enter Russian economic and, to some degree, political life in a visible way. In fact, an association such as Great Volga never developed into a serious economic actor and, by 1994–1995, had become practically invisible, along with numerous other associations of this type.

The best known of all the interregional associations in 1992–1995 was, of course, the Siberian Agreement, or MASS, with its nineteen members. The association's original goal was to coordinate economic activities within Western and Eastern Siberia. The idea to form the group originated in Novosibirsk and was not resisted by any of the other Siberian regions.

The General Directorate of the association was centered in Novosibirsk; the Coordination Council on Foreign Economic Operations worked in Krasnoiarsk; the council dealing with the use of natural resources was located in Irkutsk; the body on power engineering was based in Abakan; and so on and so forth. As a result, according to the general director of the association, Vladimir Ivankov, in 1992–1993, "it became possible to overcome the hostility among the districts and territories. . . . Now normal working relationships have been established at the level of chief administrators."[15]

Since the very beginning of the association's formation, the leaders of the Siberian Agreement refused to view their entity as a political body and almost immediately declared that they did not have anything to do with the Siberian Republic. They consistently repudiated any accusations of separatism. According to the group's spokesperson, the Siberian Agreement was the embodiment of the struggle of the neighboring regions, which were economically dependent on each other, to stabilize their economic ties. Obviously, this purpose promoted the association's creation and helped it to survive the following years, despite much organizational restructuring.

Indeed, in 1994–1995, MASS was concerned mostly with economic issues, but these issues, however, had serious political overtones. One such issue was the protection of Siberian agriculture against cheap foreign food imports. The organization also tried to extricate from Moscow additional money for the improvement of health services in Siberia, where life expectancy dropped from seventy years in 1975, to fifty-nine years in 1995.[16]

In the beginning, federal authorities treated this association with suspicion, for they saw in it the foundations for a future Siberian Republic. Indeed, on many occasions the federal government had to confront the Siberian association's opposition on various issues.[17] Moscow rejected the association's proposal to settle the problems with their center-region relations through an agreement between the federal authorities and the whole of Siberia. As a result, the government continued in 1993–1994 to firmly adhere to its practice of signing agreements on responsibilities and powers with each of the Russian Federation's subject regions separately. However, in 1995, Moscow changed its policy toward the Siberian Agreement and decided to fully cooperate with it. Viktor Chernomyrdin's attendance at a meeting of the organization's directorate in August and his support of the organization marked a turning point.[18]

Even if the Siberian Agreement had stood out in 1992–1995 as the most active interregional organization, it would still not have integrated economic life in Siberia to a great degree. In addition, as the experts on the Siberian economy suggested, the "Siberian regions are still less linked to each other than the regions in the European part of Russia."[19]

Of the other interregional associations, let us also mention the one that emerged in the Far East. In the Soviet era, the Far Eastern Association of Economic Assistance was established. After the disintegration of the Soviet Union, it almost ceased to operate, small as it was. It was replaced by the Association of the Territories of the Far East and Transbaikal Region, with Viktor Ishaiev, the head of the Khabarovsk Territory administration, as its president. The leaders turned their attention toward economic integration à la Siberia, which was much more expedient in the current conditions.

The Divisive Nature of Regional Diversity

With a very high level of diversity among the Russian regions, it is not surprising that only rarely do their interests overlap enough to allow them to create a common front against Moscow. Certain factors—whether regions are rich or poor, large or small, exporters or not, self-sufficient in food supply or not, border on foreign countries or not, have cultural specificity or not—prevent the Russian regions from creating a common economic, social, and political program, which would help them form a strong alliance against the center. Such an alliance, however, can emerge—and very quickly, as in cases of emergency, for example, at times when Moscow is engulfed in a political crisis.

PART FOUR

The Effect of Regionalism on Russian Society

Regionalization is an extremely complicated and contradictory process. As a product of the democratization of Russian society, the process of regionalization is important because it presents an obstacle to the authoritarian tendency in post-Communist Russia. In addition, the autonomy of regions is a condition for the globalization of the Russian economy. At the same time, however, regionalization is fraught with danger, posing risks to the unity of the country and to the preservation of the human rights of people living in the provinces.

In this respect, contemporary Russia resembles numerous other countries where the growing autonomy of regions has produced negative as well as positive results in both the political and the economic realms. In analyzing the regionalization of Russia, as with other countries, a simplistic assessment of this serious social process is to be avoided.

18

THE CONTRADICTORY CONSEQUENCES
OF REGIONALIZATION

Particularization, and regionalization as one of its forms, is in many respects a valuable process for groups and regions of all types. In the mid-1990s, members of any ethnic group in the United States cannot be too proud of their origin and culture. Most decidedly, a group should not, as was common in the past, imitate WASP culture in any way, nor should it be ashamed of its customs and language. Likewise, any region in Russia or Spain can now defend itself against the central government and entertain relations with the world without the capital's permission.

However, the cost of further regionalization is not small, particularly if the relationship between the center and the periphery does not have a solid legal basis, as well as rules on how to change it that are recognized by all players. An outburst of regionalization radically changes the character of the modern nation-state and the character its citizens' lives. It encourages, along with other forms of particularism, differentiation and divisiveness within societies—even stable societies such as that of the United States.

In 1992–1995, regionalism in the world was a powerful process that could not be stopped without betraying the principles of democracy. In countries such as India, Canada, Russia, China, and to some degree, the United States, particularism, and especially regionalism, is one of the major social and political processes. In Moscow, the two political adversaries—the president and Parliament—in the struggle involving the new Constitution assumed that without the support of regional leaders they had no chance of winning.

The citizens and governments of many countries face the difficult task of finding ways to reconcile particularism with the interests of the majority and with the necessity of preserving the advantages of their large unified state. Politicians in the United States and Russia, as well as the rest of the world, who make decisions for or against modern forms of particularism should carefully weigh the costs and benefits to their entire societies.

Positive Consequences

Regionalization in Russia had several positive effects on life in the country. Many of the arguments that appeared in the regionalists' ideology, as discussed previously, were confirmed by the Russian experience in 1991–1995. First of all, the increase in regional autonomy weakened the authoritative tendencies in the country and created a powerful obstacle to the restoration of totalitarianism in Russia.

Second, high regional autonomy was an important condition for greater economic progress. This factor would have been positive even with the preservation of the central planning system. Soviet economists since the late 1950s had insisted on economic decentralization. Indeed, Nikita Khrushchev, as previously explained, tried to implement his ideas with the introduction of the *sovnarkhoz*. In a market economy, regional autonomy could be even more propitious for economic growth than in a central planning system. Autonomy allowed local firms to contact firms anywhere in the world, to export their products abroad much more easily than in the past, and to cooperate with foreign firms without Moscow's permission.

Third, regional autonomy fostered cultural and intellectual progress in the provinces, while depriving Moscow of its monopoly on the country's best talents.

At the same time, regionalization as it is developing since 1992 has had controversial effects on various areas of life in Russia. For Russian democrats, most of the effects of regionalization are ultimately positive, and they believe that the Communists' and nationalists' major value—that the state's might is more important—is rather negative. The attitudes of Russia's neighbors and those of the world in general are quite ambivalent. For many foreign actors, regionalization, as a factor weakening the centralized Russian state, is quite positive. However, for others, regionalization is fraught with the danger of the country's disintegration and imminent anarchy, which they believe presents a palpable danger to the rest of the world.

Fostering Legal Chaos

The first big question to answer concerns regionalization's impact: Does it present a "clear and present danger" to Russia's future as a country that has existed since the sixteenth century? In investigating this topic, we must stipulate that the current trends outlined in the list that follows—trends that are typical for the country—must be maintained over the next couple of decades. In brief, these trends are as follows:

1. The appearance of local legislation that does not supplement all-Russia legislation but, instead, contradicts it, that is, the "war of laws," or, in fact, lawlessness.

2. The ignoring of illegal acts in localities' decrees and decisions issued by the central government's bodies, which results in low, if not zero, management efficiency of the Russian government.
3. The absence of cooperation between law enforcement bodies, central and regional, which opens broad opportunities for criminal elements.
4. The absence of control over local governing bodies, which leads to despotism by local authorities and flourishing corruption.
5. The formation and functioning of regional lobbying groups in central government bodies, which leads to the adoption of decisions by these bodies in contradiction to general state interests and serves only as a breeding ground for corruption.
6. The effective opposition in some regions to the processes of democratization, economic liberalization, and political education of the people.

The Danger of Extreme Particularism

Regionalism in modern Russia exacerbated the problem of small ethnic groups living in the Russian regions. The upsurge of nationalism greatly affected them, and almost all of these groups, regardless of size, started to claim sovereignty and refused to obey regional authorities.

Some of these small groups used to have autonomous regional status because of their small size, unlike the "old" autonomous republics like Tatarstan or Bashkortostan, and were included in larger administrative units as small units called *krai*. After 1991, they were able to achieve republican status, and there are now new republics on the map, such as the republics of Altai, Khakasia, Adygeia, and Karachaevo-Cherkessia.

However, the most significant frictions in 1993–1995 were generated not by these new republics but by those ethnic groups that remained a part of larger units with the status of "district" (*okrug*). However, these districts were simultaneously recognized as "subjects of the federation" and were mentioned as such in the 1993 Constitution (Article 65). Among the most politically important are Chukotka in the Magadan Region, Taymyr in Krasnoiarsk, Khanty-Mansiy and the Iamalo-Nenetsky District in the Tiumen Region, and the Koriak District in Kamchatka.

After noticing the impunity with which the larger regions' leaders acted, many of the bureaucrats of small ethnic districts, referring to their status as "subjects of the federation," regularly clashed with their regional executive and legislative powers. The local elite sought to expand its power by demanding autonomy, and even independence, from the regional centers. Indeed, they often displayed blatant anti-Russian tendencies, even when the majority of the district's population was Russian.[1] It is remarkable that in ethnic units, not only are local ethnic leaders trying to exploit their autonomy for their own purposes, but Russian administrators are also doing the same.

Taymyr, formally the Dolgan-Nenets District (named after two small ethnic groups), with 55,000 residents, is an excellent example. In 1992–1995, this district was constantly fighting with the Krasnoiarsk Region, trying to avoid paying taxes to it and insisting that it pay them directly to Moscow.

A particularly vigorous fight emerged over determining the administrative status of Norilsk, a Taymyr city with a famous nickel factory that attracts a lot of foreign currency. This city, even though it was in Taymyr's territory, has long been subordinated to Krasnoiarsk. In 1995, plant managers instigated a demand to change the status quo and switch governance of the city to the Taymyr District. If this were to happen, plant leaders would be able to gain almost total control over the district, since the well-being of the district's population depended on the plant.[2] Finally, Boris Yeltsin defended Krasnoiarsk's position and disallowed the Taymyr District's decision, and on September 6, 1995, the battle over the status of Norilsk ended.

In another development, the Bilibin District, an administrative unit in the Chukotsk Republic with a population of a few thousand, demanded separation from its republic and unification with the Magadan Region. At the same time, the Smidovich District in the Jewish Autonomous Region, a part of the Khabarovsk Territory, demanded to be removed from this region in order to formally join the territory.[3] Such developments created hundreds of problems and exacerbated the difficulty of maintaining peaceful relations among much of the population. These problems demonstrated that the schism between the New Russia and its regions seemingly had no limit. Such conflicts between ethnic units and regions also fueled all the other regional conflicts raging throughout the New Russia.

A Dangerous Blend: Local Authorities and the Army

Moscow's constant lack of the resources required to satisfy all of the needs proclaimed to be nationally important led, in 1991–1995, to the central administration's consistent inability to provide the army, as well as law enforcement agencies, with promised funding. In 1994–1995, reports of cases of malnourishment among soldiers, fuel shortages, and a delay of several months in paying officer's salaries became a common fixture in the Russian media.

Under the existing conditions, the army and the Ministry of Internal Affairs' agencies looked for the support of local authorities, who sympathetically reacted to their call for help. Thus, in the beginning of 1996, Sakhalin's local government decided to help the border troops and took up a collection from state and private enterprises.[4] In 1995, the governor of Volgograd greatly assisted the Eighth Guard Army Corps, which, with its headquarters in Volgograd, was fighting in Chechnia. General Lev Rokhlin, who became prominent in this war, could not help but praise the governor for his help and asked the central government to allow the local government to hold back some of its federal taxes to compensate the region for supporting the lives of the soldiers, officers, and their family.[5]

The rapprochement between the army and local authorities, if it continues, represents a serious tendency toward making regions somewhat more independent from the center. Political confrontations, over political differences between the regions and the center and over the loyalty of military units to specific regional leaders, can generate dangerous consequences for Russia. Past Russian rulers, before and after the revolution, were adamant about the idea that the army must obey only the center and in no way serve the whims of local authorities.

The Impact of Regionalization on Internal Economic Ties

The economic effects of Russian decentralization, as observed in 1992–1995, are contradictory, as are many of its other consequences. On the one hand, it is evident that the decline of central control over the provinces, along with the abolishment of central planning and privatization of the economy, was quite favorable, at least theoretically, for economic progress. On the other hand, regionalization, as it took place in Russia, created numerous new problems and worsened older problems in the country's economic life and, consequently, in its political life. This statement becomes particularly apt if we use as a criterion the country's national interest on the whole and not the interests of particular regions or even individual companies.

First, regionalization weakened economic ties between some regions. Interregional transportation of goods in Russia decreased by 31 percent in 1992, compared to the previous year. These figure dropped by 36 percent more in 1993, using 1992 data as a comparison. This decline was only partially a result of a decrease in production (which dropped by only 18 percent in 1992) and was, to a great degree, determined by the cutting off of economic relations between regions.[6]

Regionalization caused some to be unwilling to establish new ties, and this led to despecialization of production, a situation in which managers collect or produce their own inputs separately to continue production. As the experiences of 1992–1995 showed, regionalization evidently restricted the country's common economic space, as compared to the Communist past.

Another economic factor that differentiated regions in Russia and influenced their policy toward the center and each other was food supply. Being now responsible for sustaining an adequate food supply for their population, local leaders shaped their policy to fit vital issues such as pricing of basic foods, attitudes toward foreign imports of food, and exports of agricultural products from their regions, depending on their ability to solve the food problem for their regions. As a rule, regions with a developed agricultural sector took a significantly different position than that taken by industrial regions, which were not able to produce their own food stocks. Ignoring the center and behaving like independent states, these needy regions, which were able to feed their population only if they kept all of their agricultural output, supported various measures prohibiting the export of food. In other words, the scarcer a region's food resources, the higher a region's tendency to hinder food exports to other regions in the federation.

Ulianovsk and Voronezh serve as excellent examples.[7] Here, local authorities banned food exports to other regions. Indeed, local authorities even put militiamen at customs points along roads in order to prevent goods, especially agricultural goods, from being taken out of the region.[8]

Regions' position on food imports also differed. Whereas Moscow, St. Petersburg, Ekaterinburg, along with several cities located along international borders and cities with ports and large industrial centers, were interested in keeping their low prices and customs fees on foreign food imports, those regions that exported food to industrial regions held the opposite opinion.

Indeed, the elimination of import restrictions and the lowering of customs duties on certain goods imported to Russia rather significantly affected producers in those regions that produced similar goods, even if they were made to meet the needs of their own region. It has been proved that the gradual decline of Russian agriculture in 1991–1995, particularly in the production of meat and dairy products, was a direct consequence of the competitiveness of cheap foreign goods.

Serious disagreements concerning energy and raw material prices also emerged between regions. The Khabarovsk *krai*, for instance, complained that the price of electrical power in Irkutsk, on whose territory the area's main power station is located, was six times cheaper there than what Khabarovsk was charged.[9]

For various reasons, restrictions against neighboring regions became a normal phenomenon in Russian life. In 1992, according to the calculation of Vladimir Leksin and Elena Andreeva, regional restrictions on the transfer of goods from one region to another absorbed between 5 and 20 percent of production and, in some cases, even 30 to 50 percent.[10] The economic separatism further advanced in 1993 and 1994 to become a serious issue preoccupying the government.[11] According to the Council of Foreign and Defense Policies' report, by mid-1992, twenty-three territories had introduced their own restrictions on exports beyond their administrative borders. To implement these decisions, local security bodies and specially formed "voluntary formations" built customhouses and customs points in order to inspect traded goods.

Second, regionalization significantly widened the country's economic and social differentiation. It increased the gap between regions in a number of ways, as previously mentioned. It tremendously widened the gap between the prices of consumer goods and services in comparison to the Communist era. In post-Communist Russia, the ratio of food prices between regions reached 1:18 and stood at 1:15 for other consumer goods.[12]

Third, regional autonomy drastically reduced the pool from which a region could cull its management cadres. In the past, highly qualified directors of large factories were often sent by the center, but now they are mostly chosen from a local stock of specialists. The choice of the local political and economic elite can now be dictated, much more than in the past, by flagrant nepotism, ethnic and clan connections, and political loyalty.[13]

Regionalization and Democracy

The impact of regionalization on democratization in Russia was also very contradictory. As previously explained, the advocates of regionalization often argued, with significant reason, that the autonomy of regions prevented the center from becoming a base for totalitarianism and made it impossible to concentrate power in a single person, a point that Thomas Jefferson eloquently defended. Regionalists also insisted that autonomy increases the rate of democratization inside a region.[14]

At the same time, it is evident that regional autonomy can seriously endanger democratic freedoms. The crux of the debates between the Federalists and their opponents at the end of the eighteenth century in the United States was over the following question: Is liberty better protected in larger or smaller societies? James Madison argued in *The Federalist Papers* that liberty would be better served in a large country. The history of the United States, as well as that of some other countries, shows that only a powerful central government is able to protect the interests of a minorities against "the domination within each subsystem."[15] The Russian experience showed that Madison, at least with respect to post-Communist Russia, was correct: Given Russian traditions, the powerful democratic center can better guarantee political freedoms than small, powerful regions.[16]

In many places, regionalization delivered a serious blow to the fledgling democracies in the provinces, creating a set of regional dictatorships. In most regions, the executive branch of government apparently gained the upper hand, overpowering legislators who lost significant influence in their regions because most strategic decisions were made by governors. The attempts of local parliaments, where the members of the administration played the leading role, failed in most regions.[17]

In 1993–1995, regional leaders were far more conservative than federal leaders. From an objective point of view, the struggle of the regions against the center often assumed a reactionary character, turning into a struggle not for the rights of the region but for the right of a leader to rule in the region as in a private domain.

Election Procedures

During the 1993–1995 elections in several regions, freedom of choice decreased significantly in comparison to elections in 1989. Local authorities, feeling themselves immune to any legal action after violating the law, resorted to various illegal and even flagrantly criminal deeds in order to destroy an undesirable candidate—a potential political rival.

In Saratov, during the November-December 1993 election campaign, Governor Yurii Belykh, and the city mayor, Yurii Kitov, resorted to various tricks in order to eliminate Dmitrii Aiatskov, vice mayor of Saratov as a candidate for the State Duma against Kitov. The vice mayor was denied the use of his government car, and telephone service to his office was shut off. The police were instructed not to permit people to enter the mayor's building to visit him. People in various enterprises and offices were harassed in a number of ways, including arrest if they revealed their support of the vice mayor. Students were forced to sign petitions in support of Kitov.[18] The falsification of election returns by Governor Mikhail Narolin in 1993 in Lipetsk was even recognized by the local court, but the election was not canceled because "the falsification could not influence the outcome of the election."[19]

In Vologda, local authorities almost predetermined the December 12, 1993, election of a deputy for the Council of Federation because one of the candidates was Governor Nikolai Podgornov. Journalists who dared to criticize him were removed from their jobs or the financial subsidies to their newspapers were restricted.[20] The conduct of the Ulianovsk administration concerning democratic elections was even more aggressive. It was established that some of the December 12, 1993, election results were falsified and that local leaders were also ready to "influence" local election results by having prepared false ballots in advance.[21]

The pressure on the population was particularly high in the countryside. Several Russian experts asserted that the relative success of the Agrarian Party in the election on December 12, 1993, had to be ascribed to the direct intervention of local bosses in the election. As indirect evidence, they cited the fact that the number of people who participated in the election was much higher in the countryside than in the city.

The Plight of the Media and Individual Rights

After the dizzy days of democracy in 1991, in many, if not most, regions, local leaders placed the media under harsh control. Since almost all local newspapers cannot survive without state subsidies, governors were able to dramatically limit the freedom of the press and impose their political views on the media.[22] In many regions, governors fired unsubmissive editors and journalists. In some regions, journalists were brutally beaten and even murdered. Afterward, the authorities did very little to find, let alone punish, the culprits.

The Maritime Territory became notorious in 1993–1995 for harassing journalists and for closing several newspapers that supported the critics of Governor Evgenii Nazdratenko.[23] Several other regions in the country, including Khabarovsk and Taymyr (Dolgan-Nenets), have also become notorious for their abuses.[24]

There were no advantages in regionalization for ordinary people's human rights. Without a strong center able to protect citizens against the arbitrariness of local officials, which Moscow had done to some degree in the Soviet era, the regional elite found it possible to violate individual human rights much more than in the past. In 1994–1995, the Russian media declared that many regional authorities were free do what they wanted with individuals whom they disliked for one reason or another.[25]

Violation of Democratic Freedoms in Non-Russian Regions

Regionalization probably had even more contradictory consequences for the ethnic republics than for the Russian regions. The ruling elite in ethnic republics enjoyed even more freedom of action than in the Russian regions from 1992 until 1995, a result of the various factors described previously.

The high autonomy of local authorities in the ethnic republics made the violation of human rights even more intensive than in the Russian regions. Some ethnic leaders, such as Kirsan Iliumzhinov in Kalmykia, behaved like dictators. In 1994–1995, Iliumzhinov tried to eliminate all opposition to his rule. Indeed, he liquidated the parliament and replaced it with a presidential council, which the Kalmyk leader convened at his pleasure. He then decided toward the end of 1995 to restore the parliament and "elect" it in very bizarre ways: Iliumzhinov permitted only people with a certain level of income to take part in the election, and he personally appointed one-third of the parliament. The local government, consisting of his emissaries, or *akhlachi*, was totally under the control of the "great leader" of Kalmykia. Moreover, Iliumzhinov organized his own reelection as president in December 1995 and, in the process, violated all laws of the Russian Federation that applied. Despite his blatant flaunting of the federation's laws, he was not even reprimanded by the Kremlin.[26] Iliumzhinov openly recruited high officials among his relatives and friends and tried to depose the republican attorney.

The same high level of arbitrariness reigned throughout 1994–1995 in Bashkortostan, as in several other non-Russian republics.[27] Beatings in police stations in the Mordovian Republic became a norm, and even the republic's president, Vasilii Guslianikov, a democrat who was ousted from his position by the Communist parliament, had been beaten.

The violation of democratic procedures during many elections is of special importance. The elite in ethnic republics conspicuously reduced democratic procedures, for they were determined to control the outcome of any election. Tatarstan and Bashkortostan, for instance, adopted an election law that provided only for the election of deputies in single districts and completely rejected voting for parties' lists of candidates (Russian federal election laws provides for both types of voting).[28] Under the conditions established in both republics, where local leaders controlled the election process, such a law made it impossible to elect opposition candidates. This is exactly what happened in March 1995 during elections in both republics. In both instances, the number of opposition candidates elected to the republican parliaments was insignificant. Furthermore, the authorities in both republics openly obstructed the activities of opposition candidates. For instance, they did not allow them to open bank accounts to facilitate their campaign financing.[29]

The corruption of local elites was particularly strong in the non-Russian republics, where their autonomy from the center was usually greater than that of the elite in Russian regions. Iliumzhinov, for instance, during the Kalmyk presidential election and afterward, remained under investigation in connection to using credit from Moscow, which he received in 1992 as the head of a corporation called San. However, several years later, he was still president.[30] His conduct as an omnipotent tsar and his contemptuous disregard of federal laws are already legendary.[31] In fact, one of the numerous articles devoted to his election was entitled "The Man Who Bought the Republic."[32]

But, of course, corruption has reached Homeric proportions in Chechnia. There are many indications that Dzhokhar Dudaiev himself was at the center of the corrupt activities in his republic.[33]

The Conduct of the Ethnic Elite in Russian Regions

Growing regional autonomy accounts for much of the exacerbation of ethnic conflicts and for the increasing number of cases of direct persecution of ethnic groups in the country. One of the most egregious cases is found in the North Caucasian Russian regions, in Krasnodar and Stavropol. In these areas, ethnic tension increased tremendously in 1991–1994. This was mostly a result of the migration of many Caucasian people, especially Armenians, who felt that this was their home because they had found refuge here from discrimination in Azerbaijan. As a result of this migration, ethnic tension became a "normal" element of everyday life in these regions. Of course, the Chechen War in 1994–1996 enormously increased anti-Chechen sentiments in these regions as well as in other areas, such as Saratov.[34]

Several local leaders have exploited ethnic tension in their own interests. They have presented themselves as defenders of the Russian population, which suffers from the invasion of non-Russians, people who are generally richer than the local residents.[35]

Mild Discrimination Against Russians in Non-Russian Regions

Upon the independence of the former Soviet republics, Russians were almost immediately treated as second-class citizens, even in Ukraine.[36] Russians in the republics of the Russian Federation were in much better positions, even if their status as an imperial, dominating nation declined significantly in 1991–1994. In Bashkiria, for instance, Russians as well as Tatars, who together comprise a majority in the republic, had a much smaller chance of joining the bureaucracy than Bashkirs.[37] The new Bashkir Constitution declared that the right of self-determination would be exerted not by the whole population of the republic but only by the "Bashkir nation."[38] In some cases, Russians started to leave non-Russian republics, as in Kalmykia.[39]

Politicians and intellectuals representing non-Russian ethnic groups have tried to expand the role of their native languages. In fact, some of these languages, for example, Ezria and Moksha in Mordovia, have almost disappeared. Some ethnic groups have resorted to using history in order to present Russians, correctly or not, as rude invaders, going so far as to demonize the Russian people.[40] However, at the same time, local non-Russian intellectuals and, to some degree, some politicians have preached the segregation of non-Russians from Russians. Some have even advocated the resettlement of entire peoples in order to create ethnically homogeneous districts, an action that spread fear among many Russians.[41] These developments provide Russian nationalists with additional ammunition in their quest for the elimination of non-Russian republics.[42]

The Center's Lack of Control over the Local Elite

Regional elites were never so immune to any control over their conduct as in 1991–1993. Indeed, the center increased the autonomy of the regional elites and almost lost effective control over the appointment of most local bureaucratic positions.

Central government agencies, such as the Office of the Attorney, which, in the past, was independent of local authorities and often intervened in cases to maintain the laws, lost their previous stature and were almost completely at the mercy of local bosses.[43] At the same time, the fledgling democratic institutions did not work well enough to exercise control over the local elite from below.

The center started to sue local officials for violations of the law only in rare cases. Governors and people whom they protected felt much more immune to reprimands from above than even the all-powerful first party secretaries had in Brezhnev's times. The Russian media reported, in 1993–1995, many instances of such confidence by governors and their myrmidons, their wives, and other relatives.[44] In 1994–1995, Russian governors, in the perception of the Russian people, were greedy and power-hungry individuals, and, for many, they were worse than first party secretaries.[45] Tsarist governors were described by Nikolai Gogol in his novel *The Inspector-General* (1836) and by Mikhail Saltykov-Shchedrin in *The History of a Town* (1869–1870). Their descriptions accurately capture the demeanor and activities of some of these post-Communist bosses.[46]

At the same time, hundreds of thousands of officials elected to local parliaments used their deputy immunity to prevent them from criminal investigation.[47] Even in the Brezhnev era, which is presented in history as a paradise for bureaucracy, high officials could be taken to task by the central administration, even if this rarely happened.

Moscow's loose control over the regions allowed regions bordering foreign countries or rich in natural resources to become a springboard for illegal trade with foreign countries. First of all, regions such as Kaliningrad became an export conduit for raw materials, sold at dumping prices abroad.[48] The so-called oil regions, like Tiumen, were involved in mass illegal exports of their resources.[49] The great autonomy of local leaders makes them very much exposed to the corruption of foreign firms, including Chinese firms, a factor of enormous political significance for the future.[50]

Semilegal and Illegal Activities

The illegal activity of local elites in this period primarily centered on grabbing state property in the process of privatization.[51] The media in this period were full of stories describing the various facts of illegal seizure of state property by local officials.[52]

The intertwining layers of authorities and criminals reached an extremely high level, and in many regional centers, the cooperation between local political power and the Mafia became almost conspicuous. The situation in Krasnoiarsk in 1994–1995 is typical of many regions. In Krasnoiarsk, close interaction between local political power, businessmen, and criminals emerged around the production and sale of aluminum. Alexei Tarasov, a very knowledgeable journalist for *Izvestia*, summarized this cooperation between the three forces as follows: "The blend of the criminal world and the world of the aluminum business has ended, and criminal 'authorities' take active part in the economic negotiations of the directors of the industrial giants, while high-ranking police officials invite the leaders of organized crime to their meetings."[53] The close cooperation between banks, producers of titanium and uranium, law enforcement forces, and organized crime was very strong in Ekaterinburg as well. In this case, as in Krasnoiarsk and many other Russian cities, "criminal authorities" were "legalized" and almost openly took part in various economic enterprises.[54]

In several regions, criminals went so far as to create their own political organizations, as was done in Khabarovsk when a recidivist criminal, Vladimir Podataiev, established the political association called Unity. In the quest for respectability, numerous other recidivists joined this organization. Protected by the aura of this association, Podataiev became a star on local TV, was enrolled in the Human Rights Committee, and was even sent to Geneva to take part in a international conference.[55] There is also much evidence of the participation of organized crime in the election of local governors and dumas.[56]

In Soviet times, the local elite always corrupted the central elite in order to obtain from Moscow the necessary conditions for achieving personal or even regional goals. It was, of course, the Soviet southern republics, especially Georgia, that were the champions in corrupting Moscow officials.

In post-Communist Russia, the relations between the central and the local bureaucracy changed somewhat. On the one hand, with their new autonomy, local elites seemingly needed much less help from Moscow bureaucrats for the attainment of their objectives. But, on the other hand, Moscow's cooperation became even more important. In the past, good relations with central institutions were necessary to reduce the plans for regional enterprises, to receive resources for the fulfillment of these plans, or to build a big factory in a given region. The personal gains that local officials made through the corruption of Moscow apparatchiks took the form of higher prestige and promotion as a result of successes in public performance. Of course, in many cases, the protection of Moscow bosses was also important for gaining immunity to law enforcement bodies and party committees, since local apparatchiks often violated laws and party ethics in their quest for personal enrichment, taking bribes and engaging in other forms of corruption. However, the existing order imposed quite strong limits on the accumulation of wealth and even on nepotism.

In post-Communist Russian life, the goals and opportunities of local officials, as well as Moscow's role, changed drastically. The need for Moscow's help in plan fulfillment and in resource allocation evaporated. However, Moscow's role rather increased in the sphere of direct personal enrichment. The government continued to be the principal owner of financial resources, and it continued to decide how to distribute them either as subventions to local budgets or as credits. This time around, the local elite could directly profit in various ways from the financial assistance of the central administration.

Of no less importance was the control of foreign trade licenses, still monopolized by Moscow. Foreign trade and, principally, the export of raw materials and weapons was the major source of hard currency for local bosses. To some degree, Moscow's cooperation with the ruling local elite was also useful for success in local election campaigns; with Moscow subsidies, it was easier to keep inflation in control, particularly in relation to basic food commodities.

At the same time, under new social conditions, corrupting Moscow executives became much easier than in the past, when not everybody in the administration was open to bribes. In post-Communist Moscow, the involvement of officials at all levels, from the highest office to lowest position, became a norm.

The relationship between the elite in Ekaterinburg and Moscow was typical in this respect. The best way to corrupt officials in post-Communist Russia is through the inclusion of Moscow dignitaries and their relatives in various partnerships and as stockholders or employees of firms involved in foreign trade. This technique was used exactly this way in this Ural city. Among the "workers" listed for the rich firm InterUral was not only the daughter of Governor Eduard Rossel but also the son of Yurii Petrov, a former high-level member of Boris Yeltsin's administration and the head of the State Investment Corporation; Boris Yeltsin's son-in law; and the wife of the former deputy minister of foreign trade. For the promotion of the local elite's interests, Ekaterinburg created in Moscow a special lobby called the Interrepublican Association for the Advancement of the

Development of the Ural Region, which consisted of many high dignitaries in Moscow, mostly former officials in Sverdlovsk.[57]

The ties of corruption were particularly strong, as had been the case in the past, between Moscow and the non-Russian republics. In fact, there was almost a consensus among Russian experts that since 1991, there had been close cooperation between Moscow power structures and Dudaiev's regime in Chechnia and that this cooperation did not stop when the war started in December 1994.[58]

A Weakening Common Culture

Regionalization has had a significant effect on the cultural map of the country. For one thing, a radical revolution occurred within the mass media. In the Soviet period, the Moscow press was absolutely dominant countrywide, and the role of the local media was minimal. According to a survey conducted by one of the authors of this book in the 1960s and 1970s, whereas 80 percent of Russians read central newspapers, only 20 percent read local periodicals.

In post-Communist Russia, the situation has changed radically. The ratio between the circulation of Moscow and local newspapers and journals has been reversed. With the increased freedom of the press, the Moscow media, particularly newspapers and other periodicals, have also ceased to be major sources of information, which has allowed the local press and even TV to become competitors.[59]

Even Moscow TV has lost its previous dominance in the provinces. In 1994–1995, local TV stations began to compete successfully with the major programs of central TV networks. According to a survey conducted by the foundation Public Opinion, residents of sixteen cities, in a sample of twenty-two, included local TV stations as one of the three most interesting channels that they watch regularly.

The cultural splitting in Russia has also been manifested in the different attitudes displayed about the Westernization of culture in Russia. Moscow and St. Petersburg, along with a few other large cities in the European part of the country, have responded quickly to Westernization. The Russian provinces, particularly their younger Russian residents, are also under the strong influence of Western culture. However, these provinces have turned into a repository of Russian national culture and traditions, a circumstance with significant political consequences for the future.[60]

The Foreign Factor

The foreign factor is also important in assessing the effects of regionalization, as it has had some effect on Russian relations with foreign countries. However, its effect has not been as great as the collapse of the Soviet empire.

Western countries, such as the United States and the nations of Western Europe, viewed the growing autonomy of the Russian regions as a manifestation of the democratic development of Russian society. They also welcomed the opening of Russian regions to the world market, which meant new opportunities and markets for Western firms. At the same time, the West was clearly against the disintegration of the country and repeatedly demonstrated this stance, particularly during the war in Chechnia and in its opposition to the growing influence of Russian Communists and nationalists.[61]

The position of the countries neighboring Russia, especially China and Japan, is much more complicated. These countries regard the Asian part of Russia, particularly the Far East, with different emotions than the United States or Germany. Of course, the impact that the growing autonomy of the Russian regions in the Far East has on Russian relations with China is of special significance.

Previously, the Soviet Union and China had a closed border, with their armies and citizens in a state of confrontation. Therefore, the differences in population size on either side of the border were not politically significant. However, the situation radically changed after 1991 when the borders were opened. In 1995, 8 million residents of the Far East—32 million if Siberia is included—faced 100 million people in the Chinese provinces directly across the border. At the same time, the number of residents living east of the Ural Mountains, which separate Europe from Asia, tends not to increase but rather to diminish.[62] As Sergei Shakhrai noted, "If unfavorable economic and demographic processes do not stop in the big expanse east of the Urals, only 8 to 10 million people will live there by the year 2010."[63]

The vast and practically empty territories, now relatively accessible, are a magnet for the industrious and ingenious Chinese. This will be particularly true if these regions gradually lose their ties with Moscow. The exact number of Chinese currently living and working in the Far East and Siberia is unknown; however, some local politicians and journalists speak of about 1 to 2 million Chinese now living in these territories.[64] Even in 1995–1996, should the relationship with China suddenly deteriorate, the mass deportation of Chinese from the Far East would be almost technically, if not legally, impossible.

In 1991–1995, many politicians built their careers on Russian nationalism, including Yurii Nozhikov, the governor of the Irkutsk Region; Evgenii Nazdratenko, governor of the Maritime Territory; Viktor Ishaiev, governor of the Khabarovsk Territory; and two other governors of Far Eastern regions, Boris Ivanov and Vladimir Diachenko. These officials were particularly active in sounding the alarm against "Chinese assimilation" and threatened that "we can lose the ability to control our own territory, resources, and economy." They even obstructed the Russian-Chinese agreement on clarifying the demarcation of the common border between the two countries, which had been an issue since the conflicts in 1969.[65]

The position of many members of the lower levels of the administration and, particularly, the position of businesses have been quite different. They, as well as managers, have profited from importing the Chinese labor force to work in local enterprises, particularly in the construction industry, because the Chinese are less demanding about rights and wages than Russian workers. Because of this, these managers turn a blind eye to the problems brought about by these *Gastarbeiters* (guest workers).[66]

In 1991–1995, whereas the regional elite held ambivalent attitudes toward the "Chinese threat," Moscow politicians and their experts as a rule were rather pessimistic and even defeatist on this issue.[67] They did not exclude the possibility that in the future "an authoritarian 'Great China,' which has unresolved territorial disputes with Russia, might solve its demographic problems by military means," exploiting the alienation of the Far East from the motherland.[68] Some Russian experts hope that China will follow Russia's example and shed its unitarian structure—if it does not disintegrate first—reverting to the China of the 1920s and the 1930s, with warlords fighting each other. In the opinion of these Russians, a federated China with many autonomous regions would be the best solution to the problem that China poses for Russia because China would then be as feeble as Russia.[69]

CONCLUSION

In the next few decades, relations between the center and regions will be among the most important political, economic, and social issues in Russia as well as in numerous other countries.[1] The sheer number of actors involved in these relations (for example, there are over one hundred regional units involved) is daunting—and they differ strongly from each other in dozens of crucial aspects. Among these actors are the regional elite, central dominant elite, and opposition elite, the masses, intellectuals, neighboring foreign countries, international organizations, and international companies. Such diversity in the number of Russian actors illustrates just how complicated these relations are and how difficult it is to predict their outcome.

However, it is evident that Russia, as a centuries-old geopolitical power, will become very different over the next few decades. The "old" Russia, spanning from the Baltic Sea to the Pacific Ocean, could exist as a unitarian state only on the basis of authoritarian or totalitarian rule, combined with a strong patriotic and nationalistic ideology. In the new world, Russia, with its market economy and democratic institutions, is destined to change as a nation-state.

Among the most important factors that will influence the creation of a new Russian nation-state are these:

1. The country's size and high transportation costs in a "common economic space."
2. The gravitation of some of Russia's regions to stronger foreign countries for economic ties rather than to other Russian regions.
3. The strong, growing ethnic and cultural antagonism between Russian and non-Russian regions.
4. The strong separatist sentiments in several republics, such as Chechnia, Tatarstan, and a few others.
5. The extranormally large cultural, economic, and social differences among Russian regions.
6. The lack of a stable political system able to create a consensus on major values.
7. Moscow's loss of prestige as the unifying center of the country.

8. The lack of the threat of foreign invasion.

9. The lack of a strong national idea able to cement the Russian nation.

All these factors lead one to suppose that Russia will never again, at least in the foreseeable future, be as centralized as it has been for almost five centuries. However, in no way does this book suggest that Russia will completely disintegrate or even that its territories far removed from Moscow will secede, creating their own states.

There are a number of factors that hinder the disintegration of Russia as a nation-state. Among them are (1) the hostility to Russian culture in the countries bordering Russia in the south and Far East, (2) the threat that foreign bodies in the Far East and south will expand their influence and perhaps even annex some Russian territories, (3) the common cultural and lingual heritage of Russians living in the most remote regions with the rest of the Russian population, and (4) the interest of most regions in the maintenance of a greater nation-state for political, economic, and social reasons.

The combination of centrifugal and anticentrifugal forces will most likely push Russia to shed the unstable semiunitarian and semifederal state that was dominant in 1991–1995 and adopt some sort of confederation with high provincial autonomy. As has been historically true, in the future there will also be an oscillation in relative power between the center and the periphery, depending on various internal and external circumstances.

Several other scenarios can also be envisaged. For a while, Russia might again become a strong, centralized state. However, it is also possible that it could become a very loose confederation that would still contain most of its regions, much as the Holy Roman Empire did.

Speculation about Russia's future has to be placed in the context of worldwide trends in the relationship between the center and the periphery. Some authors have predicted that the existing trend toward regionalization, coupled with the trend toward the independence of even small ethnic groups, will lead toward the disintegration of the world's leading countries. The United States, Canada, and Brazil in the Americas; China, India, Afghanistan, and the Philippines in Asia; Russia in both Europe and Asia; Spain, France, Belgium, Norway, and Sweden in Europe; and Australia will either lose large sections of their territories or will be replaced by a number of new, smaller states.[2]

Other authors speak of the end of an era of universalism and the beginning of a period of fragmentation or Balkanization in the world.[3] The demise of communism, one of the most universalist ideologies in the history of mankind, has significantly contributed to the global trend of fragmentation in the territory of the former Soviet Union and Yugoslavia.

Abbreviations

The names of Russian journals and periodicals will be abbreviated if cited more than once in any chapter. When first cited in that chapter, the full name of the journal or periodical will be used, for example, *Izvestia*, 30 October 1973. Thereafter, the name of the journal or periodical will be given in abbreviated form, as follows:

AiF.	*Argumenty i Fakty*
Fiz.	*Finansovyie Izvestia*
Iz.	*Izvestia*
K.	*Kommersant*
KP	*Komsomol'skaia Pravda*
LG	*Literaturnaia Gazeta*
LR	*Literaturnaia Rossia*
ME	*Megalopolis Express*
MK	*Moskovskii Komsomol'ets*
MN	*Moskovskie Novosti*
NG	*Nezavisimaia Gazeta*
NV	*Novoie Vremia*
O.	*Ogoniok*
P.	*Pravda*
R.	*Respublika*
Reg.	*Region*
REZh.	*Rossiiskii Ekonomicheskii Zhurnal*
RG	*Rossiskaia Gazeta*
Seg.	*Segodnia*
SG.	*Sibirskaia Gazeta*
SR	*Sovietskaia Rossia*
UR	*Uralskii Rabochii*
Z.	*Zavtra*

NOTES

Chapter 1

1. Among the most important books on the economic issues surrounding regionalism in the last decade are Walter Isard, *Introduction to Regional Science*, Englewood Cliffs, NJ: Prentice-Hall, 1975; William Miernyk, *Regional Analysis and Regional Policy*, Cambridge: Oelgeschlager, 1982; N. Vanhove and L. Klaasen, *Regional Policy: A European Approach*, Aldershot, England: Avebury, 1987; Edgar Hoover and Frank Giarratani, *An Introduction to Regional Economics*, 3d ed., New York: Knopf, 1984; and Geoffrey Hewings, *Regional Industrial Analysis*, London: Methuen, 1977.

On the economic issues surrounding regionalization in Russia, see Nikolai Nekrasov, *Regionalnaia Ekonomika*, Moskva: Nauka, 1978; Leonard Kozlov, *Regionalnaia Ekonomika: Novye Podkhody*, Moskva: Nauka, 1993; Alexander Granberg, "Regionalnaia Ekonomika i Regionalnaia Nauka v Sovietskom Soyuze i Rossia," *Region*, no. 1, 1994; V. Chichkanov and R. Menakir, *Analiz i Prognozirovanie Ekonomiki Regiona*, Moskva: Nauka, 1984.

2. See Donald Campbell and Julian Stanley, *Experimental and Quasi-Experimental Designs for Research*, Chicago: Rand McNally, 1963; Vladimir Shlapentokh, *Problemy Dostovernosti Statisticheskoi Informatsii v Sotsiologicheskikh Issledovaniakh*, Moskva: Statistika, 1973.

Chapter 2

1. V. Kaganskii has suggested that "regionalization" can be used in four different ways, meaning (1) a "sovereignization" of structural, including spatial, elements; (2) a dismantling of the hierarchical system's upper level; (3) a "collapse" of sovereign regions; and (4) the restructuring of the relationship between the center and the regions (V. Kaganskii, "Realnosti Regionlizatsii: Osnovnye Aspekty Protsessa," in *Kuda Idet Rossia? Alternativy Obshchestvennogo Razvitia*, T. Zaslavskaia and L. Arutiunian, (eds.), Moskva: Interpraks, 1994, pp. 171–175).

2. For more on the differences between regionalism and nationalism, see Walker Connor, "Ethno-nationalism in the First World," in *Ethnic Conflict in the Western World*, M. Esman (ed.), Ithaca: Cornell University Press, 1977. For more on mininationalism, see Louis Snider, *Global Mini-Nationalism, Autonomy, and Independence*, Westport, CT: Greenwood, 1982.

3. Talcott Parsons and Edward Shils (eds.), *Towards a General Theory of Action,* Cambridge: Harvard University Press, 1959, pp. 77–82; Talcott Parsons, *Sociological Theory and Modern Society,* New York: Free Press, 1967, pp. 200–202.

4. Talcott Parsons, *The Evolution of Societies,* Englewood Cliffs, NJ: Prentice-Hall, 1977, pp. 193–194.

5. Talcott Parsons, *Social Structure and Personality,* New York: Free Press of Glencoe, 1964, p. 347.

6. Parsons, 1977, p. 185.

7. Most Sovietologists do not even raise the issue of regionalism. Among the advocates of the totalitarian model, see Richard Pipes, *Russia Under the Bolshevik Regime,* New York: Alfred A. Knopf, 1993, and Zbigniew Brzezinski, *Ideology and Power in Soviet Politics,* New York: Praeger, 1967. However, even the "revisionists," who denied the applicability of the totalitarian model to Soviet society and looked for various conflicts within society, did not mention the issue. See Alexander Dallin, George Breslauer, and Stephen Cohen, *Rethinking the Soviet Experience: Politics and History Since 1917,* New York: Oxford University Press, 1985; Moshe Lewin, *The Gorbachev Phenomenon,* Berkeley: University of California Press, 1988; Robert Tucker, *Political Culture and Leadership in Soviet Russia,* New York: Norton, 1987; and Daniel Orlovsky (ed.), *Beyond Soviet Studies,* Washington, DC: Woodrow Wilson Center Press, 1985.

There have been a few books in which the authors dealt with regional administration and were inclined to see "pluralism" and "conflicts" in Soviet society. See Jerry Hough, *The Soviet Prefects: The Local Party Organs in Industrial Decision Making,* Cambridge: Harvard University Press, 1969; Philip Stuart, *Political Power in the Soviet Union: A Study of Decision Making in Stalingrad,* New York: Bobbs-Merrill, 1968; Joel Moses, *Regional Party Leadership and Policy Making in the USSR,* New York: Praeger, 1974. Even in these books, however, the authors did not discuss the relationship between the center and regions as being prone to conflict. They only debated the degree to which the Kremlin delegated power to its emissaries in the provinces.

Moreover, this issue has even been ignored in the more expansive books on Soviet society published after 1991. See Martin Malia, *The Soviet Tragedy: A History of Socialism in Russia, 1917–1991,* New York: Maxwell Macmillan International, 1994; Moshe Lewin, *Russia USSR Russia,* New York: Free Press, 1995; Stephen White, *Gorbachev and After,* Cambridge University Press, 1994. As an exception, we can point to Richard Sakva's book, *Russian Politics and Society,* London: Routledge, 1993, pp. 179–200, which devotes attention to regionalism in Russia; and Elizabeth Teague, "Center-Periphery Relations in the Russian Federation," in *National Identity and Ethnicity in Russia and the New States of Euroasia,* ed. Roman Szporluk, New York: Sharpe, 1994, pp. 21–58.

8. On regionalism in Italy, see Raimondo Strassoldo, "Globalism and Localism: Theoretical Reflections and Some Evidence," in *Globalization and Territorial Identity,* ed. Zdravko Mlynar, Aldershot: Avebury, 1992, pp. 47–55.

9. See Robert Putnam, *Making Democracy Work,* Princeton: Princeton University Press, 1993.

10. V. S. Naipaul, "India: A Wounded Civilization," in *Facing the Twenty-First Century,* ed. Barbara Crossette, Bloomington: Indiana University Press, 1993.

11. Regionalization in China has been of special significance because it presents a potential threat to the integrity of the country, as it does in Russia. There is a consensus among experts on China that after Mao's death, decentralization was gaining momentum

in the country because of the revival of such strong traditions as regional warlords fighting each other (Gerald Segal, "Beijing's Fading Clout," *New York Times*, 25 May 1994; see also Patrick E. Tyler, "Beijing Party Decapitated by President," *New York Times*, 8 May 1995).

12. See Jerry Gray, "Facing the Budget Alligators," *New York Times*, 14 January 1995.

13. See Arthur Schlesinger, *The Disuniting of America*, New York: Norton, 1992. Some authors even predict the emergence in the not-too-distant future of new states within the territory of the United States. For instance, a new Mexican-American state is seen as being possible (Peter Brimelow, *Common Sense About America's Immigration Disaster*, New York: Random House, 1995).

14. See Vladimir Streleltskii, "Grozit li Kirgizii raskol," *Nezavisimaia Gazeta*, 3 March 1993; Igor Rotar, "Vzorvetsia li Sredniia Azia," *NG*, 21 January 1993; Oleg Blotskii, "Tadzhikistan: Zelenoie-krasnoie," *Literaturnaia Gazeta*, 4 November 1992; K. Baialinov, "Prostoi padishakh s neprostymi zamashkami," *Komsomol'skaia Pravda*, 28 October 1992; Sergei Alexashenko, Andrei Neshchadin, and Sergei Kosarenko, "'Osobyi rayon' Narvy," *Moskovskie Novosti*, 22 November 1992; Garri Raagmaa, "New Enterprises and Regional Development in Estonia," in *Local and Regional Development During the 1990s Transition in Eastern Europe*, ed. Markki Tykkylainen, Aldershot: Avebury, 1995, pp. 29–46.

15. Parsons, 1977, p. 194; Talcott Parsons, *Action Theory and the Human Condition*, New York: Free Press, 1978, p. 345; and B. Russet, *International Regions and the International System*, Chicago: Rand McNally, 1967.

16. "Regional literature" had already begun to flourish by the beginning of the late eighteenth and nineteenth centuries. The Romantic movement, which idealized provincial life and its noble and simple people as well as the proximity to nature, contrasted the virtues of remote regions to the wickedness of the capital and its residents. This group of writers includes Jean-Jacques Rousseau, with his glorification of provincial life in several novels such as *New Eloise*. Among others are William Wordsworth and Samuel Coleridge, renowned for their poetry. Others fitting this description are Sir Walter Scott, who described the cult of medievalism and the joy of life in the provinces in his historical novels. Among French authors, the regionalist sentiment was quite strong in François Chateaubriand, Victor Hugo, Dumas Père, Alphonse de Lamartine, Alfred de Musset, and George Sand. In Russia, both of the greatest poets of the first half of the nineteenth century, Alexander Pushkin and Mikhail Lermontov, were also known for their sympathy for life outside the capital.

From the mid-nineteenth to the mid-twentieth century, many of the bards of regionalism spread the philosophy throughout the world. In American literature, prominent writers became known for their regionalist sympathies, including Henry Thoreau, Nathaniel Hawthorne, James Fenimore Cooper, Frank Norris, Robert Penn Warren, and William Faulkner. Several authors in Latin America were also known for their interest in regional life, including such notables as Chico Alencar, Juarez Tavora, and Antonio Candido.

Regionalism was quite strong in Russian literature in the nineteenth and twentieth centuries. Among the most well-known regionalists were Pavel Melnikov (pseudonym Pecherskii), Dmitriy Mamin-Sibiriak, Gleb Uspenskii, and Vladimir Korolenko. Regionalism was quite visible in Soviet literature in the post-Stalin era. The authors of so-called rural prose (Valentin Rasputin, Vasilii Shukshin, Viktor Astafief, and Vasilii Belov were the most important representatives of this school) can be described as regionalists who demonstrated a great hatred of Moscow combined with the glorification of the life in the province.

On regionalism in literature, see David Jordan, *New World Regionalists*, Toronto: University of Toronto Press, 1994; Ludmila Iakimova, *Literaturnaia Kritika v Sibiri: Sbornik Nauchnykh Trudov*, Novosibirsk: Nauka, 1988; and Piksanov, *Oblastnye Kulturnye Gnezda*, *Istoriko-Kraevedcheskii* seminar, Moskva, 1928.

17. See Charles Tilly (ed.), *The Formation of National States in Western Europe*, Princeton: Princeton University Press, 1975, p. 15.

18. For more on the rationale of centralization and the nation-state, see Raphael Zariski and Marc Rousseau, "National Power and Local Government: Problems and Perspectives," in *Regionalism and Regional Devolution in Comparative Perspective*, Raphael Zariski and Marc Rousseau (eds.), New York: Praeger, 1987, pp. 1–43.

19. For more on traditionalist theories and their critique, see Michael Keating, *State and Regional Nationalism: Territorial Politics and the European State*, New York, London: Harvester Wheatsheaf, 1988; R. Rose and D. Urwin, *Regional Differentiation and Political Unity in Western Nations*, Professional Papers in Contemporary Political Sociology, 06–007, London: Sage Publications, 1975; W. Folz, "Modernization and Nation Building: The Social Mobilization Model Reconsidered," in *From National Development to Global Community*, R. Merrit and B. Russet (eds.), London: Allen and Unwin, 1981; John Agnew, *Place and Politics*, London: Allen and Unwin, 1987. For more on modernization theories, see Alex Inkeles and David Smith, *Becoming Modern: Individual Change in Six Developing Countries*, Cambridge: Harvard University Press, 1974; Robert Alford, *Party and Society: The Anglo-American Democracies*, Chicago: Rand McNally, 1963; Martin Lipset and Stein Rokkan, *Elites in Latin America*, New York: Oxford University Press, 1967; Tom Nairn, *The Breakup of Britain: Crisis and Neo-Nationalism*, London: NLB, 1977; Barrington Moore, *The Social Origins of Dictatorship and Democracy*, Boston: Beacon, 1966.

20. Keating, 1988, p. 22.

21. See Keating, 1988; Jean Gottmann, *Center and Periphery Spatial Variation in Politics*, Beverly Hills: Sage Publications, 1980, pp. 218–219; Owen Lattimore, "The Periphery as Locus of Innovation" in Gottmann, 1980.

22. Gottmann, 1980, p. 19.

23. As recently as 1988, Michael Keating said that "peripheral regionalism is not necessarily a relic of the past nor evidence of incomplete modernization. Indeed, in some cases it may be possible to reverse the old orthodoxy which saw peripheral assertion as a 'revolt against modernity'" (M. Lipset, *Consensus and Conflict: Essays in Political Sociology*, New Brunswick, NJ: Transaction Books, 1985; Keating, 1988, p. 18).

24. It is also true for nationalist regionalism in many other countries. Quebec or Catalonia, for example, should not be considered backward provinces of their countries.

25. The concept of "internal colonialism" was developed by Antonio Gramsci (*Antonio Gramsci: Selections from His Political Writings*, London: Lawrence and Wishart, 1978) and was supported by many radical ideologies from the 1950s until the 1970s (R. Lafont, *La Révolution Régionaliste*, Paris: Gallimard, 1967; Michel Hechter, *Internal Colonialism: The Celtic Fringe in British National Development*, Berkeley: University of California Press, 1975).

26. For more on the regional problems in England, see P. Madgwick and R. Rose (eds.), *The Territorial Dimensions in UK Policy*, London: Macmillan, 1982.

27. See Vitalii Portnikov, "Unitarnaia Rossia budet predstavlena v parlamente," *NG*, 14 December 1993; Hans Van Zon, *Alternative Scenarios for Central Europe*, Aldershot: Avebury, 1994, p. 42.

28. In this respect, the situation in East Germany is a special case because several years after the reunification, East Germany was still significantly different from the western part of the country. Many people, mostly the elderly ("Ostiens") in East Germany, had a sort of nostalgia for several elements of their socialist past and tried to preserve their specificity.

29. Of course, the North League does not overlook the opportunity to speak about the glorious past of Lombardy and its capital Milan, which is now the economic and financial heart of modern Italy. Prior to becoming the capital of Lombardy, Milan was the past capital of Rome's Western Empire and a Christian center. The league's ideology, of course, incorporates boasting about the famous rulers of Lombardy, from the Viscontis to the Sforzas (see Spencer di Scala, *Italy: From Revolution to Republic, 1700 to the Present*, Boulder: Westview Press, 1995; for more on local movements in Italy, see Giancarlo Rovati, "Political Localism and National Identity in Italy: The Case of Regional Leagues," in *European Transformation: Five Decisive Years at the Turn of the Century*, ed. Ronald Pohoryles, Aldershot: Avebury, 1994, pp. 244–253).

In the same vein, Scotland glorifies its heroes, such as Robert the Bruce or Mary Queen of Scots, while the various provinces in Spain, such as the Basque country, Andalusia, and Galicia, all of which received special rights in 1979, also exploit as much as possible their historical heritage (Alan Riding, "As Social Ills Stir, French Premier's Ratings Sag," *New York Times*, 19 March 1994).

30. See Walker Connor, *Ethnonationalism: The Quest for Understanding*, Princeton: Princeton University Press, 1994; Tony Judt, "The New Old Nationalism," *New York Times Book Review*, 26 May 1994, pp. 44–51; Yael Tamir, *Liberal Nationalism*, Princeton: Princeton University Press, 1993; and Michael Ignatieff, *Blood and Belonging: Journies into the New Nationalism*, New York: Farrar, Straus and Giroux, 1994.

31. It was Alexis de Tocqueville who noted that centralization is a necessary condition for the development of democratization and egalitarism (Raimondo Strassoldo, "Center-Periphery and System Boundary: Culturological Perspectives, pp. 27–57, in Gottmann, 1980, p. 37).

32. Totalitarianism, as we understand it from the classic works of Hannah Arendt, Zbigniew Brzezinski, and Samuel Huntington, is defined as a system of government and ideology in which all social, political, economic, intellectual, cultural, and spiritual activities are subordinated to the purposes of the rulers of a state. Several important features distinguish totalitarianism, a form of autocracy peculiar to the twentieth century, from such older forms as despotism, absolutism, and tyranny. In the older forms of autocracy, people could live and work in comparative independence, provided they refrained from politics. In modern totalitarianism, however, people are made utterly dependent on the wishes and whims of a political party and its leaders. The older autocracies were ruled by a monarch or other titled aristocrat who governed by a principle, such as divine right, whereas the modern totalitarian state is ruled by a leader, or dictator, who controls a political party (see Hannah Arendt, *The Origins of Totalitarianism*, New York: Harcourt Brace, 1951; Brzezinski, 1967; and Carl Friedrich and Zbigniew Brzezinski, *Totalitarian Dictatorship and Autocracy*, Cambridge: Harvard University Press, 1956).

33. Even in 1985, Kenneth Boulding's book, *The World as a Total System* (Beverly Hills, CA: Sage Publications, 1985) appeared almost sensational.

34. See Zdravko Mlynar (ed.), *Globalization and Territorial Identity*, Aldershot: Avebury, 1992, p. 1.

35. Anthony McGrew et al., *Global Politics*, Cambridge: Polity Press, 1992, pp. 233–249; S. Gill and D. Law, *The Global Political Economy: Perspectives, Problems, and Policies*, Brighton: Harvester Wheatsheaf, 1988; J. Kolko, *Restructuring the World Economy*, New York: Pantheon Books, 1988.

36. See R. Cappellin and P. Batey (eds.), *Regional Networks, Border Regions, and European Integration*, London: Pion, 1993, pp. 2, 6; Janush Slugocki (ed.), *Regionalism in Europe: Traditions and New Trends*, Bydgoszcz-Geneva: European Center for Regional and Ethnic Studies, 1993.

37. For more on the combination of both tendencies, "globalization" and "individuation," see Mlynar, 1992, pp. 35–59; and Antoni Kuklinski (ed.), *Baltic Europe in the Perspective of Global Change*, Warsaw: Oficyna Naukowa, 1995.

38. See Strassoldo in Gottmann, 1980, pp. 38–39.

39. H. Mowlana, *Global Information and World Communication*, New York: Longman, 1986.

40. R. Apple, "Washington, 1995: Echoes of a 200-Year Debate," *New York Times Week in Review*, 24 December 1995.

41. Strassoldo sees more evidence that the concept of centrality is deeply rooted in Western civilization in the orientation toward "circle" and "center" in the European arts until the end of the nineteenth century. He also sees such evidence of this in modern architecture (Strassoldo, in Gottmann, 1980, pp. 28, 35–36).

42. The predominance of "centrality" in totalitarian and stable states was evident to ancients such as Plato, whose state has a strong center controlling the periphery in order to deter any unnecessary contact with the outside world. Influenced by Plato's laws, the famous German philosopher, Johann Gottlieb Fichte, advocated in 1800 a closed, centralized, and autarkic state that had to protect its citizens against the pernicious influence of the French Revolution. In his turn, Fichte influenced another famous apologist of territorial "centrality," Johann Von Thuenen, who, in his book *The Isolated State* (Oxford, New York: Pergamon Press, 1826, 1966), also justified the necessity of strong spatial centrality, this time with economic arguments.

43. Vladlen Loginov resolutely explained today's fragmentation, as well as that of 1917–1920, by "the crisis of statehood" (*MN*, 27 July 1993).

44. Many Russian intellectuals were inspired to compose odes dedicated to both capitals (for an example, see Alexander Pushkin, "Copper Horseman" [*Mednyi Vsadnik*], Moskva: Izd-vo Literatury, 1937; see also Fedor Dostoyevskii in general).

45. See Michael Keating and Barry Jones, *Regions in the European Community*, Oxford: Clarendon Press, 1985, pp. 2–3.

46. See Karl Deutsch, *Decentralization: Sketches Toward a Rational Theory*, Cambridge, Massachusetts: Verlag A. Hain, 1980; A. Etzioni, *The Active Society*, New York: Macmillan, 1968; J. Miller, "Living Systems: Basic Concepts," *Behavioral Science* 10:3, 1965a, and "Living Systems: Structure and Process," Behavioral Science, 10:4, 1965b; H. Simon, *The Sciences of the Artificial*, Cambridge, Massachusetts: MIT Press, 1969 and also in J. Gottmann, 1980.

For works on complex organizations, see Peter Blau, *The Structure of Organizations*, New York: Basic Books, 1971; Richard Hall, *Organizations, Structures, Processes, Outcomes*, Englewood Cliffs, NJ: Prentice-Hall, 1991, pp. 48–83; Jerald Hage, *Social Change in Complex Organizations*, New York: Random House, 1970; Paul Lawrence and Lorsch, *Differentiation and Integration in Complex Organizations*, Boston: Harvard University, 1967;

Charles Perrow, *Organizational Analysis: A Sociological View*, Belmont, CA: 1970, pp. 32–35; Raymond Miles, *Theories of Management: Implications for Organizational Behavior and Developments*, New York: McGraw-Hill, 1975, p. 78.

47. From this point of view, the comparison made by Alfred Meyer in *The Soviet Political System: An Interpretation* (New York: Random House, 1965) between Soviet society and large corporations, although of dubious applicability in many respects, is quite reasonable for the analysis of the relations between the various levels of hierarchy (see also Gottmann, 1980).

48. See Hall, 1991, p. 78.

49. For more on the parallels between post-Communist Russia and early feudalism in Western Europe, see Vladimir Shlapentokh, "Russia: Privatization and Illegalization of Social and Political Life," *Washington Quarterly* 19 (1) (Winter 1996).

50. Lewis Coser, *The Functions of Social Conflict*, Glencoe: Free Press, 1956; Randall Collins, *Conflict Sociology: Toward an Explanatory Science*, New York: Academic Press, 1975, and *Three Sociological Traditions*, New York: Oxford University Press, 1985; Ralf Dahrendorf, *Class and Class Conflict in Industrial Society*, Stanford: Stanford University Press, 1959, and *Conflict After Class: New Perspectives on the Theory of Social and Political Conflict*, London: Longmans, for the University of Essex, 1967, and *The Reflections on the Revolution in Europe*, London: Chatto and Windus, 1990; Raymond Aron, *Progress and Disillusion*, New York: Praeger, 1968; Robert Lauer, *Perspective of Social Change*, Boston: Allyn and Bacon, 1991.

51. Several authors tried to use game theory for the analysis of various political and social processes without speaking about economics. The first area of the application of this theory to social issues is connected with John Neumann and Oskar Morgenstern's famous book, *The Theory of Games and Economic Behavior* (Princeton: Princeton University Press, 1944). In the social sciences, n-person game theory has interesting uses in studying, for example, the distribution of power in legislative procedures. Individual and group decision-making are also amenable to such study. Several authors have tried to use the game theory approach for the analysis of such processes as transition to democracy (Joseph Colomer, *Game Theory and the Transition to Democracy: The Spanish Model*, Aldershot: Edward Elgar/Ashgate, 1995). Among recent books on the application of game theory to the social issues of economics are Mark Casson, *The Economics of Business Culture: Game Theory, Transactions Costs, and Economic Performance*, Oxford: Clarendon Press, 1991.

52. A similar approach to the study of territorial issues is advanced by Mlynar, 1992, pp. 15–34.

53. As Vladimir Shubkin, a famous Russian sociologist, noted once, the relationship between the center and provinces reminds one of a yoke—if one bucket is higher, another will be lower (see V. Shubkin, "The Ruling Siberian Elite," paper presented at the Conference on The New Elite in Post-Communist Society, Michigan State University, November 1994).

It was amusing to observe how Russian leaders, beginning with Mikhail Gorbachev, followed by Boris Yeltsin, tried to ignore this principle, calling for a society "with a strong center and strong republics" and then for "a strong center and strong regions." The single fact—the necessity to divide taxes between central and local administrations—is an evident argument that the interests between both actors are in substance antagonistic. This is true of any society, including America, with permanent conflicts between the central and local administrations over the distribution of resources.

54. See Mancur Olson, *The Logic of Collective Action*, Cambridge: Harvard University Press, 1965.

55. See Yanis Varoufakis, *Rational Conflict*, Oxford: Blackwell 1991, p. 6; and Henry Hamburger, *Games as Models of Social Phenomena*, San Francisco: Freeman, 1979, pp. 197–228.

56. Some interesting insights useful for the analysis of the CP relationship can be borrowed from the concept of "loose coupling," which describes situations in which organizational units have a low level of interdependence (see Karl Weick, *The Social Psychology of Organizing*, New York: Random House, 1979; Howard Aldrich, *Organizations and Environments*, New York: Prentice-Hall, 1979; David Whetten, *Inter-organizational Coordination Theory, Research, and Implementation*, Ames: Iowa State University Press, 1982).

57. If involved in this process at all, intellectuals concentrated their efforts on the cultural dimensions of regionalization.

58. Three different groups participated in the *rissorgimento* in Italy. Revolutionary groups, such as the Carbonari, produced intellectuals like Alessandro Manzoni and Ugo Foscolo, oppositional politicians such as Giuseppe Mazzini, and also the official politicians who favored unification under the house of Savoy.

59. For more on rational behavior in game theory, see Varoufakis, 1991, pp. 10–11, 15–35.

60. See Snider, 1982, pp. 251–256.

61. See Rovati, 1994, p. 247.

62. Lansing Lamont describes the possible breakdown of Canada in the most apocalyptic way, particularly in relation to the United States. He contends that the United States would suffer great economic damage, lose an important ally in NATO, make its northern borders unstable, and so on. To make his point stronger, Lamont describes as a scenario the possible success of a Red-Brown putsch in Moscow and the dissolution of the Canadian center. With Canada's air defense in disarray, the United States would now be very vulnerable to the penetration of Russian bombers loaded with nuclear weapons through the polar ice cap. In conclusion, Lamont wrote, "A breakup of Canada would in all likelihood send the world a message of despair . . . Canada's disintegration would instruct the world, particularly its less favored people, that even the richest, freest, and the most developed democracies can die when the will to unify has atrophied" (Lansing Lamont, *Breakup: The Coming End of Canada and the Stakes for America*, New York: Norton, 1994).

Chapter 3

1. Anonymous, *Povest Vremennykh Let*, Moskva: Izd-vo Akademii Nauk SSSR, 1950.

2. Boris Grekov, *Kievskaia Rus'*, Moscow: Foreign Languages Publishing House, 1959.

3. See Igor Froianov, *Kievskaia Rus'*, Leningrad: Izd-vo Leningradskogo Universiteta, 1974.

4. For instance, see the conversation of general Alexander Lebed with Alexander Prokhanov, the editor of *Zavtra* (no. 34, August 1995, p. 3).

5. Lev Gumilev, *Drevniaia Rus' i Velikaia Step*, Moskva: Mysl', 1989.

6. V. Pashuto et al., *Drevnerusskoe Nasledie*, Moskva: Mysl', 1977, p. 21.

7. *Rossia, Entsiklopedicheskii Slovar*, St. Petersburg: F. Brokgauz-I. Efron, 1898, p. 452.

8. See Gumilev, 1989, p. 555.

9. See, for instance, Nikolai Nosov (ed.), *Kratkaia Istoria SSSR*, Leningrad: Nauka, 1978, p. 99.

10. See Gumilev, 1989, p. 562.

11. Ibid.

12. Alexander Zimin, *Vitiaz na Rasputie*, Moskva: *Khud-ia Literatura*, 1991.

13. See Naum Korzhavin, *Vremena-Izbrannoe*, Frankfurt-Main: Posev, 1976.

14. Viktor Paneiakh, "Panorama Istorii Rossii XY-XYI," *Otechestvennaia Istoria*, no. 6, 1991, pp. 75–78.

15. See Zimin, 1991.

16. See Sergei Kurginian, "V lovushke," *Argumenty i Fakty*, no. 35, August 1995.

17. For example, see Nikolai Bolshakov, "Fenomen Ziuganova," *Sovietskaia Rossia*, 24 October 1995.

18. *Ekonomicheskaia Istoria Kapitalisticheskikh Stran*, Moskva: *Nauka*, 1973, p. 76.

19. Stepan Veselovskii, *Issledovania po Istorii Klassa Sluzhilykh Zemlevladeltsev*, Moskva: *Nauka*, 1969, p. 78.

20. See *Rossia, Entsiklopedicheskii Slovar*, 1898, p. 458.

21. See *Rossia, Entsiklopedicheskii Slovar*, 1898, pp. 185–186.

22. Vladimir Shlapentokh, *Soviet Public Opinion and Ideology*, New York: Praeger, 1986.

23. Nikolai Eroshkin, *Ocherki Istorii Gosudarstvennykh Uchrezhdenii Dorevolutsionnoi Rossii*, Moskva: Moskovskii Gosudarstvennyi Arkhivnyi Institut, 1960, p. 29.

24. Even in civil cases, guilty parties received sentences in the criminal category, such as corporal punishment. For instance, insolvent debtors were sentenced to beatings with whips. Moreover, for every one hundred rubles of debt, a person was beaten over the course of a month. Interrogations in criminal cases were always accompanied by torture, and in accordance with the *Sobornoye Ulozhenie* (Fundamental Law) of 1649, capital punishment was meted out in sixty cases, including cases of infractions such as noninformation on state crimes. See Eroshkin, 1960, pp. 44–45.

25. Ibid., p. 45.

26. *Rossia, Entsiklopedicheskii Slovar*, 1898, p. 467.

27. See Eroshkin, 1960, p. 84.

28. See *Sovietskaia Istoricheskaia Entsiklopedia*, Moskva: Sovietskaia Entsiklopedia, vol. 4, 1963, pp. 868–869.

29. See Eroshkin, 1960, p. 90.

30. Ibid.

31. Ibid., p. 120.

32. Ibid., p. 120.

33. Ivan Blinov, *Gubernatory*, Istoriko-Iuridicheckii Ocherk, St. Petersburg: Tipografia Pentkovskii, 1905, p. 85.

34. Ibid., p. 127.

35. Ibid., p. 86.

36. *Rossia, Entsiklopedicheskii Slovar*, 1898, p. 477.

37. Eroshkin, 1960, p. 119.

38. *Rossia, Entsiklopedicheskii Slovar*, 1898, p. 477.

39. Eroshkin, 1960, pp. 120–122.

40. Ibid., p. 126.

41. Ibid., p. 124.

42. Ibid., p. 125.

43. Ibid.

44. *Rossia, Entsiklopedicheskii Slovar*, 1989, pp. 473, 483.

45. Ibid., p. 485.

46. Nikolai Gogol, *Mertvye Dushi*, Moskva: Khudozhestvennaia Literatura, 1982, pp. 240–242.

47. Mikhail Saltykov-Shchedrin, *Poshekhonskaia Starina*, Moskva: Gos. Izd-vo Khudozhestvennoi Literatury, 1980, pp. 235–253.

48. Alexander Pushkin, *Sochinenia v trekh tomakh*, vol. 2, Moskva: Izd-vo Akademii Nauk SSSR, 1962, pp. 312–314.

49. See Gogol, 1982, pp. 350–353; Alexander Ostrovskii, *Polnoe Sobranie Sochinenii*, vol. 5, Moskva: Khudozhestvennaia Literatura, 1950.

50. *Rossia, Entsiklopedicheskii Slovar*, 1898, p. 483.

51. Ibid., pp. 486–487.

52. The best book on the history of the zemstvo is still that of Boris Veselovskii, *Istoria Zemstva za Sorok Let*, vols. 1–4, St. Petersburg: Izdatel'stvo Popovoi, 1909–1911; see also Alexander Kizevetter, *Mestnoie Samoupravlenie v Rossii*, The Hague and Paris: Mouton, 1970; Ivan Belokonskii, *Zemskoie Dvizhenie*, Moskva: Zadruga, 1914; Natalia Pirumova, *Zemskoie Liberalnoe Dvizhenie*, Moskva: Nauka, 1977; George Fisher, *Russian Liberalism*, Cambridge: Harvard University, 1958; and Charles Timberlake (ed.), *Essays on Russian Liberalism*, Columbia: University of Missouri Press, 1972.

53. See Paul Vinogradoff, *Self-Government In Russia*, London: Constable, 1915, pp. 52–53.

54. For instance, as previously mentioned, the reforms of Ivan IV shifted some of the responsibility for local affairs onto the local population. Some of these elements of self-government were also present in the time of Catherine the Great (see L. Lapteva, *Zemskie Uchrezhdenia v Rossii*, Moskva: In-t Gosudarstva i Prava RAN, 1993, pp. 22–31).

55. During, and particularly after, the self-government reforms, Russian law experts vehemently discussed the role of the zemstvo in the Russian empire. These debates are quite similar to those that later took place in the 1990s over the role of self-government in post-Communist Russia. Boris Chicherin, a famous scholar close to the government, insisted on the necessity of the separation of political power and public activity in local affairs, substantiating in this way the necessity of the ultimate superiority of the state over self-government (see B. Chicherin, *O Narodnom Predstavitelstve*, Moskva: Tipografia Gracheva, 1866, p. 755).

Following Chicherin, some authors suggested the necessity of viewing the zemstvo as simply a part of the state machinery. The Communists did exactly this after the Russian Revolution of 1917, making all so-called public organizations, such as trade unions, the Young Communist League, and others "the cogs of the party (or state) machine" (Alexander Gradovskii, *Sobranie Sochinenii*, vol. 9, St. Petersburg: Stas I Ulevich, 1908, pp. 5–29). Several other Russian authors, such as Vladimir Bezobrazov and Konstantin Kavelin, in one or another way supported this approach to the zemstvo during this period. At the same time, there were a lot of authors who wanted to see the zemstvo as an independent body that could make decisions on local affairs and as a foundation for the democratization of Russia (see Ivan Petrunkevich, *Iz Zapisok Obshchestvennogo Deiatelia*, St. Petersburg, n.p., 1907; Vasilii Skalon, *Mnenia Zemskikh Sobranii o Sovremennom Polozhenii Rossii*, Berlin-Paris: Behr, 1883; and Lapteva, 1993).

56. Eroshkin, 1960, p. 231.

57. Veselovskii, vol. 3, 1909, pp. 1–2.

58. *Sovietskaia Istoricheskaia Entsiklopedia*, vol. 5, Moskva: Sovietskaia Entsiklopedia, 1967, p. 682.

59. See, for instance, Lapteva, 1993, pp. 59–65.

60. The hopes that the role of the zemstvo as an institution would be able to transform the centralized, authoritarian character of Russia was particularly strong in the period of reform under Mikhail Loris-Melikhov, Alexander II's minister of internal affairs in the 1860s, who saw the zemstvo as a leading institution for the implementation of liberal changes (see Belokonskii, 1914, pp. 23, 53, 103).

61. For more on the attempts of the Russian autocratic state to curb the activities of the zemstvo as much as possible, see S. Witte, *Samoderzhavie i Zemstvo*, Stuttgart: Dietz, 1903; and Richard Pipes, *Russia Under the Old Regime*, New York: Charles Scribner, 1974, p. 303.

62. Nikolai Novikov, *Tverskoe Zemstvo*, Tver: Knizhnoe Izd-vo, 1984, pp. 11–14.

63. Eroshkin, 1960, pp. 229–230.

64. Ibid., p. 236.

65. The persecution of the zemstvos was especially strong in 1869–1874 before the murder of Alexander II (Pirumova, 1977, pp. 31–34).

66. See Boris Veselovskii, *Iubileinyi Zemskii Sbornik*, St. Petersburg: Izd-vo T-va O. N. Popovoi, 1914 (Ann Arbor, MI, 1963], pp. 327, 334, 423.

67. Eroshkin, 1960, p. 223.

68. See B. Chmykhalo, "Literaturnye Vzgliady Pozdnikh 'Oblastnikov,'" in *Literaturnaia Kritika v Sibiri*, ed. Liudmila Iakimova, Novosibirsk: Nauka, 1988, pp. 113–129; and V. Korzhavin, V. Mirzoiev, and G. Ianovskii, "K kharakteristike Sibirskogo oblastnichestva," *Sibirskie Ogni*, no. 12, 1971.

69. For more on Grigorii Potanin and Nikolai Iadrintsev, see *Golos Minuvshego*, no. 1, 1915; M. Sesiunina, "K voprosu ob evoliutsii sibirskogo oblastnichestva," *Voprosy Istorii Sibiri*, vol. 3, Tomsk: Izd-vo Tomskogo Universiteta, 1967; M. Sesiunina, *G. N. Potanin and N. M. Iadrinsev–Ideologi Sibirskogo Oblastnichestva*, Tomsk: Izd-vo Tomskogo Universiteta, 1974; M. Sesiunina, "I. Razon, I. Plotnikova, G. N. Potanin v gody sotsialisticheskoi revolutsii i grazhdanskoi voiny v Sibiri," *Voprosy Istoria Sibiri*, vol. 2, Tomsk, 1965; M. Sheinfeld, "Sibirskoie oblastnichestvo i borba s nim marksistov v gody pervoi mirovoi voiny," *Istoria Sibiri*, vol. 1, Krasnoiarsk: Krasnoiarskii Gosudarstvennyi Institut, 1969; and P. Vibe, A. Mikheiev, and N. Pugacheva (eds.), *Omskii Istoriko-Kraevedcheskii Slovar*, Omsk: Otechestvo, 1995.

70. Mark Bandman, *Dezintegratsionnyie I Integratsionnye Protsessy v Sibiri*, ed. Grigorii Kostinskii, Moskva: Institut Geografii RA, 1995, p. 60.

71. The movement's main periodicals during its first period of development were *Vostochnoie Obozrenie* and *Sibir*.

72. See Varlen Soskin, *Sibir v Proshlom i Nastoiashchem: Vzgliady na Budushcheie*, Novosibirsk, 1996 (manuscript), p. 17.

73. The main opponent of the *oblastnichestvo* among these exiled revolutionaries was N. Chuzhak, associated with the Siberian magazine *Bagulnik*.

74. Some members of the movement even entered the government of General Kolchak, a fact that partially explains why in the Soviet Union, and particularly under Stalin, the sympathy for *oblastnichestvo* was equated with state treason. Indeed, many peo-

ple who were arrested in Siberia in the purges of the 1930s were accused as being Siberian separatists and followers of *oblastnichestvo* (see Vladimir Shubkin, *Nasilie i Svoboda*, Moskva: Na Vorobievykh, 1996, pp. 111–116).

75. See Vivian Itin, "Literatura sovietskoi Sibiri," *Sibirskie Ogni*, no. 5, 1934, p. 94.

76. N. Chuzhak, B. Zherebtsov, and particularly V. Zazubrin, the editor of the magazine *Sibirskie Ogni*.

77. The title of the book *Essays on Russian Literature in Siberia* (*Ocherki Russkoi Literatury v Sibiri*, Liudmila Iakimova, Novosibirsk: *Nauka*, 1987) is typical of this phenomenon. Any attempt to speak about the specific character of Siberian literature created the opportunity for some zealot, such as G. Kungurov, to denounce those who tried to restore *oblastnichestvo*, or regionalism, among Siberian authors. However, in the milder post-Gulag atmosphere, some authors dared to argue cautiously with party hacks and defended the right of "literarary regionalism" to exist (see L. Iakimova, "Problema literaturnogo regionalizma v osveshchenii literaturnoi kritiki v Sibiri," in Iakimova, 1988, pp. 22–47).

Chapter 4

1. See *Sovietskaia Istoricheskaia Entsiklopedia*, vol. 13, Moskva: Sovietskaia Entsiklopedia, 1967, p. 582.

2. See, for instance, Richard Pipes, *Russia Under the Old Regime*, New York: Charles Scribner, 1974.

3. The soviets established their power in thirty cities without the help of military-revolutionary committees (see Samuil S. Khesin, *Stanovlenie Proletarskoi Diktatury v Rossii*, Moskva: Nauka, 1975, p. 214, and *Soviety v Pervyi God Proletarskoi Diktatury*, Moskva: Nauka, 1967, p. 49).

4. By the end of the Russian Civil War, the number of vacancies in the soviets of fifty-three *gubernii* totaled 275,000. This far exceeded the number of employees, which was about 198,000 (see *Soviety v Epokhu Voennogo Kommunizma*, chap. 2, pp. 82–86).

5. S. Leonov, "Sovietskaia gosudarstvennost: Zamysly i deistvitelnost' (1917–1920)," *Voprosy Istorii*, no. 12, 1991, p. 35.

6. Efim G. Gimpel'son, *Soviety v Gody Inostrannoi Interventsii i Grazhdanskoi Voiny*, Moskva: Nauka, 1968, p. 141.

7. The Siberian Republic was established and existed for four months, from 4 July until 3 November 1918. After the expulsion of the Bolsheviks by the Czechoslovakian Legion, the local government created by the Tomsk Duma endorsed "the Declaration of the provisory Siberian government on the state independence of Siberia." However, as early as September 1918, this government dissolved itself and transferred all of its power to the All-Russian Government (see *Sibirskaia Gazeta*, no. 26, July 1993). For more on another Siberian independent region created by peasant groups, see Sergei Zalygin's novel, *Commission*, De Kalb: Northern Illinois University Press, 1993.

8. The Kaluga Republic existed formally between 1917 and 1920. However, it did indeed enjoy some independence (see *Kaluzhskii Gubkom RKP, Krasnyi Oktiabr, 7 Noiabra 1917–1920 goda*, Kaluga, 1920; *Tri Goda Oktiabrskoi Revolutsii v Kaluzhskoi Gubernii*, Kaluga, 1920; and *Kaluzhskaia Pravda*, 25 January 1918).

9. For instance, the Smolensk Regional Party Committee was bold enough in 1920 to refuse to fulfill a command from Moscow, retaining personnel that the center had decided

to transfer to the central apparatus. Such cases would be unthinkable a few years later (see Merle Fainsod, *Smolensk Under Soviet Rule*, New York: Vintage Books, 1958, pp. 38–39).

10. Timofei Sapronov, *Stat'i i Doklady po Voprosam Partiinogo i Sovietskogo Stroitel'stva*, Moskva: Gos. Izd-vo Politicheskoi Literatury, 1920; *Soviety v Epokhu Voennogo Kommunizma*, ch. 2, pp. 82–86; Gimpel'son, 1968, p. 252; *UIII S'ezd RKP(b), Stenograficheskii Otchet*, Moskva: Gos. Izd-vo Politicheskoi Literatury, 1954, pp. 202, 221; Yakov Sverdlov, *Izbrannye Proizvedenia*, Moskva: Gos. Izd-vo Politicheskoi Literatury, 1957–1960, p. 260.

11. A. Nelidov, *Istoria Gosudarstvennykh Uchrezhdenii SSSR (1917–1936)*, Moskva: Gos. Izd-vo Politicheskoi Literatury, 1962, pp. 230–231.

12. Nelidov, 1962, p. 234.

13. See the description of local life in the first decades of Soviet history in Anastas Mikoian, *V Nachale Dvadtsatykh*, Moskva: Politizdat, 1975.

14. See Sergei Kuleshov (ed.), *Nashe Otechestvo: Opyt Politicheskoi Istorii*, Moskva: Terra, 1991, pp. 131–132.

15. The arbitrariness of local authorities in their disregard for elementary laws often reached Herculean proportions. A typical example is a case in the Ladeipol District, where local Bolsheviks, having learned of the murder of Wilhelm Liebknecht (a leader of the German Communists and Third International) decided to kill a few members of the local bourgeoisie (*VIII S'ezd RKP(b), Stenograficheskii Otchet*, p. 202).

Local authorities in Vladimir decided to implement a course of action against the family as a bourgeois institution and to guarantee the equality of men in their access to women. An edict of the local soviet declared that women between the ages of eighteen and thirty-two were considered to be "state property," which must be distributed among all men. In Ekaterinodar, the local soviet issued to vanguard red soldiers a voucher that declared that "the owner of this voucher has the right to socialize in the city of Ekaterinodar with ten girls in ages between sixteen and twenty, who would be selected by this comrade" (see *Argumenty i Fakty*, no. 52, December 1995, p. 9).

16. In the first few years, members of *sovnarkhozy* were elected by workers at their enterprises (Vladimir Chuntulov, *Ekonomicheskaia Istoria SSSR, Epokha Sotsializma*, Moskva: Vysshaia Shkola, 1969).

17. At the Tenth Party Congress, advocates of "democratic centralism" (*"dezisty"*) were condemned along with other groups critical of Lenin's policy. After that time, *dezisty* were labeled enemies of the Communist Party (see, for instance, Boris Ponomarev (ed.), *Istoria Kommunisticheskoi Partii Sovietskogo Soyuza*, Moskva: Politizdat, 1976, p. 306; Thomas Remington, *Building Socialism in Bolshevik Russia*, Pittsburgh: University of Pittsburgh Press, 1984, pp. 63–74; and Kuleshov, 1991, pp. 77–78).

18. See Sapronov, 1920.

19. Nelidov, 1962, p. 249.

20. Ibid., pp. 252–272.

21. *TsSU SSSR, Narodnoie Khoziaistvo SSSR v 1979*, Moskva: Statistika, 1980, p. 60.

22. See *Pervyi S'ezd Narodnykh Deputatov SSSR, Stenograficheskii Otchet*, vol. 3, Moskva: Verkhovnyi Soviet SSSR, 1989, p. 326.

23. Fainsod, 1958, p. 74.

24. Petr Pavlenko, *Shchastie*, Moskva: Khudozhestvennaia Literatura, 1953, p. 52.

25. As compared to the regional executive committee of the Stalin epoch, the zemstvo office was a government of a sovereign state. The zemstvo administration was subordinated to the governor, whereas the executive committee was under the control of the first

secretary of the regional party committee, who combined in one person the posts of both the former governor and marshal of nobility.

The zemstvo administration was free to make decisions on the structure of farming and economic ties within the *gubernia*. A good example can be found in the period of collectivization during the Soviet era, when specialization in farming in *gubernii* was abolished, so all regions began to grow grain crops. Before the revolution, the Tver *gubernia* could survive on its own grain only for nine months; however, the zemstvo administration of the *gubernia* refused to expand areas cultivating grain in view of low yields in swampy regions but intensively developed livestock breeding in the hope of getting grain through interregional exchange. In contrast, the leadership of the Soviet Tver Region had no option but to increase the area of grain crops, a move that was extremely ineffective. All this was executed, although deep in their hearts, the local leaders knew the policy was flawed; they could not persuade Moscow that such a policy would lead only to the semistarvation of the population.

26. One documentary movie in a BBC series on life in the Soviet Union (1985–1986) was devoted to the life of the soviet secretary in the city of Nakhodka, a woman named Tatiana. This lady presented herself in the movie as an elected official who bluntly and sincerely said to a journalist that "she got all directives from the city party committee." She made this statement without even a bit of awareness that this confession undermined her statements regarding the democratic character of the soviet that she represented.

27. Fainsod, 1958, p. 396.

28. See Boris Grushin and Lev Onikov, *Massovaia Informatsia v Promyshlennon Gorode*, Moskva: Politizdat, 1980, p. 383.

29. See Yu. Klimov and V. Smirnov, *Novaia Ekonomicheskaia Politika v Promyshlennosti Kalininskoi Oblasti 1921–1925 g.*, Kalinin: Knizhnoe Izd-vo, 1989, p. 26; *Konstitutsii i Konstitutsionnye Akty RSFSR (1918–1937)*, Moskva: Gos. Izd-vo Politicheskoi Literatury, 1940, pp. 82–83, 86; Gimpel'son, 1968, p. 128; and Sapronov, 1920.

30. For more on the role of the regions in collectivization, see Robert Conquest, *The Harvest of Sorrow: Soviet Collectivization and the Terror-Famine*, London: Hutchinson, 1986; and Sheila Fitzpatrick, *Stalin's Peasants*, New York: Oxford University Press, 1994, pp. 54–55.

31. The range of duties of the first leader of the region included problems that would have seemed fantastic to any tsarist governor. For instance, it was not uncommon that he acted as the chief producer of the local theater and, increasingly more frequently, as the coach of the local football team. Football fans remember all too well that for each game, the players of the Leningrad *Zenit* team (higher league) in the 1950s were appointed personally by the secretary of the regional party committee. There were rumors that the same was true of the Lugansk *Zarya* (also higher league), although both teams were headed by first-rate football professionals.

32. *XVII S'ezd VKP(b), Stenograficheskii Otchet*, Moskva: Gos. Izd-vo Politicheskoii Literatury, 1934, p. 35.

33. See Egor Ligachev, *Zagadka Gorbacheva*, Novosibirsk: Interbuk, 1992, pp. 44–45.

34. Among post-Stalin supreme leaders, Nikita Khrushchev, Leonid Brezhnev, and Mikhail Gorbachev all served as regional secretaries. However, Georgii Malenkov, Yurii Andropov, and Konstantin Chernenko did not. For more on the importance of the position of regional secretary in party careers in the USSR, see Helene Carrere d'Encausse, *Confiscated Power: How Soviet Russia Really Works*, New York: Harper, 1980, pp. 124–139.

35. In the 1960s and 1970s, seventy regional party secretaries made up one-third of the Central Committee. Consequently, it was the largest professional group in this body.

36. See "The Decision of the Plenum of the TsK VKP(B) in January 1938," in Richard Kosolapov, *Slovo Tovarishchu Stalinu*, Moskva: Palei, 1995, pp. 143–153; and Fainsod, 1958, pp. 405–408.

37. Nelidov, 1962, p. 237.

38. Ibid.

39. *Reabilitatsia. Politicheskie Protsessy 30–50 godov*, Moskva, 1991, pp. 311–322.

40. Although Iosif Stalin formally denounced this practice at the Seventeenth Party Congress in 1934, it still flourished until the time of his death.

Chapter 5

1. It is possible to suppose that Khrushchev's regional policy was also dictated by his willingness to curtail the power of regional party secretaries by creating a sort of antidote for them in the regions.

2. For example, thirty Moscow officials were sent to the small Iaroslavl Economic Council. After the abolishment of this agency, almost all of them returned to Moscow (Vasilii Pavlov, *Budni Odnogo Sovnarkhoza*, Moskva: Profizdat, 1958).

3. Sixty councils were formed on the basis of one region, and eight controlled the economies of several regions (A. Vikentiev, *Sovnarkhozy v Deitstvie*, Moskva: Izd-vo Politicheskoi Literatury, 1958).

4. See David Granick, *The Red Executive*, London: Macmillan, 1960, pp. 162–166.

5. Wright Miller was the first writer in the West to realize the importance of this aspect of Khrushchev's economic reforms (*Russians as People*, New York: Dutton, 1961, p. 194).

6. The new economic regional bodies that had replaced the economic superministries were now responsible for the economy, and their interests began to conflict with the interests of the national economy, despite the designers' wishes to the contrary. The Kremlin saw in these councils a collection of national agencies that would represent, at the regional level, the interests of the state. While these councils existed, the media published many factual cases that illustrated the predominance of regional interests over those of the national economy. The hoarding of deficit raw materials is only one such example (see, for instance, *Pravda*, 13 January 1958; *Iz Opyta Raboty Sovnarkhozov Pribaltiki*, Moskva: Izdvo Politicheskoi literatury, 1958).

7. V. Petrovichev, "Proizvodstvennyi printsip v partiinom stroitelstve," *Kommunist*, no. 18, 1962, p. 24.

8. *Obshchaia Gazeta*, 14 January 1994.

9. It was only said that Khrushchev tried to control the regional policy and guard it from the interference on the part of his comrades-in-arms. In his report to the October Plenary Meeting, which was fatal for Khrushchev, Mikhail Suslov said that Khrushchev was always angry when some of the Presidium members expressed a desire to visit this or that region. "Go, if you have nothing to do. Want to travel a bit?"—such was his sarcastic response to the seemingly quite logical suggestions of top party officials (*Istoricheskii Arkhiv*, no. 1, 1993).

10. It is remarkable that the new Brezhnev government tried to hide the political meaning of its decision to abolish Khrushchev's innovations in regional policy and presented them as a purely administrative action.

11. It was said that "it is necessary to return to the principle of the territorial-production structure of the party organizations and thus to set up in each region [territory] one re-

gional [territorial] party committee and to reorganize the party committees at territorial production collective farm-state farm departments into former district party committees" (see *KPSS v Rezoliutsiiakh*, vol. 10, p. 419, Moskva: Izd-vo Politicheskoi Literatury, 1986).

12. See the detailed description of Soviet territorial planning in Nikolai Tsapkin, V. Gichkin, and Yurii Belik, *Planirovanie Ekonomicheskogo i Sotsialnogo Razvitia SSSR*, Moskva: Ekonomika, 1983, pp. 396–407; Boris Orlov and Ruvin Shnipper, *Ekonomicheskaia Reforma i Territoriialnoe Planirovanie*, Moskva: Ekonomika, 1969; and Jonathan Schiffer, *Soviet Regional Economic Policy: The East-West Debate over Pacific Siberian Development*, New York: St. Martin's Press, 1989.

13. See Vladimir Shlapentokh, *The Politics of Sociology in the Soviet Union*, Boulder and London: Westview Press, 1987.

14. See Andrei Danilov, Viktor Kistanov, and Stepan Ledovskikh, *Ekonomicheskaia Geografia SSSR*, Moskva: Vysshaia Shkola, 1983, pp. 9–10. Among translated books, see Walter Isard, *Location and Space Economy*, Cambridge and New York: Technology Press of Massachusetts Institute of Technology/Wiley, 1966.

15. One such work is that of Nikolai Nekrasov, *Regionalnaia Ekonomika*, Moskva: Ekonomika, 1978.

16. For an example, see V. Andreev, *Partinoie Rukovodstvo Ekonomikoi v Period Razvitogo Sotsialisma*, Leningrad: Izd-vo Leningradskogo Universiteta, 1982, pp. 102–103; Volodar Feodoritov and Tatyana Brodskaia, *Regionalnoe Vosproizvodstvo v Sisteme Sotsialisticheskikh Proizvodstvennykh Otnoshenii*, Leningrad: Izd-vo Leningradskogo Universiteta, 1984, p. 80.

17. See Igor Birman, *Transportnaia Zadacha Lineinogo Programmirovania*, Moskva: Izd-vo Economicheskoi Literatury, 1962.

18. The regional factor became particularly strong in the works of mathematical economists when they began to use the multilevel model of optimization of economic activity, which supposed that the best plan can be devised only after the interaction between the center and regions (see Alexander Granberg, "Regionalnaia ekonomika i regionalnaia nauka v Sovietskom Soyuze i Rossia," *Region*, no. 1, 1994; Abel Aganbegian, *Optimalnoe Territorialno-Proizvodstvennoe Planirovanie*, Novosibirsk: Nauka, 1969; Aron Katsenelinboigen et al., *Vosproizvodstvo i Ekonomicheskii Optimum*, Moskva: Nauka, 1972; Viktor Volkonskii, *Problemy Sovershenstvovania Khoziastvennogo Mekhanizma*, Moskva: Nauka, 1981).

19. Although mathematical economics encouraged regional studies with its focus on the optimal distribution of producers and consumers, another trend in this school was rather inimical to regional studies, focusing on the optimization of the national economy on the whole. Indeed, the major argument of the advocates of regional studies and regional economic autonomy lay in the statement that the center, by definition, could not amass and process all of the information needed for central planning and, therefore, had to delegate some power to the provincial authorities and managers of enterprises. During the same time period, several economists and mathematicians, including Viktor Glushkov and Anatolii Dorodnitsyn, insisted in the 1960s that, with the help of computers, it had become possible to collect any amount of information, making it possible for the *center* to formulate the best decisions (see Aron Katsenelinboigen, *Soviet Economic Thought and Political Power in the USSR*, New York: Pergamon Press, 1980; Vladimir Shlapentokh, *Soviet Intellectuals and Political Power*, Princeton: Princeton University Press, 1990.

20. See, for instance, Feodoritov and Brodskaia, 1984, p. 18; Schiffer, 1989.

21. See Leonard Kozlov, Boris Shtulberg, and Igor Il'in (eds.), *Regionalnaia Ekonomika: Novye Podkhody*, Moskva: Nauka, 1993, pp. 4–5; Valerii Chichkanov and P. Menakir (eds.), *Analiz i Prognozirovanie Ekonomiki Regiona*, Moskva: Nauka, 1984.

Chapter 6

1. Lifetime tenure was guaranteed only to the most loyal supporters of Brezhnev and his "gray cardinal," Suslov, who was responsible for the cadre policy. Those about whom there was the slightest doubt were immediately dismissed. Thus, within the Brezhnev period, seven out of fourteen (excluding two others who died suddenly) members of the Politburo were dismissed.

2. This signified that the first point in the CPSU rules, introduced by Nikita Khrushchev and especially disliked by regional secretaries, was abolished. In accordance with this point, it was compulsory to elect all new party leaders at each new election—up to and including the Central Committee and its Presidium.

3. See *Stenograficheskii Otchet XXIII S'ezda KPSS*, Moskva: Politizdat, 1966; *Stenograficheskii Otchet XXV S'ezda KPSS*, Moskva: Politizdat, 1971; *Stenograficheskii Otchet XXVI S'ezda KPSS*, Moskva: Politizdat, 1981.

4. See *Sovershenstvovat Rabotu Sovietov*, Moskva: Politizdat, 1978, p. 290.

5. As Seweryn Bialer suggested, "Regional leaders assumed the role of king makers during Khrushchev's rise to power." Bialer assumed that in post-Stalinist society, especially during the succession periods, "the regional struggle for resources" could only intensify (Seweryn Bialer, "The Political System," p. 35, in *After Brezhnev: Sources of Soviet Conduct in the 1980s*, ed. Robert Byrnes, Bloomington: Indiana University Press, 1983, pp. 1–67).

6. See Sergei Kuleshov (ed.), *Nashe Otechestvo: Opyt Politicheskoi Istorii*, Moskva: Terra, 1991, pp. 480–482; Sergei Khrushchev and Georgii Arbatov, *System: An Insider's Life in Soviet Politics*, New York: Random House, 1993, pp. 100–137; Fedor Burlatskii, *Vozhdi i Sovietniki*, Moskva: Politzidat, 1990, pp. 271–281.

7. Jerry Hough, for instance, pointed to "the devolution of power to the major institutional centers." He suggested that upon seeing the "institutional pluralism" in Soviet politics, he could locate many centers of decisionmaking in the Soviet Union, including regional leaders. Hough's views constituted a direct challenge to the adherents to the totalitarian model, who maintained the belief that after Khrushchev's ouster from power, Soviet society was run by a supreme leader (Jerry Hough, *Soviet Leadership in Transition*, Washington, DC: Brookings Institution, 1980). Bialer was sure that this policy to exert pressure was made by the Central Committee, where regional party secretaries made up no less than one-third, or in some cases even more, of the body's members (Bialer, 1983, pp. 6, 35; see also Bialer's *Stalin's Successors: Leadership, Stability, and Change in the Soviet Union*, Cambridge, New York: Cambridge University Press, 1980, p. 295; and Seweryn Bialer and Thane Gustafson, *Russia at the Crossroads: The 26th Congress of the CPSU*, London, Boston: Allen and Unwin, 1982).

8. It is particularly evident now that it was hardly interesting to know which regional secretary supported whom in the Politburo, since regional bosses had no influence on Moscow politics (see Thomas Henry Rigby, "The Soviet Regional Leadership: The Brezhnev Generation," *Slavic Review*, March 1978, pp. 1–24).

9. A milkmaid, being in full control of her cow, nevertheless tries to cajole her in order to increase the amount of milk that she gets from her "subordinate."

10. See, for instance, Fyodor Burlatskii, *Andrei Gromyko: Memoirs,* New York: Doubleday, 1989; Yurii Arbatov, *The System,* New York: Times Books, 1993; Fyodor Burlatskii, *Vozhdi i Sovietniki,* Moskva: Politizdat, 1991.

11. See Vladimir Shlapentokh, "Russian Patience: A Reasonable Behavior and a Social Strategy," *Archives Européen de Sociologie* (European Journal of Sociology), no. 2, February 1995.

12. In this southern city, there was a strike and protest march of 7,000 angry workers. They approached the police station, demanding the release of their comrades. The Kremlin was so terrified by this event that two members of the Politburo, Anastas Mikoian and Frol Kozlov, were dispatched to the city and the whole military district, under the command of General Issa Pliev, was put on alert and troops were ordered to fire on the people. Twenty-four people were killed during this upsetting time, and seven were later executed. The potential for the riots to spread to other factories made Khrushchev and the other Kremlin leaders mad with fear (for more on the Novocherkask incident, see David Remnick, *Lenin's Tomb: The Last Days of the Soviet Empire,* New York: Random House, 1993, pp. 414–419).

13. Thus, it is not surprising that when Brezhnev learned about labor unrest in Poland in summer 1980, he immediately ordered the revision of the next five-year plan in order to increase the production of consumer goods.

14. In Brezhnev's time, local apparatchiks stopped being afraid of complaints about their actions being sent by ordinary people to the Kremlin or to the mass media. As a rule, Moscow sent letters that accused regional leaders of something back to the people who were the object of such grievances. This change of Kremlin policy toward the "letters of the toilers" was one significant element in the country's new order.

15. It is not by chance that there were rumors that there were tens of thousands of such criminal cases stored in Yurii Andropov's files in almost every region of the country in the hope that, with time, they could be brought to court (naturally, after Brezhnev's death or removal from office). This would have meant a veritable cadre revolution, and many people cherished hopes that after coming to power, Andropov would carry out such a revolution. It is impossible to say now what his real intentions were. Still, he had enough time to remove the leadership of some of the regions.

16. There was only one case of an open removal of a regional leader under Brezhnev. However, in this case, too, the real circumstances remained a secret even to the population of the said region. On 8 February 1971, information appeared in the Voronezh regional newspaper *Kommuna* on the dismissal of First Secretary Miroshnichenko by the plenary meeting of the regional party committee for "serious drawbacks in his work." Not even the deputy chief of the Organizational Department of the Central Committee was present at this meeting. An ordinary employee, Vitalii Vorotnikov, former chairman of the Kuibyshev Regional Executive Committee, was elected first secretary. Later, Vorotnikov became a member of the Politburo.

What was meant by "serious drawbacks" remains unknown. This all happened on the eve of the Twenty-Fourth Party Congress. At the end of February, a Voronezh regional party conference was convened. But neither in the report nor in the speeches of the delegates was there any mention of Miroshnichenko's case–it was as if he had never existed. As for the replacement of other regional leaders, there was a simple blurb in the press that a certain person had been dismissed by a plenary meeting of the regional (territorial) party committee and had been replaced by such-and-such a person (*Kommuna,* 8, 27, and 28 February 1971).

17. Using as a source of information the published reports of the plenums of twenty-five regional party committees in the early 1970s, Joel Moses tried to find regional differences in the subjects chosen for discussion at these meetings but failed to do so in the end. For all the variables selected to differentiate regions, he used the frequencies of various subjects and also looked at urbanization and education, finding that the subjects were all almost uniform (Moses, 1974, pp. 61–103). Moses's conclusions were not very surprising, simply because even the agenda of the plenums was guided by Moscow.

18. As Vitalii Vorotnikov, former chairman of the Presidium of the Supreme Council of the Russian Soviet Federation of the Soviet Republic and first Voronezh party secretary, when recounting the role of regional party secretaries, noted, "As politicians, we were nothing and dealt only with the economy" (Vitalii Vorotnikov, "Stranu derzhit tolko inertsia sotsialisma," *Sovietskaia Rossia*, 20 January 1996; see Rigby, 1978).

19. Egor Ligachev, *Zagadka Gorbacheva*, Novosibirsk: Interbuk, 1992, p. 60.

20. Yeltsin recounted how regional secretaries easily joined the campaign besmirching Yeltsin at the October 1987 Plenum of the Central Committee, where the future Russian president tried to criticize party leaders (Boris Yeltsin, *Ispoved na Zaddanniu Temu*, Sverdlovsk: Sredne-Uralskoie Knizhnoie Izdatelstogo, 1990, p. 171).

21. Robert Kaiser, *The Geography of Nationalism in Russia and the USSR*, Princeton: Princeton University Press, 1994, p. 328.

22. Egor Gaidar, *Gosudarstvo i Evolutsia*, Moskva: Evrazia, 1995, pp. 125–127.

23. See Timothy Colton, *The Dilemma of Reforms in the Soviet Union*, New York: Council on Foreign Relations, 1986, pp. 91–92, 104–105.

24. According to the apocryphal data, Fikriat Tabeiev, the first secretary of Tatarstan, was able to persuade Brezhnev to build a huge car plant at Naberzhnye Chelny in his republic while he was on a train that carried the general secretary from Kazan to Moscow.

25. Hough, 1980, p. 65.

26. Jonathan Schiffer (*Soviet Regional Economic Policy: The East-West Debate over Pacific Siberian Development*, New York: St. Martin's Press, 1989, pp. 124–180) was hardly correct when he described the process of distributing resources, for instance, between the western and eastern USSR, in terms of conflicts between various groups, the resolution of whose conflicts depended on the power of political actors. In fact, resource distribution involves a struggle for the Kremlin's ear, and its outcome was determined by the arguments presented to the top leaders.

27. For more on regional party secretaries, see Jerry Hough, *The Soviet Prefects*, Cambridge: Harvard University Press, 1969; Philip Stuart, *Political Power in the Soviet Union: A Study of Decision Making in Stalingrad*, New York: Bobbs-Merill, 1968; Blair Ruble, *Leningrad: Shaping a Soviet City*, Berkeley: University of California Press, 1990; Grey Hodnett, "The *Obkom* First Secretaries," *Slavic Review*, no. 4 (December 1965), pp. 636–652.

28. Among the most notorious apologetic books on first party secretaries were those by Vsevolod Kochetov (*Secretary of the Regional Committee*, Moskva: Khudozhestvennaia Literatura, 1962) and Fedor Panferov (*Volga—Mother River*, Moskva: Khudozhestvennaia Literatura, 1960).

29. See Vladimir Shlapentokh, *The Public and Private Life of the Soviet People*, New York: Oxford University Press, 1989.

30. See Andrei Danilov, Viktor Kistanov, and Stepan Ledovskikh, *Ekonomicheskaia Geografia SSSR*, Moskva: Vysshaia Shkola, 1983, pp. 72–83; Volodar Feodoritov and

Tatyana Brodskaia, *Regionalnoe Vosproizvodstvo v Sisteme Sotsialisticheskikh Proizvodstven-nuykh Otnoshenii*, Leningrad: Izd-vo Leningradskogo Universiteta, 1984, pp. 28–29, 55–101; Schiffer, 1989.

31. See Vladimir Shlapentokh and Vladimir Kontorovich, *Organizational Innovation*, The Carl Beck Papers, Pittsburgh: University of Pittsburgh, 1986.

32. See Feodoritov and Brodskaia, 1984, pp. 28–29, 55–101.

Chapter 7

1. See John Park, *Kremlin in Transition*, vol. 2, Boston: Unwin and Erwin, 1991, p. 30.

2. A typical example from this document is a passage that calls for the Soviet people "to strengthen the centralized principle in the management of the national economy . . . to broaden the rights . . . of Soviets of People's Deputies, to raise their responsibility for the timely and successful solution of the problems of economic and social development . . . to resolutely fight against all the manifestations of departmental attitudes and *mestnichestvo*" (*Osnovnyie Napravlenia Ekonomicheskogo i Sotsialnogo Razvitiia SSSR na 1986–1990 Gody*, Moskva: Politizdat, 1986, p. 267).

3. Mikhail Gorbachev, *Perestroika i Novoe Myshlenie Dlia Nashei Strany i Dlia Vsego Mira* (*Perestroika* and New Thinking for Our Country and the Whole World), Moskva: Politizdat, 1988.

4. See *Sovietskaia Kultura*, 7 May 1988, 26 May 1988, and 3 September 1988; *Moskovskie Novosti*, 22 May 1988, 29 May 1988, 5 June 1988, and 12 June 1988; *Literaturnaia Gazeta*, 18 May 1988; *Izvestia*, 7 June 1988; *Pravda*, 17 May 1988.

5. After the Nineteenth Party Conference, the press indicated an increasing number of cases when local party committees, with the utmost impunity, made short work of so-called perestroika activists (for more on the events in the Smolensk Region, see *LG*, 31 August 1988; in Kazakhstan, see *Iz.*, 10 September 1988; in Moldavia, see *Sovietskaia Rossia*, 3 September 1988; in Kirgizia, see *Iz.*, 27 July 1988; and in Karelia, see *Iz.*, 12 November 1988 and 21 December 1988).

6. See V. Leksin and E. Andreeva, "Territorialnaia desintegratsia Rossii," *Rossiskii Ekonomicheskii Zhurnal*, no. 8–9, 1992, pp. 32–42.

7. See *Materialy XIX Vsesouznoi Konferentsii*, p. 35; and Stephen White, *After Gorbachev*, New York: Cambridge University Press, 1993, pp. 34–38.

8. Yurii Afanasiev, *Inogo ne Dano*, Moscow: Progress Publishers, 1988; Fridrich Borodkin, Leonid Kosals, and Rozalina Ryvkina (eds.), *Postizhenie*, Moscow: Progress Publishers, 1989; Viktor Kazakov (ed.), *Perestroika*, Moscow: Progress Publishers, 1989; *Sovietskii Pisatel'*, Moscow: Progress Publishers, 1989; A. Protashchik and Leonid Batkin, *Cherez Ternii*, Moscow: Progress Publishers, 1990.

9. Among the contributors to the series were prominent figures such as academicians Vitalii Ginsburg, Tatyana Zaslavskaya, Andrei Sakharov, and Nikita Moiseyev; historians, sociologists, and political scientists Yurii Afanasyev, Leonid Batkin, Fedor Burlatsky, Mikhail Gefter, Andranik Migranian, and Andrei Nuikin; publicists Alexander Bovin, Yurii Burtin, Len Karpinsky, Yurii Karyakin, and Vasilii Selyutin; economists Mikhail Lemeshev, Larisa Piyasheva, Gavriil Popov, and Grigorii Khanin; writers Ales Adamovich, Daniil Granin, Sergei Zalygin, and Naum K. Rorzhavin, among others.

10. For instance, in his article "On Ways of Improving the Political System of Socialism," Evgenii Ambartsumov cited Vladimir Lenin (from his work *State and Revolution*),

who complained that "insufficient attention has been paid and continues to be paid in our party propaganda and agitation to the question of the federative and centralist republic, and local self-government." Ye. Ambartsumov supplemented the citations from Karl Marx and Frederick Engels by demanding the transfer of a significant part of the enterprises subordinated to ministries to the subordination of local authorities, who, in his view, should be given the right to lodge complaints against ministries. This is the end of his "treatise" on the problem of regionalism, to which less than two pages are devoted. Characteristically, this article is the only one in the whole series that "deals" with the problem of regionalism.

11. See, for instance, the interview given to *Komsomolskaia Pravda* in 1988 by Professor Ruslan Khasbulatov, "an absolute progressist," at the beginning of his climb to the top, who insisted at that time that with economic equality, all other problems would disappear (*KP*, 17 June 1988).

12. It is not by chance that the following anecdote about a Soviet director on probation in the United States was very popular. After some time, the American manager went on a business trip leaving the Russian director in charge. When the manager came back the Russian readily reported: "Everything is OK! There were plenty of orders, but I managed to ward off all of them."

13. For example, in 1990, grain yields were 15 percent higher than the average annual level in 1985–1991. In 1991, grain yields fell drastically to 12 percent below that same average level.

14. Contrary to the liberals' expectations, the conference delivered a serious blow to the single most significant achievement of the Gorbachev era—glasnost. Through attacks on the press, on anti-Stalinist authors, and on informal organizations, glasnost was blasted in nearly every speech and was ridiculed both through catcalls and by the small proportion of slogans that were applauded (the ratio of applause for and against glasnost was 1:4). Only a few delegates defended glasnost and its liberal principles, and they did so rather timidly.

15. For instance, Ivan Polozkov, then the first secretary of Krasnodar and a leading party conservative acting in the capacity of the first secretary of the Russian Communist Party in 1990–1991, lambasted the existing order, which did not permit local authorities to even establish a new nursing position at the local hospital (*XIX Vsesouznaia Konferentsia Kommunisticheskoi Partii Sovietskogo Soyuza, 28 Iunia–1 Iulia 1988, Stenograficheskii Otchet*, vol. 2, Moskva: Politizdat, 1988, p. 36).

16. Party leaders in Leningrad refused to listen to the warning of sociologists who predicted their failure in the election. Indeed, all five leading city apparatchiks lost the election.

17. The hostility toward Gorbachev was so strong that he left the meeting with the first city and district secretaries after a stormy shouting match with several of them.

18. For example, in 1987–1991, Soviet film directors made a number of movies challenging the existing system, such as *Little Vera* and *The Extraordinary Event of District Importance*. Regional party secretaries in Leningrad, Volgograd, and several other cities banned the showing of these movies (see Vladimir Shlapentokh and Dmitrii Shlapentokh, *Soviet Cinematography 1918–1991: Ideological Conflict and Social Reality*, New York: Aldine de Gruyter, 1993).

19. See Andrei Zdravomyslov, *Sotsiologia Konflikta*, Moskva: Aspekt Press, 1994, p. 174; Alexander Tsipko, *"Spor o Rosssi," Novoye Vremia*, no. 50, 1990, p. 7; John Dunlop, *The Rise of Russia and the Fall of the Soviet Empire*, Princeton: Princeton University Press, 1993, pp. 62–63.

20. For more on the use of the Russia card, see ibid.

21. Almost no one in the Soviet Union, including the harshest Stalinists, doubted the truth of the so-called Leningrad affair in the late 1940s and early 1950s. It was evident that only Stalin's paranoia could instill in his mind that Leningrad's apparatchiks wanted to use the "Russia card" for self-promotion and planned to make Leningrad the capital of the Russian Federation, thereby undermining the role of Moscow and his leadership. But, and this is truly a twist in history, for four decades Yeltsin followed the scenario presumably born in a wild dream of some faceless KGB prosecutor who knew of Stalin's fear of any type of nationalism, even Russian nationalism, even though Stalin himself had used it profusely for official ideology since the early 1930s.

22. See *Iz.*, 31 May 1990; *KP*, 1 June 1990.

23. The January 1990 protest of Russian mothers in Stavropol against the army provided clear evidence of the Russian opinion on the preservation of the empire. Chanting "We do not want our sons dying for the empire," the Russian women vehemently protested the recruitment of reservists for use in crushing the rebellion in Azerbaijan. In 1994–1995, Russian mothers fighting the war in Chechnia went much farther than Russian women in 1990—they created a special association called Mothers Against the War in Chechnia. Furthermore, they not only carried out numerous demonstrations in the capital but traveled en masse to Grozny in order to find their sons and take them back home.

24. See *Sovietskaia Tataria*, 8 and 12 August 1990; *Sovietskaia Bashkiria*, 14 August 1990. During his trip across Russia in August 1990, he made many important statements regarding the support of unlimited sovereignty in the ethnic regions of the Russian Federation. At this time, Yeltsin also revealed that he even nurtured in his "initial program" the division of Russia into "seven Russia states," but then he "understood that it would be a serious mistake and this development should be so far prevented from occurring" (*Uralskii Rabochii*, 16 August 1990; for more on Yeltsin's flirtation with the autonomous republics, see Nikolai Gulbinskii and Marina Shakina, *Epizody Politicheskoi Biografii Alexandra Rutskogo*, Moskva: Lada-M, 1994, p. 90).

25. See Yurii Baturin, "Shakhmatnaia diplomatia v Novo-Ogarevo," *Democratizatsia*, vol. 2, Spring 1994, pp. 212–221; A. Weber, V. Loginov, G. Ostroumov, and A. Cherniaev (eds.), *Soyuz Mozhno Bylo Sokhranit: Belaia Kniga*, Moskva, April, 1995, pp. 172–184.

26. Later, Gorbachev and people loyal to him accused Yeltsin of responsibility for the destruction of the Soviet Union and for generating the destructive specter of regionalism in the Russian Federation (see Weber et al., 1985).

Chapter 8

1. See Vitalii Portnikov, "Unitarnaia Rossia budet predstavlena v parlamente," *Nezavisimaia Gazeta*, 14 December 1993.

2. For instance, at Mikhail Gorbachev's instigation, the April 1990 "USSR Law on the Delimitation of Powers Between the USSR and the Subjects of the Federation" declared that the Autonomous Republics were "the full subjects of the Federation which enters into the ranks of the Union-republics" (*Izvestia*, 3 May 1990).

3. See John Dunlop, "Russia: Confronting a Loss of the Empire," in *Nations and Politics in the Soviet Successor States*, Ian Bremmer and Ray Taras (eds.), Cambridge: Cambridge University Press, 1993; Victor Zaslavsky, "The Evolution of Separatism in the

Soviet Union Under Gorbachev," in *From Union to Commonwealth: Nationalism and Separatism in the Soviet Republics,* Gail Lapidus and Victor Zaslavsky with Philip Goldman (eds.), Cambridge: Cambridge University Press, 1992; and Sergei Parkhomenko, "Bolshinstvo otsutstvuet," *NG,* 11 November 1992.

4. Egor Gaidar, in his speech at the Seventh Congress of Peoples' Deputies (*Rossiskaia Gazeta,* 4 December 1992) and the Congress of the Russian Parliament, asserted, "Regionalization is our main task since it is impossible to implement reforms without it." He demanded "the perpetual the extension of the rights and the opportunities of regions in the management of their own economy." He also added that "we plan to expand the rights of regions also in foreign economic activity" (E. Gaidar, *RG,* 4 December 1992; see also Boris Nemtsov, "Esli budet diktatura ia uidu," *Pravda,* 12 November 1992).

5. When Evgenii Nazdratenko became governor of the Far East in summer 1993, he composed a draft of the presidential edict with the characteristic title, "On the Expansion of the Rights of the Administration of the Maritime Territory for the Solution of Urgent Social and Economic Problems." Among other things, this edict would have permitted the regional administration to dispose of all taxes collected in its territory, including federal tax revenues. However, this draft was not endorsed by the Kremlin (Valerii Sharov, "Premier trebuiet rasshirenia svoikh prav," *Iz.,* 2 September 1993).

6. For more about the ethnic regions' offensive against the Russian Federation, see Ramazan Abdulatipov, *Vlast i Soviest,* Moskva: Slavianskii Dialog, 1994, pp. 56, 79, 140. As Mikhail Nikolaiev, president of Sakha-Iakutia, declared, "It is not arguable that republics, which in the past were autonomous formations, are now becoming republics looking for special relations with Russia" (Mikhail Nikolaiev, "Vozvrata k proshlomu net," *RG,* 8 December 1992).

7. As Dzhokhar Dudaiev said then, "If Russia threatens the security of the Chechen people and their state, we would take the extreme measures. *Gazavat!* And by the end of the last Chechen! We didn't have any intention to sign the Federal Treaty and are not planning to do so" (in an interview with Dudaiev, *Komsomol'skaia Pravda,* 28 October 1992).

8. In 1992–1995, Moscow tried to avoid direct confrontation with the confederation. For instance, having arrested Yurii Shanibov, the leader of the Confederation of the Caucasian People in 1993, the authorities released him without even an attempt to pursue their accusations against him of illegal activities.

9. See Lidia Malash, "Tatarstan: Tsentr razvala Rossii," *Megalopolis Express,* 23 June 1993.

10. See *Iz.,* 11 March 1993; Malash, 1993. At the same time, Russians in the republics berated the same leadership for its cooperation with nationalists and for its attempts to undermine Russia's unity (Malash, 1993). It is significant that only 12 percent of all Russians living in Tatarstan speak the Tatar language (Malash, 1993).

11. The Chuvashian nationalists, according to *Pravda,* are also preparing for strong actions in order to gain parity with the Tatars. Among other things, they have the paramilitary organization called Detachment of the Grey Wolf (*P.,* 11 December 1992).

12. See *NG,* 12 December 1992; *NG,* 23 October 1993.

13. In 1992–1994, the chairman of the Krasnoiarsk *kraisoviet* Novikov, claimed that the republic's proclamation of sovereignty would be "a bomb placed under the future of Russia." He even promised in 1993 to obstruct the adoption of a new constitution if the integrity of Russia was not secure (see Radik Batyrshin, "Rodina prezidenta—suverennoe gosudarstvo?" *NG,* 6 July 1993).

14. Mikhail Nikolaiev, "Period trudnostei nado skoree proiti. Minovat' etot otrezok nevozmozhno," *Literaturnaia Gazeta*, December 1993.

15. Mikhail Nikolaiev, "Artika: Gosudarstvo i liudi," *NG*, 14 March 1993.

16. The result of a content analysis of 473 articles, which were used to find the frequency of articles written about non-Russian republics, published in 1993–1995 in thirteen Russian newspapers (*Izvestia, Moskovskie Novosti, Segodnia, Den'-Zavtra, Pravda, Sovietskaia Rossia, Komsomol'skaia Pravda, Moskovskii Komsomol'ets, Literaturnaia Gazeta, Nezavisimaia Gazeta, Argumenty i Fakty, Megalopolis Express,* and *Literaturnaia Rossia*) support this relationship between the center and ethnic republics.

17. See Radik Batyrshin, "Yeltsin ukrepliaet svoi pozitsii," *NG*, 21 November 1992.

18. See the interview with Vasilii Likhachev, the vice president of Tatarstan, *NG*, 3 November 1992.

19. *Iz.*, 27 October 1992.

20. *Iz.*, 24 June 1993; *SR*, 8 July 1993; *Sibirskaia Gazeta*, June 1993. For instance, the governor of Sverdlovsk Region, Eduard Rossel', justified the decision to create the Ural Republic and presented himself as a fighter against "the discrimination of the majority of Russians' interests," by referring to the behavior of the leaders of the ethnic republics. This behavior, according to the computations of Leonid Smirniagin in 1992, is illustrated by the amount paid in taxes and received as subventions by non-Russian republics. For example, Tatarstan paid 93 million rubles in taxes, while receiving 38 billion rubles in subsidies, an amount that is more than that given to a dozen Russian regions from the European part of Russia, even though they paid more taxes than Tatarstan (see Emil Pain, *NG*, 25 July 1993).

Another author compared the Sverdlovsk Region and the Kalmykia Republic. She found that in March 1993, the republic got 63,000 rubles in subsidies per capita, whereas the region got nothing. Despite the fact that the Sverdlovsk Region paid six times more in taxes to the budget than the republic, public expenditures per single resident in Kalmykia were two times higher than in the region (see Liudmila Perzevaia, "Rodina prezidenta khochet stat respublikoi," *Moskovskie Novosti*, 4 July 1993).

21. A group of researchers, headed by A. M. Salmin, prepared a report and presented it to the Council for Foreign and Defense Policy on 17 November 1992. This report summarized the group's opinion on the importance of separatism in the provinces to Russia's unity: "The actual threat not only for the vital interests of Russia in separate regions and spheres of the economy and politics but also for its very existence issues more from regional than national-territorial separatism. While today it basically stems from the economic crisis and the desire to use local (mostly temporary) advantages, it is hardly going to disappear in the foreseeable future, for the regions would inevitably be differentiated in the course of the reform."

22. Vladimir Emelianenko, "Revansh Kalashnikova," *MN*, 27 June 1993.

23. Vasilii Kononenko, "Podgotovka k referendumu perekhodit v prakticheskuiu ploskost," *Iz.*, 6 February 1993.

24. Alexander Afanasiev, "Gubernator Sakhalina," *Komsomol'skaia Pravda*, 23 October 1992.

25. Boris Nemtsov, "Ukaz ne vygodnyi nikomu," *MN*, 1 October 1995.

26. Having no special supporting apparatus and no finances, as well as no real administrative power, the presidential representatives often lost the war against the governors or heads of regional administration and lost the support of the president.

27. Tatarstan, for example, through its prime minister supported not the Federal Treaty but the "interstate relations" between Russia and non-Russian republics (Abdulatipov, 1994, p. 206).

28. *Konstitutsia Rossiiskoi Federatsii,* Moscow: Judicial Literature Publishers, 1993.

Chapter 9

1. See Grigorii Iavlinskii, "Pogranichnaia situatsia," *Literaturnaia Gazeta,* 28 October 1992.

2. See Victor Trushkov, "Nad Rossiei slyshen krik Obidy," *Pravda,* 9 September 1993.

3. *Sovietskaia Rossia,* 8 July 1993.

4. See *Izvestia,* 9 July 1993.

5. *Den',* which is regarded as the organ of the advocates of a strong state, also publishes articles that call for "the separation of the regions from the criminal center" (*Den',* 21 November 1992; see also *Moskovskie Novosti,* 13 December 1992). A nationalist suggested in *Literaturnaia Rossia* that in the past it was not Moscow, but the provinces that saved Russia. This reflects the attitudes of Kuzma Minin and Dmitrii Pozharskii, who headed the popular struggle against Polish intervention in the beginning of the seventeenth century from their headquarters in Nizhniy Novgorod.

6. Aman Tuleev, "Ne verte v ostrova protsvetania," *Pravda,* 22 November 1992.

7. *Den',* No. 29, November 1992.

8. The same references to the Time of Troubles were advanced by several other nationalists and Communists (Boris Polevanov, "Rodina prevyshe vsego," *Zavtra,* no. 46, November 1995).

9. See Ruslan Khasbulatov, "Sovershenstvovanie parlamentarizma: Put k demokratii," *Rossiskaia Gazeta,* 7 November 1992; *Nezavisimaia Gazeta,* 21 November 1992.

10. See Viktor Filippov, "Neprimirimaia oppozitsia nanosit udar oppozitsii v provintsii," *Iz.,* 9 July 1993.

11. In the opinion of Emil Pain, Yeltsin's opposition had the majority of the regions' support until the April referendum of 1993 (Emil Pain, "Separatizm i federalizm v sovremennoi Rossii," in *Kuda Idet Rossia? Alternativy Obshchestvennogo Razvitia,* T. Zaslavskaia and L. Arutiunian (eds.), Moskva: Interpraks, 1994, p. 164).

12. See *NG,* 12 and 27 May 1993.

13. See Elizabeth Teague ("Center-Periphery Relations in the Russian Federation," in *National Identity and Ethnicity in Russia and the New States of Euroasia,* ed. Roman Szporluk, New York: Sharpe, 1994), who cites the geographer Lee Schwartz, p. 48.

14. See the interview with Nikolai Travkin in *LG,* 11 November 1992.

15. See A. Uglanov, "Razvalitsia li Rossia," *Argumenty i Fakty,* no. 2, 1993.

16. See Leonid Shebarshin, "Vopros o granitse—eto vopros o vlasti," *Ogoniok,* 25 June 1993.

17. One year later, in November 1993, in the aftermath of the parliament's defeat, he radically changed his view and became very optimistic about Russia's future as a unitary state.

18. During 1992–1993, innumerable scholars thought it very likely that Russia's collapse was due to heightened regionalization (L. Nikiforov, "Smeshannoie obshchestvo: Perspektivnyi variant obnovlenia Rossii," in T. Zaslavskaia and L. Arutiunian, 1994, pp.

13–22; Alexander Vladislavlev and Sergei Karaganov, "Tiazhkii krest Rossia," *NG*, 17 November 1992; Andranik Migranian, "Bitva na relsakh v tupike," *LG*, 28 October 1992). Lilia Shevtsova, a prominent political scientist, tuned to the same ideas at the end of 1992. In her article with its notable title "The Pangs of Powerlessness," she suggested that "we are seemingly on the eve of a gigantic redistribution of power between the center and regions which has to change radically our political system" (Lilia Shevtsova, "Muki bezvlastia," *Iz.*, 3 November 1992). Valerii Pisigin, a known liberal, wrote, in his turn, that "a new life and new politics is being born in the provinces" and that "the new local political elite" would change the course of Moscow political processes (*MN*, 15 November 1992). In his article "Either Regionalization, or the Disintegration of Russia," the well-known Moscow social scientist Anatolii Antonov advanced the same view (Antonov, "Libo regionalizatsia libo razval Rossii," *Megalopolis Express*, 1 September 1993). See also Iosif Diskin, an ideologue of "the Civil Union" in 1992, "Appatatnyi revansh: Pugalo ili blief," *LG*, 28 October 1992.

19. *NG*, 12 January 1996.

20. The participants of a Heritage Foundation seminar held in May 1993 adhered to similar views. In discussing the problems of the center-periphery relationship, the seminar's speakers, almost all of whom, with the exception of Sergei Arutiunov, were Americans, concluded that "the center is more or less capable of managing the country" and that "changes in the balance of forces bear a basically spontaneous and uncontrollable character" (see *Regiony Rossii v Perekhodnyi Period*, Moscow: Russian Union of Industrialists and Entrepreneurs, November 1993, p. 4, and *Ekonomika i Obshchestvo*, nos. 9–10, 1993; Elizabet Tigue, "Regionalizm v Rossii: 'Ekonomicheskii Aspekt,'" in *Federalizm, Regionalizm i Konstitutsionnaia Reforma v Rossii*, Washington: Heritage Foundation, Russian edition, 1993, p. 32; and Mark Zlotnik, "Vliianie regionalnykh factorov na razvitie Rossiiskoi Federatsii," in *Federalizm, Regionalizm i Konstitutsionnaia Reforma v Rossii*, Washington: Heritage Foundation, Russian edition, 1993, p. 78).

This idea was clearly expressed by Mark Zlotnik, a prominent American expert on Russia, who said: "The presence of centrifugal tendencies could be explained in fact by the absence of a strong power in the Center, as well as by the inability of Moscow to effectively resolve the tasks of managing the country. As a result, in the conditions of democratization this right began to be delegated to the regions."

21. See Nikolai Troitskii, "Brounovskoie dvizhenie v Rossii," *ME*, 21 July 1993.

22. See *MN*, 1 August 1993; and *ME*, 14 July 1993.

23. The draft, however, was rejected by the local Soviet (see Radik Batyrshin, "Krai i oblsati trebuiut sebe prava respublik," *NG*, 20 March 1993).

24. See Sergei Gutnik, "Sibiri ne po puti dazhe s 'democraticheskoi: Rossiei,'" *Sibirskaia gazeta*, no. 8, 1993.

25. The regional movement in Siberia attracted special attention because a political movement—*oblastnichestvo* (regionalism)—had been born here, headed by Grigorii Potanin, before the revolution. During the revolution, this movement suggested that each region of Russia be an autonomous entity with parliaments and ministries. It was recommended that in the New Russia, these bodies should control only those issues that regions considered to be of mutual interest (see Boris Shishlo, "Regionalizm, separatizm i avtonomia," in *SG*, no. 36, September 1992).

It is remarkable that this newspaper published a resolution from August 1917 of the Siberian Conference of Public Organizations on Siberian autonomy. It noted that this resolution gave Siberia more autonomy than the federal treaty and that Siberia was still considered a colony by Moscow (*SG*, no. 14, April 1992; no. 32, August 1992; see also *ME*, 3 March 1993; *Krasnoiarskii Rabochii*, 29 August 1992).

26. As in Ekaterinburg or St. Petersburg, 88 percent of the Vologda residents answered positively to the question "Do you think that all *oblasti* and *kraia*, including Vologda, must have the same constitutional rights as republics?" (see Dmitrii Shevarev, "Poshla pisat gubernia," *Komsomol'skaia Pravda*, 30 June 1993).

27. See *Iz.*, 15 May 1993. Separatist provisions of the Vologda Constitution were reborn in the Charter of the Vologda District, drafted under the editorship of Governor Nikolai Podgornyi. In particular, the charter declares that the natural resources of the district are to be the property of its inhabitants.

28. See Dmitrii Olshanskii, "Nabravshis vlasti po Moskve ne goriuiut," *KP*, 7 July 1993.

29. For more on the Central Russian Republic, see *NG*, 1 September 1993.

30. A referendum on the Neva Republic was held on April 25. Most of the city's residents supported the creation of a city republic (see Radik Batyrshin, "Rodina prezidenta—suverennoie gosudarstvo," *NG*, 6 July 1993; and Nikolai Volynskii, "Krugom odni respubliki," *P*, 14 August 1993).

31. Sergei Kostromin, chairman of the Cheliabinsk Soviet, declared in August the creation of the Southern Ural Republic, appointing himself president, vice president, and chairman of the government. He also introduced customs checks at the region's borders. These actions resulted in no consequences, since Moscow ignored them. However, as a Moscow journalist noted, they "show the collapse of the state and the spreading of anarchy" (see German Galkin, "V Cheliabinske odnovremenno obiavilis prezident i tsar," *Iz.*, 28 August 1993; and *RG*, 14 July 1993).

32. See Sergei Razin, "Nam est chem skrepit odeialo iz loskutov," *KP*, 7 July 1993; and Nikolai Troitskii, "V Rossii voznikaiut novye respubliki," *ME*, 7 July 1993.

33. See *Iz.*, 10 August 1993; Elena Matveieva, "Ot velikogo do smeshnogo," *MN*, 18 July 1992; and Razin, 1993.

34. See Sergei Alexeiev, "Provintsia khochet svobody," *Iz.*, 9 July 1993.

35. Although the district center was renamed Ekaterinburg, the name of the district itself was preserved as the Sverdlovsk District.

36. See the description of the Constitution of the Ural Republic in *KP*, 27 October 1993.

37. See Vitalii Portnikov, "Uralskaia Respublika provozglashena," *NG*, 30 October 1993; Lidia Malash, *NG*, 3 November 1993; Alexander Pashkov and V. Kononenko, "Uralskaia Respublika nachinaiet zhit po svoei konstitutsii," *Iz.*, 2 November 1993.

38. Alexander Pashkov, in his article "The Escalation of the Debate Among the Subjects of the Federation: The Proclamation of the Ural Republic," expressed the opinion that the blame lay with those officials who gave a negative review of the drafts (Alexander Pashkov, "Eskalatsia spora subektov Federatsii: Provozglashena Uralskaia Respublika," *Iz.*, 2 July 1993).

39. *Iz.*, 10 July 1993. Vadim Chelikov, "Pervoprokhodtsy s Urala," *MN*, 11 July 1993. A. Matrosov, chairman of the Sverdlovsk District Deputy Control Committee, in trying to justify and explain this step wrote in *Izvestia*: "We consider June 26, 1993, as one of the blackest days for us, for it was the day when the drafting of the Constitution of the Russian Federation was completed, which will for many forthcoming years put the regions

and territories into a vassal-like dependence now not only on the Center, but, in fact, on the national republics. The decision of the Sverdlovsk District Soviet on the formation of the Ural Republic should be considered as a serious warning of the inadmissibility of the formation of Russia according to nationalistic principles; on the inadmissibility of the adoption of the Constitution, which fails to provide for the equality of all the subjects of the Federation; and on the inadmissibility of adopting any legal acts on federal power and management, concerning the interests of the subjects of the Federation without the agreement of the latter."

40. See the interview with Eduard Rossel, "Uralskaia Respublika ukrepit Rossiu," *Iz.*, 17 September 1993. Addressing the State Duma in April 1994, Rossel, former head of the Sverdlovsk District Administration and a member of the Council of the Federation, told the audience that he once visited eighteen ministries and departments in Moscow with the goal of unifying six territories into the Ural Republic. He left Moscow with a total of exactly eighteen rejections.

41. See Ilia Ioffe, "Ural: Respublika ili region," *Federatsia* (The Newspaper of the Russian People), 10 August 1993.

42. Some Moscow observers insisted that, as in July when the idea of the Ural republics emerged for the first time, the final proclamation of the Ural Republic was an act made by Rossel only with the explicit or tacit support of the Russian president. The Russian president was seen as continuing to use the regional card against the presidents of the non-Russian republics, who were much less impressed by the shelling of the White House than the leaders of the Russian regions. These authors cited the meeting of the Russian Council of Ministers on 2 November 1993, where Yeltsin indirectly backed Rossel, who was then already the head of the Ural Republic.

43. Later, in December 1993, Rossel recognized that "we made a first important breakthrough to the new division of Russia—territorial" (Eduard Rossel, "Desiat dnei Uralskoi Respubliki," *LG*, 29 December 1993).

44. It was principally the leaders of Tatarstan and Bashkortostan who denounced the Russian regions' drive to gain the status of republics and who opposed them as "the subjects of the Federation" (see Radik Batyrshin, "Nastalo vremia rasplachivatsia za oshibku," *NG*, 7 July 1993).

45. In accordance with the well-used principle of "divide and conquer," Viktor Chernomyrdin conducted an extended session of the Council of Ministers, during which he accused the Ekaterinburg authorities of desiring to secure "ungrounded advantages over other subjects of the Federation," i.e., other regions, for the Sverdlovsk District wanted only to be equal with the national republics and did not want to gain advantages over other regions.

46. *NG*, 20 August 1993.

47. Later, Rossel contended that the president "did not know the essence of our Ural Constitution" (Eduard Rossel, "Rossia Uralom pribyvat budet," *Na Smenu*, 30 December 1994).

48. The former governor complained about the illegality of Yeltsin's action and "the Kremlin's games" (see *Kommersant*, 3 November 1993; *NG*, 21 November 1993; and *Iz.*, 16 November 1993).

49. Boris Yeltsin, "Kak prezident, ia bolshe drugikh zainteresovan v sotsialnoi stabilnosti," *Iz.*, 11 November 1994.

50. See *Respublika*, 23 February 1995.

51. See *AiF.*, 31 October 1994.

52. See *LG*, 24 November 1993.

53. The Congress of Transformation of Ural, which met in April 1995, was made up of delegates from all the cities in the Sverdlovsk region and the representatives of the local branches of several national parties, which used the "regional card" in their policies, such policies as those on economic freedom and on the party of Russian Unity and Concord (*Materialy i Dokumenty*, Ekaterinburg: Poligrafist, 1995, p. 3).

54. See *MN*, 21 November 1993; *Iz.*, 24 November 1993.

55. Among them was a resolution of the Supreme Soviet of the Russian Federation titled "On the Rehabilitation of Cossacks," 16 July 1992. Other resolutions included a presidential edict on the state support of Cossacks and structural military reforms in the zones of their residence, passed on 15 March 1993.

56. There were eleven such districts by the beginning of the twentieth century, such as the District of Don Troops, the District of Kuban Troops, etc.

57. See Eduard Bagramov et al., *Razdelit li Rossia Uchast Soyuza SSSR?*, Moskva: Mezhd-yi Fond Rossiiskogo Edinstva, 1993, pp. 79–86.

58. Some ideologies of the movement insist that the Cossacks were Russified and in fact belonged ethnically to the Polovets, a Turkish nomadic people (M. Adzhiev, *My Iz Roda Polovetskogo*, Rybinsk: Knizhnoe Izd-vo, 1992).

59. *AiF.*, October 1992.

60. For instance, the draft decision of the Cossack Assembly of the Terek Cossack Troops mentioned the formation of the Terek Cossack Republic, which would include several regions currently located within neighboring national republics: Kizlyar, Dagestan; Mozdok, North Osetia; Prokhladnyi, Kabardino-Balkaria; and Sunzhensk, Ingushetia. In this draft, claims were also laid on a portion of Chechnia, although it is true that these claims were removed from the final version of this decision.

61. V. Veselov, chairman of the Economic Council of the Terek Cossack Troops, while meeting with the then first vice prime minister Vladimir Shumeiko, said that "if we assume a formal attitude to Article Three of the 'Law on the Peoples Subject' to Repressions, we would have insisted on the restoration of the borders existing prior to 1916 . . . The Cossacks always were the guarantors of stability in Russia. Our motto is order, legality, statehood. We are fully aware of the real situation in our country. We do not need war" (Vakhtang Dzhanashia, "Kazaki stremiatsia poluchit status subiektov Federatsii," *Segodnia*, 24 August 1993).

62. See Liana Minasian, "Donskie kazaki v ozhidanii 'gosudarstvennoi sluzhby,'" *NG*, 1 July 1993.

63. See *Iz.*, 8 September 1995; *MN*, 28 January 1996.

64. See Denis Dragunskii, "Vykhod iz krizisa: Konfederativnoie Sobranie," *NG*, 24 February 1993; Anatolii Antonov, "Razval Rossii neizbezhen," *ME*, 12 February 1993; Vladimir Emelianenko, "Rossia rukhnet, esli po-prezhnemu budet delitsia na vassalov i suzerenov," *MN*, 7 February 1993; and Bagramov, 1993, p. 44.

65. See *ME*, 31 March 1993.

66. See, for example, interviews with Boris Nemtsov, governor of Nizhniy Novgorod, in *P.*, 12 November 1992; and with Valentin Fedorov, governor of Sakhalin, in *KP*, 23 October 1992.

67. Yeltsin's speech in Petrozavodsk, the capital of the Karelian Republic, on August 12 was an example of Yeltsin's determination to use the "regional card" against the parliament (*Iz.*, 14 August 1993).

68. See *Iz.*, 14 August 1993.

69. See Leonid Smirniagin, "Soviet Federatsii v politicheskoi perspektive," *NG*, 23 September 1993.

70. *Russkie Vesti*, 4 August 1993.

71. The most fervent supporters of the president were the heads of administration in St. Petersburg, Moscow, Ekaterinburg, Khabarovsk, Vladivostok, Chita, Rostov, and Kemerov.

72. For more on the role of regional leaders during the crisis, see *Rossia*, 26 October 1993.

73. See Kirsan Iliumzhinov, "Strategia razvala Rossii," *Literaturnaia Rossia*, 29 October 1993.

74. On October 2, Yeltsin announced in a special edict the convening of the Federation Council. The next day at 11:00 P.M. on the eve of the storming of the parliament building, when the status of president was particularly shaky, Yeltsin sent cables to all the regions moving up the meeting of the council on October 4. However, after Yeltsin's victory the council meeting was postponed to the next day and then canceled (see Vladislav Dorofeiev, "Politiki v regionakh v osnovnom podderzhivaiut Tsentr," *K.*, 10 October 1993).

75. Iliumzhinov contends that on October 4 at a meeting in the Kremlin, the governors had already drastically changed their views and, in the bout of loyalty to the president, demanded to "kill all deputies" (Iliumzhinov, 1993).

76. At the same time, Yeltsin was less categorical toward ethnic entities, only recommending that they take into account his edict in reforming their local government (*K.*, 17 October 1993).

77. See Alexei Mikhailov, "Voina ili mir," *MN*, 24 October 1993.

78. Although Yeltsin calls the regions' desire for greater independence "natural," at the same time he recognizes the existence of the "potential for Russia's disintegration." It is noteworthy that with the exception of the section "Federalism and Inter-National Concord," the president speaks about regions without dividing them into ethnic and Russian categories. He perceives the danger to Russia's unity not as national but as regional separatism. Yeltsin enumerates three manifestations of Russia's disintegration on the part of regional authorities: "It should not be tolerated when contrary to the Constitution the regional authorities restrict the freedom of economic, scientific, technical, and other contract relations between enterprises of different subjects of the Federation, hamper the movement of goods, financial resources and people across the administrative boundaries of territories and violate the unity of the principles of taxation" (Message of the president of the Russian Federation to the Federal Assembly, "Ob ukreplenii Rossiiskogo gosudarstva," in *Osnovnye Napravlenia Vnutrennei i Vneshnei Politiki*, p. 39).

79. Prime Minister Viktor Chernomyrdin's behavior was typical of this period. During a meeting in Tomsk, he quickly lost his temper because of the stubbornness of the Siberians with the "Siberian Agreement" and openly declared that "there will be no strong Russia with strong regions" (*Seg.*, 23 January 1993, based on information from Reuters).

80. See *Iz.*, 13 October 1993; *RG*, 10 October 1993; *NG*, 9 October 1993.

81. See Natalia Pechegina, "Oblsoviety gotovy uiti," *NG*, 9 October 1993.

82. See his article in *NG*, 11 November 1993; see also the article in support of the Ural Republic, *P.*, 2 November 1993.

83. See Mikhail Nikolaiev, "Vozvrata k proshlomu net," *RG*, 8 December 1992.

84. As early as 1992, 1,411 Muscovites were asked what the best political structure for the Russian Federation was. Of these respondents, 25 percent voted for the elimination of

the national republics as administrative units (Yurii Arutiunian, [ed.], *Rossiane: Stolichnye Zhiteli*, Moskva: Institute Ethnologii i Antropologii, 1994, p. 134).

85. The program of the party adopted in December 1991, at the Third Party Congress, contains the following statement: "In the final count, the strategic aim is the rejection of the national-territorial principle of the state structure of Russia. This aim should be achieved through gradually equalizing the rights of territories, regions and autonomies" (see *Iz.*, 7 November and 28 December 1991).

86. See Sergei Valentei, "K probleme federalizma," *NG*, 11 February 1995.

87. See Gavriil Popov, "Problemy nashego konstitutsionnogo protsessa," *NG*, 26 January 1993.

88. This principle was actively propagated by Austrian Marxists in the early twentieth century and found clearest definition in the works of Otto Bauer. Bauer put forward the program of transforming the Austro-Hungarian multinational empire into an aggregate of territorial regions, "followed by the constitution of the national minority within each self-governing region into a public-legal corporation" for the solution of questions on education and culture (Otto Bauer, *Die Nationalit Atenfrage und die Sozialdemokratie*, Wien: Verlag der Wiener Volksbuchhandlung, 1924).

89. Among others, Vyacheslav Novikov, the head of the Krasnoiarsk Parliament, called on all the Russian regions to create a greater Russian Republic as a move to extend the legal rights of each region (*Novoye Russkoye Slovo*, 16 July 1993).

90. *NG*, 12 October 1993.

91. *NG*, 18 February 1995.

92. See Volgograd's attempts to create self-government, *NG*, 9 November 1994.

93. See Alexander Solzhenitsyn's "Speech Before the State Duma," 28 October 1994; *Moskovskii Komsomol'ets*, 1 November 1994; *P.*, 2 November 1994; and *P.*, 29 October 1994.

94. Such was the position of the leader of Tatarstan, Mintimer Shaimiev, and the leader of Bashkortostan, Murtaz Rakhimov (*Iz.*, 22 December 1993).

95. *NG*, 18 December 1993.

96. *LG*, 27 October 1993.

97. Zhirinovsky said that "it is necessary to 'close' autonomous republics, regions and so on and immediately restore *gubernias* with governors at the head. There is nothing to discuss. Those who refuse to be transformed into governors should, without delay and much ado, by the decree of the respective sovereign presidents, be moved to Moscow summer cottages for 'interviews.' Let them rest a bit, eat some sour cream, watch TV, but sit tight . . . for the sake of their own security. We should forget this federation like a nightmare. A federation is a wrong form for our conditions. We should have a united state, envisaging strong democracy in the localities and the development of all national cultures" (Vladimir Zhirinovsky, "O sobiratelnoi roli Rossii i molodykh volkakh," *Iz.*, 23 April 1994).

98. Of course, not all unitarists offered such a dictatorial program. Sergei Shakhrai and Nikolai Travkin were in favor of a gradual transition to a new form of the federation. Shakhrai says in support of this view that "it is vital to understand: within the entire transitional period Russia is going to develop as an asymmetric federation. That is why, by making the territories and regions equal from the economic and legislative points of view, we still won't be able to overcome the national specific features, including the republican form of management in these regions" (*Iz.*, 17 November 1993).

99. Viacheslav Kostikov, Yeltsin's press secretary, declared, "I am for *gubernii*. Russia has to return to the historical experience that was tested successfully over two centuries.

Despite skepticism toward Vladimir Zhirinovsky's slogans, I have to say that he is one of very few who promotes the idea of *gubernia*" (*K.*, no. 44, 7 October 1993). The same view was expressed by Mikhail Leontiev, deputy editor in chief of *Segodnia*, one of Russia's most liberal newspapers (Mikhail Leontiev, "Vybory," *Seg.*, 9 December 1995).

100. "Rossia dolzhno byt edinym gosudarstvom, a ne lzhefederatsiei," *Iz.*, 6 October 1993.

101. Vasilii Likhachev, vice president of Tatarstan, "Vzaimnaia Otvetstvennost," *NG*, 29 November 1994; see Dmitrii Mikhailin, "Tatarstan nakhodit novykh druzei, i ne zabyvaet starykh," *RG*, 17 February 1993.

102. *Seg.*, 5 April 1995; Dmitrii Olshanskii, "Vizantiistvo politiki," *NG*, 19 April 1995.

103. See Buriat president L. Potapov's statement after the signing of the treaty with Chernomyrdin in summer 1995, *Seg.*, 12 July 1995.

104. See the presidential declaration on this issue, *Seg.*, 1 September 1995.

105. Such was the position of the Perm and Rostov Regions, whose statutes do not mention the necessity of the separation of power between the region and center (see *Ustav Permskoi Oblasti*, Bulletin no. 5, Perm, November 1994; *Seg.*, 26 August 1995).

106. Open Media Research Institute (former Radio Liberty, Prague, Czechoslovakia), 21 November 1995.

107. See Vladimir Lysenko, "Vne federalizma net demokraticheskogo budushchego," *NG*, 10 December 1995.

108. See Nikolai Gritchin, "V Dagestane vse gromche zvuchat antirossiikie lozungi," *Iz.*, 17 January 1996; see also *Iz.*, 20 January 1996.

109. See the interview with Nikolai Fedorov, "Nikolai Fedorov," *MN*, 9 April 1995; *P.*, 8 April 1995; and *LG*, 22 February 1995. See also Valerii Vyzhutovich, "V nashem dome chlen pravitel'stva ne uzhivaetsia s chlenom partii," *Iz.*, 16 May 1995; "Lipetskii gubernator ostaetsia na postu," *Iz.*, 6 May 1995; and also "Bolshoi konvoi dlia prezidenta malenkoi respubliki," *Iz.*, 1 April 1995.

110. See the interview with Boris Nemtsov, "Yeltsin khotia by na odin den dolzhen lichno vozglavit peregovory po uregulirovaniu v Chechne," *Iz.*, 3 February 1996; and Boris Nemtsov, "Ukaz, nevygodnyi nikomu," *MN*, 1 October 1995.

111. Even in Tatarstan, the Chechen War sobered many people, and the influence of separatists declined significantly. In any case, during the December 1995 elections to the Russian Parliament, they failed (Gusel Faisulina, "Kazan mezhdu Groznym i Moskvoi," *MN*, February 11 1996).

112. See the interview of Sanobar Shermatovoi with Ramazan Abdulatipov, "Raduev ushel zhivym—eto poshchechina Dagestanu," *MN*, 28 January 1996.

113. Even some democrats, such as Kemerovo's governor, Mikhail Kisliuk, under the influence of the Chechen War, supported the idea of gubernization in order "to reduce conflicts between the center and periphery" (Open Media Research Institute, 20 September 1995).

114. Nemtsov, 1995.

Chapter 10

1. See Vitalii Portnikov, "Unitarnaia Rossia budet predstavlena v parlamente," *Nezavisimaia Gazeta*, 14 December 1993.

2. Vladlen Loginov resolutely explained the fragmentation of Russia in 1991–1993, as well as that experienced in 1917–1920, as "the crisis of statehood" (V. Loginov, "Vse eto uzhe bylo," *NG*, 27 July 1993).

3. This process surfaced particularly during the Chechen war, in 1994–1996, when in several regions, especially in the North Caucasus, regional authorities began to take several measures to protect their populations against eventual attacks by Chechen terrorists.

4. For more on the history of Soviet Moscow, see Timothy Colton, *Moscow: Governing the Socialist Metropolis,* Cambridge: Cambridge University Press, 1995.

5. Even for several Western scholars who took Soviet official propaganda about the Soviet capital at face value, Moscow, with its long-term planning system was a somewhat model city (see Ervin Galantay, "Moscow: Model of a Socialist Metropolis," in *The Metropolis in Transition,* ed. Ervin Galantay, New York: Paragon, 1987, pp. 187–202).

6. Nikita Khrushchev used this opportunity in 1953, when he moved from the position of Moscow party secretary to that of the first party secretary. Viktor Grishin also had similar opportunities to do the same in the aftermath of Yurii Andropov's death. Boris Yeltsin's ascension to power is also correlated with his work as Moscow's first party secretary between 1985 and 1987.

7. Yurii Poliakov, "Moskva . . . kak mnogo v etom zvuke," *Pravda,* 29 September 1993.

8. The most famous song about the capital, "My Moscow," was composed by Isaak Dunaievskii, an extremely talented official Soviet composer, with lyrics by Marc Lisnianskii and Sergei Agranian, in 1942 after the Soviet victory over Germany in the battle for Moscow in World War II.

9. Blair Ruble accurately captured the changing mood in the country in regard to Moscow when he wrote, "Though many leaders of the Russian Federation want exactly the opposite, Moscow will soon resemble not so much Paris, but rather Rome: as a Russian asset, it will remain a symbol of a greater Russian nation for Russian regions, which are more and more poised toward their own political and economic connections" (Blair Ruble, "Devolutsia, desintegratsia, detsentralizatsia i democratizatsia–chetyre 'D' sovremennoi politiki Rossii," in *Federalizm, Regionalizm i Konstitutsionnaia Reforma v Rossii,* ed. Ariel Cohen, Washington, DC: Heritage Foundation, 1993, pp. 23–32).

10. Vasilii Belov, a prominent Russian writer and ardent nationalist, described Moscow as "a giant blister that sucks from the country all its juices" (Vasilii Belov, "Pokhishchenie Moskvy," *Zavtra,* no. 3, January 1996, pp. 5–6).

11. *Moskovskii Komsomol'ets,* 4 October 1995. The survey of 1,000 Novosibirsk residents in September 1995 found that one-third of them supported this idea. In 1994, 20 percent of Novosibirsk's residents voted in favor of this proposal (*Ogoniok,* no. 43, October 1995).

12. See Boris Grushin's survey of experts, *NG*, 31 July 1996.

13. For instance, many of the candidates for the Russian Parliament from the Maritime Territory during the election campaign leading up to the December elections were Muscovites (Elena Matveeva, "Brosok na Vostok," *Moskovskie Novosti,* 22 October 1995).

14. See A. Treivish and T. Nefedova, "Ekonomicheskoie Prostranstvo Rossii: Problemy Regionalnogo Rassloenia" in *Rossia i SNG: Dezintegratsia i Integratsionnye Protsessy,* ed. G. Kostinskii, Moskva: Institut Geografii, 1995, p. 44.

15. In 1993, Moscow made up only 8.3 percent of all industrial production in Russia, but about 37 percent (50 percent in 1990) of all joint enterprises in the country were located there (Treivish and Nefedova, 1995, p. 45).

16. Because of the gigantic influence of foreign companies as well as the emergence of a large number of "New Russians," or newly rich Russian people, prices of apartments in Moscow soared sharply in 1992–1995, probably by ten times. Muscovites are now in a privileged position again in comparison to the residents of the provinces, because their dwellings are several times more valuable than housing in the provinces. As a result, many Muscovites could significantly improve their well-being, as compared to provincial dwellers, by renting or selling their apartments.

17. *Goskomstat Rossiiskoi Federatsii, Sotsialno-Ekonomicheskoie Polozhenie Rossii,* Moskva, 1995, p. 338.

18. By 1994, as VTSIOM's data show, Muscovites were already more satisfied with their life than were people in the rest of the country. In 1994, 21 percent of Muscovites were extremely discontented with their life, whereas in Siberia, 29 percent of the residents were not happy with their present situation.

Muscovites were less afraid of unemployment than those who lived in the provinces. Only 17 percent of all Muscovites were concerned about their jobs, whereas in the central portions of European Russia, 31 percent were worried, as were 32 percent of all Siberians.

19. Moscow's aggressive stance, by the end of 1995, had reached such a point that some political scientists in Moscow started to assert that "Moscow opposes the rest of Russia and is almost about to declare its sovereignty" (Konstantin Katanian, "Luzhkov nesprosta obidel Chernomyrdina," *NG,* 4 January 1996).

20. It is remarkable that Muscovites, although differing radically from the rest of the country in their political attitudes by being generally more supportive of liberals, Westernizers, and democrats, by the end of 1995 held very similar views to other Russians on the major plagues of Russian post-Communist society. Moscow and the country on the whole, in answering a question on "the most menacing problems of society" (respondents were urged to use no more than five or six alternatives), ranked in the first two places the rising prices (70 and 74 percent, respectively) and the rising crime rate (72 and 63 percent), followed by the economic crisis (52 and 50 percent) and growing unemployment (38 and 51 percent) (*Segodnia,* 23 February 1996).

21. L. Smirniagin (ed.), *Rossiiskie Regiony Nakanune Vyborov,* Moskva: Iuridicheskaia Literatura, 1995, p. 181.

22. *Izvestia,* 26 January 1996.

Chapter 11

1. See Vladimir Shlapentokh, "Russia: Privatization and Illegalization of Social and Political Life," *Washington Quarterly,* 19 (1), 1996, pp. 65–85.

2. *Moskovskie Novosti,* 24 December 1995; Open Media Research Institute, 28 February 1996.

3. Anonymous analysts, "Politicheskie nastroienia regionalnoi administrativnoi elity," *Nezavisimaia Gazeta,* 26 January 1996.

4. The "Kuriginian center," an exotic analytical organization that served in 1992–1994, made up of mostly Communists and nationalists, had the right to say, even if it was somewhat exaggerated, that "votes are becoming a new property of political power," that "regional elites practically took control of this property," and that "the selling out of votes is going on in a grand scale in the political market" (Kurginian Center, "Vybory kak sistema," *Zavtra,* no. 38, September 1995, p. 3).

5. *NG*, 8 February 1996. However, many governors were not very successful, whether intentionally or not, in supporting the governmental party Our Home Russia during the December 1995 elections. The president, in a fit of revenge, fired some of them (Lilia Shevtsova, "Vybory: Igra so mnogimi neizvestnymi," *Izvestia*, 24 February 1996).

6. In the opinion of a group of Russian experts who studied the ideology of Yurii Skokov, this politician wanted to transform the Russian Federation into a federation of large economic regions (the Greater Volga, North Caucasus, Western Siberia, Ural, and Central Russia) and "make regional elites responsible for the solution of concrete issues leaving to the center the role of arbiter" (*Segodnia*, 10 October 1995; for the opposing view, see Gennadii Ziuganov, *Derzhava*, Moskva: Informpechat, 1994, pp. 68–69).

7. Open Media Research Institute, 13 February 1996.

8. *MN*, 11 February 1996; OMRI, 14 February 1996.

9. Viacheslav Nikonov, "Prezidentskiie vybory i vlast," *NG*, 21 February 1996.

10. A journalist opposing the Federation Council as a serious body in comparison to the Duma with its "factions, groups, stupid political intrigues and ambitions, marginal deputies living with ideological chimeras" described this chamber as a place filled "with regional elite, princes, tsars and feudals for whom in their home, in their 'subjects of the Federation,' they have the same carpet lane as Yeltsin's in Moscow" (Iulia Kalinina, "My vse budem rvatsia k dengam," *Moskovskii Komsomol'ets*, 24 January 1996).

11. See Igor Kliamkin's speech published in Mikhail Gorbachev (ed.), *Rossia Na Pereputie: Trudnosti Posttotalitarnoi Modernizatsii i Ideologicheskaia Situatsia v Strane (Masterialy Seminara)*, Moscow: Gorbachev Foundation, 1994, p. 83.

12. Oleg Kiuchek, "Regionam predlozheno vykhodit na mezhdunarodnuiu arenu," *Seg.*, 26 August 1995.

13. See R. Cappelin and P. Batey, *Regional Networks, Border Regions, and European Integration*, London: Pion, 1993, p. 41.

14. This kind of independence stems from vague statements in basic documents. Article 72 of the Constitution contains regulations on "international and foreign economic ties of the subjects of the Russian Federation" (*Konstitutsia Rossiiskoi Federatsii*, Moscow, Judicial Literature Publishers, 1993, p. 29).

The Treaty of the Federation also contains a similar statement. As V. Pustogarov, a doctor of law, justly remarked, the Constitution distinguishes between "international relations" and "international ties," where the former are considered to be within the competence of the federation itself, but where the difference lies is not clear. "There is no explanation either in the Constitution, or in foreign laws, or international law" (V. Pustogarov, "Bolshe voprosov, chem otvetov," *NG*, 24 March 1994).

15. B. Alexandrov, "Oblast' podpisala soglashenie s gosudarstvom," *Seg.*, 25 September 1993.

16. Gennadii Ziuganov, *Rossia i Sovremennyi Mir*, Moskva: Informatsionnoe Izd-vo Obozrevatel, 1995, p. 69.

17. See Boris Nemtsov, "Oblast stabilna, no zhivet trevogami," Megalopolis Express, 17 March 1993; Evgenii Krestianinov (chairman of the Nizhniy Novgorod Soviet), "Gde v Rossii stolitsa reform," *Argumenty i Fakty*, September 1993.

18. *Komsomol'skaia Pravda*, 12 November 1992.

19. See *Respublika*, 2 March 1995.

20. See *Iz.*, 11 March 1993; *Rossiskaia Gazeta*, 17 February 1993; *ME*, 24 November 1993.

21. *Seg.*, 29 December 1995.

Chapter 12

1. VTSIOM, *Ekonomicheskie i Sotsialnyie Peremeny: Monitoring Obshchestvennogo Mnenia*, no. 4, 1995, pp. 61–62.

2. Boris Nemtsov, the liberal media's and central government's most touted governor, was reelected in December 1995. However, Nizhniy Novgorod was full of various rumors referring to the governor's suspicious deals, his connections and friendships with people who ultimately found themselves behind bars. Many other governors' reputations, such as those of Evgenii Nazdratenko in Vladivostok, Nikolai Podgornov in Vologda, and Alexander Deriagin in Kaluga, were, in 1994–1996, much worse than Nemtsov's.

3. Few regional leaders who tried to be in the vanguard of reforms were defeated by the regional conservative elite. For example, in Mordovia, President Vasilii Gusliannikov was forced to resign in 1994, having lost to the alliance of various political forces against him.

4. In the first half of 1991 before the events of August, when the new post-Communist regime was emerging and seeking out the support of the masses, local leaders of these regions ignored the decisions of the Presidium of the Supreme Soviet, which wanted to diminish the party bosses' power and did ban the combination of the positions of chairman of regional soviets and first party secretary. These same local leaders again, in accordance with their territories' mood of hating Boris Yeltsin, tried to obstruct the referendum for the installation of the Russian president's position, which was evidently coupled with his own election to the post. Local leaders were also among the most active supporters of the abortive effort of August 1991. Alexei Titkov, a Russian geographer, insisted that these regions were particularly conservative even in prerevolutionary times (Alexei Titkov, *"Umret li Moskva," Nezavisimaia Gazeta*, 10 July 1993).

5. See, for instance, Ivan Szelenyi et al., "The Development of Social Stratification and Recruitment of Elites in Eastern Europe After 1989," *Sociologisky-Casopes*, 1991, pp. 3, 27.

6. It is remarkable that after 1991, apparatchiks of the second and third echelons of the *nomenklatura* came to power in the regions.

7. In general, the elite in the executive branch was, in these years, much stronger than its counterparts in the legislature. First, a great number of politicians in the executive branch managed to be elected to local dumas and thereby combined the might of both powers. Among the deputies elected during the spring elections of 1994, 31 percent were officials from the executive branch and 21 percent were directors of large enterprises.

Those local bosses, who united in their hands the administrative, economic, and legislative power, were somewhat more powerful than the members of the old party *nomenklatura*. Indeed, they had immunity as deputies that party apparatchiks never had. Furthermore, in controlling the public money and the process of privatization, they could enrich themselves far more than the old *nomenklatura* could even dream of in the past. According to the law, many dumas could not work as permanent acting bodies because, among other reasons, deputies elected in villages and small cities, for example, 60 percent of the deputies in Perm and 72 percent of the deputies in Orenburg, did not have the opportunity to get apartments in the regional center.

Secondly, in most regions the Duma was convened only once every two months and only two-fifths of the deputies worked on a permanent basis, making it easier to manipulate these deputies by local administration. Under these circumstances, it is difficult to consider most deputies as a real part of the local elite (Mikhail Afanasiev, "Krai derzhavnogo piroga," *Segodnia*, 21 February 1995).

8. Directors of former state enterprises or of those that were turned into joint stock companies had similar political attitudes toward regional legislators and, like them, supported various forms of authoritative ideologies.

According to Elena Avraamova's data, in 1993, 62.6 percent of all directors voted for the "statist-patriotic ideology," with the state as the decisive agent in society, whereas 10.9 percent of heads of regional administration supported this ideology. Further, 35.4 percent of directors and 76.4 percent of administrative heads supported the "social democratic model"; and 0.0 percent and 2.6 percent, repsectively, supported the "liberal model." It is remarkable that the political attitudes of directors are the closest of the other elite groups to the views of the masses. In Avraamova's survey, 64.1 percent of all people in the general population voted for the "statist-patriotic model," 29.4 percent voted for the "social democratic model," and 3.9 percent voted for the "liberal model."

9. For instance, the governor of the Maritime Territory was furious at Moscow's indifference to the problems of his *krai*. He angrily exclaimed in September 1994 that "Moscow pushes us out of the country."

10. In 1996, Boris Nemtsov and Aman Tuleev, as well as the governor of Omsk, Leonid Polezhaiev, were considered by various organizations as candidates for president (*Argumenty i Fakty*, no. 5, January 1996; Galina Kovalskaia, "Aman Tuleev govorit s liudmi," *Novoie Vremia*, no. 42, October 1995, p. 12). Egor Stroiev, after the parliamentary election of December 1995, was elected the chairman of the Federation Council and immediately began to play a prominent role in the political life of the country (Anna Ostapchuk, "Bespartiinyi Stroiev," *Moskovskie Novosti*, 4 February 1996; see also *Ogoniok*, no. 5, January 1996; and Andrei Vladimirov, "Stroiev ustraivaet vsekh," *AiF.*, no. 6, February 1996, p. 3).

11. For instance, in view of the catastrophic state of Russian civil aviation, seventeen governors and heads of administration sent a letter to Yeltsin demanding radical measures for improvements in this vitally important sector of the economy (*Izvestia*, 11 January 1995).

12. The Chechen War, revealing the ineptitude of the central administration, introduced unusual activities of governors in several spheres of social life. The Novosibirsk governor, Vitalii Mukha, for instance, was involved in the rescue of Novosibirsk policemen who were captured by Chechens. It was he, and not President Yeltsin, whom residents of Novosibirsk addressed, begging that he do something in order to save the lives of their countrymen (*MN*, 28 January 1996).

13. *NG*, 21 June 1995.

14. Among them were Alexander Volkov, chairman of the parliament of Udmurtia; Yurii Luzhkov, Moscow's mayor; Eduard Rossel, Sverdlovsk's governor; Nikolai Sevriugin, head of the Tula administration; and Egor Stroiev, head of the Orlov administration (*NG*, 9 December 1995).

15. The strong nationalistic orientation of the local elite in non-Russian regions was the object of vehement criticism in 1991–1993 by Russian politicians and intellectuals (and the leaders of former Soviet republics were even more impassioned), who accused them of national egotism, manipulation of their people, and speculation on nationalism for their own personal interests (Arkadii Popov, "Idoly i zhretsy," *NG*, 11 November 1992).

16. See Midkhat Farukhshin, "Praviashchaia elita v Respublike Tatarstana," paper presented at the Conference on the New Elite in the Post-Communist World, 2–4 November 1994. It is remarkable how the Tatar local elite justifies the preponderance of its own ethnic group in the highest echelons of power. The members of this elite indicate that the

Tatars, whose population ranks second in size after Russians and Ukrainians in the Russian Federation, held only a very few positions in the Moscow establishment.

17. Nikolai Biriukov, the former party committee secretary of Mordovia and chairman of the Mordovia Supreme Soviet, defeated the democrat Vasilii Gusliannikov in the election for president in this republic (Irina Ovchinnikova, "Moskovskii stsenarii na mordovskoi stsene," *Izvestia*, 5 January 1993).

18. It is not surprising that Tatarstan's leaders enjoy greater support in the republican capital of Kazan (56 percent support), which has a higher proportion of Russians, than they receive in the countryside (25 percent support).

19. The case of Kirsan Iliumzhinov is of special interest. After being elected president, he promised to turn his poor republic into another Kuwait within one to two years. However, nothing like this happened. Despite his evident failure as a leader, in 1992–1995 Iliumzhinov played an extremely visible role in Russian politics and even, to some extent, in international affairs. As previously mentioned, he tried to be a power broker during the conflict between Yeltsin and the parliament in September 1991. He implemented various, mostly exotic, political ideas in his republic, including the cancellation of the Constitution, the elimination of Parliament, the proposal to eliminate the republican status of Kalmykia, and so on. As all these "innovations" became public, he continued his active role and was even elected the president of the FIA, the World Chess Federation.

20. Andrei Melville and Galina Bashkirova, "Public Attitudes and the December Election in Russia," paper presented at the Sixteenth World Congress of the International Political Science Association, Berlin, 21–25 August 1994.

21. Of course, the regional and globalistic feelings of Russians did not go as far as those of the residents of Lombardy, who, according to Giancarlo Rovati's study, thought of themselves first of all as Lombards (about 60 percent), then as Europeans (40 percent), and only after that as Italians (25 percent) (Giancarlo Rovati, "Political Localism and National Identity in Italy: The Case of Regional Leagues," in *European Transformations: Five Decisive Years at the Turn of the Century,* ed. Ronald Pohoryles, Aldershot: Avebury, 1994, pp. 248–249).

Chapter 13

1. *Uralskii Rabochii*, 26 September 1995.

2. See Richard Pipes, *Collected Essays on Russian and Soviet History,* Boulder: Westview Press, 1989, pp. 160–161.

3. Egor Gaidar, in his speech to the congress of the Russian Parliament, asserted that "regionalization is our main task since it is impossible to implement reforms without it." He also demanded "the perpetual extension of the rights and the opportunities of regions in the management of their own economy." He added that "we plan to expand the rights of regions also in foreign economic activity" (Egor Gaidar, speech at the Seventh Congress of People's Deputies, *Rossiskaia Gazeta*, 4 December 1992; see also Boris Nemtsov, "Esli budet diktatura ia uidu," *Pravda*, 12 November 1992).

4. For example, the leader of the Russian Communists, Gennadii Ziuganov, wrote, "In fact, in Russia today the process of a truly feudal split is now being encouraged . . . The expanding epidemics of sovereignization . . . is nothing but a naive attempt to survive on one's own, which is obviously doomed to failure and which only tends to deepen the crisis

and devastation. Its logical outcome could be only completely 'independent' individuals each sitting in his cellar with a sawed-off gun at the ready" (Gennadii Ziuganov, *Drama Vlasti. Stranitsy Politicheskoi Avtobiografii*, Moskva: Paleia, 1993, p. 153).

5. Exactly such argumentation flourished during the election campaign in Ekaterinburg in summer 1995. While Eduard Rossel focused on the revenues that fled to Moscow, his opponent, Alexei Strakhov, asserted that as the post-Soviet experience showed, the exploitation of the provinces by the capital was a lie.

6. In a typical regionalist statement, Rossel, praising his defunct Ural Republic, said on 15 April 1995 at a congress of his association, Transformation of Ural, "When it became real that the Sverdlovsk region was breaking the ring which stifles the self-dependence of regions that threatens the bureaucracy in the center with the loss of their unrestrained control over the regions, Moscow reacted in clear ways: to disband the council and to cancel all decisions related to the Ural Republic" (*Materialy i Dokumenty i S'ezda*, on the public nonparty alliance Transformation of Ural, Ekaterinburg: Poligrafist, 1995, p. 7).

7. See Igor Kliamkin's speech, published in Mikhail Gorbachev (ed.), *Rossia Na Pereputie: Trudnosti Posttotalitarnoi Modernizatsii i Ideologicheskaia Situatsia v Strane (Masterialy Seminara)*, Moscow: Gorbachev Foundation, 1994, p. 82.

8. Kliamkin, 1994, pp. 88–89.

9. Aman Tuleev, a populist in Kuzbass, formulated that "regional isolationism is perceived by local authorities, political leaders and industrialists as the single means of the salvation and defense of their interests" (*P.*, 22 October 1992).

10. See Elizabet Tigue, *"Regionalizm v Rossii: 'Ekonomicheskii Aspekt,"* in *Federalizm, Regionalizm i Konstitutsionnaia Reforma v Rossii*, Washington: Heritage Foundation, Russian edition, 1993, p. 35.

11. *Segodnia*, 17 February 1995.

12. See Vladimir Shlapentokh, *Soviet Public Opinion and Ideology*, New York: Praeger, 1986.

13. As Yurii Skokov, a prominent conservative politician, complained, "The Russian people begin to lose their place in history, the feelings of their role in the state and begins to dissolve into the sea of numerous national moves." He also deplored the connection with "the strengthening of political tendencies toward closed regional enclaves" (Yurii Skokov, "Strana u kriticheskoi cherty," *Nezavisimaia Gazeta*, 22 April 1995; see also V. Shlapentokh, "Russia: Privatization and Illegalization of Social and Political Life," *Washington Quarterly*, 19 (1) (Winter 1996); V. Shlapentokh, "Russian Patience: A Reasonable Behavior and a Social Strategy," *Archives Européen de Sociologie* (European Journal of Sociology), no. 2, 1995.

14. Ramazan Abdulatipov, "Natsionalnaia ideia i natsionalizm," *NG*, 28 April 1995.

15. See Vladimir Shlapentokh, *Public and Private Life of the Soviet People: Changing Values in Post-Stalin Russia*, New York, Oxford: Oxford University Press, 1989.

16. See Vladimir Shlapentokh, *Soviet Public Opinion and Ideology: The Interaction Between Mythology and Pragmatism*, New York: Praeger, 1986, and *Soviet Ideologies in the Period of Glasnost*, New York: Praeger, 1988.

17. VTSIOM, no. 5, 1994, p. 58; VTSIOM, no. 1, 1995, p. 11; Timon Riabushkin and Gennadii Osipov, *Sovietskaia Sotsiologia*, vols. 1–2, Moskva: Nauka, 1982.

"Jungle individualism" manifested itself blatantly in offices and factories in 1992–1994. When asked in 1994 "How does the fear of being fired affect the behavior of your colleagues," only 2 percent of respondents pointed to "increasing solidarity," and 1 percent referred to "the planning of collective actions against firing" (VTSIOM, no. 1, 1995, p. 30).

Lev Gudkov, a leading Russian liberal sociologist, cited with great satisfaction data showing the rejection of social values by Russians as evidence that Russians are abandoning Communist ideology and now concentrate only on their individual life (see L. Gudkov, *Dinamika Etnicheskikh Stereotipov: Sravnenie Zamerov 1989 i 1994*, VTSIOM, no. 2, Moscow: Aspect Press, 1995, and *Etnicheskie Stereotipy Naselenia: Sravnenie Dvukh Zamerov*, VTSIOM, no. 3, Moscow: Aspect Press, 1995). The same satisfaction was expressed by Yurii Levada when he cited similar data in writing about "destatization" and "privatization" of the average Russian (see Yu. Levada, VTSIOM, no. 1, 1995, p. 11; see also *Moskovskie Novosti*, 9 January 1994).

18. Conversely, according to VTSIOM's data (April 1995), 74 percent were against keeping Chechnia in Russia (*Seg.*, 18 July 1995).

19. Here are some examples of the headlines in the local press in January 1995: "Today Blood in Chechnia, Tomorrow in Briansk," in Briansk; "If You Have Power You Do Not Need Brains," in Lipetsk; "The March to Chechnia—The Last March," in Ulianovsk (Nikolai Petrov, "Regiony ne bezmolvstvuiut," *NG*, 20 January 1985).

20. Alexander Lebed spoke at the end of 1995 about "the discrimination" of the Russian regions and opposing the "five million people in the Sverdlovsk Region" to "three hundred thousand people in Kalmykia" totally supported Eduard Rossel in his willingness to elevate his region to the status of republic (Alexander Lebed, "U gosudarstva ischezla volia," *Seg.*, 10 November 1995). Russian extremists even praised Adolf Hitler, who, "having deprived the German Lands of independence, united Germany" (Alexander Sevastianov, "Uroki Hitlera," *Zavtra*, no. 41 October 1995, p. 8).

21. Calculated from data presented in *Narody Rossii, Bolshaia Sovietskaia Entsiklopedia*, Moskva: Sovietskaia Entsiklopedia, 1994, pp. 19, 227, 249, 381.

22. *MN*, 25 April 1993.

23. Among these characteristics are the differences between prices, the role of other sources of income, and the existence of "illegal salaries" used by firms in order to avoid taxes.

24. In the Volga Region in 1985, the average wage level in the national republics equaled the wage average for the territory, and in 1990 the level was a little bit higher than the average, though lower than in such districts as Volgograd and Samara.

However, even with the average salary at the same level, the standard of living, even in such a developed republic as Tatarstan, was lower than in Russia on the whole. According to Midkhat Farukshin's study in 1990, the average consumption of meat and milk in the republics was lower than the average level in the Russian republics (Farukshin, "Praviashchaia elita v Respublike Tatarstan," paper presented at the Conference on the New Elite in the Post-Comunist World, 2–4 November, 1994). Whereas the number of cars per thousand people in the republic was 38, versus 52 in the Russian republics, the average size of personal savings in the republic was 1,025 rubles, versus 1,147 in Russia.

25. Whereas the average wage for a collective farmer in 1992 in the Volga-Vyatka Region was 2,675 rubles, in the Mari-El Republic it was 2,510 rubles; in the Mordovian Republic it was 2,465 rubles; and in the Chuvashia Republic it was 2,010 rubles, i.e., much lower than in the Russian districts.

The same picture can be found in the Volga Region, where the average pay was 3,116 rubles, but people received 2,360 rubles a month at Tatarstan collective farms and 3,116 rubles at the collective farms in Kalmykia. The gap is much wider in the North Caucasus. For example, in Adygeia, the average monthly wage amounted to 2,758 rubles, and in Kabardin-Balkaria only 2,547 rubles; in North Osetia it was 2,577 rubles and even less in

Daghestan, at 875 rubles, whereas the average wage for the region as a whole was 3,391 rubles. In the Urals, a collective farmer in Bashkortostan received 2,264 rubles a month, whereas in the Sverdlovsk District, he got 4,776 rubles, but he received only 4,030 rubles in the Cheliabinsk District (the average figure for the region was 2,994 rubles). Although it is true that in Udmurtia the wage was higher than the average figure by one hundred rubles, the republics of Western and Eastern Siberia also had lower wages than in Russian districts.

26. *Goskomstat Rossii, Rossiiskii Statisticheskii Ezhegodnik 1994*, Moskva: Goskomstat, 1994(a), pp. 510–512.

27. *Goskomstat Rossii*, 1994(a), pp. 736–742.

28. *Goskomstat Rossii, Sotsialnoie Polozhenie Regionov Rossiiskoi Federatsii*, Moskva: Goskomstat, 1994(b).

29. Certainly, in 1992 such a distortion in favor of the republics was exaggerated when compared to the preceding years due to the fact that Tatarstan and Bashkortostan make a show of not paying taxes to the federation. Tatarstan, which has powerful industries and a population of 3.7 million people, paid only 93 million rubles in federal taxes, nine times less than Tuva, with its population of 300,000 people. But although not paying taxes to the federation in order to firmly stress its own sovereignty, Tatarstan nevertheless took 38 billion rubles from federal resources. However, if we eliminate Tatarstan and Bashkortostan from our estimates, the comparison of the republics with the Russian regions is obviously not to the benefit of the latter (data published in *Seg.*, 25 June 1993. The mistakes in the publication have been corrected by the authors).

30. A. Treivish and T. Nefedova, "Ekonomicheskoe prostranstvo Rossii: Problemy regionalnogo rassloenia," in *Rossia i SNG: Dezintegratsionnye i Intergratsionnye Protsessy*, ed. G. Kostinskii, Moskva: Institut Geografii, 1995.

31. The situation could, to a certain degree, be explained in the case of the Transcaucasian republics by the specific features of their geographical location and of their history. For example, the explanation for the need to compensate for the losses suffered during the deportation of some of the national peoples under Stalin and their return to their native lands several decades later does not suit other national regions. Their reason for rejection is probably due to political and not economic or geographical factors.

32. For more on the struggle for the preservation of the older buildings and monuments, see Blair Ruble, *Money Sings: The Changing Politics of Urban Space in Post-Soviet Iaroslavl*, New York: Woodrow Wilson Center Press, 1995, pp. 76–103.

Chapter 14

1. In the late 1980s, regions enhanced their role in the budget process. For instance, they earned the right to retain their surplus from previous fiscal years and to introduce some local taxes (see Lev Freinkman and Stepan Titov, *The Transformation of the Fiscal System in Russia: The Case of Iaroslavl*, Washington: World Bank, 1994, p. 6).

2. Freinkman and Titov, 1994, p. 15.

3. Alexander Granberg, "Regionalnaia ekonomika i regionalnaia nauka v Sovietskom Soyuze i Rossia," *Region*, no. 1, 1994, p. 23.

4. Freinkman and Titov, 1994, pp. 6, 17.

5. Freinkman and Titov, 1994, pp. 7–9.

6. See Emil Pain, "Separatizm i federalizm v sovremennoi Rossii," in *Kuda Idet Rossia? Alternativy Obshchestvennogo Razvitia*, ed. T. Zaslavskaia and L. Arutiunian, Moskva: Interpraks, 1994, p. 160.

7. *Moskovskie Novosti*, 19 September 1993.

8. For example, the Iaroslavl District reduced the percentage of the value-added tax transferred to the center from 80 to 50 percent, which meant that it had at its disposal 20 million rubles originally owed to the federal authorities. The Altai Territory deprived Moscow of approximately the same sum, whereas the Voronezh District went much further: Its leadership decided to transfer to the federal budget only 20 percent of all taxes (See Radik Batyrshin, "Nalogovaia voina tsentra i regionov," *Nezavisimaia Gazeta*, 1 September 1993).

9. See Alexander Deikin, "Prizrak budzhetnogo federalizma vse eshche brodit po Rossii," *Finansovyie Izvestia*, 28 September 1995.

10. *Izvestia*, 3 September 1993.

11. *Iz.*, 4 November 1995.

12. The leaders of Tatarstan denied this accusation levied against them by the Moscow press and politicians. Mukhammat Sabirov, the prime minister, contended that his republic continued in 1992–1993 to make its contribution to the federal budget. However, he recognized that the sum was much smaller than Moscow required—only 19 percent of the income instead of the requisite 57 percent (see M. Sabirov, "My vnosim nalogi v federalnuiu kaznu," *NG*, 10 October 1993).

13. See Vladimir Emelianov, "Nastuplenie provintsii na Kreml'," *MN*, 3 October 1993.

14. See Evgenia Pismennaia, "Regiony nedovolny nalogovo-buzhetnoi politikoi federalnogo pravitelstva," *FIz.*, 1 December 1995.

15. See the textbook edited by Alexei Rumianstev, *Political Economy*, Moskva: Politizdat, 1985, pp. 310–319; see also A. Prokhorov (ed.), *Sovietskii Entsiklopedicheskii Slovar*, Moskva: Sovietskaia Entsiklopedia, 1989, pp. 729, 1261–1262.

16. In the past, in several cities and even in whole regions, managers of large state enterprises under all-union control, mostly belonging to the industrial-military complex, were subordinated only to Moscow (such as the Volga auto plant in Toliatti, Kuibyshev Region) and had more power than the local authorities. The well-being of one-half to two-thirds of the residents (in some cities, even more) depended totally on the enterprise managers, who often openly flouted the wishes of the local administration. These local administrators had no choice but to accommodate the real masters in their own sphere of authority. Even the first party republican and, even more so, the regional secretaries, had to be cautious in their dealings with the directors of the large military complex. Vera Panova, in her famous novel *Kruzhilikha* (Moskva: Sovietskii Pisatel, 1948) vividly described such a Soviet industrial baron in the postwar Soviet Union.

17. See *Goskomstat SSSR, Narodnoie khoziastvo SSSR v 1988*, Moskva: Finansy i Statistika, 1989, p. 332; *Goskomstat SSSR, Narodnoe Khoziastvo SSSR v 1990*, Moskva: Finansy i Statistika, 1991, p. 351.

18. See Dmitrii Babich, "Skolko respublik budet v Rossi," *Komsomol'skaia Pravda*, 26 June 1993.

19. *Konstitutsia Rossiiskoi Federatsii*, Moskva: Iuridicheskaia Literatura, 1993, pp. 28–29.

20. Before 1985, Tatarstan could control only 2 percent of all enterprises. In 1994, this figure increased to 65 percent (see Midkhat Farukshin, *Praviashchaia elita v Respublike Tatarstan*, paper presented at the Conference on the New Elite in the Post-Communist World, 2–4 November 1994).

21. For an example, see Mikhail Nikolaiev, president of the Sakha Republic, "Sakha (Iakutia) Rossia—derzhava severnaia," *Literaturnaia Rossia*, 31 March 1995.

22. *Goskomstat, Sotsialnoie Polozhenie Regionov Rossiiskoi Federatsii*, Moskva, 1994, pp. 578–80; see also Mikhail Nikolaiev, "*Vozvrata k proshlomu net*," *Rossiskaia Gazeta*, 8 December 1992.

23. See the interview with Mikhail Nikolaiev, president of Iakutia, in *Literaturnaia Gazeta*, 1 December 1993; and Vladimir Todres, "Bashkiria poka dovolna dostignutym suverinitetom," *Segodnia*, 7 February 1995.

24. See Article 22, *Ustav (Osnovnoi zakon) Orenburgskoi Oblasti*, Orenburg, 1994.

25. See *RG*, 11 February 1995; A. Kirillov, B. Kirillov, and A. Ryzhkov, *Ural: Stanovlenie oblastnykh zakonodatelnykh organov vlasti*, Ekaterinburg, 1995, pp. 126–127; *Seg.*, 23 August 1995.

26. The Tiumen Region elaborated its own ideology of property relations, which supposes the existence of three types of property in the district's territory: regional, district, and joint property of both subjects on the most valuable resources (see Sergei Sobianin, "Severianam dostaiutsia krokhi ot neftianykh bogatsv," *Seg.*, 20 October 1995).

27. See Alexander Bekker, "Terpenie i trud vse peretrut," *Seg.*, 11 November 1995.

28. As a Moscow journalist wrote, "The threat to deny sewage permits by local authorities causes them to quickly find 'common ground' with any manager" (see Vladimir Gurevich, "Chrezvychainyi rynok," *MN*, 24 October 1993.

29. See V. Leksin and E. Andreeva, "Territorialnaia dezintegratsia Rossii," *Rossiiskii Ekonomicheskii Zhurnal*, no. 9, 1992, p. 40.

30. About the changes in the relations between the local political elite and the economic bosses in Toliati in 1992, see Ekaterina Vasilchenko, "Vse mogut 'Koroli,'" *RG*, 26 November 1992.

31. Mikhail Zadornov, the head of the Duma's Budget Committee complained in 1995 that "the active practice of the distribution of resources according to 'special' decisions of the country's highest leaders undermines . . . the new budget structure of the Russian Federation" (*FIz.*, 28 September 1995).

32. Indeed, Iakutia obtained the right to sell abroad one-third of its diamond production even if 98 percent of the entire diamond reserves were concentrated there (see also the interview with Nikolaiev, 1993).

33. See Sergei Glaziev, *Ekonomika i Politika: Epizody Borby*, Moskva: Gnosis, 1994, pp. 240–241.

34. In the struggle with the center, the Murmansk District won the right to leave 40 percent of its currency revenues from export trade for state purposes and all of the revenues from border and coastal trade with foreigners. The regions of the Far East and Transbaikalia allocate a portion of the currency revenues due to the federation to their reserve fund.

35. See Vladimir Todres, "Sibir voiuet za prava exportera," *NG*, 14 January 1993; *Argumenty i Fakty*, no. 2, 1993, p. 2.

36. See Vladimir Emelianenko, "Dvadtsat tri vandei," *MN*, 17 October 1993.

Chapter 15

1. The sample included *Izvestia, Moskovskie Novosti, Segodnia, Den'-Zavtra, Pravda, Sovietskaia Rossia, Komsomol'skaia Pravda, Moskovskii Komsomol'ets, Literaturnaia Gazeta, Nezavisimaia Gazeta, Argumenty i Fakty, Megalopolis Express*, and *Literaturnaia Rossia*.

2. *Goskomstat, Sotsialnoie Polozhenie Regionov Rossiiskoi Federatsii*, Moskva: Goskomstat, 1994, pp. 441–443.

3. *Goskomstat, Sotsialno-Ekonomicheskoie Polozhenie Rossii*, Moskva: Goskomstat, January-June 1995, pp. 158–160.

4. The first secretaries of economically powerful regions were elected to the Central Committee as full members as well as to the Soviet Parliament, whereas their colleagues, representing weaker regions, only had the opportunity to be appointed to the position of "candidate to be a member of the Central Committee" and to be members of the Parliament of the Russian Republic.

It was also unthinkable that the party secretary of an economically weaker region would have the chance to be invited to Moscow for a leading position on the Central Committee as the head of a department or to be a secretary of the Central Committee. Only those who served in the larger regions had such opportunities. These insights on the regional composition of party positions are gleaned from the personal biographies of Feodor Kulakov, Mikhail Gorbachev (who advanced from a position as Stavropol *krai* party secretary to a position as the secretary of the Central Committee), and Andrei Kirilenko and Boris Yeltsin, who were both promoted to leading party roles in Moscow from Sverdlovsk.

5. The Tiumen case is of special interest. As major producer of oil and gas in the country, the region was strictly under Moscow's control. This control was maintained because the leaders of the oil and gas companies, which control the region's economy, were strongly interested in supporting Moscow in order to retain the right to export oil and gas.

6. It did not formally proclaim itself to be a republic, but appropriated, in practice, republican rights and powers. The declaration states that the district "exercises full state power within its territory," except those powers that are the prerogative of the federal bodies. The district leadership thus obtained the right to issue legislative acts that are to be in force in their territory. The laws of the Russian Federation can be applied in the territory only on questions of responsibility that the district has decided to pass on to Russia's federal government. "The federal bodies of state power," states the Declaration, "have no right to issue legal acts on questions within the jurisdiction of the district bodies of state government." The Voronezh District was declared "an independent participant in international and foreign trade relations. Its leadership should conduct negotiations with the federal government and formalize their results in mutual agreements. The state bodies of the Russian Federation have the right to introduce a state of emergency in the district only upon the consent of the district bodies of state power."

7. Gennadii Ziuganov (ed.), *Sovremennaia Russkaia Idea i Gosudarstvo*, Moskva: Obozrevatel', 1995, p. 69.

8. According to the data supplied by the Merkator group, only in the case of the Far East, in 1993, did the percentage of profit-losing enterprises in the Kamchatka, Magadan, and Sakhalin Regions and Maritime Territory exceed 30 percent. Thus, there is nothing surprising in the fact that in the Kamchatka, Sakhalin, and Amur Regions, local budget expenditures exceeded revenues by 30 percent. The respective figure for the Maritime Territory and the Magadan District is only slightly less. The same picture could be observed in other regions as well.

9. L. Vardomskii, "Problemy i protivorechia regionalnogo razvitia Rossii," in *Rossia i SNG: Dezintegratsionnye i Integratsionnye Protsessy*, ed. G. Kostinskii, Moskva: Institut Geografii, 1995, p. 48.

10. *Goskomstat*, 1994, pp. 459–461.

11. The Spearman coefficient of correlation between export and per capita income was 0.84 for 1994 (Vardomskii, 1995, p. 49).

12. See A. Treivish and T. Nefedova, "Ekonomicheskoie prostranstvo Rossii: Problemy regionalnogo rassloenia," in G. Kostinskii, 1995, p. 46.

13. Vardomskii, 1995, p. 51.

14. When it became clear that there was a diamond-bearing area in the Arkhangelsk Region, which, according to some estimates, was as rich as the Iakutian deposit, there almost immediately emerged the idea of forming a Coastal Area Republic (Pomorye), which turned into a sort of regionalist movement in Arkhangelsk.

15. In discussing the role of Russia's size in the post-Communist political process, Vadim Poegli, a Russian journalist, noted, "'Russia is too big a country, and, therefore, reforms here are not possible'—written two hundred years ago by some travelers. Seventy years of Communism had only crystallized this issue" (*MK*, 19 December 1995).

16. Vladimir Kontorovich, "The Future of Soviet Science Research Policy," vol. 23, 1994, p. 115.

17. Vladimir Polevanov, governor of the Amur Region in 1994, cited the existence before the revolution of the "Cheliabinsk threshold"—a ban on increasing railway tariffs levied on the transportation of commodities from the Russian Far East to Europe. This ban allowed goods made in the Far East to compete with European ones (Vladimir Polevanov, "Rodina prevyshe vsego," *Zavtra*, no. 46, November 1995).

18. See *Goskomstat Rossii, Rossiiskii Statisticheskii Ezhegodnik*, Moskva: Goskomstat, 1994, pp. 391, 396.

19. See, for instance, Treivish and Nefedova, 1995, p. 44.

20. See V. Aksamentova, "Ovdovevshii sever," *SR*, 22 August 1995.

21. For more on life in Murmansk, see Alexander Senin, "Zakryt otkrytyi port," *NG*, 7 February 1996.

22. Vadim Dubnov, "Prusskie Russkie," *Novoie Vremia*, no. 35, 1995, p. 13; Alexander Kondrashov, "Zloveshchaia ten prodannoi Aliaski nad Kaliningradom," *P*, 19 January 1996.

23. This view was heartily supported by Vladimir Polevanov, who was governor of the Amursk Region, a part of the Khabarovsk Territory. In his opinion, "the Far East is on the edge of extinction" (Polevanov, 1995).

24. See E. Bagramov et al., *Razdelit li Rossia Uchast Soyuza SSR?* Moskva: Mezhdunarodnyi Fond Rossiiskogo Edinstva, 1993, pp. 69–70. Indeed, how is it possible, on the basis of geography, to explain why there are no signs of overt regional separatism in the Murmansk District, which has an outlet to the sea that does not freeze over in the winter? By contrast, a move toward regional separatism can be detected in the Arkhangelsk Region, which has close ties with the neighboring regions through a developed network of highways and which is unable to use its seaport for several months in the winter! Why then does the Vologda District, which is not on the periphery, want so passionately to become a sovereign republic? How can one explain why, in the traditionally stable non-black soil zone, regionalism finds refuge in the Voronezh District? Other factors that differentiate regions also have repercussions on the level of regionalism. Among those of special importance are the region's economic status.

25. The foreign trade of the Far East is coupled almost exclusively with its immediate foreign neighbors. China attracts 93 percent of all of the Chita Region's foreign trade and 43 percent of the Maritime Territory's trade, and Japan makes up 51 percent of Sakhalin's trade (Vardomskii, 1995, p. 50).

26. Indeed, as discussed in note 24, regionalist tendencies were quite weak in the Murmansk District but were stronger in the Arkhangelsk Region.

27. L. Vardomskii and V. Chasovskii analyzed the changes that occurred in the Briansk Region, which, since 1991, borders Ukraine and Byelorussia. In their conclusion, even in 1994, this region was a victim, along with similar regions, of the "general economic crisis and disintegrative processes" (L. Vardomskii and V. Chasovskii, *Dezintegratsia 'Soyuznogo' Ekonomicheskogo Prostranstva: Pogranichnye Regiony Rossii (Primer Brianskoi Oblasti)* in G. Kostinskii, 1995, pp. 67–69.

28. Vardomskii, 1995, p. 50.

29. Samuel Huntington, *The Clash of Civilizations and the Remaking of World Order,* New York: Simon and Schuster, 1996.

30. Many Russians would prefer to speak about the special "Russian civilization" (especially Russian nationalists) or the "Soviet-Russian civilization" (those Westernizers who focus on the Soviet past).

Chapter 16

1. Official prices of consumer goods were, in some zones, no more than 10 to 15 percent higher than in most other zones in the country. The greatest differences were in the prices of products in "collective farm markets." In some regions, the prices on vegetables and fruits were up to four times higher than in the "cheapest" regions. Even if the Russian population spent no more than 5 to 10 percent of its consumer expenditures (the figures varied a lot across the country) in these markets, the collective farm markets would still have instilled in the public conscience the notion that life in one region was "better" or "worse." At the same time, the state provided people living in remoter regions with additional bonuses, thus making the differences relatively small, a factor that was beneficial for the unity of the country.

2. The Kremlin created few oases for scholars. Dubna in the Moscow Region, Pushchino in Tula, and Akademgorodok in Novosibirsk were cities where the standard of living was immensely higher than in the rest of the region in which they were located (Vladimir Shlapentokh, *Soviet Intellectuals and Political Power,* Princeton: Princeton University Press, 1990).

3. As mentioned earlier, these markets were named "collective farm markets," even though most vendors were individual peasants or workers who were selling products grown on private plots. In fact, prior to 1985, produce grown on these plots provided up to one-third of the country's food supply.

4. These differences are illustrated by a striking episode in Vladimir Dudintsev's novel, *Not by Bread Alone* (Miunkhen: Izdanie Tsentralnogo Obedinenia Politicheskikh Emigrantov iz SSSR, 1957), one of the first relatively realistic novels in the post-Stalin era. In this scene, a woman, who came from Moscow to a small provincial city, was peeling an orange, to the great amazement of the local children who had never seen such a fruit, during her walk.

5. The ratio between regions with the highest and lowest levels of consumption was 1:3 (Alexander Granberg, "Regionalnaia ekonomika i regionalnaia nauka v Sovietskom Soyuze i Rossia," *Region,* no. 1, 1994, p. 22; A. Treivish and T. Nefedova, "Ekonomicheskoe prostranstvo Rossii: Problemy regionalnogo rassloenia," in *Rossia i SNG: Dezinte-*

gratsionnye i Integratsionnye Protsessy, ed. G. Kostinskii, Moskva: Institut Geografii, 1995, p. 41; and L. Vardomskii, "Problemy i protivorechia regionalnogo razvitia Rossii," in Kostinskii, 1995, p. 48).

6. The ratio of the exchange of apartments between cities serves as an amusing indicator of the differences in the quality of life in the country. Since most city apartments, particularly large apartments, belonged to state citizens moving from one place to another, only they could exchange them. In this market, one room in a communal apartment in Moscow was equivalent to a three-room apartment in a city such as Kursk or Volsk (the Saratov Region). There was a typical rate of exchange between cities that took into account dozens of factors influencing the quality of life, including the supply of goods, climate, ecological conditions, and so on.

7. In 1985, only 21 percent of all regions had housing conditions close to the national average, while 30 percent of the regions deviated from the average by more than 10 percent. The situation had not radically changed by 1993 (*Goskomstat, Sotsialno-Ekonomicheskoie Polozhenie Rossii, Ianvar-Oktiabr*, Moskva: Goskomstat, 1995; *Goskomstat, Sotsialnoie Polozhenie Regionov Rossiiskoi Federatsii*, Moskva: Goskomstat, 1994).

8. The death rate due to lung cancer in the country ranged from 36.2 per 100,000 people between the ages of birth to sixty-four years old (Kurgan Region) to 16.3 per 100,000 (Karachaevo-Cherkesskii) (Murray Feshbach [ed.], *Environmental and Health Atlas of Russia*, Moscow: Paims, 1995, p. 18).

9. See Feshbach, 1995.

10. The value of a basket of nineteen basic foods varied enormously across the country. Furthermore, the value of this food basket varied enormously even within the same region. For example, in the Volga Territory, the ratio of the value of this basket in the most expensive (Volgograd) and least expensive region (Ulianovsk) was almost 1:2 (see *Goskomstat*, 1995).

11. Granberg, 1994, p. 22; Treivish and Nefedova, 1995, p. 41; Vardomskii, 1995, p. 48.

12. A Russian author contended that the dangers generated by the large gap in regional standards of living in Russia are similar to those found in Yugoslavia: "Yugoslavia was blasted out by the sevenfold differences between republics in income" (Vardomskii, 1995, p. 51).

13. Communists and nationalists were the victors in the 1995 parliamentary election: The Communists received 21 percent of the votes in the parties' lists and the nationalists took second place with 11 percent. *Yabloko*, a democratically oriented party, won only 8 percent and the progovernment block, Our Home Russia, received 10 percent. Meanwhile, in Moscow, as well as in St. Petersburg, the latter two parties were in first place.

14. The platforms of most of the local politicians in Kursk, in spring 1994 (see Alexei Sobianin, *Demokratia, Ogranichennaia Falsifikatsiami*, Moskva: Proektnaia Gruppa po Pravam Cheloveka, p. 122) declared that "pseudo-democrats destroyed the great country, demolished industry, which was created with such great efforts, undermined the legitimacy of the Supreme Soviet, libeled our past, created the conditions for interethnic wars, and destroyed agriculture as a common good." In Tambov, the leading block during the spring 1994 elections was the very nationalistic and antireformist group called Russia. Of fifty deputies elected in March 1995 to the Orlovskaia Duma, thirty were Communists (see also Nikolai Lysenko, chairman of the Republican Party, "Demokraty terpiat porazhenie," *Sovietskaia Rossia*, 1 December 1994; Svetlana Shiunova, "Posev i zhatva," *Nezavisimaia Gazeta*, 2 December 1994; *Segodnia*, 6 December 1994).

15. In Penza, 59 percent voted against the draft of the constitution; in Tambovsk, 57 percent; in Bzinsk, Smolensk, and Orel, 56 percent each; in Kursk, 55 percent; and in Belgorod, and Voronezh, 54 percent each. See Sobianin, 1995, pp. 197–210.

16. See *NG*, 18 December 1993. In Siberia, Krasnoiarsk was one of the opposition's bastions of support. It was here that the Communists first restored their regional party organization in the country after the ban on the party in 1991. Russian nationalists were more active here than in other districts, publicly professing their most extremist slogans and ascribing democracy in Russia to a Zionist plot.

Alexander Sterligov, Vladimir Zhirinovsky, Eduard Limonov, and other leaders of the Russian nationalist movement regularly visited the city. The director of local enterprises, especially Piotr Romanov, director of the chemical complex, Enisei (he was elected to the Federal Council in December 1993), conspicuously supported Russian nationalists as well as Communists. Even the presidential emissary, I. Moskvich, demonstrated his respect for the opposition's leaders when they visited Krasnoiarsk.

In 1992–1994, the local newspaper, *Krasnoiarskaia Pravda*, attacked privatization, the market economy, and the entire regime (see Alexei Tarasov, "Prizrak kommunizma voskresnet v kraie Stalinskikh lagerei," *Izvestia*, 25 February 1993; "Oppozitsia torit dorogu v Kreml cherez provintsiu," *Iz.*, 3 December 1992). It was not surprising that, in the December 12 election, one-third of the residents voted for Zhirinovsky (*Iz.*, 18 December 1993).

Another center of oppositionist activity was Irkutsk, where the main organization hostile to the regime was the local Cossack alliance supported by the local administration (see Alexander Krutov, "Iz Sibiri s nenavistiu," *Moskovskie Novosti*, 14 February 1993).

17. These data are based on VTSIOM's exit polls.

18. The political differentiation of regions determined the radical differences in the composition of local administrations. A high proportion of legislators in a number of "non-black-soil" regions are chairmen of collective farms or those stock companies that replaced them. In the Kirov Region, for instance, this group is the most numerous, making up 29 percent (whereas heads of administration made up 24 percent) of the administration. Entrepreneurs were the most significant group in Ural, whereas in Perm they made up about 42 percent, 38 percent in Cheliabinsk, 28 percent in Orenburg.

19. See *Pravda*, 14 March 1995.

20. In seventeen Russian regions, less than 20 percent of all apartments were privatized; in another twenty-eight regions, between 20 and 30 percent were privatized; and in yet another eleven regions, more than 30 percent were privatized (*Rossiiskii Statisticheskii Ezhegodnik*, Moskva: Goskomstat, 1994, pp. 459–461).

21. *Rossiiskii Statisticheskii Ezhegodnik 1994*, Moskva: Goskomstat, 1994, pp. 477–479.

22. See Boris Nemtsov, "Sviaz s premierom ia derzhu dazhe cherez babushku v razdevalke," *Komsomol'skaia Pravda*, 21 June 1995; Nemtsov in an interview with *Literaturnaia Gazeta*, 3 August 1994.

23. Nizhniy Novgorod became a mecca for Western politicians and businessmen, for whom this city and region symbolized a new Russia with a market economy. Nemtsov also promoted a Western style of life with innumerable shows and receptions celebrating the visits of famous intellectuals, both Russian and foreign (Arbakhan Magomedov, "Politicheskii ritual i mify regionalnykh elit," *Segodnia*, 31 December 1994).

Margaret Thatcher, who visited Nizhniy Novgorod in 1993, remarked that she had come to the capital of reforms. However, not only foreigners but the prime minister of the Russian government, Viktor Chernomyrdin, also spoke highly of the Nizhniy Novgorod experience in implementing successful agrarian reforms (V. Savichev, "Gde v Rossii sto-litsa reform?" *Argumenty i Fakty*, no. 34, September 1993).

24. See the Iavlinskii interview, *LG*, 11 November 1992.

25. Ulianovsk authorities used both these methods. In mid-1993, for instance, every citizen in the region could buy once each month 1.5 kg of meat, 2 kg of sugar, 400 kg of butter, 400 kg of vegetable oil, 15 eggs, and 300 g of candies at low prices. Bread and other perishables were not rationed and were sold at fixed prices. Export of all subsidized goods was prohibited. Besides special ration coupon shops, the region also has so-called commercial shops, which sell the same goods, but at free prices. The price difference is spent on subsidies.

26. Specialists of the Expert Institute of the Russian Union of Industrialists and Entrepreneurs, who have analyzed the results of these two models in operation, concluded that "it is impossible to arrive at a conclusion: it would be more proper to speak about two strategies, each of which has its own price for the region and is different for each of the regions. One is the strategy of a quick breakthrough, while the other strategy is more of a smooth and prolonged transition."

They simultaneously remarked that the strategy of the Ulianovsk leaders "obviously hampers the process of decentralization and allows the regional authorities to keep power in their hands for a longer period."

27. Zhana Mindubaiev, "Zagadki deshevoi korziny," *LG*, 3 March 1993; Valentin Razboinikov, "Ulianoivskoie 'Chudo' ekonomiki obnaruzhivaet priznaki upadka," *Iz.*, 3 December 1994.

28. In 1993, the officially registered unemployment rate in Ulianovsk was lower than in Nizhniy Novgorod (0.8 percent of all labor, versus 1.2 percent); the death rate was also lower than in Nizhniy Novgorod (13 per thousand, versus 16.1); and the annual increase of saving was higher (9.4 percent of money income, versus 8.4). Most important, the proportion of the value of a basket of nineteen basic foods to per capita income was 21 percent versus 31 percent in Nizhniy Novgorod (Goskomstat, 1994, pp. 450–451, 459–460, 507–508, 510–511).

29. Voronezh, with its governor Alexander Kovalev and his policy of economic intervention, was clearly closely aligned to Ulianovsk, whereas Sverdlovsk, with its governor Eduard Rossel, was definitely in the same camp as Nizhniy Novgorod (see Valerii Konovalov, "Gde na Rossii zhit khorosho, khuzhe i sovsem plokho," *Iz.*, 28 June 1995).

30. Magomedov, 1994; Irina Demina, "V regionakh poiavilis priznaki ekonomicheskogo pod'ema," *MN*, 9 August 1995; Razboinikov, 1994, and "Ulianovskii zapovednik," *Iz.*, 17 February 1996.

31. See Magomedov, 1994.

32. See, for instance, Razboinikov, 1996; Otto Latsis, "Kuda idut nashi dengi," *Iz.*, 1 July 1995.

33. See Mintimer Shaimiev, "My nanizany na edinuiu nit," *NG*, 10 December 1993; Viktor Minin, "Opyt ekonomicheskikh reform Tatarstana," *KP*, 29 March 1995.

34. See Celestine Bohlen, "Out in the Hinterland, Moscow's Din Is Muted," *New York Times*, 28 March 1993.

35. Boris Yeltsin, in a February 1994 message to the Federal Assembly, was forced to say that "different starting conditions and different policies of local authorities widen the gap between various regions, thus forming the potential for Russia's disintegration."

Chapter 17

1. Egor Stroiev, governor of Orel and a former secretary of the Central Committee of the Communist Party, was the head of this association in 1995. In some journalists' opinion, this position helped him to be elected as the chairman of the Federal Council, which was created after the December 1995 parliamentary election (see *Moskovskii Komsomol'ets*, 25 January 1996).

2. It was dissolved in October 1993 (see *MK*, 17 February 1995; *Nezavisimaia Gazeta*, 20 January 1995; *Segodnia*, 6 January 1995).

3. The republics were quite active during the Chechen War and intensively maintained their contact with each other. In January 1995, they also gathered in Cheboksary and Petrozavodsk.

4. In the Duma elected in 1993, a faction emerged called New Regional Policy, headed by Vladimir Medvedev, a prominent politician (see Aleksei Makhrovskii, "Glubinka protiv Moskvy," *Literaturnaia Gazeta*, 15 February 1995).

5. For instance, the Party of Constitutional Democrats, led by V. B. Zolotarev, which was similar to the Party of Economic Freedom, made the following entry in its program: "Subjects of the Federation shall be legally equal, self-governing lands and republics with their own constitutions, independent systems of state power and management, as well as tax and legislative systems." The faction of Radical Democrats formed within the framework of the Congress of People's Deputies of Russia, in early 1993, coordinated by S. N. Yushenkov, also supported the idea of eliminating regions.

Some authors, like Moscow journalist Lidia Malash, called upon the government to look at the unification of regions as large territorial blocks, as "a major condition for the preservation of the unity of Russia." Malash explained that unification was needed since these associations would make, among other things, the investment process more effective than before, because large investment firms need only big territories (see Lidia Malash, "Parlament reshil: 'Mukhi otdel'no, kotlety otdel'no,'" *Megalopolis Express*, 3 March 1993).

6. Hence, Moscow made attempts in 1993–1995 to "tame" the associations and, still better, to turn them into bodies of the central government. According to press reports, the problem of giving the interregional associations full state and legal status was discussed by Vladimir Shumeiko, the speaker of the Council of the Federation, with representatives of all eight associations.

7. *Konstitutsia Rossiiskoi Federatsii*, Moskva: Iuridicheskaia Literatura, 1993, p. 32.

8. The following example illustrates the conflict between the large and small regions. In 1993, the Far Eastern authorities tried to follow in the footsteps of Ekaterinburg in its attempt to create the Ural Republic, uniting all of the Ural regions. A referendum was being prepared in Vladivostok on the question of the formation of the Maritime Republic, which was supposed to incorporate more than just the Maritime Territory alone. However, the leaders of the other regions, such as the governor of the Sakhalin Region, Evgenii Krasnoiarov, refused the transfer of their territories into republics, and the whole idea subsequently failed.

9. For more on the Association of Eastern Territories, see a Vladivostok newspaper, *Tikhookeanskaia Zvezda* (Pacific Star), 24 October 1992. See also L. Vardomskii, "Problemy i protivorechia regionalnogo razvitia Rossii," in *Rossia i SNG: Dezintegratsionnye i Integratsionnye Protsessy*, ed. G. Kostinskii, Moskva: Institut Geografii, 1995, p. 55; *Argumenty i Fakty*, no. 6, February 1996, p. 3. For more on the Great Volga organization, see

Alexei Chirkin, "Povolzhskaia respublika: Plany i realnost'," *ME*, 11 August 1993. See also *Kommersant*, 3 October 1993.

10. *Pravda*, 19 September 1995.

11. In 1995, several regions discussed the creation of a "Bank of Provinces" (*P.*, 19 September 1995).

12. For example, they laid claim to the role of distributors of resources, allocated by the federal bodies. Alexander Danusia, director general of the Central Russia Association, openly declared that by mid-1994, interregional associations had become "the sole body capable of coordinating and implementing all decisions in the localities."

13. See Artem Tarasov, "Pochemu kazhdyi tretii krasnoiarets golosoval za Zhirinovskogo," *Izvestia*, 18 December 1993.

14. See Radik Batyrshin, "Ekonomicheskii soyuz Izhevska, Kazani i Ufy," *NG*, 8 July 1993.

15. *Seg.*, 20 November 1993.

16. See Vladimir Emelianenko, "Sibirskoie nesoglasie s Moskvoi," *Moskovskie Novosti*, 2 April 1995.

17. There are many examples to prove this point. On 4 March 1994, the Great Council of the association Siberian Agreement demanded that the government significantly extend the region's rights in the sphere of exports. Without Moscow's consent, they argued, export quotas should be raised to 20 percent of total output. Export duties should be reduced in Siberia's case, and import duties on foodstuffs, medicines, and equipment should be abolished altogether. Moreover, the percentage of duty and excise taxes that remained in Siberia should be raised to at least 30 percent.

The center's reaction was unambiguous. The chief of the Main Department on Coordination of Foreign Economic Activity of the federation's subjects, A. Gumilevsky, said that "such privileges cannot be given to any individual territory" and suggested that Siberia wait for foreign trade reforms, when quotas and licenses would be gradually replaced with customs duties. However, it seems that the Siberians do not want to wait for favors from the government and are ready to implement some of the proposed changes without preliminary permission.

18. *P.*, 9 August 1995.

19. See M. Bandman, V. Kuleshov, and V. Seliverstov, "Intyegratsionnye protsessy v Sibiri," *K.*, 1995, pp. 56–62.

Chapter 18

1. See Elena Matveieva, *Moskovskie Novosti*, 18 July 1993; the Krasnoiarsk newspaper, *Svoi Golos* (Own Voice), 23 September 1992; *Priamurskie Vesti* (Amur Register), 29 August 1992.

2. For more on the Taimyr case, see *Krasnoiarskii Rabochii* (Krasnoiarskii Worker), 27 August 1992; Aleksei Tarasov, "V Sibiri mozhet obrazovatsia respublika 'Norilskii Nikel,'" *Izvestia*, 7 September 1995, and *Iz.*, 8 September 1995.

3. See *Tiumenskaia Pravda* (Tiumen's Truth), 18 November 1992; *Nezavisimaia Gazeta*, 9 July 1993.

4. See Elena Matveieva, "Fond golodaiushchikh pogranichnikov," *MN*, 11 February 1996.

5. See Lev Rokhlin, "Stroi synovei, a ne pasynkov," *Literaturnaia Gazeta*, 4 October 1995. Stavropol's governor, Piotr Marchenko, declared that in a case of state emergency, the president permitted him "to take control over all military units on his territory" (*Iz.*, 17 November 1995; and *Iz.*, 6 January 1996).

6. Alexander Granberg, "Regionalnaia ekonomika i regionalnaia nauka v Sovietskom Soyuze i Rossia," *Region*, no. 1, 1994, pp. 20–21.

7. Ulianovsk's regional authorities, led by Yurii Goriachev, the regional first party secretary prior to 1991, chose a social and economic policy radically different not only from the policies of such regional reformers as Boris Nemtsov of Nizhniy Novgorod but also from the Kremlin's.

8. Valerii Mirolevich, "Voronezhskie vlasti vveli krepostnoie pravo," *Iz.*, 11 November 1995. This practice has its roots in the Communist past. Those who used to vacation on the Caucasian Black Sea coast during the summer in the 1970s and 1980s often witnessed how collective farmers, who were trying to bring into Russia their own tangerines, were thrown out of the trains.

9. See Viktor Ishaiev, head of the Khabarovsk administration, "Territoria i Tsentr," *Iz.*, 30 June 1993; V. Polevanov, "Rodina prevyshe vsego," *Zavtra*, no. 46, November 1995.

10. Vladimir Leksin and Elena Andreeva, "Territorialnaia dezintegratsia Rossii," *Rossiiskii Ekonomicheskii Zhurnal*, no. 9, 1992, p. 35.

11. Underlining the necessity of legal measures to stop the region's attempts to split Russia's single economic space, Yeltsin warned: "At the same time, the struggle against economic separatism of the regions should not result in the infringement on their rights and lead to the restoration of a unitarian state. The course of passing over to the regions of more powers should continue" (Poslanie prezidenta Rossiiskoi Federatsii sobranuiu, "Ob ukreplenii Rossiiskogo gosudarstva" [Moskva: Ofitsialnoe Izd-vo, 1994], p. 47).

12. Citing these data, two Russian authors commented that "our situation is reminiscent of the early Middle Ages or periods of barbarian colonization" (Leksin and Andreeva, 1992, pp. 34–35).

13. On the selection of cadres in Dagestan, see Anatolii Tkachev and Alexander Shinkin, "Na otkatnoi volne," *Pravda*, 12 November 1992.

14. Jeffrey Sachs, for instance, like many other Western experts on post-Communist Russia, is also confident that if "regions took more power and responsibility into their hands . . . it had to lead to the expansion of democracy and the emergence of governments sensitive to the needs of their citizens" (*Rynochnaia Ekonomika i Rossia*, Moskva: Ekonomika, 1994, p. 116).

15. Robert Dahl, *Dilemmas of Pluralist Democracy: Autonomy Versus Control*, New Haven: Yale University Press, 1982, p. 104.

16. Vadim Poegli noted, "When [Sergei] Shakhrai and [Alexander] Solzhenitsyn deplore that all politics of the Russian state are made in Moscow and suggest to transfer the political process to regions, I shudder to think that I would like to see Russia governed by politicians from Omsk, Tomsk and Vladivostok!" (*Moskovskii Komsomol'ets*, 19 December 1995).

17. For instance, in February 1995, the parliament of the Maritime Territory tried to curtail the right of Governor Evgenii Nazdratenko and again did not succeed (Oleg Kriuchok, "Evgenia Nazdratenko popytalis urezat v pravakh," *Segodnia*, 22 February 1995; Andrei Novikov, "'Novye' politiki—plokho zabytye 'starye,'" *LG*, 1 December 1993).

18. Alexander Krestnikov, "Streliate po kolesam," *Komsomol'skaia Pravda*, 7 December 1993.

19. *Iz.*, 6 May 1995.

20. A journalist who described the election campaign in Vologda sarcastically noted that the list of candidates was used as a telephone directory of local officials. There were practically no candidates in the election who did not belong to the local administration (*Iz.*, 19 November 1993).

21. Valentin Razboinikov, "Ulianovskii zapovednik," *Iz.*, 3 December 1994.

22. Yurii Goriachev, governor of Ulianovsk and former first regional party secretary, took total control over the major local newspaper, *Ulianovskaia Pravda*, which glorified the local leader more often than, as a Moscow journalist noted, "it mentioned Stalin in 1948" (Valentin Razboinikov, "Nachalstvo predpisano liubit," *Iz.*, 2 November 1994; Open Media Research Institute, 8 December 1995).

23. The beating of A. Petrachenko, a journalist in Vladivostok in 1994, became well known because it drew the attention of the Moscow media (Lidia Malash, "Geroi nashego vremeni," *ME*, 2 November 1994). Another Vladivistok journalist, Alexei Sadykov, was tortured by policemen who wanted confessions from him useful for the governor. Several journalists also received various threats for their publications (I. Golembiovskii and V. Simonov, "Pechat molchania sniata?" *Iz.*, 21 December 1994; Igor Kots, "Potom oni stali gasit sigaretu o moiu spinu," *KP*, 29 November 1994; see also *Iz.*, 19 March and 6 April 1994; *MN*, 14 August 1994; Malash, 1994; and Natalia Ostrovskaia, "Ruchnaia pressa: Ideal gubernatora," *Iz.*, 27 October 1994).

24. Viktor Filippov, "Svoboda slova v provintsii: Prodaisia ili umri," *Iz.*, 11 January 1995.

25. For more on the violation of human rights in Tambov, see Elena Iakovleva, "Tambovskaia militsia planiruet okrutit golovu poslednim demokratam," *Iz.*, 24 March 1995.

26. The only oppositional newspaper was regularly persecuted, leading to its often needing to be published outside the republic in 1995. Thus, it is very difficult to buy it even in Elista, the regional capital (*Iz.*, 11 November 1995; *NG*, 28 October 1995).

27. See Valerii Lebedev and Dmitrii Sevriukov, "Dopros po-mordovski s pristrastiem i protivogazom," *KP*, 25 March 1995; on developments in Bashkortostan, see Iosif Galperin, "Khronika pikiriushchego sovieta," *Rossiskaia Gazeta*, 27 October 1993.

28. See, for instance, Bashkortostan's election law, *Vecherniia Ufa*, 7 December 1994.

29. See *Seg.*, 23 February 1995. In Bashkiria, for instance, the 1994 election law permitted political parties to nominate only one candidate for each of the two chambers of the republican Parliament. One requirement for the nomination of candidates, which is to gather a significant number of signatures (for example, in Bashkiria, no less than 5 percent of the district's population), could be met only by local bosses. Only these bureaucrats and directors of large enterprises could meet this stipulation for candidacy by using their apparatuses or employees in order to achieve this goal.

The March election of the local parliament in Tatarstan, for instance, was closed to journalists and was not monitored by independent observers. Even the representatives of candidates and the Russian Duma deputies were not permitted to watch the tabulation of election results. It was local officials who controlled the whole process (see *P*, 14 March 1995).

30. Kirsan Iliumzhinov himself was involved in a "wool case" and was suspected of illegally enriching himself and embezzling federal money. However, the investigation was dragged out over years without any results (see Olga Senatova, "'Drug stepei' a vsekh velikikh priatel," *LG*, 12 April 1995; Iulia Kravchenko, "Feodalnaia respublika v

demokraticheskoi federatsii," *NG*, 28 October 1995(a), and "Bespredel kak privelegia," *NG*, 19 October 1995(b)).

31. For instance, he publicly, and without condemnation from Moscow, intimidated all 130 members of the parliament into "unanimously voting for its own dissolution." He also eliminated the Council of Ministers and several other bodies and suspended federal privatization laws and continues to perpetrate countless other brazen activities.

For a view of his personal demeanor, read his self-aggrandizing interview (*Obshchaia Gazeta*, 16 July 1993). Recently, Italian journalists in Moscow commented that the elevation of people like Iliumzhinov would have been absolutely impossible even in Italy (*LG*, 14 June 1993). For more on Iliumzhinov, see also *Argumenty i Fakty*, April 1993; *P*., 10 April 1993; *KP*, 24 April 1993; *RG*, 30 April 1993; *Megalopolis Express*, 5 May 1993.

32. *KP*, 30 April 1993.

33. See Emil Pain and Arkadii Popov, "Kriminalnyi regim," *Iz.*, 8 February 1995.

34. The Cossacks in these regions lead in the harassment of the Armenians. According to one source, Cossacks are forcibly making Armenian families leave the area, lashing them, attacking police workers, and beating people of Caucasian nationality (Correspondent, People's Deputy of Russia, "Vlast molchit. Ruzhie streliaet," *RG*, 20 October 1992; on the anti-Caucasian mood in Saratov, see *MN*, 11 February 1996).

35. N. Kondratenko, one of the conservative leaders in the Krasnodar Region, declared in 1992 the necessity to fight "non-Russian minorities, Zionists and private business" (*RG*, 11 November 1992).

36. See Vladimir Shlapentokh, Munir Sendich, and Emil Pain (eds.), *The New Russian Diaspora: Russian Minorities in the Former Soviet Republics*, Armonk, NY: M. E. Sharpe, 1994.

37. See Vladimir Todres, "Sibir voiuet za prava exportera," *NG*, 14 January 1995.

38. *AiF.*, no. 2, 1993, p. 1.

39. Kravchenko, 1995(a).

40. By rejecting the Judeo-Christian religion and calling for a return to the paganism of their remote ancestors, Mari-El historian Patrushev presented Russians as a people who, under the impact of "Semitic irrationality," are deprived of spiritual values. In Mari-El, 8 percent of the population are pure Paganists and 21 percent are a combined form of Russian Orthodoxy and paganism (Dmitrii Epstein, "Kak sozdaietsia vnutrennee zarubezhie," *MN*, 11 February 1996).

41. See Liudmila Narovchatskaia, "Velikoe pereselenie narodov," *LG*, 20 January 1993.

42. Alexander Vengerovskii, one of the leading figures in Vladimir Zhirinovsky's party, spoke about the "emergence of an Ugro-Finish circle around Russia" and the necessity of incorporating non-Russian republics into *gubernias* (Epstein, 1996).

43. The case of Krasnoiarsk attorney Nelli Zhukova, an official with an impeccable reputation in the city, is typical. She was fired from her position in 1995 because of her "great attention to the activities of local authorities" (*Iz.*, 3 March 1995).

44. Evgenii Nazdratenko, governor of the Maritime Territory, along with his close aides, became a symbol in Russia of the corrupted regional bosses. The major instrument for obtaining the local bureaucrats' illegal incomes, including Governor Nazdratenko and his deputies, Nikolai Pavlov and Igor Lebedinez, was the company Pakt (Natalia Ostrovskaia, "Primorskii 'pakt,'" *Iz.*, 1 December 1993). In 1994, the Moscow audit commission asked the president to remove the governor "for abuses of power and corruption," but the Kremlin refused to do it (Irina Savvateieva, "Evgenii Nazdratenko kak zerkalo rossiiskikh reform," *Iz.*, 1 December 1994; *Seg.*, 1 November 1995).

The Tiumen governor, Leonid Roketskii, was one of those regional officials strongly tainted by corruption. His wife, an entrepreneur, was involved in evidently criminal action, but the local procurator dropped legal action against her. Many other prominent dignitaries, including the presidential emissary, G. Shcherbakov, were also noted to be involved in various suspicious deeds. However, all of them avoided any punishment (Fedor Sizyi, "Zhena gubernatora vne podozrenii," *KP*, 15 March 1993).

Yurii Vlasov, governor of the Vladimir Region, used his power for a number of purposes, from building his luxurious home to obliging the head of the local highway police to accompany his wife on her trip to a Black Sea resort in an official car (*Sovietskaia Rossia*, 24 December 1994).

Alexander Deriagin, governor of Kaluga and a doctor of mathematics and physics who supported the democrats in 1991, also turned out to be corrupt. He was accused for abusing his power for his personal enrichment (see *NG*, 6 February 1996).

The developments around Vologda's governor were also remarkable. The head of the administration in Vologda, Nikolai Podgornov, continued to receive a salary as director of a state farm in addition to his administrative head salary. He also managed to improve his housing conditions as soon as he became governor, building himself an actual castle. Further, he manipulated public funds, depositing money that the center had sent to purchase grain in private banks in order to collect the interest on the deposited funds (Viktor Filippov, "Rechi gosudarstvennye: Tseli lichnye," *Iz.*, 21 December 1993 and *Iz.*, 11 October 1995; *Iz.*, 26 September 1995; Iz, 15 November 1995; *Iz.*, 7 February 1996).

Finally, Boris Yeltsin, in starting his election campaign in February 1996, fired the corrupt governor. Governors of several other regions, such as Perm and Ulianovsk, were also accused by the media of blatant corruption (see Valentin Razboinikov, "Ulianoivskoie 'Chudo' ekonomiki obnaruzhivaet priznaki upadka," *Iz.*, 3 December 1994; Mikhail Lobanov, "V torzhestvo spravedlivosti ne veritsia," *Iz.*, 24 January 1995). Consequently, in 1992–1995 the media published materials on the corruption of the leaders of several other regions (on the Altai bosses, see *Iz.*, 1 December 1995; on Penza, see *Iz.*, 12 January 1996).

45. Even the most popular of Russian governors, Boris Nemtsov, was associated by many people in Nizhniy Novgorod with murky business and criminals (Sergei Chugaiev, "Iz podpolia v gubernatory nameren podatsia nakhodiashchiasia v rozyske lichnyi drug Nemtsova," *Iz.*, 3 October 1995).

46. Mikhail Saltykov-Shchedrin himself served as a vice governor in Tver from 1860 until 1862. A post-Communist Russian newspaper, with evident allusion to the governors of that time, commented on his sterling qualities: "competent, active, selflessness, demanding of subordinates" (*NG*, 6 February 1996).

47. See the interview with E. Lisov, deputy general procurator of the Russian Federation, *LG*, 11 November 1992.

48. In Kaliningrad Oblast, officials randomly checked 3 trains, 6 ships, and 7 airplanes. Consequently, they detained and confiscated 700 tons of nonferrous metals, 6 tanks of gasoline, 10,000 packs of cans and 29 kilograms of amber. Over the last eight months, more than 500 attempts to illegally export raw materials have been suppressed (Vladimir Kuznetsov, "Dva dollara—vziatka za tonnu nefti," *RG*, 20 October 1992).

49. F. Sizyi (special correspondent), "Pokhozhe, vorov stalo bolshe chem skvazhin," *KP* Tiumen-Moscow, 27 October 1992.

50. See Igor Ilushmin, a Vladivostok journalist, about the corruption in this city ("Borba privedenii," *LG*, 11 May 1994).

51. See Mikhail Gorbachev (ed.), *Materialy Situatsionnogo Analiza Seminara M. S. Gorbacheva*, Moscow: Gorbachev Foundation, 1994, pp. 89–92.

52. One of the main objects of privatization was land. As the author of the article "The Farmer-Apparatchiks" wrote, "Everywhere power holders started to seize what is probably the most valuable now—land, and the most fertile, the closest to the centers settlements and to roads." As an example, the author cites the developments in Tambov Region, where high officials and their relatives got the land as farmers but that they then rented to former collective farmers (Viktor Kozhemiako, "Nomenklaturnye fermery," *P.*, 26 December 1992).

53. Alexei Tarasov, "Novye zhertvy aliuminievoi voiny," *Iz.*, 21 April 1995.

54. In 1994, the authorities of Ekaterinburg accepted the division of the city into three criminal structures as a fundamental fact of life and cooperated with the criminals in various ways. The major criminal figures gained full respectability in the city, and local authorities did not object to the huge, solemn funeral conducted in 1992 for one of the slain bandits.

The killing of businessmen reluctant to observe their obligations became a norm in this Ural city in 1994. At the same time, banks and other firms helped criminals to transfer their money abroad (Stanislav Govorukhin, *Strana Vorov Na Doroge k Svetlomu Budushchemu*, Narva: Shans, 1994, pp. 222–239; Sergei Plotnikov, "'Kozhannyi zatylok' nad belym vorotnichkom," *KP*, 21 February 1995). During the gubernatorial elections in summer 1995, competing candidates actively looked to criminal elements for support, a fact that was openly discussed in the media at the time.

55. See Boris Reznik, "Kto tam riadom s prezidentom," *Iz.*, 6 January 1995.

56. The Russian media pointed out the activities of organized crime in the gubernatorial elections in Ekaterinburg in summer 1995 (Alexander Pashkov, "Vybory gubernatora na kriminalnom fone okazalis bezresultatnymi," *Iz.*, 8 August 1995).

57. Lidia Malash, "Ekaterinbrug polozhil Moskvu na lopatki," *ME*, 8 December 1993.

58. The famous financial scheme, operated by citizens of Chechnia in 1993–1994, where billions of rubles were withdrawn from Moscow banks using false documents, was possible, in the opinion of Moscow experts, only with the help "of the Russian state and bank structure" (Pain and Popov, 1995; see also *Moskovskie Kuranty*, 16 February 1996).

59. By the beginning of 1996, 68 percent of all newspapers to which Russians subscribed were local periodicals (Open Media Research Institute, 12 December 1995). According to a VTSIOM survey taken in 1995, 31 percent of Russians did not read periodicals at all, 50 percent preferred regional papers to their national counterparts, and 19 percent preferred national papers to regional editions (*KP*, 19 November 1995).

60. See Evgenii Sidorov, "Vykhod v svobodnom federalizme," *Seg.*, 31 August 1995.

61. See, for instance, Alexander Tsipko, "Bunt Yeltsina stal neozhidannostiu dlia Vashingtona," *NG*, 8 February 1996, and "Prezidentskie vybory v Rossii nado otmenit," *NG*, 20 February 1996; see also the interview with Evgenii Primakov, the director of the Russian intelligence services, *KP*, 20 December 1995.

62. In 1991–1993, the population of the Far East declined by 2 percent (see the Russian Statistical Yearbook, *Rossiiskaia Federatsia v 1992*, Moskva: Respublikanskii Informatsionno-Izdatelskii Tsentr, 1993, p. 93).

63. See Sergei Shakhrai, "Neobkhodimo imet strategiu v otnosheniakh s Kitaem," *Iz.*, 20 May 1994.

64. See *Iz.*, 21 November 1993; Valerii Sharov, "Kitaiskaia karta," *LG*, 27 October 1993; Sergei Baburin, "Trevogi Amura," *SR*, 3 August 1995.

65. See Alexei Tarasov, "Kto prirastet mogushchestvom Sibiri, esli eie budut osvaivat' kitaitsy," *Iz.*, 16 April 1994; *Seg.*, 25 March 1995.

66. For example, after his trip to China in 1993, V. Vopilov, head of the Foreign Economic Department in the Krasnoiarsk administration, offered a large developmental program in his region with the help of Chinese workers. He referred to the Chinese as the ones who "have to build factories and plants, railroads and greenhouses." This official, however, was soon removed from his position (*Iz.*, 16 April 1994).

67. Valerii Sharov spoke, without fear of using racial epithets in a liberal weekly, about the "yellow invasion" and the conscientious intentions of the Chinese to "penetrate Russian life." He accused the Chinese of attempting to create "special lobby structures inside Russia" and of ultimately seeking to "obtain by peaceful means the lands which allegedly belonged to China in the past" (Sharov, 1993). Sharov is seconded by Sergei Andreiev, a journalist from a liberal nationalist newspaper, *Komsomol'skaia Pravda*. His article on illegal Chinese immigration has the remarkable subtitle "Stanet li Vladivostok prigorodom Kharbina?" (Will Vladivostok Become a Kharbin Suburb?) (Sergei Andreiev, "Litsa Kitaiskoi natsionalnosti po gorodu kruzhatsia. Stanet li Vladivostok prigorodom Kharbina?," *KP*, 19 April 1994).

68. Musing about the offensive between the "oriental civilization" and "European civilization", Miasnikov called on his compatriots to prepare themselves for the mass penetration of Chinese into the country. He stated that this would occur because "Russia has a large, rich territory and a relatively small population of only one hundred fifty million" (see Vladimir Miasnikov, "Vtoroi Russko-Kitaiskii raund," *Seg.*, 2 September 1994).

Alexei Voskresenskii, deputy head of the Russia-China Center in Miasnikov's Institute of Far East Studies, in his article "The Zone of Cooperation or Potential Conflict" invited Russia to reconcile with "the mass penetration of Chinese in the Far East" as an unavoidable development. He did, however, try to alleviate this "bitter pill" with the promise that Beijing would not consider the millions of Chinese in Russia as a reason for its expansion. Rather, he claimed, China would do its best to disown those Chinese as citizens and would refuse to cooperate with its former compatriots (Alexei Voskresenskii, "Zona sotrudnichestva ili potentsialnyi konflikt," *NG*, 3 June 1994).

69. Russian alarmists reminded their readers that Stalin, when he helped Mao Tse-Tung in the autonomous regions as the best prospect for Russia in 1949, had not wanted the full disappearance of Chiang Kai-Shek from the continent. He desired the existence of both Chinas, just as he preferred two Germanies and two Koreas (Alexei Voskresenskii, deputy director of the Russia-China Center, "Vyzov Kitaiskoi Narodnoi Respublike I Rossiiskie interesy," *NG*, 16 September 1994).

Conclusion

1. Russian experts regularly put this issue at the forefront of Russia's many current and future problems (VTSIOM, no. 2, 1993).

2. See *Izvestia*, 22 January 1993.

3. Patrick Glynn, "The Age of Balkanization," *Commentary*, July 1993, pp. 22–25.

About the Book and Authors

Written in the spirit of comparative and historical analysis, this book addresses the relationship between the center and its provinces—an important issue in any society—using Russia as a case study. The authors investigate the historical stages of Russia's past, with special focus on the post-Communist era.

Vladimir Shlapentokh is professor of sociology at Michigan State University; Roman Levita is professor of economics at the Open University, Moscow; and Mikhail Loiberg is professor of history at the Open University, Moscow.

INDEX